DATE DUE

FEB 17 1997 MAR 17 2000 MAR 3 0 2000	
BRODART	Cat. No. 23-221

Social Capitalism

Christian democracy has been the most successful political movement in post-war Western Europe, yet its crucial impact on the development of the modern European welfare state has been critically neglected. In this study Kees van Kersbergen demonstrates the precise nature of the links between Christian democracy and the welfare state.

Using a variety of sources the author describes the origin and development of the Christian democratic movement and presents comparative accounts of the varying degrees of political entrenchment of national Christian democratic parties. Drawing upon cross-national indicators of welfare state development he identifies and explains the existence of a distinctly Christian democratic (as opposed to a liberal or social democratic) welfare state regime which he labels social capitalism.

This book compares the different national contexts in which Christian democratic social theory has been turned into political action. Kees van Kersbergen shows how the different social policy performances of crucial cases (Germany, Italy and the Netherlands) have been affected not just by prevalent power structures but also by the coalitional strategies and political abilities of Christian democratic parties.

Kees van Kersbergen is a Lecturer in Political Science, Department of Political Science and Public Administration, Vrije Universiteit, Amsterdam.

Social Capitalism

A study of Christian democracy and the welfare state

Kees van Kersbergen

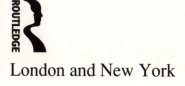

London and New York

First published 1995
by Routledge
11 New Fetter Lane, London EC4P 4EE

Simultaneously published in the USA and Canada
by Routledge
29 West 35th Street, New York, NY 10001

© 1995 Kees van Kersbergen

Typeset in Times by LaserScript, Mitcham, Surrey
Printed and bound in Great Britain by
TJ Press (Padstow) Ltd, Padstow, Cornwall

British Library Cataloguing in Publication Data
A catalogue record for this book is available from the British Library

Library of Congress Cataloging in Publication Data
A catalogue record for this book has been requested

ISBN 0–415–11670–8

Contents

Tables

Acknowledgements

Christian democracy has attracted surprisingly little scholarly attention. Whereas studies of social democracy could easily fill a small library, monographs on the Christian-inspired movements of Western Europe would probably scarcely fill a single bookshelf. Given the political importance of Christian democracy I have always found such lack of concern with the phenomenon quite perplexing. In the course of my studies I have noticed that occupying oneself with Christian democracy out of intellectual curiosity tends to bring out scepticism from those who have never seriously thought about the topic. They have sometimes doubted my motives. Each time I presented my work somewhere, somebody always felt obliged to ask whether I was perhaps religious myself. Apparently, it is difficult to imagine that Christian democracy can be an intriguing object of study in itself. One does not have to believe in the Christian democratic project in order to study it, just as one does not have to be a fool to study madness. The most cordial reaction I ever got was when someone praised my courage to tackle the topic, probably contending that masochism is a prerequisite for martyrdom. Trying to explain that Christian democracy is related to the welfare state has not been an easy matter either. The possibility of the connection seems to be excluded in the minds of many 'critical' social scientists. It is 'common wisdom' that Christian democracy inhibits a happy life for all. But how do we know? Let us postpone value judgments until knowledge permits us to assess the movement's virtues and vices properly.

Fortunately, the academic entourage of the European University Institute in Florence has provided me with an intellectual environment wherein my original attempt to make sense of Christian democracy and the welfare state has been more than encouraged. Here I have come across very little prejudice. The Institute's openness and its international character have given me a unique opportunity to carry out this study. I am grateful to the

Dutch Ministry of Education and the European Community for providing me with the grants that allowed me to write a dissertation on the topic and survive financially.

If altruism and generosity have lost much of their content in contemporary personal relationships, Gøsta Esping-Andersen has certainly made a great effort to refresh the genuine meaning of the concepts (and note that – unlike charity – altruism does not imply the submission of the recipient to the benefactor). His influence on this study is unmistakable and I do not regret it for a moment. It is certainly not a 'bad idea' to ask under what conditions some do and some don't. I thoroughly disagree with him on only one minor detail. The first rule of sociology *is* that 'everything took longer'.

The initial idea for this study was conceived when I was at the Political Science Department of the University of Amsterdam. I wish to thank Uwe Becker for making me aware of the fact that Dutch exceptionalism may be as much due to the peculiarities of this nation as to the hidden assumptions of theories of the welfare state. He taught me the importance of a critical spirit. The collaboration with Dietmar Braun has contributed much to my understanding of Christian democracy and the original project was a direct result of a seminar on Christian democracy that we held in 1986–7. I also wish to thank him for his critical suggestions.

During my stay in Florence I participated in several seminars which gave me the opportunity to present the preliminary results of my research. I wish to thank all the participants for their efforts to read and comment upon my usually too wordy papers. My gratitude goes especially to Mary Daly, Johan De Deken, Bernhard Ebbinghaus, Maurice Glasman, Stephen Hopkins, Jürgen Kohl, Philippe Marlière, Veronica Muñoz Dardé, Declan Murphy, James (Jim) Newell, Fritz von Nordheim-Nielsen, Lasse Ringius, David Thomas, Philippe van Parijs and Axel West Pedersen. If you read this work carefully, you will certainly recognise bits and pieces of your own remarks and miss the most important ones. My friend Zina Assimakopoulou deserves special mention. Together we found out how tedious empirical research sometimes can be. Steven Lukes has encouraged me to think harder, and even harder. Harald Sonnberger has helped me to understand many things, but above all the importance of econometric testing. I wish I could blame him for all the remaining statistical mistakes I have made, but unfortunately they are the result of my own obstinacy.

Franz-Xaver Kaufmann, Hans Keman, Roger Morgan and John Stephens kindly gave me their critical comments when this work was still a doctoral thesis. I am also much indebted to the anonymous reader of Routledge for his or her constructive criticism. The participants of the conference on 'Comparative Studies of Welfare State Development:

Quantitative and Qualitative Dimensions' (Bremen, September 1992)
allowed me to test the plausibility of the argument. I am especially grateful
to Christoph Sachße for his extensive comments.

If it were not for the Swedish Institute for Social Research in Stockholm,
I would never have been able to write this book. I would like to thank
Walter Korpi for allowing me to use the data-set, Joakim Palme for preparing the data, sending me updates and telling me what I did wrong, and
Olli Kangas for sending me such excellent and extensive comments. I also
would like to thank Jorma Sipilä for his comments, Eugen Shoenfeld for
making me rethink my ideas on charity, Alex Hicks for sending me an
encouraging letter at a time I was ready to abandon the whole project, and
Bertjan Verbeek for helpful comments. The section on social democracy as
a model of the welfare state (Chapter 2) is an adopted and partly amended
and extended version of Esping-Andersen and van Kersbergen (1992:
190–95) and is reproduced, with kind permission, from the *Annual Review
of Sociology*, vol. 18, © 1992, by Annual Reviews Inc.

I know it is common practice to be critical of the administration of a
university. Unfortunately, in the case of the European Institute I cannot
think of anything important to complain about. The staff of the EUI library
have been helpful in many ways. I particularly would like to thank Peter
Keneally. The Department of Political Science and Public Administration
of the Vrije Universiteit, Amsterdam kindly allowed me to return to Italy
for some months to prepare the manuscript.

I also wish to thank Andreas Frijdal and Chris Colinet for their friendship, hospitality and for the many occasions on which they gave me the
opportunity to satisfy some of my non-academic needs. Beatrijs de Hartogh
has taught me, among other things, what 'harbour the homeless' as one of
the positive connotations of charity means. The people from Faella, particularly Anna, Roberto, the late Primo, Anita (Stella), Giuliana, Bistino,
Beppe and Filomena, have introduced me to real Italian life.

Bep and Corry, my parents, have contributed to this work in their own
peculiar manner. I can show my gratitude now that – for the moment at least
– we are all back in the Netherlands. Of course, I should also thank my wife,
Inger Stokkink, but I already did that yesterday and today, and I will do so
again tomorrow.

Abbreviations

ARP	Anti-Revolutionaire Partij
CDA	Christen Democratisch Appèl
CDU	Christlich-Demokratische Union
CGT	Confédération Générale du Travail
CHU	Christelijk-Historische Unie
CNEL	Consiglio Nazionale dell'Economia e del Lavoro
CPB	Centraal Planbureau
CSP	Christlich-Soziale Partei
CSU	Christlich-Soziale Union
CVP/PSC	Christelijke Volkspartij/Parti Social Chrétien
DC	Democrazia Cristiana
DGB	Deutscher Gewerkschaftsbund
ENEL	Ente Nazionale di Energia Elettrica
ILO	International Labour Organisation
INAIL	Istituto Nazionale per le Assicurazioni contro gli Infortuni sul Lavoro
INAM	Istituto Nazionale per l'Assicurazione contro le Malattie
INPS	Istituto Nazionale della Previdenza Sociale
IRI	Istituto per la Ricostruzione Industriale
KP	Katholieke Partij
KVP	Katholieke Volkspartij
MRP	Mouvement Républicain Populaire
NU	Nederlandse Unie
NVB	Nederlandse Volksbeweging
OECD	Organisation for Economic Cooperation and Development
ÖVP	Österreichische Volkspartei
PC	Parti Catholique
PCI	Partito Comunista Italiano
PDP	Parti Démocrate Populaire

PPI	Partito Popolare Italiano
PRI	Partito Repubblicano Italiano
PSB/BSP	Parti Socialiste Belge/Belgische Socialistische Partij
PSI	Partito Socialista Italiano
PvdA	Partij van de Arbeid
RKSP	Rooms Katholieke Staatspartij
SDAP	Sociaal Democratische Arbeiderspartij
SER	Sociaal-Economische Raad
SPD	Sozialdemokratische Partei Deutschlands
SPÖ	Sozialistische Partei Österreichs
SSIB	Svensk socialpolitik i internationell belysning
SSN	Servizio Sanitario Nazionale
StvA	Stichting van de Arbeid
USL	Unità Socio-sanitarie locali
VVD	Volkspartij voor Vrijheid en Democratie

1 Introduction

Christian democracy has been one of the most successful political movements in post-war Western Europe yet its crucial impact on the development of the modern European welfare state has been critically neglected. This book describes the origin and development of the Christian democratic movement and presents comparative accounts of the varying degrees of political entrenchment of national Christian democratic parties. Drawing upon cross-national indicators of welfare state development the existence of a distinctively Christian democratic (as opposed to a liberal or social democratic) welfare state regime, called social capitalism, is identified.

These social capitalist nations also manifest marked degrees of variation among themselves. Identifying the common ideology that unites them, the different national contexts under which Christian democratic social theory has been turned into political action are compared. Focusing on the essential peculiarity of Christian democracy – its ceaseless effort to accomplish a settlement between possibly opposed social interests – this study attempts to show how the different social policy performances of crucial cases (Germany, Italy and the Netherlands) have been affected not just by prevalent power structures but also by the coalitional strategies and political abilities of Christian democratic parties.

Generally, welfare state research has been dominated by the social democratic model. This model assumed a linear relationship between the power of the social democratic labour movement and welfare capitalism. The development of the welfare state was essentially seen as the social democratisation of capitalism. If one relaxes one of the main, although usually hidden suppositions of this model, namely that wage-earners in capitalist societies are by nature social democrats, it becomes possible to understand the development of welfare capitalism in nations where social democracy does not rule as the Christian democratisation of capitalism.

Chapter 2 provides a survey of welfare state literature. It demonstrates that the recent discussion on the relative role of Catholicism or Christian democracy in patterning social policy regimes is an effect of the inability of the social democratic model to deal successfully with exceptional cases. However, the literature still lacks a thorough account of Christian democracy and its possible bearing on the welfare state. This is because the departure from the social democratic model is still not radical enough and because in many ways Christian democracy is still an enigmatic political phenomenon.

Politically, Christian democracy is neither a substitute for conservatism nor a duplicate of social democracy; it is a distinctive political actor. Religious inspiration affects virtually every matter of policy. An articulate social theory of capitalism emphasises the vital role of social organisations and the subsidiary role of the state. A specific political ethic aims at reconciling conflicts and accomplishing social integration. Particularly relevant for social policy is the politics of mediation: the religiously inspired, ideologically condensed and politically practised conviction that conflicts of interests can and must be reconciled politically in order to restore the natural and organic harmony of society. The politics of mediation is a common characteristic of the Christian democratic movements of Western Europe. However, the precise configuration of interest representation and accommodation within these movements has led to different outcomes in terms of social policy performance.

In other words, it is incorrect to make too general claims on the association between Christian democracy and the development of a distinctive welfare state regime. There is a need for methodological prudence here, because the distinctiveness of Christian democracy forces one to think from the outset in terms of both similarities and variations. Comparative social research has tended to glorify generalisations and to treat exceptions to the general rule only as annoying 'outliers'. Case studies, by contrast, are inclined to the predictable conclusion that cases are so unique that generalisations are not warranted. The position on method taken here, however, is that exceptions are normally interesting, because they have the disposition to clarify or attenuate sweeping generalisations, and that 'unique' cases are usually fascinating not solely in their own right, but also because they are capable of generating hypotheses for further comparative research. Disputes over techniques have too often created artificial and quarantined 'methodological schools', where in reality methodological cross-fertilisation and open, intellectual intercourse are called for. If this betrays a fairly utopian conception of the scientific community, so be it.

In order to make sense of the often hypothesised, but rarely well-understood affiliation between Christian democracy and the welfare state, it is indispensable first to document the political entrenchment of the movement. Christian democracy is essentially a phenomenon of the period after the Second World War. It was the successor of the kind of social and political Catholicism that developed roughly between 1870 and 1940. In general, Catholic politics was characterised by the attempt to integrate the entire Catholic population into a unitary movement (Chapter 3). The extent to which this succeeded or failed accounts for considerable cross-national variation both in strength and complexion among the European Catholic parties. The level of integration that the post-war Christian democratic parties achieved greatly facilitated their development into dominant political actors. In the first decades after the Second World War the Christian democratic parties of Germany, Italy and the Netherlands gained at least a plurality of the vote, became the pivot of the political system and developed into government parties *par excellence*. This defined their dominant position. However, the historical conditions under which these movements came to power and under which they started to implement their political projects varied considerably. A closer comparison of the German, Italian and Dutch cases documents the diverging roads of power mobilisation and the effects on the political complexion of the movements (Chapter 4). This reinforces the critical view that empirically oriented cross-national comparisons of Christian democratic welfare states will have to be more sensitive to intragroup variations. The empirical questions are whether and to what extent Christian democracy, despite variations, promotes a distinctive path of welfare state development and whether and to what extent empirically observed variations are related to the different complexions and histories of national Christian democratic movements.

The existence of a Christian democratic welfare state regime and its variations can be documented and tested empirically (Chapters 5–7). A quantitative study of social expenditure (Chapter 5) manifests that Christian democratic politics does matter, but in a specific sense. Christian democracy and social democracy are well matched in terms of social spending, but spending is particularly promoted when competition between the two is fierce. The analyses reveal, however, that the German welfare state – at least in the 1960s – spent more than predicted. A closer study of this case is therefore imperative in order to find out why.

Because it is by now a well-established fact that levels of social spending tend to conceal crucial differences in the quality of social security arrangements, one needs to go beyond spending and study more qualitative indicators of welfare state development (Chapter 6). Yet if one looks at replacement rates and coverage ratios of major social security schemes, one

does not find significant differences between social and Christian democratic nations. Again competition is found to be an important factor in
explaining the relative generosity of social security schemes. An empirical
finding is that the Dutch welfare state is more generous than expected and
a case study of the Netherlands clarifies the reasons why. This case study
also uncovers that the distinctiveness of Christian democratic welfare states
is most likely to be found in how social rights are defined and to whom they
are granted. Further cross-national comparisons indicate that social
capitalist regimes are characterised by a family bias in their tax-benefit
systems and by a heavy reliance on benefits in cash rather than in kind. In
other words, welfare states redistribute equally large sums of money, but
they do so in fundamentally different ways. Christian democratic welfare
states are passive, transfer-oriented systems. These characteristics are then
hypothesised to have a definite impact on labour force participation.
Regression analysis indicates that such a hypothesis is indeed plausible.

The Dutch case study also provides another proposition for cross-
national examination. Christian democrats seem to have a clear preference
for a specific organisational structure of the welfare state that aims at
reducing the direct control of the state over the implementation of social
policies and that reinforces social differentiation. Empirical analysis
demonstrates that the movement is indeed positively related to these characteristics (Chapter 7). The organisation of Christian democratic welfare
states is generally characterised by a minimalisation of state control, the
reproduction of status differentials and the fragmentation of major
schemes. In terms of the latter feature, however, the Italian welfare state
stands out, which justifies a closer inspection of this case.

Bringing together the findings of the cross-national comparisons and the
evidence from the case studies (Chapter 8), the twofold thesis can be
defended, first, that there is indeed – despite variations – a core of social
policies that is distinctively Christian democratic and, second, that the
variations around this common core can by and large be explained by the
different historical conditions under which Christian democratic parties
have assumed central positions of power and by the different political
contexts in which they have functioned. It is this common kernel which is
termed social capitalism. The explanation of social capitalism and the
Christian democratic project draws upon a clarification of the ideal concept
of citizenship that Christian democracy fosters, upon an elaboration of the
key ideological concepts of the movement and upon a delineation of the
ideal-type of social capitalism.

Where does social capitalism come from? What were the historical
sources of Christian democracy and social capitalism? Why is the ideal

political economy of Christian democracy both social and capitalist? The answers to these questions (Chapters 9 and 10) suggest that Christian democracy and its core theory of social capitalism are related to the continental European movements of political and social Catholicism, i.e. the main 'little tradition' of Roman Catholicism. It was this political tradition which managed to formulate an appealing alternative to both liberalism and socialism. The 'grand tradition', i.e. Vatican doctrine, has contributed little more than perhaps a legitimation of the efforts of social and political Catholics all over Europe to find a distinctive political place. Vatican social teaching has always lagged behind the ideological and practical solutions that Christian democracy has nourished in the course of its political struggles in the twentieth century.

The main conclusions of this study (Chapter 11) allow for a discussion and elaboration of the accidental yet crucial finding that social capitalism was not only the outcome, but also the medium of Christian democratic power mobilisation. A further explanation of the mechanisms of power accumulation typical for Christian democracy demonstrates that social capitalist arrangements have been crucial for the movement's political project. These considerations also make clear that the contemporary de-composition of Christian democracy, particularly exemplified by the downfall of the Italian party and the decline of dominance of the Dutch movement, is not so much (or at least not only) caused by secularisation, but rather (or primarily) by the increasing difficulties of upholding social capitalism and the social contracts it embodies as a medium of power accumulation.

In a recent paper, Therborn (1994:106) wrote the following: 'Was there ever a specifically Catholic social policy embodied in modern institutions? At least as far as the significant latterday welfare states are concerned, the answer must be no' (see Castles 1994). The whole point of the present enterprise is that the answer must, instead, be yes.

2 The welfare state and Christian democracy

An introduction

The debate on the origins, growth and nature of the welfare state has been flourishing for more than two decades now. It has been an exciting controversy with many outstanding contributions.[1] The extensive body of literature finds its justification in the fact that the welfare state is a fundamental structural component of contemporary capitalist democracies.[2] The purpose of this chapter is to introduce the field of comparative welfare state research and to justify the need in the literature for a more thorough analysis of the often conjectured, but rarely well-appreciated association between Catholicism (or Christian democracy) and welfare state development.

First, a short review is offered of the leading approaches, methods of research, methodological disputes and current developments that are representative for this field of comparative research. Then follows an examination of the literature in somewhat greater detail. The discussion concentrates on theories and empirical studies that attempt to explain the growth of the welfare state and the cross-national variations in the development of social policies in advanced capitalist democracies. In other words, the focus is on empirically oriented theories that attempt to identify the causal forces and mechanisms promoting the development of the welfare state.[3]

The analysis below shows that the dominant 'social democratic model' of welfare state development largely evolved as a critique of the 'logic of industrialism' approach. The problem of the relative role of Christian democracy in shaping welfare state regimes, in turn, primarily surfaced as a by-product of the social democratic model. Time and again inexplicable exceptions were found to the leading hypothesis of this approach, namely that variations in the levels of social spending across nations are largely explained by the strength and rule of the social democratic labour movement.

As is often the case when theories do not fit the facts, there are two possibilities: there might indeed be something very peculiar about the exceptional case (empirical reason) or there is something wrong with the elementary axiomatic structure of the theory (theoretical reason). A solution for exceptionalism may then consist of rethinking one's basic assumptions, i.e. arguing beyond the unsuccessful theory, or relaxing some major empirical hypothesis, i.e. explaining away the exception within the theoretical framework. Understandably, it was mainly the latter option that initially was chosen in order to deal with the empirically observed association between Catholicism and the welfare state.

The solution for exceptionalism was sought in hypothesising that quasi-social democratic welfare policies could be carried out by non-social democratic actors, too. Another account of welfare capitalism without social democracy was given by the suggestion that the specific properties of Catholic social theory and the pro-welfare stance of the Church also promote social policy. More generally, Catholic parties were argued to be functionally equivalent to social democracy. Under conditions of economic prosperity and depending on the extent to which various parties were backed by affiliated organisations of the working class, Christian democracy and social democracy were both big spenders. However, these in themselves useful attempts to solve the problem of exceptional cases left largely unquestioned a number of fundamental, yet usually unreasoned assumptions of the social democratic model. A critical discussion of these presuppositions in the conclusion of this chapter passes into a preliminary argument on Christian democracy and the possible identification of a distinctively Catholic type of welfare state.

THEORIES, METHODS AND RECENT DEVELOPMENTS

There are three main theoretical approaches in the comparative, empirical literature on the welfare state. First, functionalist theories understand the growth of the welfare state in developed nations by and large as the response of the state to the growing needs of its citizens. Second, class mobilisation or interest group theories seek the causes for cross-national differences in welfare policies and expenditure among industrial democracies primarily in the varying capacities of collective political actors (labour movements, interest groups, political parties) to articulate, politicise and implement welfare demands. Institutionalist theories, finally, argue that institutions (the rules and regulations of democratic policy-making), operating relatively autonomously from social and political pressures, determine the growth and shape of the welfare state. These contrasting approaches do not simply differ in how they construct the causal logic of their argument; above all they vary with respect to how they grasp the explanatory problem of welfare state evolution. The principal interest of functional accounts lies in finding an answer to the question why different nations adopt similar social and economic policies. Their explanatory problem concerns the convergence of social policies among nations that have reached an advanced stage of economic development. Political and institutionalist theories, on the other hand, deal with the question of cross-national variations in social and economic policies among nations that are very similar in their economic and social structures. Their explanatory focus is on the divergence of welfare state development in nations that are largely comparable in other respects.

The range of research designs and methods is probably as wide as the theoretical approaches that can be distinguished. Nevertheless, two distinct and opposite methods figure prominently in the literature. First, the cross-national quantitative research strategy, which is variable-oriented, includes many cases and makes use of statistical techniques to test causal relations between variables. Second, the comparative historical design, which is case-oriented, examines many variables and offers an in-depth study of a single or limited number of cases by looking at complex historical conditions and sequences (Ragin 1987, 1991; Rueschemeyer, Stephens and Stephens 1992). As Ragin (1987) has shown, the goals of the two major strategies of comparative social science differ radically. Whereas the comparative historical, case-oriented design acknowledges the complexity of social and historical events and, accordingly, is reluctant to seek general explanations that go beyond the complex and unique conditions of a single case, the cross-national, variable-oriented strategy seeks general explanations precisely by disregarding (or holding constant) many of the distinctive features and historical conditions of single cases. Both methods, moreover, contrast with respect to the role of theory in research: 'the case-oriented approach uses theory to aid historical interpretation and to guide the identification of important causal factors; the variable-oriented strategy, by contrast, usually tests hypotheses derived from theory' (Ragin 1987:55).

As a result of the co-existence of these two contrasting methods, the discipline of comparative welfare state research – like other areas of comparative research (e.g. Rueschemeyer, Stephens and Stephens 1992:12–39) – has tended to yield opposite substantial results, particularly when studying the explanatory relevance of political variables. Thus, case-oriented studies typically deny a simple link between social interests and political outputs, whereas numerous variable-oriented analyses consistently show the causal association between, for instance, the strength of left political parties and social spending or other measures of welfare state development.

In her comparative case study of health politics in France, Switzerland and Sweden, Ellen M. Immergut (1992:243) concludes that 'in contrast to approaches that seek the roots of political activity in social forces, the cases discussed here have shown that politics can be independent of social power'. However, in his macro-comparative analysis of 18 welfare states, Esping-Andersen (1990:1) argues that 'the history of political class coalitions is the most decisive cause of welfare-state variations.'

One of the major problems of the field is that until recently representatives of both research traditions have rarely attempted to discuss seriously what sets them apart and what explains the continuous contradictions of their respective findings. True, the research strategies are difficult to fuse, because they set separate priorities: universality and generalisations versus historical precision; testing of hypotheses versus theoretical argument. The important point that Rueschemeyer, Stephens and Stephens (1992) have made is that such controversies cannot be attributed to an epistemological conflict alone. Wherever different research strategies lead to conflicting results, it is empirical evidence and theoretical improvements that ought to resolve disputes, not philosophical or technical reasoning. The bearing of this point will be stressed below.

The state of the art of welfare state research is even more confusing if one remembers that inconsistency of findings and contradictory results are not only found between studies that employ radically different methods, but plague the quantitative field as a whole. As a result, new methodological disputes have arisen. Thus, O'Connor and Brym (1988) have concluded that many of the inconsistent findings in the literature can be attributed to inconsistencies in the divergent manner in which the strategic (both dependent and independent) variables are conceptualised and operationalised. In addition, the reliance on cross-sectional multiple regression analyses lowers the reliability of findings because of the low case-to-variable ratio and the presence of high correlations among the independent variables.

The current literature is largely characterised by four related theoretical and methodological developments. First, theoretical attempts have been made to move away from the unsatisfactory conceptualisation of the welfare state in terms of social spending alone; other indicators of welfare state development are introduced that capture better the variations in social policies. Second, there is an increasing tendency to refine the quality of data-sets (pooling cross-sectional and time-series data), statistical techniques and operationalisations of dependent and independent variables. Third, there appears to be a potentially productive willingness among various theorists to abandon the traditional trenches of methodological warfare and strive for a settled peace by integrating each other's insights and methods. Finally, the age of 'Swedocentrism' (Shalev 1983) and the social democratic bias of much of the literature seems largely over, opening up the intellectual, theoretical and normative space needed for making sense of the possible existence of a Christian democratic welfare state type.

THE COMPARATIVE STUDY OF WELFARE STATES: TWO DECADES OF RESEARCH

Functional accounts

Theories which stress the causal primacy of industrialisation typically argue that the welfare state is largely the answer of society to the growing needs of its population. Industrialisation creates the demand for welfare by destroying the traditional bonds of kinship, family ties and the guilds, which were the main institutions providing social security. The development of industrial society (and its correlates of economic growth, urbanisation, demographic change) at the same time creates the possibility of new forms of social security of a more comprehensive character: the welfare state. The prime explanatory problem for these theories concerns the very existence of, rather than the variation among, Western welfare states (Wilensky and Lebeaux 1965; Kerr *et al.* 1973; Cutright 1965; Pryor 1968; Rimlinger 1971; Jackman 1975; Wilensky 1975).

For theories that accord causal centrality to modernisation (economic development, secularisation, democratisation) comparable considerations hold. The welfare state is seen as an effect of modernisation and as one of the mechanisms restoring disrupted societal integration. The explanatory object typically involves the timing rather than the existence of social policy in modern society. The introduction of major social programmes is seen as directly associated with the rhythm and tempo of modernisation (Flora and Heidenheimer 1981a, 1981b, 1981c; Flora and Alber 1981; Alber 1982; Kohl 1983; Flora 1983, 1986; Alber 1989).

Both the argument of the 'logic of industrialism' and the major thesis of the 'logic of modernisation' stress that societal development created the demand for social security that could only be met by means of state intervention. In other words, the politics of social welfare is a function of the industrialisation and modernisation of societies. Economic development, industrialisation and modernisation are preconditions for welfare state development in a dual sense: the welfare state is 'a product of both the new *need* and the new *resources* generated by the process of industrialization' (Pierson 1991:16). The developmental perspective of the 'logic of industrialism' is most clearly exemplified in the work of Wilensky (1975).

Theories of industrialisation and modernisation argue in favour of an objective problem pressure of societal integration. Both industrial and modernisation theories are functional accounts, because they assume that societal problem pressures emerge from the wide disruption created by development and that the welfare state, in turn, is the automatic and functional response to such disruption. A natural consequence of this reasoning is that all nations sharing the experience of modernisation and industrialisation are assumed to converge in their adoption of social policies. The further nations are on the scale of industrial development, the more they are likely to advance social policies, and the more they will tend to look alike. However, it remains obscure how needs and demands can create their own fulfilment. There is little or no account of political inter-mediation, other than that the growth of the welfare state 'is hastened by the interplay of political elite perceptions, mass pressures, and welfare bureaucracies' (Wilensky 1975:47). As theories of the differences between modern welfare states, moreover, they lack the analytical tools because the main variables show no variation among the advanced industrial nations. Schmidt (1989) has argued that an industrialism thesis does account for differences in social spending between rich and poor nations, but cannot cope with 'exceptions' that either spend too much or too little, given their level of development.

Marxist theories of the welfare state (Piven and Cloward 1972; O'Connor 1973; Ginsburg 1979; Gough 1979; Lenhardt and Offe 1984; see also Mishra 1984) share the functional reasoning of the industrialist and modernisation theories. Although it is usually admitted that the welfare state in one way or another embodies a real improvement in the condition of wage labour within capitalism – i.e. warranting the (limited) possibility of reform – the welfare state is primarily analysed as a capitalist state. Such a state first and foremost (or, if you like, 'in the last instance') fulfils the function of assuring the profitability of capital. Welfare arrangements are secondary effects of this function. The mitigation of the harmful and oppressive character of capitalism is an accidental side-effect. Since all nations considered are capitalist nations, social policy produces the same effect everywhere. Political determinants are irrelevant, since the welfare state is a function of the logic of the capitalist economy. The Marxist argument is that social policy exists because capital needs it.

Within the Marxist paradigm there is a general tendency to confuse effects and functions. Thus, when O'Connor (1973:138) redefines the meaning of social insurance as mainly an insurance for capitalists and corporations to create stability and security among workers, which, in turn, guarantees capital accumulation, he mistakenly holds this possible effect as its function. Gough's (1979) very definition of the welfare state as the use of power to modify the reproduction of labour and to maintain the non-working population in capitalist societies, determines this confusion of effects and functions. The transformation of non-wage-labourers into wage-labourers and their maintenance as such may have been an important effect of social policy (Lenhardt and Offe 1984), but cannot be taken to explain its emergence and character. The justified criticism of Marxist functionalism does not necessarily imply, however, that one has to abandon a critical analysis of social policy altogether. No doubt, social policy may have a legitimising effect. But it is not always because of this effect that states pursue social policies. Admittedly, the state might facilitate the accumulation of capital, but such a phenomenon is the *explanandum* not the *explanans*, let alone an account of cross-national variation. In short, Marxist functionalist theories point to the possibility of (unintended) effects of social policy that may (or may not) be advantageous to the survival of capitalism. Favourable effects, however, cannot be taken to explain phenomena of which they are the effect, not even if one recognises unintended effects (see Elster 1989:98–9).

In general, the functional accounts of industrialism, modernisation or capitalism assume convergence among economically developed nations. Political explanations are neither necessary nor useful. The problem of the causal (political) mechanisms that might explain how societal needs or demands are converted into effective policies and social rights is largely left untouched. Most importantly, variations in welfare state development among advanced nations with similar economic structures cannot be explained.

Social democracy as a model of the welfare state

The debate on the social democratisation of capitalism has naturally centred on equality, either in terms of the distributive end result, or in terms of the institutional commitments of welfare states, such as universalism, solidarity, the generosity of social rights and their capacity to 'de-commodify' workers (Esping-Andersen 1990; Western 1989).

The first generation of research was primarily a debate with the 'logic of industrialism' thesis as discussed above, but increasingly also with the 'median voter' view of democratic politics as represented in particular by Jackman (1975, 1986). Hence, the objective was twofold: to demonstrate that politics matters and that the party composition of the polity makes a decisive difference. Hewitt (1977) was one of the first to examine explicitly the capacity of social democratic labour movements to affect redistribution in both these senses. His argument is that the mere presence of democratic structures could not sufficiently explain gains in equality and that social democratic rule is a necessary condition of egalitarian outcomes.

The causal effect of social democracy on welfare state outcomes was subsequently corroborated by a large number of studies that employed the variety of research designs identified above. In the comparative case-approach, some studies emphasised the Scandinavian experience in particular, primarily because of the seemingly close association between social democratic dominance and advanced welfare states (Castles 1978; Korpi 1978, 1983; Esping-Andersen and Korpi 1986, Esping-Andersen 1985a). Others sought to identify the social democratic effect via matched comparisons between 'failed' and 'successful' cases, such as Higgins and Apple's (1981) and Pontusson's (1988) British–Swedish contrast, Esping-Andersen and Korpi's (1984) or Scharpf's (1984) comparison of Austria, Germany and Sweden, and Hage, Hanneman and Gargan's (1989) four-nation comparison. By comparing nations in which the welfare state outcomes seemed to diverge despite social democratic movements of similar strength, these studies served to identify more concretely the conditions under which social democratic movements are capable of introducing change. Three key conclusions emerge from these studies. Castles (1978) emphasises the weakness of the right as a basic precondition; Stephens (1979a) and Higgins and Apple (1981) were among the first to suggest that the political efficacy of social democracy is contingent on trade union strength or cohesion; and Castles (1978) as well as Esping-Andersen (1985a) hold that the social democratic model can only be pursued effectively through the building of political coalitions (especially with the agrarians).

The dominant approach, however, has been the cross-national, quantitative design to test the social democratic thesis on the basis of 16–20 advanced nations (Hewitt 1977; Korpi 1983; Swank and Hicks 1984, 1985; Esping-Andersen 1985b). Most analyses are cross-sectional, but (pooled-) time series analyses have become common in recent years (Alvarez, Garret and Lange 1991; Griffin *et al.* 1986, Griffin, O'Connell and McCammon 1989; Korpi 1989). Using a variety of different measures of both social democratic strength and the policy outcomes (from social spending and redistribution to various institutional characteristics), most of these studies have in common a theory of working-class mobilisation of political power, i.e. the social democratisation of capitalism depends on the degree to which the balance of power favours labour. In most cases, the political parties were identified as the chief causal agents. Swank and Hicks (1985), for example, test a number of competing explanatory hypotheses on social spending (transfers) and equality, such as level and rate of economic growth, the role of democratic institutions, political power of labour and capital, and increasing needs. They find that the most consistent explanation concerns class-based political actors. The degree of unionisation significantly influences transfer spending as does the presence of large monopoly-sector firms. In addition, the finding is that lower- and working-class protest (demonstrations, strikes) positively affects social spending.

The power resources argument has been most fully developed by Korpi (1983) and the fully developed social democratic model can be summarised as follows. The more the mass of the population is organised as wage-earners within the social democratic movement, the higher the quality (universalism, solidarity, redistribution) of the welfare arrangements tends to be and, as a result, the higher the extent of equality. A developed welfare state, therefore, is evidence for a decisive shift in the balance of power in favour of the working class and social democracy. The distribution of power resources between the main social classes of capitalist society determines political intervention in the economy and the extent of inequality.

This basic power resources model has been subject to several amendments, precipitating the emergence of a second generation of research. Apart from the emphasis on the relative weakness and fragmentation of the right (Castles 1978, 1985) and on the distinctiveness of political class alliances (Esping-Andersen 1985a, 1985b) mentioned above, there is a consensus in the literature that the political efficacy of left parties depends on the extent to which they count on strong trade unionism (Stephens 1979a) and, especially, on a centralised, neocorporatist industrial relations system (Cameron 1978, 1984; Schmidt 1983; Scharpf 1984, 1987; Hicks, Swank and Ambuhl 1989).

As Shalev (1983) has pointed out, many of these studies assume the social democratic welfare state to be a leap in the direction of socialism or, indeed, an early image of the future 'good society'. At the very least, the social democratic welfare state represents an intermediary stage between capitalism and socialism (Korpi 1983; Stephens 1979a; Stephens and Stephens 1982). Several authors have challenged this kind of embryonic socialism assumption. Tilton's (1990) analysis of Swedish social democratic ideology argues that its dominant values have their roots in a radical–liberal commitment to freedom of choice rather than to socialism. Baldwin (1990) rejects the causal link between social democracy and solidaristic social policies since, in his analysis, their mainsprings are not necessarily in the working classes. His contribution to the debate is innovative for two reasons. First, he shows that while growing equality may be a characteristic of modern welfare states, it has not been its goal. The welfare state is more about reapportioning risks than about the redistribution of wealth. Equality refers to risk redistribution. Second, the theory of risk and distribution allows for a rejection of what Baldwin calls the labourist account (i.e. the social democratic model with its stress on class power and class coalitions), but at the same time protects the social interpretation of the development of the welfare state. The main problem with the labourist approach has been its narrow focus on the working class as the only risk category. The critical insight is that class may, but rarely does, coincide with a risk category. The labourist view mistakenly assumes that welfare policies are explained in terms of a victory of the working class over the bourgeoisie. Certain risks, of course, have tended to coincide with class. Occupational injuries and unemployment come with the position of an industrial worker. It is this coincidence that has led to the labourist interpretation. More often, however, risk categories cut through the cleavage of class, a fact that establishes the possibility of varying risk coalitions. The welfare state is a pooling of risk rather than of resources (Baldwin 1990:19). Baldwin's crucial claim is that what historically has determined the solidarity of social policy was not working-class strength, but, on the contrary, the fact that 'otherwise privileged groups discovered that they shared a common interest in reallocating risk with the disadvantaged' (Baldwin 1990:292).

Similarly, Heclo and Madsen (1986) and Therborn (1989) argue that the principles of solidarity and equality that characterise Swedish social democracy have less to do with socialism than with the Swedish historical tradition. Thus, it may very well be Swedish history, and not social democracy, that constitutes the root cause of reform. The implication is that the Swedish model is inapplicable elsewhere, so that even if Sweden did arrive at socialism, it is doubtful that the next candidate in terms of labour movement power mobilisation even would approximate Swedish-style achievements (see Milner 1989).

In the debate with the functionalist 'logic of industrialism' and modernisation theses (and their Marxist equivalents), the explanatory power of left parties cum trade union strength seemed to hold up against standard demographic and modernisation variables, such as age structure and level of economic development. Yet, the results depend very much on differences in variable measurement and methodological design. Left power explanations tend to vanish when controlling for age structure when the outcome is measured as social expenditure ratios (Pampel and Williamson 1989; Esping-Andersen 1990) because such a large share of spending is age-dependent. As Griffin, O'Connell and McCammon (1989) show, cross-sectional and time-series models may tell different stories. Pampel and Stryker (1990) argue that cross-sectional data underestimate the effect of variables that tend to change over time (like demographic structure) and overestimate relatively stable variables (like corporatism).

Such methodological reflections and empirical findings constitute a challenge to the social democratic model as they imply that the struggle between labour and capital is not the dominant dynamic explaining growth of welfare spending and equality. A nation's demographic structure appears to be the single most influential determinant of social spending, because older people simply need more care. However, it is not at all clear that older people get the care they need because they need it. The question of how such a need was translated into an effective social right (and with what qualitative characteristics) before these programmes were inaugurated or at a time when these schemes had hardly had the time to 'mature' is largely left unanswered. It is hard to imagine how 'need' in itself can explain its fulfillment. Nevertheless, the relative advantages of cross-sectional and longitudinal analyses pose an interesting question: what type of analysis, time-series or cross-sectional, would correspond best to the research problem of variation? The current literature has mainly been preoccupied with a re-examination of what is to be explained, whether and how social democracy may be decisive and which alternatives for the cross-sectional design are appropriate.

Challenges to the social democratic thesis

The one-to-one relationship between labour movement power and welfare outcomes has been challenged in different ways. In one group one finds those who emphasise the decisiveness of neocorporatist solutions to global economic dependency. Cameron (1978, 1984) suggests that the association between strong social democracy and welfare states is linked to a country's position in the international economy. Specifically he argues that the vulnerability that small, open economies face favours the expansion of the public economy so as to reduce uncertainty via social guarantees, full employment and more active government management of the economy. As elaborated more fully in the work of Katzenstein (1985), the real causal chain would appear to be that small open nations develop democratic corporatist structures as a way to enhance domestic consensus, facilitate economic adjustments and maintain international competitiveness. While democratic corporatism is promoted by the presence of strong social democratic labour movements, Katzenstein points to Switzerland and the Netherlands to suggest that they may not constitute a necessary condition.

At this point it becomes increasingly difficult to separate the neocorporatist argument from the social democratic thesis (see also Keman 1988).

Cameron's argument has often been mistakenly interpreted as an outright rejection of the social democratic thesis: the explanatory power attached to 'openness' seems to suggest that the effect of social democracy is spurious. However, the gist of his thesis (see especially Cameron 1984) is more deeply historical, suggesting that the openness of an economy favours certain structural features in societies which, in turn, enhance the power of labour. Since small, open economies tend to be industrially concentrated, they also tend to develop strong and unified interest organis- ations. The capacity to forge broad consensus and to mobilise power is further helped by the homogeneity and concentration of the labour force (see also Hemerijck 1993).

The importance of neocorporatist arrangements for social democratic success has been stressed in the studies of Schmidt (1983), Keman (1988), and Hicks, Swank and Ambuhl (1989). They suggest that social democracy is most likely to promote (and defend) welfare statism successfully if its parliamentary power is matched by strong consensus-building mechanisms in both the polity and economy. These studies also suggest that neo- corporatist intermediation comes to play an especially important role in maintaining welfare policies during economic crisis periods – the distri- butive battles that erupt when growth declines are better managed with 'all-encompassing' interest organisations. Studying income distribution, Hicks and Swank (1984) and Muller (1989) suggest that the strength of left parties (and economic openness) influences income distribution directly, while trade unionisation and centralisation have decisive indirect effects by providing the electoral basis for social democracy. There appears to be a growing consensus that parties or unions alone have little effect and that successful social democratisation requires a configuration of strong left parties in government backed by an encompassing and centralised trade union movement.

The explanatory power of social democracy has also been questioned in terms of the historical roots of welfare state reforms. Based on a study of France, Britain, Germany, the Netherlands and the United States, de Swaan (1988) puts forward what might be termed an elite-conflict explanation, arguing that welfare states developed through conflicts and compromises struck between elites in response to their understanding of underlying social problems and needs. Moreover, the catalyst for change was not so much the rising working classes as the declining veto power of the tradi- tional *petit bourgeoisies* in combination with the decline of private property accumulation. De Swaan's argument provides indirectly some support for the kind of state-centred accounts found in Heclo (1974), in Heclo and Madsen (1986), in Weir, Orloff and Skocpol (1988), and in Skocpol (1992), but also in the interactive model of Hage, Hanneman and Gargan (1989), where the efficacy of left power depends on state responses. De Swaan's critique loses some of its bite, however, because he fails to consider key social democratic cases, Scandinavia in particular. The inclusion of the Scandinavian countries in a broader European comparison is, in contrast, what makes Baldwin's (1990) rejection of the social democratic thesis much more challenging. Trying to trace the origins of key welfare state characteristics, such as universalism and solidarity, Baldwin shows that what one typically attributes to the social democratic movements should, instead, be traced to the efforts of 'risk classes' to secure themselves. In his account, the historical role of the social democratic movements is essentially a spurious one; indeed, Baldwin goes so far as to argue that the agrarians were the real root cause of the Scandinavian model.

It may be that Baldwin exaggerates the role of the agrarians, and he certainly downplays the impact of social democratic movements in key junctures of Scandinavian reform, as Olsson (1990:90–107) has convinc- ingly shown. Yet, the real value of his study lies in unravelling the contents of the 'black box' that is, in effect, substituted for a serious analysis of how demands are transformed into party politics. Baldwin challenges adherents of the social democratic model to rethink the rela- tionship between class and politics. Is it possible that social democratic movements represent 'risk-class' alliances rather than working classes?

Aside from much greater attention to the historical process by which social democratic power translates into outcomes, the recent literature has begun rethinking what precisely the theory should explain. The choice of many (especially early) studies to gauge welfare state achievements in terms of social expenditures was defended in pragmatic terms (spending data were reliable and easy to collect), and substantially (they should reflect 'effort' or the scope of the social wage). Yet the spending variable has been criticised for its loose correspondence to the theoretical issues of social democratisation (Esping-Andersen 1990). In particular, aggregate spend- ing ratios fail to distinguish the characteristic effects of social democracy from those of other political forces.

The choice of a variable that measures income inequality and redistri- bution appears immediately to gain validity to the extent that equality is the traditional socialist goal. Since the early study by Hewitt (1977), there is considerable evidence in favour of a social democratic effect on income distribution (Bjorn 1979; Stephens 1979a; van Arnhem and Schotsman

1982; Hicks and Swank 1984; Swank and Hicks 1985; Muller 1989; Hage, Hanneman and Gargan 1989). Still, income distribution is for several reasons a problematic variable. On technical grounds, aggregate data available until the recent arrival of the Luxembourg Income Study (see Smeeding, O'Higgins and Rainwater 1990; Mitchell 1990) are not truly comparable. On theoretical grounds, income distribution is problematic to the extent that the kinds of universalistic and generous welfare programmes associated with successful social democratic politics may lose their redistributive effect because they increasingly favour the middle classes (LeGrand 1982; Goodin and LeGrand 1987; Esping-Andersen 1990). Ringen (1987) argues that large welfare states will generate greater equality, but this may be true only of transfers. With the rising importance of collective services, any firm conclusion must await more research on non-cash income distribution.

There is some evidence to suggest that the social democratic effect is more evident when measured against institutional characteristics of welfare states. This is the case in Myles' (1989) study of pension systems, Korpi's (1989) and Kangas' (1991) studies of sickness insurance, Palme's (1990) study of pension rights and Esping-Andersen's (1990) study of welfare state attributes such as universalism, the public–private mix, the importance of means tests, and active labour market policies. Yet, as research has moved in the direction of studying the institutional properties of welfare states, it has also been forced away from the kind of linear 'more or less' or 'the bigger, the better' social democratisation conception that has dominated the literature. Thus Kangas' (1991:52) study of social expenditures and social rights concludes that 'the biggest are not necessarily the best, but the best are rarely the smallest'.

One of the major insights of the contemporary debate is that to equate social democracy and the welfare state may have been a mistake. There is considerable variation on both the independent (social democracy) and the dependent (the welfare state and equality) variables (Keman 1988). Titmuss (1974) argued that welfare states differ fundamentally as to their institutionalisation of solidarity and equality. Only his 'institutional redistributive' type comes anywhere near the social democratic ideal. Furniss and Tilton (1977) offer a distinction between the social security state and the social welfare state, only the latter representing the social democratic ideal. Therborn (1986a; 1987) has stressed the vital criteria of social policy and a commitment to full employment. Without the commitment to full employment there is no social democratic welfare state. He therefore argues in favour of a regeneration of welfare state theory (Therborn 1987:239).

Esping-Andersen (1985b; 1990) has accepted this challenge, arguing that there is a striking conceptual indifference in the literature with respect to the object of study itself, the welfare state. Starting from the judgment that 'expenditures are epiphenomenal to the theoretical substance of welfare states' (1990:19) and the reflection that 'it is difficult to imagine that anyone struggled for spending *per se*' (1990:21), he suggests that the study of welfare states has much to gain by looking at the quality of social rights, the typical patterns of stratification and the manner in which the state, the market and the family interact in the production of social welfare. There does not exist any causal linearity between societal power and welfare statism. Welfare states cluster along qualitative and political dimensions.

Esping-Andersen distinguishes three types of welfare state regimes: a social democratic, a liberal and a corporatist or conservative regime. These regimes differ with respect to the major institutions guaranteeing social security (the state, the market or the family); the kind of stratification systems upheld by the institutional mix of these institutions (the extent of status and class differentiation, segmentation and inequality typically implied in social security systems); and the degree of decommodification (i.e. 'the degree to which individuals, or families, can uphold a socially acceptable standard of living independently of market participation' (Esping-Andersen 1990:37)). The social democratic regime is characterised by a political commitment to equality; it reduces status and class differentials and modifies greatly the market dependence of wage-labour. Particularism and an unwillingness to alter the status and class structure are major features of the conservative regime, which also favours a social policy that privileges and preserves the family. In the liberal welfare state regime the market predominates and social rights are generally modest and attached to performance on the labour market. The variations in welfare state regimes are by and large explained by the distinct modes in which classes (particularly the working class) became politically mobilised, the diverging structuration of class alliances and class coalitions, and the different national policy legacies.

Current developments

Four theoretical and methodological improvements characterise current developments in the debate on the welfare state. These concern the reconceptualisation of the strategic variables in an attempt to respecify both the welfare state and the causal forces fostering its development (Esping-Andersen 1990; Huber, Ragin and Stephens 1993; Hicks and Misra 1993; Castles and Mitchell 1993; Janoski and Hicks 1994), the endeavour to master contradictory and inconsistent empirical results (Griffin, O'Connell and McCammon 1989; Hage, Hanneman and Gargan 1989; Korpi 1989; O'Connor 1988; O'Connor and Brym 1988; Pampel and Williamson 1989; Hicks and Swank 1992; Hicks and Misra 1993; Huber, Ragin and Stephens 1993; Huber and Stephens 1993), the attempt to reconcile methodological controversies and propose alternatives (e.g. Amenta 1993; Janoski and Hicks 1994), and a slow but gradual farewell to approximately 15 years of dominance of the social democratic model.

In the attempts to reconceptualise the welfare state, Esping-Andersen's (1985b, 1990) work stands out as having decisively changed the direction of theoretical and empirical research. In effect, much of the up-to-date literature provides (sometimes overly) critical discussions of the theory of welfare state regimes, but is at the same time greatly indebted to the suggestion that there are various configurations of market, state and the family, and that variations in welfare state development are 'not linearly distributed, but clustered by regime-types' (Esping-Andersen 1990:26).

Recent studies increasingly highlight distinct welfare state types and accept the idea that the social democratic welfare state is but one variant. Castles and Mitchell (1993) attempt to refine the theory of welfare state regimes by arguing that the liberal regime identified by Esping-Andersen in reality includes a 'fourth world of welfare capitalism'. The means-tested, residual type of welfare state found in Australia should be considered as the result of a coherent social democratic strategy once one takes into account labour's success in establishing guaranteed employment and wage growth, accompanied by occupational social rights. Looking at welfare expenditure and benefit equality, taxes and transfers, and redistribution of incomes, Castles and Mitchell show the relevance of their proposed four-quadrant typology of welfare states. Particularly interesting is their attempt to link these welfare state types to distinct political configurations, which clearly single out a liberal, a conservative, a 'radical' and a social democratic regime. The existence of a radical regime is explained in terms of a distinct historical, political pattern, 'consisting of a labour movement unable to obtain a degree of partisan control commensurate with its political support base in the community and of an historical legacy of radical egalitarianism' (Castles and Mitchell 1993:123). Esping-Andersen (forthcoming) argues that this point is theoretically relevant, because it shows that the biased focus of much of the literature on the welfare *state* runs the risk of underrating the possible effects of private or less straightforwardly political interventions in the market.[4] It has to be stressed that – except for the radical regime – Castles and Mitchell's analysis largely reproduces the worlds of welfare capitalism distinguished by Esping-Andersen. For the present purposes it is important to note that on different indicators – household transfers, average benefit equality, income and profit taxes – Austria, France, Germany, Italy and the Netherlands consistently fall into one group. An intriguing finding, however, is that in terms of the political configurations that correspond to the four worlds, only Germany, Italy and the Netherlands perfectly fit in the conservative group. The welfare states in these nations are apparently very similar and are characterised by high levels of social expenditure and a considerable degree of equality, whereas the political characteristics of these nations are low trade union density and high non-right incumbency. Anticipating the argument below, *prima facie* these three cases seem to lend themselves very well to a closer comparison.

The debate over strategic variables and contradictory or inconsistent empirical findings has had a slight tendency to slip into a predominantly technical squabble, confusing statistical techniques, methodology and substance. Such controversies are exemplified by the critical exchange between O'Connor (1990) and Pampel and Stryker (1990). Introducing more sophisticated statistical techniques alone cannot settle unresolved issues. The more fundamental methodological issue pertains to the necessity of relating findings of quantitative analyses back to the theoretical assumptions of the various models. Huber, Ragin and Stephens (1993) show that different conceptualisations, operationalisations, and measurements of the welfare state and the factors that encourage its development may satisfy diverging theoretical interests, but cause empirical confusion (see also Huber and Stephens 1993). Moreover, although more sophisticated statistical techniques have helped overcome problems inherent to the linear, cross-sectional (ordinary least squares, OLS) model (such as multicolinearity and the low case-to-variable ratio), multiplying the number of cases by pooling time-series and cross-sectional data does not necessarily solve this.

Hicks and Misra (1993) identify theoretical fragmentation as the root cause of inconsistent and contradictory findings. Rather than attempting to resolve these discrepancies by technical sophistication, they strive after a theoretical reconciliation of diverging approaches, because – so to speak – every theory has a point. Their 'political resource' theory is therefore not so much a theory but a collection of causes of welfare state development adopted from other theoretical frameworks. The originality of their enterprise, as Hicks and Misra readily acknowledge, lies in underscoring the fact that the causes of welfare state development are too complex to be comprehended fully by the limited perspectives of mainstream theories.

In his comment on both Hicks and Misra (1993) and Huber, Ragin and Stephens (1993), Amenta (1993) makes the point that refined quantitative studies have done much to solve unsettled disputes with respect to spending efforts, but fall short of providing convincing accounts of social policy phenomena that are not easily operationalised in terms of aggregate expenditures. In fact, he goes so far as to suggest that comparative historical analyses of one or a few cases will be theoretically more fruitful, because this type of research 'can untangle issues of causality for which quantitative indicators are too highly correlated to interpret' (Amenta 1993:760). Amenta might be overstating his case to the extent that he suggests that only in-depth case studies or close comparisons can provide the hypotheses to be tested in macro-comparative analyses. There is no reason to assume that cross-fertilisation should be unidirectional. Stressing the absolute friction between macro comparisons and case studies not only threatens to paralyse the search for generalisations but also denies the possibility of welcoming rather than explaining away 'outliers', exceptional cases and 'unexplained variations'. The analysis of residuals in quantitative studies, for instance, constitutes a potentially rich source of new hypotheses that can be tested in closer examinations of individual yet crucial cases. Amenta's point on spending, however, remains important. It is curious to note that, although current studies seem to evolve around the conviction that spending or welfare effort may be a misleading indicator of welfare state development, there is the continuous hazard of plummeting into the pitfall of this variable. The most sensible position is to acknowledge that spending matters, but that focusing on spending data alone is theoretically problematic.

THE PROBLEM OF CHRISTIAN DEMOCRACY AND THE WELFARE STATE

A commentary on current comparative welfare state studies

The departure from the social democratic bias in much of the literature deserves special attention, since it has once again put the political causes of variations in social policies prominently on the research agenda. The reconsideration of the model began with the undeniable fact that early welfare state reforms rarely, if ever, were initiated by the socialists, and that several countries (e.g. the Netherlands) pursue equality and welfare statism without the advocacy of a strong social democratic labour movement (Castles 1978, 1985; Stephens 1979a; Wilensky 1981; Skocpol and Amenta 1986). This suggested the need to elaborate the political process of welfare state construction. The most influential answer came from those who show that Christian democracy (or Catholicism) constitutes a functional equivalent or alternative to social democracy. This point was raised early on by Stephens (1979a:100), who argued that 'it seemed possible that anti-capitalist aspects of Catholic ideology – such as notions of fair wage or prohibitions of usury – as well as the generally positive attitude of the Catholic church towards welfare for the poor might encourage government welfare spending'. As a result, one of the constitutional assumptions of the social democratic model, namely that the power of labour equals the power of social democracy, had to be relaxed. Stephens suggests that Christian democratic parties operating in the centre enjoy considerable working-class support and are commonly backed by powerful Catholic unions (see also Shalev 1983), and that this political constellation is highly favourable to welfare state development. Schmidt (1980, 1982) asserts that social democracy and Christian democracy can be functionally equivalent, at least during periods of economic prosperity, and Wilensky (1981) argues that the two movements overlap considerably in ideological terms, and that Catholicism indeed constitutes a more important determinant of welfare statism than does left power.

These attempts to improve upon the social democratic model have culminated in Esping-Andersen's (1990) thesis that Christian democracy and social democracy result in fundamentally different kinds of welfare states. Most importantly, Christian democracy is reluctant to expand collective social services and does not demonstrate the kind of full employment characteristic of the social democratic model. Current research (e.g. Huber, Ragin and Stephens 1993; Huber and Stephens 1993; Castles and Mitchell 1993) corroborates these findings. These analyses embody real improvements in understanding the political forces that shape welfare state outcomes. However, the farewell to the social democratic model is still not radical enough to allow of a thorough innovation in the power resources tradition that can fully grasp the still problematic association between Christian democracy and welfare state development. There are two main reasons for this. First, the critique of the assumptions of the social democratic model needs to be developed further. Second, the understanding of Christian democracy is still inadequate and needs to be improved.

The usually unreasoned assumptions of the social democratic literature (and of some of the current studies as well) can be summarised as follows: class and class structure are the determinants of political power and the political power of the working class is founded by the degree of organisation of its main political representative, social democracy; a developed welfare state is the incarnation of social democracy in power; a high level of social spending is a token of a developed welfare state and therefore of a powerful labour movement.

The latter two assumptions are major points of reference in Esping-Andersen's (1985b, 1987, 1990) critical contribution to welfare state theory. The first assumption, however, still figures in the theory of welfare state regimes. In particular, it is imperative to modify the presupposition of equating labour power and social democracy. Like Baldwin (1990), Esping-Andersen makes the observation that dominant theories of working-class mobilisation fail to explain the origins of social policy, because they are 'essentially premised on the laborist, socialist, or social democratic model of collective action, a model that was far from being dominant until well into the twentieth century' (Esping-Andersen 1990:109). This suggests that class reductionism should be explicitly avoided since one 'cannot assume that socialism is the natural basis for wage-earner mobilization' (Esping-Andersen 1990:17). However, it seems impossible to imagine any other form of labour power mobilisation than one that stresses de-commodification, equality and solidarity, i.e. the typically social democratic values. Apparently, the liberal and conservative clusters of welfare states are largely defined by emphasising the elements in which they differ from the social democratic world. Therefore, the assumption of the welfare state as basically being the fruition of social democratic power mobilisation is left intact. Such a presupposition is not only historically problematic but also theoretically unsatisfactory when studying qualitative differences of welfare regimes. Even Baldwin thinks in terms of the social democratic paradigm when he argues that 'the fully, generalized, comprehensive welfare state most closely embodies institutionalized solidarity' (Baldwin 1990:29). The very vocabulary ('fully, generalised') reveals the shared fixation of so many a study in the field on the social democratic model and a tendency to relapse into the linear 'more or less' or 'the bigger, the better' social democratisation conception identified above.

It is only in the context of the social democratic presumption that the thesis of wage-earner mass movements converging around the social democratic model makes sense. In the course of the analyses, wage-earners' parties are equated with left parties. And only in this way could it be possible to defend the thesis that the development of the welfare state is the 'social democratisation of the welfare state'. And if social democratisation means 'the capacity to substitute for the characteristics dominant in either a liberal or conservative regime, a comprehensive, universalistic, "de-commodifying", full employment welfare state' (Esping-Andersen 1990:110), other regimes and their political determinants can never assume a theoretical status comparable to, or at the same level of, the social democratic model.

It is the assumption of the fundamentally social democratic essence of the position of wage-labour in capitalist societies that makes it so difficult to consider in a theoretically convincing way the relative and independent role of other political actors. Other parties, for instance, can only take the role of 'filtering' labour demands, which would otherwise be social democratic in nature. And what about the countries where Christian democratic parties have been dominant? Here, such parties have been decisive 'in the interpretation of labor's social policy needs' (Esping-Andersen 1990:111). In other words, labour has autonomous social policy needs which would normally lead to social democratic power mobilisation concentrated around the goals of solidarity, equality and universalism, unless these demands are 'filtered' and 'interpreted' (and implicitly assumed to be 'distorted') by other movements, notably Christian democracy.

The alternative assumption to the 'socialist essence' conception of social power, which is more helpful for understanding the development of social citizenship in nations where social democracy does not rule, would be the following. There is no reason to assume that class is the only basis for the articulation of political identity (see Becker 1986). And even if there is an association between class and politics, there is no necessary relationship between the interests of the working class and the social democratic labour movement. Wage-earners are not by nature social democrats. There is a historical justification, too. The fact that in Western Europe the dominant pattern of the political mobilisation of wage-earners led to the formation of social democratic or socialist movements cannot be taken to constitute the normal course of working-class mobilisation. This historical regularity of social democratic power mobilisation is not a standard from which, for example, Christian democratic political forces of wage-labour would be a deviation. A socialist or social democratic labour movement is not *a priori* to be valued higher than its Christian democratic counterparts in its reformist capacities (van Kersbergen and Becker 1988), although Catholic unions (not the parties) tended to emerge as a reaction to the 'socialist threat' (Ebbinghaus 1993:78–82). In any case, one needs to allow for the possibility of conceptualising the power of wage earners in other forms than social democratic mobilisation. Such a view problematises the very notion of political forces that shape welfare state regimes. Perhaps one should think of a possible Christian rather than social democratisation of capitalism. But this asks for a much less cursory analysis of Christian democracy and its impact on welfare capitalism.

Towards a theory of Christian democracy

Christian democracy and its impact on social policy performance are conspicuously understudied and often misunderstood phenomena. Compared to the number of studies of social democracy or of the communist parties of Western Europe, Christian democracy has attracted surprisingly little scholarly attention. This lack of interest in one of the major actors on the continental European political scene is difficult to understand intellectually and an explanation for this is hard to provide. This theoretical and empirical deficiency of comparative political sociology and economy is unfortunate, because it has led to inadequate interpretations of the movement in various contexts of analysis (see van Kersbergen 1994:31–5) and of the political economy that the movement has fostered.

The recent publication of Hanley's (1994a) edited volume on Christian democracy in Western Europe, however, has not only increased our understanding of the movement considerably, but has also revealed significant points of disagreement that need to be elaborated. Specifically, it seems exceedingly difficult to agree on a simple, straightforward and precise definition. Undoubtedly, problems of definition are never peripheral in social science. Yet in the case of the study of Christian democracy there is a substantial reason for the problem of definition, a point well captured by Hanley (1994b:2) when he argues that 'Christian democracy is in many ways an elusive and shifting phenomenon'. The issue is how to pin down a movement that seems to escape every bid of designation. Recent research answers this question by stressing both distinctiveness and elusiveness, both the 'essence' of Christian democracy and its various national 'manifestations' and variations.

Dierickx's (1994) comparison of Christian democratic ideologies in the Low Countries shows that these are essentially systems of beliefs that stress *Gemeinschaft* rather than *Gesellschaft*, i.e. they comprise a set of doctrines rooted in a critique of modernisation. This critique is fully elaborated in the concepts of (social) personalism and solidarity. As Dierickx (1994:22) puts it: 'the ideal of a social-personalist is friendship between human beings who were once strangers and enemies to each other'. This 'essence' of Christian democratic ideology has definite and distinctive consequences for concrete political issues, such as family policy, cultural policy (particularly education), economic policy and social policy. The family is put forward in virtually every policy context; cultural pluralism characterises views on education; the virtue of responsibility is stressed in economic policies that favour centralised and decentralised co-determination of firms; an ethically founded notion of solidarity controls social policies, moderating inequalities that are considered to be unjust to the extent that they lead to an unacceptable distribution of power. In sum, the analysis leads to the conclusion that 'contrary to common wisdom Christian democracy has been able to formulate an ideology of its own not on a few but on many issues' (Dierickx 1994:28).

Van Kersbergen (1994:30) attempts to catch 'essence' and 'elusiveness' at a blow by arguing that 'Christian democracy is distinct from its competitors by virtue of its specific model of social and economic policy and because religion accords the movement an unparalleled opportunity to adapt to changing circumstances'. The distinctiveness of Christian democracy is corroborated by three elements. First, the possession of an elaborate body of (Catholic) social doctrine has historically distinguished Christian democracy from conservatism. Second, the typically centrist position of Christian democratic parties in the political systems in which they operate was not simply an effect of a pragmatic slackening of elementary principles in the course of political conflicts, but – on the contrary – a consequence of the consistent application of a distinct political ethic, that resulted in a specific political project which aimed at social integration, (class) compromise, political mediation, accommodation and pluralism. Specifically, the argument is that 'Christian democracy voices, translates, codifies and restructures societal conflict within itself in an attempt to arbitrate and accommodate societal discord. Class reconciliation and co-operation lie at the heart of what defines Christian democracy as distinctive' (van Kersbergen 1994:36). The 'essence' of Christian democracy is, therefore, that it has always attempted to be the 'embodiment' of the building of social and political consensus. Christian democratic politics has been a politics of mediation, i.e. the religiously inspired, ideologically condensed and politically practised conviction that conflicts of social interests can and must be reconciled politically in order to restore the natural and organic harmony of society. Third, the religious inspiration of Christian democracy has supplied the movement with an electoral catch-all identity of a specific type, because religion had the capacity to canvass voters from a variety of social backgrounds precisely to the extent that the religious cleavage curbed the political weight of class.

Recent empirical studies have shown the relevance of the principles of 'integration', 'accommodation' and 'mediation' to the extent that they all emphasise the institutionalisation of different social groups as recognised factions of the parties and find empirical support for the hypothesis that the electorate of Christian democracy has traditionally mirrored to a large extent the social and demographic structure of society (Lucardie and ten Napel 1994; Müller and Steiniger 1994; Broughton 1994; Donovan 1994). The Austrian Österreichische Volkspartei (ÖVP) is the most factionalised organisation, followed by the Democrazia Cristiana (DC) of Italy, the Christelijke Volkspartij (CVP) of Flanders, the combination of the

Christlich-Demokratische Union (CDU) and Christlich-Soziale Union (CSU) of Germany, and the Dutch Christen Democratisch Appèl (CDA). Although factions have been characteristic of political parties more generally, the scope of social and other groups covered and the degree of institutionalisation and recognition of factions has been a unique feature of European Christian democracy.

This factionalisation, the representation of possibly opposed interests within the parties and the established links with various affiliated social organisations have confronted Christian democratic parties with the obvious difficulty of how to appease conflicting groups. The diverging ways in which Christian democratic movements have structured the representation and accommodation of interests under different historical circumstances have caused a considerable amount of cross-national variation in the character, complexion and political impact of the movements. To put it differently, the identification of the distinctiveness of Christian democracy leads to the conclusion that what clearly differentiates the movement idealtypically might obfuscate distinctiveness empirically.

However – and this is the main point and the leading theme of what follows – the politics of mediation has been a perennial characteristic of post-war Christian democratic politics. And it is the religiously inspired politics of mediation that has governed the social and economic practice of Christian democracy. Social and economic policies, in turn, have functioned as the lubricant of a politics of accommodation by which – under favorable economic conditions – several social interests could be mediated in what was essentially a political pay-off for Christian democracy.

CONCLUSION

If, however, historical conditions matter so much in determining the national characteristics of Christian democratic parties, generalisations on the impact of Christian democracy on specific policy areas, notably the welfare state, may be difficult, if not hazardous. Two decades of welfare state research have come to a point where the possible association between Christian democracy and welfare state development has been put in the centre of research agendas. Current studies have become increasingly sensitive to how different political actors may shape social policies differently. Recent literature on Christian democracy, however, indicates that one may, in reality, be dealing with a political phenomenon which varies to such an extent historically and cross-nationally that general statements on the impact of Christian democracy on welfare statism are not easily warranted. The methodological consequence of these theoretical reflections is that in order to readdress the association between Christian democracy and welfare state development, it is necessary, first, to study the political entrenchment of Christian democracy empirically in an attempt to document where Christian democracy has been dominant and which historical conditions in different national contexts account for both similarities and differences between the various movements. Only then is it possible, next, to examine whether or not a core of distinctive social policies can be identified empirically around which Christian democratic welfare states (despite variations) tend to converge, whether or not Christian democracy, in effect, explains such a regime, and whether or not variations around this common kernel are explained by the varying conditions under which Christian democratic movements have come to power.

3 The political entrenchment of Christian democracy in Western Europe, 1870–1960

MOBILISATION OF CATHOLIC POLITICS BEFORE THE SECOND WORLD WAR

'Closed Catholicism' and political unity

The contemporary Christian democratic parties are the heirs of the Catholic parties that mobilised roughly between 1870 and 1914 and assumed important political positions in the inter-war period in Austria, Belgium, Germany, the Netherlands, and to a lesser extent, in Italy and France.[1] Catholic political mobilisation was a response to the threat of liberalism and socialism as well as a project to combine them. It was also an attempt to distance political Catholicism from the disadvantageous alliances with monarchists and extreme conservatives. At first, these parties were the political representatives of what Whyte (1981) has called 'closed Catholicism'. This 'closed Catholicism' was characterised by explicit clerical involvement in the political and social organisation of the Catholic population and the existence of an exclusively Catholic party with strong links to Catholic social movements, particularly the trade unions. The parties were to varying degrees confessional parties, explicitly established in defence of the Catholic interest, with a direct link to the Church, and primarily aimed at building and preserving the political unity of all Catholics. Between the late nineteenth century and the Second World War Catholic parties matured from essentially middle-class and upper-class, confessional movements, with little interest in social policy, to cross-class, aconfessional people's parties with an articulate social concern (Fogarty 1957:296–7), although with considerable cross-national variations.

The political entrenchment of Catholicism before the Second World War was greatly facilitated by the intimate links between the parties and the Catholic social organisations. Independent Catholic unions started to organise in the last two decades of the nineteenth century in Belgium, Germany, the Netherlands, France and Italy (Fogarty 1957:186–90). These efforts to organise the Catholic workers within their own cultural environment, however, were hampered by a set of simultaneous obstacles and led to different levels of integration and political unity. The socialist unionists viewed the initiatives of Catholic working-class mobilisation with suspicious eyes, since denominational unionism potentially dealt a deathblow to working-class unity and solidarity. The socialists essentially saw the Catholic unionists as traitors of the working class. The Catholic unionists, therefore, first of all faced the difficulty of having to define precisely what made them so different from their socialist counterparts. Anti-socialism was simply not strong enough an incentive for non-socialist working-class mobilisation. The solution consisted of an emphasis on industrial workers' participation as an alternative for what they saw as the essence of the socialist threat: nationalisation of the means of production and extensive state intervention. The Catholic unions stressed co-operation between classes and the propitious effects of class reconciliation. In addition, the struggle for social justice became a struggle for the improvement of the material conditions of the working class, without neglecting religious and cultural responsibilities (Fogarty 1957:191).

Achieving autonomy was another obstacle. Paternalism and the fear Catholic employers had of Christian socialism proved to be obstinate impediments to the self-organisation of Catholic workers. In line with corporatist ideals the model for organisation was initially guild-like, i.e. employers and workers were to act in concord within a single, usually sectoral association. According to Fogarty (1957:193) only at the turn of the century the conviction among Catholic workers spread that 'effective and honourable collaboration between classes could be attained only if each class stood firmly on its own feet'. However, it took the Catholic employers much longer to acknowledge this need for independent and separate Catholic working-class associations.

The third difficulty concerned the question whether unions were to be organised as exclusively Catholic organisations of the working class or perhaps as interdenominational associations (Fogarty 1957:193–205; Ebbinghaus 1993:70–82). This issue raged particularly in Germany and the Netherlands where Catholic unions managed to establish a satisfactory distance from the clergy as interdenominational unions (Germany) and as Protestant and Catholic unions (the Netherlands). In contrast, Italian unions were firmly under the disadvantageous authority of the clergy. After 1903, for example, the papacy attempted to regain control over left-wing Catholics who were in favour of opening unions to non-Catholic members, as a result of which Catholic unionism declined sharply (Agócs 1988:96). The question of the mobilisation of Catholic workers in separate unions time and again prompted the Church to intervene in an attempt to maintain control over its flock, particularly when the social ardour of these unions tended to drift beyond the constraints set by official Catholic social teaching.

The final problem involved the relationship between unions and parties and the precise definition of their respective tasks. As the cases analysed below indicate, the success of Catholic democratic power mobilisation to a large extent came to depend on whether the parties managed to generate cross-class appeal and on the manner in which they nourished their affiliation with the organisations of social Catholicism. Catholic labour unions sought political protection in their attempt to organise the working class independently from the paternalistic tutelage of the clerical hierarchy and the charitable benefactors of the bourgeoisie as well as from the socialist union movement. In the often fractious clashes between parties and unions, the latter so to speak attempted to Christian democratise the former by introducing a more solid social concern, while the latter sought to incorporate the unions in what was seen as the organic unity of social and political Catholicism that best served the interests of the Church and that could function as a bulwark against the various threats of modernism. On some issues parties and unions were utterly divided, on others they obviously had common interests. Universal suffrage and the abolition of plural (class) voting was ultimately to the benefit of both, whereas the representation of workers' interests within the party was quite another matter (Fogarty 1957:205). The attempts to integrate workers fully into Catholic politics failed in Austria and France, partly succeeded in Italy, and were effective in Belgium, Germany and the Netherlands.

Political Catholicism in Austria, Belgium, France, Germany, Italy and the Netherlands

Austria

The Austrian Christlich-Soziale Partei (CSP), founded by von Vogelsang's pupil Karl Luegger in 1889, rapidly became a major political force. The CSP profited from the emerging petit bourgeois critique of the governing alliance of a liberal ruling class (mainly bankers and industrialists) and conservative Catholics (nobility, the higher ranks of the clergy and large landowners), but initially was also supported by the lower classes and the lower ranks of the clergy. The Catholic party was successful in gaining political control over Vienna in 1897 and gradually also over some non-urbanised areas (Diamant 1960; Whyte 1981; Král 1983). Austrian political Catholicism steadily worked on the establishment of the unity of all Catholics. By 1907, when the estates system was abolished and the first general elections under universal manhood suffrage were held, the party won considerable support (Mackie and Rose 1991:24) and entered the national government as a leading political force, integrating at first the entire Catholic movement. Gradually losing contact with the lower class, partly as a result of successful socialist mobilisation, it lost support and the battle over Catholic unity. This was a major blow to the political entrenchment of Austrian Catholicism, especially since the membership of Catholic unions in Austria had steadily grown in the period 1900–45. The Zentralkommission der Christlichen Gewerkschaften had already organised an average of approximately 34,000 workers between 1906 and 1914, and membership had increased from 64,000 in 1920 to a peak of 112,000 in 1930. Socialist union membership, however, amounted to 655,000 in 1930 (Visser 1989:19; Ebbinghaus 1993:280–4). In spite of the troubled relationship with the Catholic labour movement, the CSP won an average of 44 per cent of seats in the Nationalrat between 1919 and 1930 (Mackie and Rose 1991:29).

The CSP never fully accepted democratic principles, was strongly influenced by a Romantic longing for an idealised past and aimed at the establishment of a corporatist social and political order that was to resemble a society of far-off days. This Romantic legacy and the inability to attract and keep the support of the working class most likely explain why during Austria's first republic the party became 'a class-based, clerico-fascist government party, unable to halt Austria's slide towards authoritarian rule' (Král 1983:31; see also Fogarty 1957:308) and the attempt to transform Austria into an authoritarian, corporative state. The Constitution of 1934 was grounded on an odd mix of Romantic, Catholic and specifically Austrian political ideas (Diamant 1960:250, 256–60). It strongly resembled the Romantic heritage and influence of the conservative Catholic movement in Austria.

Belgium

Belgium, too, has a long history of Catholic politics. The creation of the Belgian state in 1830 was, in effect, the result of a political struggle for independence from the Dutch, broadly supported by an alliance of the liberal and Catholic bourgeoisie (Irving 1979:165; de Winter 1992). Catholic politics was not properly organised on a regular basis until the 1860s and the first party was founded in 1884, signifying a decisive break with the liberals as a result of their attack on the autonomy of Catholic schools. At first, the Walloon Parti Catholique (PC) and the Flemish Katholieke Partij (KP) were class-based parties, mainly supported by Catholic segments of the bourgeoisie. Gradually, however, the parties attracted the Catholic working class and the Catholic farmers, too, which introduced a much stronger concern for the 'social question' (i.e. the social effects of industrial capitalism), resulting in a political programme in the late 1890s that also included some proposals for social insurance and factory legislation. The political process of the unification of all Catholics led to the establishment of well-defined factions within the party (1914) and eventually culminated in a major reconstruction of the party in 1921. This newly founded Union Catholique became an 'indirect party' to the extent that direct membership was excluded. It was a federation of distinct Catholic, social and political groups (a conservative association, a workers' league, a farmers' league, and a league of the middle classes), who were loosely organised, lacked a clear political programme but consistently united forces during electoral campaigns (Witte and Craeybecks 1987:202–7). Nevertheless, these factions gradually lost their political weight during an era of increasing nationalism, as a result of which a linguistically fractioned party, the Bloc Catholique Belge, was founded in 1936, consisting of the Katholieke Vlaamsche Volkspartij in Flanders and the Parti Catholique Social in Wallonia (Dunn 1983; de Winter 1992; Lucardie and ten Napel 1994).

Between 1884 and 1919, the Catholic party managed to control an absolute majority in the Chambre des Représentants, while on average it held almost 40 per cent of seats in the inter-war period (Mackie and Rose 1991:49–57). At first a profoundly conservative party, it gradually developed – as argued – a social concern for those who suffered the consequences of Belgian industrialism, mainly as a result of the influence of its labour wing (the 'Christian democrats') and Vatican social teaching (Irving 1979:171–2). The electoral and social reforms in the period immediately following the First World War (e.g. the introduction of old age pensions and a restriction of working hours) were the result of a coalition between the 'Christian democrats' and the socialists. But the party's anti-socialism prevented it from co-operating with the socialists on a more permanent basis and, instead, joined the conservative liberals in subsequent governments in the inter-war period. The factionalised character of the party, moreover, seriously hindered any further political advance. Although the attempt to overcome this internal discord – the reorganisation of the Union Catholique into the Bloc Catholique Belge in 1936 – was simply too late in the light of the terrible events that were to happen four year later, it did supply the fertile soil for post-war Christian democracy in Belgium (Irving 1979:172). The political potential for Christian democracy was furthered by the development of Catholic unionism. The Confédération des Syndicats Chrétiens/Algemeen Christelijk Vakverbond had steadily expanded from a mere 12,000 members in 1902 to 123,000 in 1914. Between 1919 and 1930 this union organised about 160,000 workers and reached a top of 340,000 members in 1939. The Belgian socialist unions organised about 57,000 members in the period before the First World War (1914: 129,000 members) and about 560,000 in the period between 1919 and 1930. At the outbreak of the Second World War, the socialist confederation with its 540,000 members was the main rival of the Catholic unions (Ebbinghaus 1993:280–4).

France

The political role of Catholics in France can only be understood in the context of the antithetical relationship between Church and State the country has known since the French Revolution. In effect, this historical event can be seen as the single major cause of the failure of a unitary Catholic political movement in this nation. A fundamental paradox of French history concerns the particular manner in which Catholicism, although the major religion of the French, never assumed a dominant influence on French political culture. The Enlightenment adopted the role played by Protestantism in other nations in engendering a militant anticlerical, laic culture. The Enlightenment developed outside the Church, while the monarchy absorbed the Church. The revolution brought down both the monarchy and the Catholic Church and an anti-clerical laic culture became dominant. In the nineteenth century the political cleavage between left and right was virtually identical to the cleavage between laic and clerical. Around the turn of the century radical politics successfully separated Church and State entirely, passing the separation law of 1905 which defined the neutrality of the state in religious matters and cancelled subsidies to religious organisations (Soltau 1965:40–3). France paradoxically became a Catholic nation whose political culture was dominated by republicanism and the legacy of the Revolution more generally. Under these circumstances political Catholicism never developed into a mass movement comparable to the movements in other nations.

Several unsuccessful attempts were made to found Catholic political movements in France. French political Catholicism was divided in opposing wings which prevented the establishment of a unitary Catholic party. First, there has always been the current of those who argued that there could be no reconciliation between Church and the Republic; these conservative and anti-Semitic Catholics usually joined various authoritarian, monarchist (i.e. anti-republican) movements, notably the Ligue de la Patrie Française (1898), the Ligue d'Action Française (1905) and the Action Française of the period after the First World War. More moderate right-wing or right-centre politicians rejected the extremism of these conservatives. This second current of Catholic politics in France prepared the way for a more indulgent attitude towards the state and held out a promise of a stronger Catholic involvement in French politics. Thus, the Parti d'Action Libérale Populaire succeeded the Conservateurs Ralliés in 1899 and this party can be seen as an attempt to found an aconfessional party that was both aiming at the protection of the rights of the Church and supporting social and political reform (Fogarty 1957:331; Irving 1973:31; Wilson 1983:285). The third wing of French political Catholicism, partly overlapping with the moderates, consisted of the 'Christian democrats', who were democratic, determined to reconcile State and Church, included the social Catholics, but above all advocated social policies as a means to stifle the socialist advance. According to Irving (1973:36) the Sillon movement (1897) and its heir, the Jeune République (1911), were genuine Christian democratic parties to the extent that they had no reservations in acquiescing to democratic principles. Their active stance in French politics, however, led to the papal condemnation of the Sillon in 1910. Prior to the First World War, therefore, political Catholicism in France did not assume any significant role and it was not until 1924 that a new Christian democratic party, the Parti Démocrate Populaire (PDP), was founded (Fogarty 1957:333; Irving 1973:42), integrating much of what was left of the Christian democratic current in French Catholicism. This party stressed social and political democracy, made a sincere attempt to bridge the gap between Catholicism and republicanism, appealed to Catholics of all social strata, but was to remain very small electorally, operating as it was in the context of a political culture determined by strong anti-clericalism (Fogarty 1957:334).

French Catholic unionism was not of much help here either. The Confédération Française du Travailleurs Chrétiens remained comparatively small and in the period between 1900 and 1918 never exceeded a total number of 9,000 members, while in the period between 1919 and 1934 total membership amounted to around 77,000. Between 1935 and 1939, however, there was a steep rise in membership, reaching a maximum of 320,000 members in 1937 (Visser 1989:67; Ebbinghaus 1993:284). The communist unions of France were incomparably stronger and dominated the organisation of the working class. The Conféderation Générale du Travail (CGT) already had around 100,000 members in 1900, over 200,000 in 1906 and 400,000 in 1912. Between 1919 and 1935 the CGT and the Confédération Générale du Travail Unitaire (split off from the CGT in 1920, but reunited in 1935) had a total membership of almost 900,000, and the reunited communist union movement experienced a fast growth in the final years before the Second World War, reaching an unprecedented strength of almost three and a half million organised workers in 1938.

It was, however, the political record of the PDP – a majority of its deputies voted against the Pétain regime and some Catholic groups were actively involved in the French resistance during the Second World War – which increased the prestige of Catholic politics to such an extent that the prospects for Christian democracy in post-war France were substantially improved.

Germany

The German Zentrumspartei or Zentrum, founded in 1870, constituted altogether a clearly confessional Catholic party and quickly matured to be the principal force in establishing the political unity of Catholics. Its strongly confessional character – the political representative of the interests of the Catholic church in Germany – is largely explained by the fact that Catholics were a large minority in the German empire, and by the *Kulturkampf*, i.e. the attempt to strengthen German unity by weakening what Bismarck conceived as the anti-national role of the Roman Catholic church in the German *Reich*. The Zentrum indeed stood in opposition to the empire, not only because its confessional character sharply contrasted with Prussian Protestantism, but also because its cross-class social composition, consisting of a variety of anti-bourgeois and anti-capitalist forces (priests, aristocrats, farmers and workers), unmistakably diverged from the political leadership of the aristocratic military and the liberal bourgeoisie (Neumann 1973:42). The *Kulturkampf*, although devastating for the position of the Church and Catholic religious, cultural and social organisations, had a favourable effect on political unification. More than 80 per cent of voting Catholics supported the Zentrum (Blackbourn 1987:189) and between 1871 and 1912 the Zentrum controlled a politically pivotal bloc of votes in the Reichstag of an average of 24 per cent (Mackie and Rose 1991:168–72). From the beginning one of the party's strongest points was its rather elaborate social and economic programme which aimed at the accommodation of the interests of various social groups (Fogarty 1957:304–5).

Catholic union and political strength was preserved even when Bismarck's anti-clerical policies ceased to be the 'grand unification force' of all German Catholics, as the *Kulturkampf* was gradually relaxed in the early 1880s and eventually abolished in 1887. Blackbourn's (1980:119) study of the Zentrum in Württemberg before 1914 shows the remarkable and characteristic ability of German Catholic politics 'to absorb and incorporate the pressure of various interest groups' and the 'willingness to placate and accommodate special interests'. This critical function of the Zentrum was greatly enhanced at the national level by its position as the pivot of the German political system between 1890 and 1914. In fact, all governments during this era depended on the support of the Catholic party. The Zentrum's position of power, moreover, was reinforced by the possibility of a coalition with the socialists, although the likelihood of such an alliance at that time must not be exaggerated (Blackbourn 1980). Societal backing came from the affiliated unions that played an important role in reinforcing the strength of political Catholicism in Germany. The blue-collar federation, the Gesamtverband der Christlichen Gewerkschaften Deutschlands, grew in the era before the First World War from slightly over 76,000 members in 1900 to a peak of nearly 351,000 members in 1912. And the white-collar Gesamtverband Deutscher Angestellten increased its numbers from 40,000 to almost 150,000 in the same period.

The Zentrum was the leading political force of the Weimar Republic, too. In the divided Reichstag, it commanded between 1919 and 1932 an average of 14 per cent of the seats (Mackie and Rose 1991:176). The party held government positions in every coalition until 1932 and provided 9 of the 22 chancellors. As Karsten Ruppert (1992) has recently shown, the Catholic party was actively engaged in parliamentary activities and virtually no law was passed without Catholic involvement in its preparation. Moreover, the party was characterised by an integration of different social interests which was even mirrored in the social composition of its parliamentarians (Neumann 1973:44). The reinforced labour faction of the party initially accorded a more left-wing orientation and facilitated the co-operation with the social democrats. Typically, the Zentrum defended anti-capitalist policies and promoted social policy, but never agreed with the social democrats on the right to private property (Johnson 1983:413; Neumann 1973:46). Between 1920 and 1928, the Zentrum controlled the Ministry of Labour and devised and implemented reformist legislation (Kaufmann 1989:108–15; Sachße 1992:17). This was a great success for the Christian workers' unions that reached a peak of over a million members in the first years of the Weimar Republic, but between 1923 and 1931 stabilised around 710,000 members, while the white-collar confederation had on average 464,000 members in the period 1919–31. However, in Germany as elsewhere, the Christian unions were no match for the socialist organisations. The Algemeiner Deutscher Gewerkschaftsbund had already reached a membership of over a million members by the early 1900s and averaged a total of one and a half million members between 1900 and 1914. In the inter-war years, the socialist confederation had almost eight million workers organised until 1923, but lost slightly less than half of its members between 1924 and 1931 (Ebbinghaus 1993:280–4).

In spite of the strength of the Catholic labour movement and the success of the left faction of the Zentrum, a gradual return to more conservative policies was noticeable in the late 1920s (Irving 1979:17). The conservative Catholic leadership that controlled the party in the early 1930s supported the appointment of Hitler as chancellor as well as the notorious 'Enabling Act' which sealed the doom of the Catholic movements and of the democratic polity of the Weimar Republic and ushered in the Nazi dictatorship (Irving 1979).

Italy

In contrast to the German Zentrum, Italian Catholics were relatively late in organising politically. It was not until 1919 that an officially aconfessional Catholic party, the Partito Popolare Italiano (PPI), was founded by the Sicilian priest Don Luigi Sturzo (de Rosa 1988). This late appearance of organised political Catholicism finds it origin in the tense relationship between the Italian State and the Vatican. The political unification of Italy, completed in 1870, turned out to be particularly harmful to the temporal power of the papacy. The Vatican had already lost the Papal States in 1862 and was deprived of its final political stronghold, Rome, in 1870. The Vatican reacted by refusing to deal with the newly established unitary state and by summoning the Catholic citizens of Italy to renounce political activity altogether. This ban on Catholic political action was lifted only gradually after the turn of the century, but was not officially abolished until 1919 (Molony 1977; Irving 1979; Whyte 1981; Candeloro 1982). And it was not until 1929 that the Italian State and the Vatican reached a settlement over the 'Roman question', the Lateran treaties, an arrangement between Mussolini's fascist regime and Pius XI (Candeloro 1982:495–508).

In spite of the papal embargo, however, Italian Catholics actively participated in social and political life before the First World War, particularly via the Catholic organisations for the laity. After the unification these organisations were to be 'the frontline troops in the Catholic *reconquista* of civil society' (Clark 1984:86). The crucial institution was the Opera dei Congressi e dei Comitati Cattolici (founded in 1874) that explicitly aimed at isolating Catholic citizens from the influence of modernism in general and from the anti-clericalism of Italian liberalism in particular (de Rosa

1953–4). The lay committees of the Opera were engaged in education, publishing and social work and were initially controlled by conservative *intransigenti*, i.e. by Catholic laymen who were unconditionally obedient to the Pope in his inflexibility towards the Italian State. Gradually, however, the Opera was turned into a more politically oriented organisation when less 'intransigent', progressive Catholics (called 'Christian democrats') assumed influential positions. These 'Christian democrats' with their stronghold in the Catholic social movements aimed at greater political independence from the papacy and were strongly in favour of a more active role of the Catholic laity in politics. Moreover, they were committed to social policies for the working classes or the poor. The 'Christian democrats' were radical to the extent that they demanded far-reaching reforms, such as the corporatist reconstruction of society, the proportional representation of social interests, decentralisation and regional and local autonomy, legal protection for labour and social insurance, agri-cultural and tax reform, control on speculation, civil and political liberties, and a pacifist defence policy (Fogarty 1957:319–20). Thus, the Opera – like the Belgian Bloc Catholique Belge – was split between the conservatives who stressed the need to defend the interests of the Church and the 'Christian democrats' who emphasised the need for Catholic action for the poor. The latter dominated the Opera around 1903 when a much more radical, modernist stance in social and political matters was assumed. The reaction of Pope Pius X was simple and quick: he dissolved the organis-ation and replaced it by the Azione Cattolica. By 1908 the five main organisations of Catholic social action provided religious education and propaganda, organised labour, capital and the farmers, mobilised the Catholic vote, and provided activities for the youth and for women (Clark 1984:147). However, the Catholic union movement (Confederazione Italiana dei Lavoratori) never grew bigger than approximately 110,000 members in the years just before the First World War and organised around a million people just before the fascist dictatorship. By contrast, Italy's socialist Confederazione Generale del Lavoro had around 300,000 members between 1907 and 1914, organised a maximum of over two million people in 1920, and gradually declined until it was finally abolished by the fascists.

Yet it was the Azione Cattolica that prepared the ground for the PPI. The direct motive for the foundation of the new party was the lifting of the papal boycott of Italian politics in early 1919. Italy's Catholic party was ex-plicitly organised as a cross-class Catholic people's party with considerable independence from the Church. Its cross-class electoral appeal, however, was limited to the extent that Catholic farmers and the urban lower middle classes were overrepresented. In effect, it lacked strong support from the working class. Moreover, its popularity was geographically distinct, because the party was mainly strong in the rural areas of the north and the urban areas of various regions, but weak in the south (Irving 1979:5). Nevertheless, similarly to other Catholic parties, the PPI consisted of various wings, representing the entire political spectrum from extreme conservatism to Christian socialism, and included farmers, workers, the middle classes, the clergy and some segments of the bourgeoisie. Its political programme comprised such demands as electoral reform (proportional representation, female suffrage), the protection of small proprietors, agrarian reform, regional and local autonomy, and the separation of Church and State. Moreover, it contained a radical analysis of the social question (Molony 1977:61), reflecting the influence of the party's labour wing, although with much less emphasis on the corporatism of the original 'Christian democrats' (Fogarty 1957:323). Ideologically, the programme stressed the importance of 'social personalism' which is also the core ideological concept of Belgian Christian democracy. The concept signifies that essentially individuals are persons only in the context of their own social group, particularly their family, class and local community. At the elections of 1919 and 1921 the PPI won about 20 per cent of the seats in the Camera dei Deputati (Mackie and Rose 1991:267). However, by 1924 the party was already in serious crisis, organisationally as a result of splitting conflicts between its factions, and electorally as a result of the introduction of a law that disproportionally favoured the fascists.

The party's governmental record is mixed. Because the socialists refused to cooperate with the PPI, the party entered government coalitions with the liberals, supported centrist governments and finally also Mussolini's Cabinet, the survival of which depended on Catholic support. The decision to ally with the fascists was dictated by the anxiety about a new election and the fascist violence that this was likely to entail, but was made dependent on demands regarding the protection of the proportional system, a halt to violence, and the autonomy of the labour unions (Molony 1977:141; Irving 1979:6). Internal conflicts over the fascist issue and Mussolini's double-crossing politics led to further splits in the party and to the amputation of its right, pro-fascist wing. The fascist 'democratic victory' at the elections of 1924, the violence that went with it, and particularly the murder in June 1924 of Giacomo Matteotti, a socialist and impassioned anti-fascist who had documented fascist crime (Molony 1977:182), finally determined the PPI's transition to the anti-fascist opposition. The party soon withered away, especially when the Vatican became increasingly sympathetic to the fascist regime, prohibited an anti-fascist alliance of the PPI with the socialists and, in general, thought a Catholic party superfluous. What remained of the PPI was outlawed in 1926 and disbanded in 1927 (Fogarty 1957:325).

The Netherlands

The evolution of Catholic politics and Christian democracy in the Netherlands must be placed against the background of the religious segmentation that has characterised this nation since the reformation and the revolt against the Spanish (1568–1648). The political impact of the fundamental religious cleavage on Dutch society, both expressed as a liberal–confessional conflict and as a Calvinist–Catholic antithesis, can hardly be overstated. Religious strife and dissension constitute one of the major continuities in the history of this nation. The religious cleavage controlled Dutch politics during the second half of the nineteenth century; it was the single most important cause for the rise of the 'pillarised' structure of the political system (1917–67), and it determined the dominance of Christian and Catholic parties during most of the twentieth century. In effect, religious conflicts and pillarisation explain why an interdenominational Christian democratic party did not arise until 1980 (van Kersbergen, Lucardie and ten Napel 1993).

Dutch Catholics were a large, oppressed minority in the nineteenth century and much of their social and political activities involved their much sought after emancipation. The re-establishment of the Catholic hierarchy in the 1850s, allowed by the liberal government, had aroused the anger of the Protestants and reinforced the Calvinist–liberal conflict, but at the same time signified the inauguration of a long and laborious struggle for Catholic liberation (Kossmann 1978:278). Nevertheless, the Calvinists were first to organise politically. The orthodox Protestants had a hard time deciding who were the bigger enemy: the Catholics or the liberals. The political issue of the public financing of private schools, however, redrafted the impact of the religious cleavage by moderating the Calvinist–Catholic antithesis and by reinforcing conflicts between the liberals on the one hand and the religious forces on the other hand. The schools issue induced the political organisation of orthodox Calvinism. Moreover, it also fundamentally reorganised the political landscape with respect to other crucial issues such as the extension of the suffrage and the social question, and supplied the foundation for the social and political pattern of highly integrated yet segregated sub-cultural organisation named pillarisation.[2]

The politically dominant liberals intended to create a universal, state-controlled and religiously neutral educational system and passed a law for that purpose in 1878. This law obviously threatened to topple the confessional schools and led to the foundation by the Calvinist minister Abraham Kuyper of the first Dutch mass party, the Anti-Revolutionaire Partij (ARP) in 1879. The party was anti-revolutionary to the extent that it rejected the tenets of the French Revolution and the Enlightenment. The term, therefore, refers to 'a distinction between "counterrevolutionaries" who would wish to reverse history and "antirevolutionaries" who, while rejecting the entire spirit of 1789, would yet recognize change' (Daalder 1966:199, fn.27). The ARP was not reactionary, but rather 'isolationist', struggling for the survival of the Calvinist minority and the limitation of state intervention in what Kuyper believed to be the vital and essentially free spheres of social life (the family, the Church, the school). It was a genuine party with a cross-class appeal, although it was disproportionally supported by the orthodox lower middle classes. The party not only organised the Calvinist electorate, but also those who were denied the right to vote. In this sense the ARP was indeed an evangelical people's party (Irving 1979:196). The ARP was successful electorally and on average controlled about 20 per cent of seats in the Tweede Kamer between 1888 and 1913. In the inter-war years its electoral appeal declined gradually to approximately 14 per cent of seats (Mackie and Rose 1991:331–5). Its record of government, however, is more impressive. During 1888–91 it formed the first confessional coalitions with the Catholics (a novelty in Dutch politics and this was repeated in 1901–5 and 1908–13), played a dominant role in government during the entire period 1918–40, controlling social and economic policy, and provided the prime minister five times.

Catholic social and political emancipation was notoriously slow and although the priest Herman Schaepman had already written a Catholic political programme in 1897, it took until 1926 before an authentic Catholic party, the Rooms Katholieke Staatspartij (RKSP), was finally founded. This does not imply, however, that Catholics, who were in many ways treated as second-class citizens, refrained from participating actively in national politics. On the contrary, as indicated, they played at first a small, but gradually a more important role in several coalition governments with the anti-revolutionaries between 1888 and 1940. Conducive to Catholic politics was the schools question which detached them from the secular liberals, whom they initially had supported because of the promise of liberty. But the liberal attack on confessional schools brought them nearer to the orthodox Protestants. The paradoxical aspect in the development of Dutch Catholic politics is that it was in fact greatly encouraged by the political progress of the Calvinists. At the time of the schools question Kuyper formulated his notorious political theory of the 'antithesis', i.e. the idea that what fundamentally divided the Dutch politically concerned the cleavage between faith (of whatever creed) and incredulity. This doctrine cemented the anti-liberal coalition of the confessional forces. Quite unexpectedly, therefore, the Catholics had found a partner in the Calvinist party through which they could exercise some political influence in their attempts to improve the situation of their brethren, particularly by moderating the Calvinists' reluctance to promote social reform.

Although the inclusion in national politics mitigated the sense of inferiority among Catholics, their leaders were eager to avoid new waves of anti-papism that they expected to follow from further Catholic mobilisation (Wolinetz 1983:648). In addition, Catholic politics was no different in its internal discord from its equivalent elsewhere in Europe at the same time, as a result of which the formation of a unitary Catholic party was further delayed (Irving 1979:199). Yet Catholics did establish electoral committees at the turn of the century that survived until the RKSP replaced them in 1926. Similar to other Catholic parties, the RKSP was an outright confessional party and comprised an amalgam of the political and social organisations of the Catholic sub-culture, which by that time was already well established. In terms of electoral strength, the various Catholic representatives-without-a-party commanded an average of over 26 per cent of seats in the Tweede Kamer between 1888 and 1925. The RKSP won about 30 per cent of seats between 1929 and 1940, almost perfectly reflecting the numerical strength of the Catholic minority in the Netherlands.

The most decisive event in Dutch political history for both Catholic and Protestant politics before the Second World War undoubtedly concerned the 'Pacification' of 1917, i.e. the simultaneous settlement of several sharply dividing issues. The new Constitution of 1917 granted the financial equalisation of public and private primary schools and introduced universal manhood suffrage (and a provision for female suffrage) under a proportional system in a single national constituency. As Gladdish (1991:28) rightly put it, 'the new electoral system recognised, reflected and reinforced the crystallisation of political sub-cultures' which was to determine Dutch politics at least until the mid-1960s.

The social and political system of pillarisation together with the proportional system was particularly beneficial to the mobilisation of Catholic power in the inter-war years. The RKSP, as the political representative of a comprehensive network of Catholic social and cultural organisations, became the single largest party in the parliament. Moreover, pillarisation contributed to the political dominance of confessionalism in more general terms. The confessional parties together systematically managed to control a comfortable absolute majority in the Tweede Kamer as well as in government. In terms of union strength, however, the record is less impressive. The Dutch Katholieke Arbeidersbeweging (Catholic) and the Christelijk-Nationaal Vakverbond (Protestant) together organised on average no more than 30,000 members between 1907 and 1914, while in the inter-war years they amounted to 145,000 (the Catholic movement) and 84,000 (the Protestant unions). The socialist union was backed by an average of 39,000 members between 1907 and 1914 and an average of 256,000 between 1918 and 1940.

Conclusion

The political entrenchment of Catholic political parties into the evolving polities of Western Europe and the power mobilisation by the Catholic sub-cultures of various nations show remarkable similarities as well as crucial differences. In all nations analysed, attempts were made to define a separate position for the Catholic social movement and the associate parties between 1870 and 1940. In some cases, notably Italy and France, clerical mediation initially inhibited the development of stable relations between party and social movements and, accordingly, suppressed the complete development of 'closed Catholicism'. In other cases, especially Germany, full-fledged confessional parties with strong connections to both the social movements and the clergy were facilitated by historical conditions under which the very existence of the Catholic sub-culture was at stake. The conflict with the liberals over cultural policies united forces in Belgium and the Netherlands. In the Low Countries, too, a 'closed Catholicism' developed gradually.

The way in which church and state have historically settled their struggle over power has caused diverging patterns of Catholic power mobilisation. In Germany, the internal threat to the survival of Catholicism during the Bismarck era produced the unintended effect of the consolidation of unitary political Catholicism. In this nation the *Kulturkampf* tempered the class-struggle within the Catholic sub-culture and expedited the coalescence of different factions and social groups. This politically effective capacity was then retained under conditions of pivotal power that the Catholic party enjoyed during the Weimar Republic and was only temporarily undone during the politically exigent and precarious final years of the Weimar Republic. The conflict between the Vatican and the French and Italian States, on the other hand, decidedly blocked the development of weighty Catholic political parties. The Revolution of 1789 virtually played the political part in France that the unification of states in 1870 played in Italy. In both cases the Vatican refused to become involved in the politics of the states and sharply renounced Catholic republicanism or liberalism, with detrimental effects on the political development of Catholicism in these nations before the Second World War. What mattered was how the Catholic political and social movements split amongst themselves over the 'Roman question' or over republicanism and the legacy of the French Revolution. In both nations, the attempts to found cross-class parties directed at the political homogeneity of all Catholics were difficult, because in order to do so a reconciliation between state and church had to be accomplished first. And as long as the Vatican consistently refused to allow any form of Catholic republicanism or liberalism, social Catholics were unable to unite their working-class support with the clerical cause.

The situation was radically different in Belgium and the Netherlands. In these nations a certain compromise on state–church relations was already established in the 1870s and here Catholic political action emerged as a reaction to the liberal attack on the right to found and maintain state-protected schools. In both nations the historical break with the liberals had a unifying effect on the Catholic political movement. However, in Belgium the very early establishment of well-organised factions of different social strata within the parties, the emerging linguistic cleavage and the parties' ardent anti-socialism continuously threatened the merger of all Catholics as a permanent force in the nation. On two momentous particulars the Dutch situation was different from the Belgian. Parallel to Germany, Dutch Catholics formed a large minority. Their precarious status as second-class citizens initially determined a more 'inward-looking' development of 'closed Catholicism' to the extent that a genuine party was slow to appear. Dutch Catholics also faced the zealously anti-papist Calvinists who, in addition, were already organised politically by the 1880s. The double threat of liberalism and of Calvinism not only gradually united the entire Catholic population behind a common political conviction, but – simplified by Calvinist–liberal controversies – paradoxically put Dutch political Catholicism in the centre of power even before it got properly organised politically.

In Austria, early victories of conservative Catholicism led to a gradual excavation of political unity. Internal and external threats to the survival of the Catholic sub-culture were largely absent and Austrian Catholics kept the reactionary, Romantic legacy very much alive. As a result anti-democratic corporatism not only inhibited the firm incorporation of the Catholic working class into a unitary political movement, but led to a corporatist authoritarianism that was strongly supported by the clergy.

These considerations largely corroborate the conclusions of the second chapter. The integration of various social interests within Catholic parties and the resulting condensation of institutionalised factions not only determined the potential for full-fledged and genuine Christian democratic parties, but also caused a considerable amount of cross-national divergence between the different movements of Western Europe. Moreover, the representation of different social interests became both a strong and a weak element in the evolution of unified political Catholicism. The historical conditions under which the attempted incorporation of the entire Catholic population into a single political party took place – particularly the extent to which internal or external threats confined the existence of a Catholic sub-culture – constrained the capacity of successful integration. The degree of integration, in turn, determined the political outlook of the movement. And it was the lack of a strong, organised labour-wing in particular that effected a much less developed social concern of political Catholicism and tended to inhibit the development of Christian democracy. Is has to be stressed that cross-class mobilisation has been a common feature of Christian democracy, but has also caused cross-national divergence.

TOWARDS POLITICAL DOMINANCE: CHRISTIAN DEMOCRACY, 1945–1960

Writing in the late 1950s and reviewing the results of his own study of Christian democracy in Europe, Fogarty (1957:340) could not conceal his astonishment at the 'remarkable heights of power' that by this time the movement had reached. In Germany, Austria, Switzerland, the Netherlands, Belgium, France and Italy, fully organised Catholic, Protestant and inter-denominational parties had come to power (see Table 3.1 for an overview of Christian democratic parties). Moreover, international co-operation had greatly contributed to the unity of the Christian democratic movement in Europe and the social movements of Catholicism flourished as never before. The post-war Conference of Catholic International Organisations, for example, united a large number of international organisations that dealt with study and education (e.g. the International Union of Social Studies), the youth (e.g. the Young Christian Workers' International), adult affairs (e.g. the World Union of Catholic Women's Organisations), social service (e.g. various societies of St. Vincent de Paul and the Catholic International Union of Social Service), economic and social affairs (bringing together the International Christian Social Union – a union of the organisations for workers, farmers and the middle classes – and the Catholic International Union of Employers' Associations), and the media (e.g. the International Federation of Catholic Journalists) (Fogarty 1957:343). An important component of the 'remarkable heights of power' consisted of the extensive reach of the Catholic press that sometimes perhaps reluctantly and critically supported the political and social organisations of Catholicism, but more often was simply controlled by the Catholic party. Other underpinnings of the power of Christian democracy concerned the extended network of church-led or church-controlled educational institutions and the wide array of other organisations of the Catholic laity. Finally, there were the churches, centres of the Catholic sub-culture and in many ways the point of reference for family and community life. The churches not only met the religious needs of the people through the Divine service, but above all provided social services, whether in the form of pastoral care, psychological relief, marriage counselling and even financial advice, or by performing important ritual functions outside the strictly religious context such as, to give but one example, the consecration of a new factory owned by Catholics.

How can one best document the political potential, entrenchment and effects of national Christian democratic movements in post-war Western Europe? The answer to this question is usually found by looking at the strength of the parties, i.e. by largely neglecting other possible resources of power. Castles (1994) is right when he asserts that the argument with respect to the impact of Christian democratic parties on public policy outcomes is not convincing because it neglects the power of the Church in Catholic nations in which there is no significant Christian democratic party. The Church influences 'politicians of all parties through its role as an elite pressure group and as a force shaping the demands of the electorate at the mass level' (Castles 1994:24). According to him, this may very well be as effective a determinant of political outcomes as the strength of political parties. Much of the analysis in the preceding pages is, in fact, an attempt to document this very point.

However, Castles seems to overstate his case when he defines 'Catholic polities with a potential Catholic policy influence' as those nations that are either predominantly Catholic or that have enjoyed considerable Christian democratic party strength. The first major problem is that the number of Catholics registered in a nation does not necessarily say much about the political potential or impact of the Church. Looking at the number of practising Catholics is obviously a better indicator for this potential, al-though data on this are scarce. But even if data were readily available, this would still be complicated, not just because of the difficulties involved in deciding what is meant by 'practising', but also because of the varying positions of the Catholic Churches in different nations. This evidently influences the extent to which the Church might function as a pressure group and the manner in which it might shape the demands of citizens. A too strong emphasis on this possible function of the Church, moreover,

Table 3.1 Christian democratic parties in continental Western Europe and Ireland

Country	Party	Pre-war predecessor(s)	Founded
Austria	Österreichische Volkspartei (ÖVP)	Christlich-Soziale Partei (CSP)	1945
Belgium	Christelijke Volkspartij (CVP)/Parti Social Chrétien (PSC)	Katholieke Vlaamsche Volkspartij (KVV)/ Parti Catholique Social (PCS)	1945
France	Mouvement Républicain Populaire (MRP)	Parti Démocrate Populaire (PDP)	1944
Germany	Christlich-Demokratische Union (CDU)/ Christlich-Soziale Union (CSU)	Zentrum	1945
Italy	Democrazia Cristiana (DC)	Partito Popolare Italiano (PPI)	1943
Netherlands	Katholieke Volkspartij (KVP)	Rooms Katholieke Staatspartij (RKSP)	1945
Switzerland	Schweizerische Konservative Volkspartei (SKV)		1912
	Konservativ-Christlich Soziale Partei (KCSP)		1957
	Christlich-Demokratische Volkspartei (CDVP)		1971
Ireland	Fine Gael (FG)[a]		1933

Note: [a]The inclusion of the Fine Gael rather than the Fianna Fáil here is controversial. Hanley (1994:191) argues that the former 'has as many (or as few) Christian democratic features as the latter'. However, it was the Fine Gael that joined the group of Christian democrats in the European Parliament in the 1970s. Perhaps a more convincing argument in favour of including the Fine Gael among the family of Christian democratic parties concerns the fact that this party was most committed to Catholic social policy (Cohan 1983).

Sources: Irving (1979); MacHale and Skowronski (1983); Jacobs (1989); Lane, McKay and Newton (1991); Mackie and Rose (1991); Hanley (1994b).

tends to overrate the direct impact of the pulpit. In fact, it becomes impossible to distinguish between church and party, which leads to the odd effect that the crucial struggles between parties and the Church over the independence of the former remain outside the scope of the analysis. In other words, the equalisation of church and party would simply miss this important aspect of Christian democracy and, accordingly, most likely leads to a mis-specification of the possibly diverging effects of both Catholicism and Christian democracy, because it abstracts from historical contexts.

The second difficulty with Castles' proposal concerns the question of the mechanisms by which the Catholic message is converted into effective political power. Depending on the historical conditions under which the Church assumes its social and political role, this message is not necessarily identical across contexts. Surely, the Church may influence and shape the demands of church-goers, but it may do so in different ways. As argued, it matters considerably for the political direction of political Catholicism how church–state relations are defined and to what extent the social movements are integrated into the party. Moreover, how – to put it rather crudely – can a sermon determine political opinions and public policy outcomes, unless the demands are backed by an infrastructure of social and political movements that mobilise support for a political party that effectively controls policy-making?

To avoid misunderstandings, Castles makes a clear point when he criticises the public policy and welfare state literature on its too narrow a focus on party politics, but stretches the argument too far. It does make sense to estimate the potential influence of the Church by looking at the number of practising Catholics. But the political entrenchment of the Christian democratic movement can only be assessed to the extent that the social and political power of Catholicism in different nations is documented empirically.

It is notoriously difficult to estimate the proportion of practising or active Catholics in different nations. The first question is what one means by 'practising'. Whyte's (1981:136–44) solution is probably the best. He follows official Catholic law by arguing that a practising Catholic attends mass every Sunday and goes to communion and confession at least once a year. His calculations, then, lead to the following aggregate picture for 1960. The Austrian population counted almost 90 per cent nominal and 36 per cent practising Catholics. In Belgium about 96 per cent of the population was registered as Catholic and almost half of the population could be classified as committed Catholics. Over 90 per cent of the population of France was officially a member of the Church, whereas only about a fourth part of the French people could rightly be said to be practising. West German Catholics numbered about 45 per cent of the population and about half of these people were actively participating in church life, indicating that about a quarter of the population could be categorised as practising

Catholics. Italy's population consisted of 95 per cent nominal Catholics, and 43 per cent were actually taking part in church activities on a regular basis. The Netherlands had about 40 per cent nominal Catholics, no less than 80 per cent of whom were observing Catholic citizens. The Swiss Catholic minority amounted to about 41 per cent of the population, half of whom were practising, as a result of which 21 per cent of the Swiss were reckoned among practising Catholics. An interesting case is provided by Ireland, because in this nation there was not much difference between nominal and practising Catholics: 85 per cent of the Irish population faithfully observed their religious duties in 1960.

One thing that these data immediately make clear is that there is no direct, positive relationship between nominal church membership and religious activity across national contexts. In fact, there is no significant correlation between the percentage nominal and the percentage practising Catholics. This corroborates the above identified problem with Castles' approach to the potential policy impact of Catholicism at large and confirms the idea that one has to look beyond such crude measures as aggregate number of Catholics in a nation for an estimate of Catholic political potential.

It is safe to say that roughly until the 1970s Catholicism was a strong cultural and political force on the European continent, although the momentum of this religion varied considerably across national contexts. The highest level of integration (approximated by the number of practising Catholics among nominal Catholics) of the Catholic sub-culture in the 1960s was reached in the Netherlands. The levels of Belgium, Italy and Austria (three almost homogeneously Catholic nations) were relatively moderate, whereas France (also homogeneously Catholic) scored very low, reflecting this nation's secular culture (Whyte 1981). An interesting question is whether the levels of integration of the Catholic sub-culture is positively related to the strength of Catholic politics and unionism in these nations (see Table 3.2). As yet the answer seems to be no, because there is no significant correlation between the degree of integration, the proportion of practising Catholics (among nominal Catholics and in the population), gross Catholic union density (the number of Catholic union members as a percentage of total dependent labour force), and the strength of Catholic parties. There is, however, a positive association between the level of integration and the level of religious fragmentation (the chance that two people in a nation belong to different religions; see Lane, MacKay and Newton 1991:21), indicating perhaps that religious heterogeneity has a positive effect on the 'closure' of the Catholic sub-culture.

These are all rough measures, and although they are not entirely without

Table 3.2 Membership and electoral strength of Catholic/Christian democratic parties in continental Western Europe and Ireland, 1945–60 (or nearest year)

Country	Party	Members	Member–party vote ratio	% votes	% seats	Catholic union density
Austria	ÖVP	534,667	.28	45.06	48.12	0.00
Belgium	CVP/PSC	213,751[a]	.10	43.80	47.51	18.85
France	MRP	n.a.	n.a.	19.00	21.20	2.84
Germany	CDU/CSU (Centre)	308,263[b]	.02	43.93	47.63	0.24
Italy	DC	1,185,358[c]	.15	41.55	45.18	10.66
Netherlands	KVP	385,500[a]	.20	30.76	31.88	11.41
Switzerland	SKV/KCSP	n.a.	n.a.	22.55	23.80	4.44
Ireland	FG	n.a.	n.a.	27.24	28.42	n.a.

Notes: 1945–60, or nearest year.
a 1960
b 1962
c Only direct members. Ancillary membership of the DC in 1960 amounted to 701,496.

Sources: Mackie and Rose (1991); Katz and Mair (1992); Ebbinghaus (1993).

significance, the post-war political entrenchment of Christian democracy cannot be substantiated by looking at data on religion alone. Table 3.2, then, shows that the electoral appeal of Christian democracy in the first 15 years after the Second World War was considerable. In Austria, Belgium, Germany and Italy Christian democracy has been particularly strong in mobilising the vote, winning on average over 40 per cent of total vote and over 45 per cent of seats in national parliaments during 1945–60. The Dutch Catholic party controlled almost a third of both votes and seats in the same era, followed by the Swiss and French parties, winning approximately 20 to 24 per cent of votes and seats. In Belgium the Catholic labour movement organised almost 19 per cent of the dependent labour force, at some distance followed by the Netherlands and Italy (10–12 per cent). The direct membership of the parties seems to have been much less important in the first years after the war than their electoral appeal. This is especially clear when one looks at the membership–vote ratios. However, the precise meaning of these ratios is better understood if compared with the ratios of the main competing parties in the different nations. Thus, although the ÖVP had a relatively high ratio of 0.28, the main competitor of this party, the Sozialistische Partei Österreichs (socialist party, SPÖ) (average membership 1945–60: 622,965; Katz and Mair 1992) had a membership–vote ratio of 0.32. The main political rival of the Belgian Christian democratic parties, the socialist Parti Socialiste Belge/Belgische Socialistische Partij (PSB/BSP) (membership in 1960: 199,000; Katz and Mair 1992) had the same ratio (0.10) as the CVP/PSC. The very low membership–vote ratio in the German case is less remarkable when compared to the 0.06 ratio of the Sozialdemokratische Partei Deutschlands (SPD; membership in 1960: 649,578; Katz and Mair 1992). The ratio of Italian Christian democracy, although comparatively speaking moderate, was no match for the communist party (Partito Comunista Italiano, PCI; average membership of almost two million in 1945–60; Katz and Mair 1992) that had a membership–vote ratio of 0.26. Finally, the relatively high ratio of the Dutch KVP is emphasised by the relatively low ratio (0.08) of the Dutch social democratic party (Partij van de Arbeid, PvdA; membership in 1960: 142,583; Katz and Mair 1992).

The political entrenchment of Christian democracy in Western Europe in the first 15 years after the war can further be studied by examining the general government record of the parties. Table 3.3 summarises some essential facts. First of all, it is clear that in the period under consideration Christian democratic parties became government parties *par excellence*. Five parties (ÖVP, CDU/CSU, DC, CVP and the KVP) have participated in all governments during the entire period. The Austrian, German and Italian

Table 3.3 Government record of Christian democracy in continental Western Europe and Ireland, 1945–60

1 Country	2 Party	3 % of possible days in government	4 Dominance in government gross	5 net (4×3)/100	6 Number of governments
Austria	ÖVP	100	.58	.58	7
Belgium	CVP/PSC	63	.72	.45	14
France	MRP	89	.30	.26	29
Germany	CDU/CSU	100	.71	.71	6
Italy	DC	100	.76	.76	16
Netherlands	KVP	100	.39	.39	6
Switzerland	CVP	100	.39	.39	16
Ireland	FG	45	.50	.23	5

Note: Austria: 18.12.45–11.4.61; Belgium: 11.02.45–01.09.60; France: 23.11.45–14.04.62; Germany: 15.09.49–13.11.61; Italy: 12.07.46–25.07.60; Netherlands: 03.07.46–18.05.59; Switzerland: 14.12.44–14.12.60; Ireland: 18.02.48–10.10.61.

Sources: Woldendorp, Keman and Budge 1993, various tables.

parties, moreover, were dominant government parties to the extent that on average they commanded a majority of posts in these cabinets. Belgian Christian democracy, if in government, held almost 75 per cent of posts on average, whereas the French, Dutch and Swiss commanded 30–40 per cent.

The sixth column of Table 3.3, finally, also makes clear that one has to be careful in interpreting these data, because the political entrenchment of Christian democracy apparently occurred under very different institutional circumstances. The democratic polities of Austria, Germany and the Netherlands can be identified as relatively stable, the more so as new elections were the most common reason for the termination of a government in these nations (Woldendorp, Keman and Budge 1993). The average number of days a government remained in power was 932 in Austria, 725 in Germany and 783 in the Netherlands. The Belgian, French and Italian political systems were evidently more unstable, with the government instability of the French fourth republic towering above all. The average number of days of a government was 407 in Belgium, 170 in France (fourth republic), and 320 in Italy.[3]

CONCLUSION: JUSTIFYING A CLOSER COMPARISON OF GERMANY, ITALY AND THE NETHERLANDS

The review of welfare state literature revealed that mainstream welfare state typologies consistently place three nations (Germany, Italy and the Netherlands) in the group of conservative welfare state regimes on the basis of similar levels of social expenditure, comparable degrees of equality and analogous characteristics of political configurations. Other Christian democratic nations (e.g. Austria, Belgium and France) less easily fit these typologies (Castles and Mitchell 1993:123, table 3.7).

These findings were taken as a first justification of a closer comparison between Germany, Italy and the Netherlands. Two further arguments, which can be distilled from the analysis presented in this chapter, support the usefulness of this choice of cases. The first concerns the different conditions under which Christian democracy developed in these nations and the effects this has had on the political complexion and the policy potential of the movements. Could it be that mainstream welfare state theories underestimate or wrongly explain the extent to which social policies differ qualitatively in these nations? Or if these theories are largely correct, why is it then that apparently dissimilar movements produce very similar outcomes? The second argument that may justify the proposed closer comparison pertains to the fact that the Christian democratic parties of the Netherlands, Italy and Germany were dominant parties (Pempel

1990) in the foundational period after the Second World War. As a result, these parties can indeed be expected to have had a strong impact on social policy, but – given their relative differences – not necessarily in an identical fashion.

The first justification can be elaborated as follows. Italy – in contrast to Germany and the Netherlands – is a nation where Catholicism constituted the religion of the majority of the population. Christian democracy here was initially hampered by the negative attitude and enmity of the Vatican towards the political activities of Catholic citizens, which also led to the difficulty of mobilising Catholics of all social strata within one movement. Its survival increasingly came to depend on the organisational infra-structure of Catholic action, particularly during the fascist dictatorship. The question is under what conditions Christian democracy nevertheless mobilised as a unitary movement in post-war Italy? In Germany and the Netherlands Catholicism has been the religion of a considerable minority of the population. In both nations the level of political integration that the Christian democratic parties achieved before the war was already high. The question is why Christian democracy emerged as a cross-confessional union of forces in post-war Germany, while in the Netherlands separate confessional blocs reappeared after the liberation of this nation?

The establishment of Christian democracy in Germany and Italy cannot be appreciated properly without reference to the respective burdens of fascist totalitarianism and warfare that these nations experienced. If any-where, it was in these nations that the terms of a new social contract (Rosanvallon 1981) had to be negotiated. Granted, the actual conditions of Italy and Germany immediately after the termination of the hostilities differed considerably. Germany was in complete disarray after its effort of total war and its unconditional surrender to the allied forces. Italy's war experience was both unique and ambiguous. Ultimately, the Italian anti-fascist resistance had been able to take up arms and participate in the liberation of the northern part of the country from Mussolini's fascists and the German armies. In Germany the economic infrastructure was thoroughly cracked. Major cities were ruined by ruthless and undirected bombing and the population was demoralised and dislocated on an immense scale. The devastation of the Italian economy, on the other hand, turned out to be much less severe than feared. The bank of Italy, for instance, calcul-ated the damage of industry at a mere 8 percent. Large parts of the nation had survived the war relatively untouched, while the refugee problem was not in any sense comparable to the German tragedy.

Yet the similarity in the nations' starting position is undoubtedly notable. Both nations faced the huge task of replacing the totalitarian state with a revitalised civil society. Political forces had to be re-established or newly instituted. An entirely new political-administrative Constitution had to be designed in which built-in safeguards against despotic threats were to be incorporated. Moreover, in both nations a state edifice had to be erected if not from scratch then at least from the remnants of what still represented the civilised world of pre-fascist democracy. The decisions taken in the first decade after the war were therefore in many ways foundational: they determined and demarcated the very settlement of state and civil society. And what is more, this was done under and went parallel with the growth of Christian democratic power. In Germany, social democrats were excluded from government until late 1966; in Italy the communists were expelled from government in 1947 and up to now have never had the opportunity to rule Italy at the national level.

In retrospect, the Second World War provided much less of a historical break in the Netherlands. The reappearance of the pre-war pillarised social and political structures and with it the surfacing of confessional politics might indicate a clear tendency towards restoration in this nation. The threat to democracy had come from outside and as a result no societal reordering in this respect was necessary. A restoration would suffice. The defeat of the German armies ushered in the immediate de-Nazification of Dutch society and the trial of traitors. Two years after the liberation, the Netherlands looked very much like the pre-war society, except for the horrendous fact that the Dutch Jewish population had been massacred in the Nazi Holocaust.[4] However, some important changes had taken place at the political level. An attempt to redesign and modernise Dutch society in the immediate post-war years had been effective in two central aspects: a substantial conversion of Dutch social democracy and the construction of a coalition between this renewed movement and political Catholicism. Unlike in Germany and Italy, the left participated in power until the social democrats were expelled from government in the late 1950s.

In Germany Christian democracy (CDU/CSU) emerged as a new alliance of political forces and became one of the leading actors actively involved in the process of economic, social and political reconstruction. After twelve years of Nazi dictatorship and six years of warfare the conditions of the first phase appeared to provide unique prospects for a fresh start. Constraints, however, on the possible configuration of societal power relations were set, not merely by the prevailing internal conditions, but above all by the presence of a coalition of foreign powers occupying the country. The *Weichenstellungen*, i.e. the constraints on possible directions of development, for the reconstruction of politics and society were set in the period 1945–50 under the leadership of Christian democracy. The cross-confessional political movement not only managed to formulate a relatively consistent plan for the reconstruction and reformation of society, but – within and in line with the exceptional structural conditions of the period – proved to a large extent to be capable of implementing the German version of capitalism: the social market economy (*soziale Markwirtschaft*), a combination of neo-liberal economic policies and traditional social policies. The questions are what explains this cross-confessional character of Christian democracy in Germany and under what conditions did the CDU/CSU come to power?

No single party in any Western democracy has been able to become so politically dominant in the first decades after the Second World War as the Italian Democrazia Cristiana. It has been the largest party in every election between 1946 and 1992, polling an average of about 41 percent between 1946 and 1963, 39 per cent between 1968 and 1979, and 32 per cent between 1983 and 1992. It has played the dominant role in every post-war Cabinet (majority of Cabinet seats) until the 1990s and the post of prime minister went to the DC in all but a few (Spadolini, Craxi, Amato) of Italy's numerous post-war Cabinets until July 1992 (Hine 1993:345–6; Hancock *et al.* 1993:540–1). The party has been the initiator, producer and main profiteer of the *sottogoverno*: the 'colonisation' of the institutions of the state and the public corporations by party loyalists, reinforcing traditional clientelism, large-scale political patronage and corruption. Titles of studies of the DC typically refer to 'The Occupation of Power' (Orfei 1976), 'The Anatomy of Power' (Cazzola 1979), 'The Christian Democratic Iceberg' (Tamburrano 1974), 'Masters of Survival' (Wertman 1981) and 'The Politics of Dominance' (Leonardi and Wertman 1989). What accounts for the unparalleled strength of Christian democracy in the immediate period after the Second World War? What were the structural and contingent conditions for the unique electoral victory of the DC in 1948 when the party won 48.5 per cent of the total vote?

Until the second half of the 1970s there was no Christian democratic party in the Netherlands that can be compared to the Protestant–Catholic combination of forces in Germany or to the powerful DC in Italy. Instead, there existed three major confessional or denominational political movements, which Irving (1979:193) has depicted as 'embryo Christian democratic' parties. Both the Dutch KVP and – although to a lesser extent – the ARP have had considerable cross-class appeal. Nevertheless, where the anti-revolutionaries had their stronghold among the protestant lower middle class of shopkeepers, the self-employed, artisans, and the like, the Catholic party up to a point managed to secure a substantial working-class backing, too. In the Netherlands it has been primarily the Catholic party that has represented the Christian democratic tradition of social concern through its labour wing, while the Protestant parties initially had no systematic view on social reforms whatsoever. Woldring and Kuiper (1980:40–51), in their study on the Protestant critique of society, have evaluated the contribution of the ARP to the solution of the social question as 'disappointing'. The ARP had developed the concept of 'sovereignty in one's own circle' primarily as a means to secure the autonomy of lower societal organs from the state. All authority was argued to derive from God and the essentially free circles of social and economic life did not have to acknowledge the authority of the state: 'the highest authority in any circle has nothing above itself but God, and the state cannot intervene and cannot command on the basis of its own power' (Kuyper 1898:79). This theory has influenced the ideology and political practice of the ARP until the 1970s. It is not surprising, therefore, that this party frequently voted against social legislation and as a government party failed to develop social policy (van Putten 1985:175). Moreover, it was the ARP that largely had been responsible for a detrimental crisis policy in the 1930s. The anti-revolutionary attempt to cope with the economic slump was permeated by dogmatic economic liberalism (Klein 1980:5) and more active state intervention in the post-war era conflicted with this traditional anti-statism of the ARP. Finally, political Catholicism has been the prime motor behind the establishment of the cross-confessional Christian democracy in the Netherlands in the mid-1970s. It was not until the Catholic party started to lose its working-class support (both electorally and organisationally with the de-confessional-isation of the Catholic labour movement in the late 1960s, see Roes 1985) that it took the initiative to establish a cross-class and cross-confessional Christian democratic movement. The merger of the confessional parties into the Christen Democratisch Appèl (CDA) was facilitated by an ideo-logical rapprochement of political Catholicism and Protestantism (Zwart 1993). In sum, it has been Catholic politics that represented the Christian democratic current in Dutch politics. What explains the 'absence' of a cross-confessional Christian democracy and the dominance of denomin-ational politics in the Netherlands?

The second justification for a closer comparison of Italy, Germany and the Netherlands is that the Christian democratic parties in these nations were dominant parties. Pempel (1990:3–4) has argued that single-party dominance exists if a party is able to gain at least a plurality of the vote in national elections; if a party enjoys a pivotal position in the political system, according it a strong governing capacity; if the electoral appeal and the government record of a party has an enduring capacity and is not accidental; and if a party uses this dominant position of power to pursue a specific political project through public policy. These criteria were fulfilled in Germany, Italy and the Netherlands.

Electoral results satisfy the first criterion. German Christian democracy won an average of 44 per cent of the vote in parliament as opposed to 31.5 per cent of the vote for the social democrats between 1949 and 1961. In Italy the DC appealed to approximately 42 per cent of the electorate, whereas the communists won an average of 21.4 per cent between 1946 and 1958. The Dutch Catholic party won an average of almost 31 per cent of the vote as opposed to the 29 per cent for the social democrats between 1946 and 1959. In Germany, Italy and the Netherlands the Christian democratic parties have been in government during the entire period 1945–60. The exclusion of communism in Italy and the inability of German and Dutch social democracy to ally with the liberals (for Germany until the late 1960s, for the Netherlands until 1994) established multiparty systems in which the Christian democratic parties became the pivot to the extent that the formation of governments without them remained infeasible. The second dimension of single-party dominance was fulfilled, too. The time criterion is more difficult to assess, because when can one safely conclude that a party is 'at the core of a nation's government over a substantial period of time, not simply for a few years' (Pempel 1990:3–4)? The government position of 15 years in the first period after the war satisfies this criterion, partly because the number of years is sufficient, but mainly because the period in which Christian democracy enjoyed substantial and continuous government power has been politically foundational. The extent to which Christian democracy has been able to exercise power to the benefit of its own political project is an empirical question that will be answered in the next chapters.

In the following chapter the focus is on nationally specific developments that have determined both the character and strength of Christian democracy in Germany, Italy and the Netherlands. Thus, for Germany the political struggle over the 'basic law' (i.e. the Constitution) and the creation of the 'social market economy' is analysed in terms of the mobilisation of bias towards the reconstruction of capitalism. This provides the context within which the establishment of Christian democracy and its rise to power is interpreted. Also for Italy the conflicts around the Constitution highlight the unique conditions of the Christian democratic road to power. Pillarisation and its structural tenacity, finally, are the relevant contextual elements for an account of the dominance of confessional politics and the strength of Christian democracy in the Netherlands. The analysis below will substantiate both similarities and contrasts between Christian democratic movements in Italy, Germany and the Netherlands.

4 Christian democracy in Germany, Italy and the Netherlands

A closer comparison

CONDITIONS OF POWER: CONSTRAINTS AND OPPORTUNITIES

Perhaps even more than in Italy or the Netherlands, 'integration' is the key for understanding the history of Christian democracy in Germany in the immediate post-war phase. The centre-right components of German politics reorganised via Christian democratic power mobilisation. German fascism and the war had thoroughly revolutionised traditional political attachments. The Weimar parties had had their day, particularly right-wing liberalism and conservative Protestantism (Heidenheimer 1960:31). In fact, it is crucial to understand that 'Christian democracy has been *the* vehicle through which German conservatives have come to accept liberal democracy' (Irving 1979:163, original emphasis). This fact already may clarify a conservative disposition of German Christian democracy. Since only the pre-war Zentrum to a certain extent had been able to resist the ideological decomposition of German politics (Heidenheimer 1960:40), the leading role of Catholics in the foundation of Christian democracy was conspicuous, in spite of the fact that the Zentrum, too, had voted in favour of the 'Enabling Act' that had brought the Nazis to power in 1933.

The main ideological and integrative theme present from the start concerned an emphasis on general Christian values, both as a moral rejection of the atheist, immoral and materialist Nazism and as a manner of distinction *vis à vis* social democracy. The thrust of the Christian democratic argument was that politics had to be founded in Christianity and that a moral recovery was a prerequisite for social and economic recuperation. It was imperative to concede the importance of Christian ethics after an epoch of such inhuman and atheist cruelty (Heidenheimer 1960:33–4; Mintzel 1982:133).

Christian democracy aimed at attracting a differentiated electorate from various groups: the pre-war supporters of the Zentrum and the highly fragmented former conservative Protestant as well as other groups (Ute Schmidt 1983:515, 1987). The attempt at integration showed itself, therefore, in the creation of an interconfessional organisation that was to overcome the confessional cleavage completely, and in the self-identification of Christian democracy as fundamentally a people's movement that could cut across class divisions (Pridham 1977:26–8).

The interconfessional character of German Christian democracy was first of all an effect of the experiences of the Weimar Republic, where the confessional as well as the class-based political cleavages had effectively blocked a robust anti-Hitler coalition of the political centre and the non-fascist right. Early Christian democracy was ardently and emotionally anti-fascist. It declared itself to be a movement that provided a clear break with the unfortunate past (Mintzel 1982:132). The strength of interconfessionalism within the early movement was partly an effect of the Nazi experience itself, when Christians of all denominations found out that in the face of such brutality they at least had a shared Christian morality. However, the *de facto* separation of Germany into a western and an eastern zone provided a material basis for these sentiments by altering the balance of denominations in favour of Catholicism, which consequently reduced the anxiety within this sub-culture over Protestant domination (Bark and Gress 1989,1:115). From the outset Christian democracy was characterised by pluralism, both socially and religiously. Its inclination was towards the right of the political spectrum, partly because of the movement being the only acceptable re-alliance of the centre-right, and partly as a result of the temperance of the influence of its union wing and of the social Catholics (Uertz 1981; see also Ute Schmidt 1983:516).

Various groups could easily identify with a Christian democratic union. Organised social Catholicism had an interest in re-establishing the political wing of the movement. The Church sought a new political defence in a changing polity. Protestant groups with a concern for politics wished to ally with fellow Christians in an attempt to safeguard a minimum of influence. German liberalism recognised the potential Catholic significance for the protection of liberal values. The anti-socialism of Christian democracy brought in bourgeois elements, while the movement's rooting in the German tradition of Catholic social theory attracted trade-unionists as well as Prussian conservatives who welcomed Christian democracy as a 'movement seeking to encompass, and reconcile, the claims of all social groups and classes' (Heidenheimer 1960:36).

This pluralism contributed to the establishment of the pivotal religious–secular cleavage of post-war German politics. As a result, both religion and class became important determinants of voting behaviour (Pappi 1984). Three characteristics of German electoral behaviour are fairly well established: Catholics were strongly in favour of the CDU, workers tended to vote for the SPD, and Protestants had a preference for the SPD. What is essential, however, is the extent to which religion 'overdetermined' class voting. This sociological fact has played a crucial part in the mobilisation of working-class support for the CDU/CSU (Linz 1967:291). Catholicism proved to be a strong cross-cutting force in the working class, but affected voting patterns of other classes as well. Among Catholics Christian democracy gained a plurality of votes from most classes and a majority from the salaried class and the farmers. In terms of class distinctiveness, the SPD disproportionally depended on the working-class vote, whereas Christian democracy relied on the middle-class vote. However, Christian democracy's difficulty of attracting voters from the working class was much less critical than social democracy's inability to get proportionate middle-class support. Christian democracy was the least class-distinctive movement, liberalism the most, whereas social democracy appeared to be somewhere in between (Linz 1967:287). These patterns of class and religious voting have been relatively stable over time (Pappi 1984; Padgett and Burkett 1986:285). The overall picture is that Christian democracy in Germany was largely successful in winning both cross-class and inter-confessional support already quite soon after its foundation. Moreover, the CDU/CSU managed to keep its pluralist character during the decades following its establishment. This integrative capacity was an important precondition for the ascendancy of Christian democracy in Germany (Ute Schmidt 1983; 1987) and for the German political system more generally.

As in the case of Germany – mainly as a reaction to fascism and the increasing strength of communism – Italian Christian democracy initially emphasised Christian morality as a constitutional foundation of politics. Christian democracy wished to represent Catholicism in Italian society and politics (Einaudi and Goguel 1952:28; Orfei 1976:29). From the start, Italian Christian democracy, too, was characterised by an integrative, cross-class capacity. But given the pre-war tense relations between political Catholicism and the Vatican the political entrenchment of the DC now critically depended on the ability to gain the direct support of the Church.

A precondition for gaining the full support of the Church consisted in the appreciation of the central role of Catholicism as a popular religion. A cluster of interrelated values and beliefs concerning private property, the vital function of the patriarchical family, the idealisation of rural life, the importance of obedience and the acceptance of one's station in life, constituted

Italy's popular religion (Prandi 1983; Allum 1990). Among other things, it had been the lack of the acknowledgment of the social, cultural and ethical role of Catholicism and its institutions in the political programme of the pre-war PPI that had made the relationship between this party and the Church fractious in the pre-war period. Ultimately, the Vatican had evaluated the fascists as the crucial force for defending the Church's interests and had used the opportunity of fascist dictatorship to solve the 'Roman question' (Irving 1979:5). The PPI's successor needed the Church, but at the same time tried to establish itself as an aconfessional party without antagonising the Vatican. As an effect, the Christian democratic politics of State and Church were often contradictory. The DC defended the Church's accumulated rights and Catholicism's special status, but was nevertheless perfectly ready to acknowledge the freedom of religion.

The organisation of the party depended on the lay organisations of the Catholic infrastructure, the Azione Cattolica (Poggi 1967; Candeloro 1982; Casella 1987; de Antonellis 1987), which had survived remarkably well during the fascist era and had been able to offer the PPI's cadre protection against fascist oppression (Einaudi and Goguel 1952:26). The non-ecclesiastical Catholic organisations, which organized a cross-section of the Catholic sub-culture, provided the new party not only with a ready available organisational network, but also with a pool of party activists and party leaders. The Catholic network functioned as a steady mobiliser of electoral support for the DC (Leonardi and Wertman 1989:193). It was, however, the direct support of the Church that turned Christian democracy from a discussion club into a mass party (Ginsborg 1990:50), since the Church controlled Catholic action.

The Catholic Church had made two improvements in its position and status during the fascist period: one materially, through the Lateran treaties of 1929 (Settembrini 1977:37–40; Spatano 1969:177–91) and one – a paradox perhaps – morally, by improving its ethical standing in Italian society. One of the 'achievements' during the 20 years of fascism was that the Church had never completely identified itself with the fascist project (Poggi 1972:137–8) and during the war the Church had succeeded in disengaging itself from the fascist regime. The position of the Church at the end of the period of totalitarianism and war appeared one of strength rather than of weakness (Poggi 1972:140). The Church itself could rely on the religious organisational resources that fascism had left almost untouched (the hierarchy), the lay organisational resources, the Catholic intellectuals and politicians, an elaborate body of social doctrine, and the active presence of the allied forces that would certainly have intervened in case of a communist insurrection. The Church pursued a strategy of maximum involvement and maximum commitment in politics. The former consisted of a vast and permanent mobilisation of resources, the latter of the deployment of these resources for the attainment of a single goal: the creation of the political unity among Catholics and the institutionalisation of a mass party (Poggi 1972:147).

A further condition for the initial success of the DC concerned the persisting political salience of the north–south division of the Italian nation and society. Italy continued to be a geographical expression rather than a nation. In effect, the different war experiences of the north and the south contributed to a deepening of the question. Whereas the south was liberated in 1943 with relatively little war damage, the north experienced a two-year war effort as well as an armed struggle of the Italian resistance. As a result, the organisation of the Christian democratic party in the north differed considerably from that in the south. Particularly, the progress of the DC in the southern provinces was an important new political fact, because the PPI had never really managed to obtain a foothold in the region in the pre-war era. Critical in this respect was the entrance of the old ruling elites into the DC, giving it – at least in the south – a conservative character (Allum 1972:114).

If it is correct to define one of the perennial principles of southern politics as 'one must belong to the groups or parties which control, or have access to, the government and state machinery, in order to preserve and advance one's own privileges' (Allum 1972:113), then one of the consequences of the 'infiltration' of the southern notables into the DC was the reconstitution of the southern system within the boundaries of the Christian democratic movement itself. In other words, what occurred in the early history of the DC is the integration of the old ruling class of southern Italy into the movement and with it the southern system of clientelism and patronage.

Another element in the account of the effective power mobilisation of Italian Christian democracy before the first general elections concerned the presence of a strong left, but above all, of the communist movement. The DC's road to power was simplified, on the one hand, by a change of tactics in the communist movement. The communists had not only postponed their anti-monarchism, but had also tried to organise a broad coalition of anti-fascist forces which they wished to extend to the period of reconstruction. The PCI considered a strong anti-clerical position to be politically inopportune under the circumstances (Ginsborg 1990:45–6, 83; de Grand 1989:89–90). On the other hand, this initially moderate anti-clericalism of the PCI was not matched by a temperance of Christian democratic anti-communism. In fact, a consequential fact for the particularity of Italian

Christian democracy – and for Italian democracy for that matter – pertains to the condition of having to compete with one of the strongest communist movements of Western Europe. Anti-communism has always played a significant role in Italian politics, as around the elections of 1948 where Christian democracy (and the Catholic Church) phrased the voters' option in terms of a choice between Christ and communism. But already before 1948 it played a determining role. For instance, before the elections for the constituent assembly (June 1946), Pope Pius XII addressed the Italian people, drumming into the voters' mind that the choice was between materialism and Christianity (Kogan 1983:25). The communists' strength also automatically defined Christian democracy as the most acceptable force to the United States and the United Kingdom (Almond 1948). The communist movement itself consisted of two currents; a political one opting for a 'progressive democracy', and a social movement of revolutionary forces, mainly originating in the resistance. The communist strategy reflected this duality by on the one hand presenting itself as a party that recognised the *status quo*, accepted parliamentary democracy, and attempted to ally with the centre, but on the other hand retaining its revolutionary potential among the former (armed) forces of the resistance (Spriano 1978:ch.19; di Loreto 1991).

The DC has always been able to gain the support of a cross-section of society in a considerably less distinctive manner (in terms of region and class) than any of the other political movements in Italy. Christian democracy attracted conservatives, moderate progressives and anti-communists alike. Decisive was the capacity to make inroads into the groups of small farmers, the farm workers and the (Catholic or at least anti-communist) working class (Catalano 1972:63). The mass base of the DC was founded upon the anti-communist and anti-socialist *classe media*, i.e artisans, the self-employed, merchants, shop keepers, employees, state officials and small businessmen. This class had constituted the backbone of the former support of Mussolini (Ginsborg 1990:76), and after the defeat of the fascists was left without political representation. The programme of Christian democracy, therefore, promised to safeguard the middle-class values of private property and private initiative in the economic realm. In addition, it sought to limit monopoly power and to protect the consumer and the small producers. Moreover, the DC promised to restore the traditional values of the family, which had been ravished by fascism. The emphasis on the family and its problems also helped to dilute the salience of class even further and appealed to women in particular (Ginsborg 1990:77). This last detail is relevant, given the fact that after the war for the first time women were given the right to vote and the women's organisations of Catholic action strenuously worked to mobilise the Christian democratic vote (Casella 1987:247–66).

The DC electorate has always been relatively sex-distinctive to the extent that women consistently made up the majority of its core electorate (Leonardi and Wertman 1989:166). Religion, the traditional view on the family and the massive mobilisation of women through the Azione Cattolica were the key factors in effecting this sex-distinctiveness. In terms of class and region, however, the DC has been the least distinctive of all political parties. Although slightly overrepresented among the small farmers and underrepresented among the skilled workers, the composition of the Christian democratic electorate was very similar to that of the electorate as a whole. Religion has been an important conditioning factor of the working-class vote in Italy and members of the working class were most likely to vote for the DC if they were embedded in the Catholic organisational infrastructure, if their religiosity expressed itself not just in a proclaimed membership, but in Church attendance in particular, and if they came from regions where the Catholic sub-culture was strongly developed (Wertman 1974:176; Kogan 1983: 59; Leonardi and Wertman 1989:209–10).

There are two main conditions that account for the 'absence' of a cross-confessional Christian democracy and the re-emergence of religiously based but denominationally divided parties in the Netherlands after the war. The first pertains to the peculiarity of Dutch political history and the pattern of pillarisation. This pillarised structuring of both society and the polity was earlier (Chapter 3, note 1) described as a system of institutionalised segmentation of religious and other groups. This social system was accompanied by political representation of co-operating elites at the top of the pillars that completed the building of separate religious and ideological sub-cultures. The second element concerns the structural tenacity of pillarisation, which – in combination with other rather more contingent catalysts – prevented the refurbishing of the political structure in the Netherlands. The persistence of pillarisation and its organisational pattern also encouraged the relatively underdeveloped anti-religious and anti-clerical disposition of liberalism and socialism in the Netherlands (van Doorn 1989:46; Zahn 1989:33; von der Dunk 1982). The Second World War provided much less of a political rupture in the Netherlands than it did in Italy and Germany. It is partly the persistence of the unique conditions of Dutch politics that explain the particularity of religiously based politics. These conditions played a decisive role in how Dutch political

Catholicism was coupled to a moderate form of social democratic reformism (van Kersbergen and Becker 1988).

Although the Netherlands is often characterised as a thoroughly Calvinist nation, the main characteristics of the political system until 1967 have to be accounted for by reference to the presence of a large and politically active Catholic minority, concentrated in the southern provinces of the nation (Bakvis 1981; Gladdish 1991:44). Within the Protestant nation Catholics formed a discriminated minority. Catholic and Protestant emancipation and protection against threats to the sub-cultures is one cause of pillarisation (Irving 1979:196). Protestants, Catholics and even socialists had attempted to free themselves from liberal dominance. The pattern that evolved in this process consisted of the establishment of a wide array of ideologically separate cultural and social organisations with elite political representation (Verwey-Jonker 1961; but see Righart 1986:29; Stuurman 1983:60).

Pillarisation was also characterised by strategies of social and political control, where sub-cultural masses were willing instruments in the power accumulation of political elites and where political elites recognised the danger of a divided nation and co-operated at the top to accommodate societal conflict (Lijphart 1975), which ultimately led to the establishment of a consociational democracy (van Schendelen 1984; Daalder and Irwin 1989). Dutch politics can be identified as a politics of accommodation. Four segments of society – Catholics, Protestants, socialists and liberals – competed and co-operated in what appeared a paradoxical situation of an extremely segmented yet stable democracy. This politics of accommodation was based on 'a high degree of self-containment and mutual isolation of the four blocs with overarching contact among the blocs limited to the elite level' (Lijphart 1975:112). Political elites intentionally attempted to reconcile conflicts that resulted from societal segmentation. The political game of accommodation among elites, who represented the blocs politically, was facilitated by a set of unwritten rules (Lijphart 1975:122–38), which secured democratic stability but at the same time reinforced social segmentation.

The politics of accommodation, however, not only originated in such prudent leadership, but was also rooted in a long tradition of pluralism (Daalder 1966, 1990). The plurality of religions was recognised early, which implied that 'once definitely discriminated minorities were increasingly free to organize openly' (Daalder 1990:39). Furthermore, parliamentarism had developed before the modernisation of society, which conditioned the formation of mass political movements, giving these a traditional leadership structure of accommodating elites and an internal division between radicalism and conservatism. Pillarisation was a slow and piecemeal process, as a result of which traditional structures of decision-making were reproduced. The pillar type of organisation that emerged in this process became a model for political mobilisation which also forced the liberals and the socialists to adopt it if they were to compete with the religious pillars at all.

Pillarisation was the manner in which 'an older pluralist world developed in a more modern world of associational politics' (Daalder 1989:15; see van Kersbergen and Becker 1988:480–1; Pennings 1991). As argued in Chapter 3, the question of the state financing of religious education produced a religious–secular cleavage in Dutch politics. The anti-revolutionary 'anti-thesis' coincided with the growing Catholic distrust of liberalism. As a result, Protestants and Catholics entered the coalitions that prepared the 'Pacification' of 1917, i.e. the financial equalisation of state and religious education and the extension of the franchise. The solution to the schools question provided the financial and organisational paradigm for the pillarisation of virtually every other social sector, particularly in the religious sub-cultures. The social democrats and liberals, however, typically lacked the density of institutions of the religious organisational network and never managed to gain the same impact on education. Most import-antly, they had no equivalent to the Protestant and Catholic Churches.

The political salience and the organisational importance of confessional cleavages made a cross-confessional political movement virtually impossible. The presence of social and economic cleavages, on the other hand, urged the confessional blocs to co-operate in their mutual aversion towards the non-religious blocs of social democracy and liberalism. The Dutch political structure developed into a three-bloc system of co-existing minorities (Daalder 1989:11), consisting of a Protestant-orthodox cluster, divided politically in the moderate ARP and the conservative Christelijk-Historische Unie (CHU), a highly integrated Catholic bloc, headed by a united Catholic party (KVP), and a rest category of secular segments, divided along class rather than any other cleavage.

The experience of the Second World War and the Nazi occupation did not bring to the Netherlands the kind of political reorganisation that both Germany and Italy were to witness, yet there was an attempt at political innovation. Politics in the Netherlands had not been severely contaminated by fascism. In addition, part of the traditional political system had escaped the country and was transferred to London, where it had continued to represent legal political authority. During the war the government had been preparing its return from England, and from this side of the Channel hardly any innovative aspirations could have been expected.

The forces opting for political reform were to be found in the occupied Netherlands. First, there was the Nederlandse Unie (NU), a movement which attempted to institutionalise the adaptation of the Dutch population to the 'new European order' of fascism (Blom 1982:67; Rogier 1980). The more promising political reform movement – not discredited by the shadow of collaboration – was found among the former leaders of political and social organisations. To a large extent, the progressive movement originated as an affair of elites that had no solid mass base. What contributed to the willingness among these elites to discuss political reform was the common enemy and the recognition of the marginality of many of the differences that had separated them in the pre-war period.

Immediately after the liberation a new political movement was launched, which had as its main objective the 'breakthrough' of the old pillarised political system. The main driving force behind the Nederlandse Volksbeweging, (NVB) (Ruitenbeek 1955; Bank 1978; de Keizer 1979) consisted of the elite of the socialist Sociaal Democratische Arbeiderspartij (SDAP) that wished to dispose of its Marxist heritage and sought to transform itself through the NVB into a broader people's party. In addition, the striving for renewal was backed by left-wing liberals and Catholic groups who shared a longing for unity of the Dutch people. The cement for this blend of miscellaneous political bricks was found in the idea of 'personalist socialism', a mixture of social democratic, liberal, and Catholic-corporatist conceptions (on the concept see Rauch 1972). The shared conservative element consisted of an emphasis on Christian values, the traditional family and community (von der Dunk 1982:197), while the progressive legacy was embodied in an ideal of a classless society and the nationalisation of crucial means of production. Personalist socialism shared quite a number of characteristics with social Catholicism. Personalism was interpreted as a more solidaristic form of individualism that at the same time rejected Marxist and fascist collectivism. Its focus on individuals and their attachment to small communities and the family was an attempt to provide an alternative for class ideologies. Socialism in the personalist interpretation was introduced as a means to stress social justice and as a way of incorporating more radical ideas on social policy without defying a commitment to the capitalist market economy (Bank 1978:20; Böhl, Nekkers and Slot 1981).

The 'breakthrough' movement was only a partial success. It was a failure in the sense, that – on three major exceptions – the pre-war political and social system of pillarisation was restored in very much its traditional outlook (Blom 1977, 1982; Bosmans 1982; Böhl and van Meershoek 1989). The failure of the 'breakthrough' must first of all be sought in the tenacity of the system of pillarisation. Apparently, historically deep-rooted sub-cultural differences and their structural condensation are not that easily vanquished, not even by war and foreign rule. In addition, the course of the war was such that the southern, predominantly Catholic part of the Netherlands was liberated in the autumn of 1944, half a year before the rest of the country. This led the Catholic conservatives sufficient room for the restoration of their traditional networks. In addition, the social democratic reformists feared that political renewal in the south would be dominated by the Catholics. They decided to postpone the foundation of the NVB and subsequently reintroduced their pre-war party. The implication was that at the time of the establishment of the NVB, the Catholics were already safe within their own pillar (Bosmans 1982:272) and the 'breakthrough' movement became an almost exclusively social democratic affair.

The three main achievements of the 'breakthrough', however, involved the foundation of a new social democratic party (Partij van de Arbeid, PvdA) with a personalist socialist and social Christian character; the modernisation of the Catholic party, according it a stronger reformist disposition; and the construction of a government coalition between the two parties. This systematised the political basis on which the post-war reconstruction of society was carried out. The potential for this alliance of social democratic and Catholic forces was greatly enhanced by the fact that the PvdA had been thoroughly influenced by religion, adding to the already considerably religious nature of Dutch politics (Rogier 1980:103).

The partial restoration of the Dutch political system came clearly to the fore in the first elections in 1946. The main pre-war parties returned to the stage at more or less the same strength as before the war. The renewal of the Dutch system appeared to be slimmed down to an ideological innovation of social democracy, without it having had hardly any effect on electoral behaviour. In fact, the PvdA came out of the first elections a little weaker than its pre-war socialist predecessor. The elections between 1946 and 1963 time and again revealed the dominance of confessionalism in Dutch politics. The three major confessional parties managed to attract roughly 49–53 per cent of the total vote in this period (Daalder and Irwin 1989:159; Irwin 1989:154–8).

Voting behaviour was utterly predictable and it almost perfectly mirrored the structure of pillarisation. Catholics voted for the KVP, members of the Dutch reformed Church and the orthodox Calvinists voted either ARP or CHU, the secular working class voted PvdA, while the secular middle-class vote was more dispersed, although almost a third of this class voted for the liberal Volkspartij voor Vrijheid en Democratie (VVD) (Andeweg and Irwin 1993:97–9). The most important determinants of voting behaviour were church affiliation, church attendance and social class (Lijphart 1974:257; Gladdish 1991:43). In terms of class, the three major Christian parties of all parties were the least distinctive. This held particularly true for the KVP, which was the least class-distinctive of the confessional groupings (Lijphart 1974:243). The social democrats were disproportionally supported by the working class and the liberals lacked substantial support from this class (van der Eijk and van Praag 1991:174).

Although the existence of two major Protestant parties in the Netherlands was an exceptional phenomenon, the confessional parties nevertheless seemed to form a kind of Christian democratic group in parliament. However, in the first decade after the Second World War there existed considerable disagreement between the Protestant parties and the Catholic party over general ideological issues, and more specifically over economic and social policy (van Kersbergen, Lucardie and ten Napel 1993) and it was the ARP that refused to accept increasing state intervention, whether legitimised by the Catholic idea of subsidiarity or by the state socialism of the PvdA. The ARP opted for something very near the neo-liberalism of the German CDU in economic policy (van Wissen 1982; Woldring and Kuiper 1980).

NEW POLITICAL ENTRENCHMENTS AND THE CONSTITUTION OF SOCIETIES

The West German 'basic law' (*Grundgesetz*) of 1949 pictured the Federal Republic of Germany as a democratic and federal social state (Hancock 1989:157–78; Conradt 1989:247–66). A crucial condition for the development of the post-war German political economy concerned the fact that the postulate of the social state (*Sozialstaatspostulat*, Hartwich 1970) was deliberately formulated in an open, undetermined way (Seifert 1989:44). The concrete materialisation of laws that were to shape the edifice of the social state was made contingent upon the evolving political power structure rather than immediately predetermined (Alber 1989:59).

Two models competed for hegemony in the immediate post-war period: the Christian democratic model of the social market economy and the model of democratic socialism as represented by social democracy (Hartwich 1970; Welteke 1976; Ambrosius 1977). These models focused on the main contents, directions and principles of the 'basic law' and on the economic and social relationships that were to evolve from it. Both the Christian democratic and the social democratic designs competed in the 1949 elections as real alternatives for charging the postulate of the social state with real content. Their differences primarily concerned the question of the fundamental construction of the societal *status quo* in terms of property relations and the role and scope of state intervention.

The Christian democratic model was first formulated fully in the so-called Düsseldorfer Leitsätze of July 1949 (Hartwich 1970:54–7; Rimlinger 1971:140–8; Pütz 1976:92–3; Ambrosius 1977:195–213; Buchhaas 1981:164–71; Leaman 1988:50–8; Bark and Gress 1989,1:191–209). The social market economy involved a reconciliation of a pro-market stance and a positive belief in the moderating capacity of social and economic policy. It was directed against both the liberal *laissez-faire* doctrine and the doctrine of the controlled or planned economy (see Müller-Armack 1989:82–3). The neo-liberal bias of the social market economy originated in the debates among the members of the so-called liberal Ordo-Kreis (Peacock and Willgerodt 1989). In this sense the economic policy proposed by the Christian democrats was barely distinct from the manifestos of the republican middle class in the Weimar Republic except for the stress on monopoly control (Leaman 1988:51).

According to the *Leitsätze* the new social and economic order of the federal republic would consist of a 'socially bound constitution of the commercial economy' (cited in Leaman 1988:52). Competition had to be guaranteed, the monetary system was to be placed under central control and prices were to be freely determined. In addition, wage moderation was called for as a lasting road to economic recovery. Private property would constitute the basis of the economic system and the spread of private property was to be encouraged as a means to overcome the socialist demand for nationalisation. Economic management should primarily consist of credit and monetary policy, although public investment was not excluded. Workers' participation in management was to be encouraged (Leaman 1988:52–3; Ute Schmidt 1983:536).

The CDU aspired to a new societal order on the basis of social justice, socially responsible freedom and real human dignity. A comprehensive social policy for all economically and socially dependent groups was needed. The family was to be protected and the value of the working person was confirmed as well as the right to co-determination. A reorganisation of the system of social security and social assistance was called for. In addition, there existed a right to work, both for men and women, although a woman ought not to be forced into a type of job that did not correspond to her female nature (Ute Schmidt 1983:538). There was to be freedom of choice for occupation, fair and equal pay, a six-day working week, labour protection and a special programme of aid and compensation for war victims (*Lastenausgleich*). Displaced Germans and refugees were to be integrated into society and a special programme for social housing was considered to be necessary.

Social policy was conceived of as fundamentally subordinate and secondary to economic policy. The social market economy was essentially a liberal ordering of economic relations, a kind of socially reformed capitalism, in which the only problematic issue concerned the extent to which social compensation would have to be allowed (Ambrosius 1977:207). The social policy implications of the essentially neo-liberal social market economy were clear from the outset. Social policy would typically be passive, reactive and compensatory in nature, since its chief aim would be compensation rather than prevention (Rimlinger 1971:143). On the account of the neo-liberal wing of Christian democracy, however, the ideal social policy was to be founded in a sound and 'healthy' economic policy.

A further implication of the social market economy concerned the inherent ambiguity as to specific social policy measures. The predicament here was that the pure neo-liberal model in its ultimate theoretical implications would inhibit the expansion of the domain of collective social security, whereas at the same time the practice would (and in fact did) allow quite different developments. In one sense, this ambiguity produced certain ideological advantages. The promise of a political economy that was efficient and just and that guaranteed economic and political freedom was a powerful instrument in the struggle for dominance in the relatively contingent historical context of Germany in the first years after the war (Rimlinger 1971:144).

It has to be stressed that the philosophy of the social state was not solely derived from classical liberal doctrines (Hallet 1973:21–4). Even in the formulation of the neo-liberal point of view in the various manifestos promoting the social market economy there were typical social Catholic elements, such as the stress on persons in their social setting rather than on the individual. Leading ideas were that the state had to protect capitalism from the capitalists (Bark and Gress 1989,1:207) and that capitalism was not at all incompatible with the 'natural order of society'. A free market economy could not function in a morally empty space, but was to be socially and morally embedded (Bark and Gress 1989,1:208). Markets produced socially unacceptable outcomes that had to be dealt with by means of political and moral instruments. Moreover, governments led by Christian democrats in the 1950s were relatively active in the realm of social policy despite the neo-liberal rhetoric. If too great an emphasis is placed on the neo-liberal economics of the social market economy one might easily underestimate or wrongly evaluate the importance of the 'social' side of the social market.

The CDU/CSU gained a plurality of the vote in the elections of 1949 with the social market as its programme. What were the conditions for this victory and what enabled the Christian democrats to win these elections and make a start with the implementation of their political project? One answer could be that the German 'basic law' was already heavily biased towards the mix of neo-liberalism and social Catholicism of the CDU/CSU-model. However, the provisional Constitution did not serve as a guidebook for social and economic policy (Seifert 1989:44). The postulate of the social state and in particular the openness of its formulation illustrate why this was the case. Both Christian democracy and social democracy – uncertain as to the actual balance of power in post-occupied Germany – had an interest in an open formulation of the social postulate. Neither movement wanted to see its own project blocked in advance by constitutional constraints and both the CDU/CSU and the SPD hoped to win the first post-war elections. However, there were extra-constitutional constraints that facilitated Christian democratic power mobilisation.

The influence of the American occupying force, the dominant role of Christian democrats in the economic council (*Wirtschaftsrat*) in the occupied zones, a range of institutional measures taken in the period preceding the constitution of the federal republic, and the elections of 1949 determined a gradual shift towards an extra-constitutional bias in favour of the social market. Only in this sense was the institutionalisation of the social market in Germany pre-determined before Christian democracy got hold of the legitimate power in the federal republic. In addition, the systematic integration of the western occupation zones into the Marshall plan, the linkage to international economic organisations and the European monetary union, and the increasing importance of the conflict between East and West, were other momentous catalysts of this development (Hartwich 1970; Welteke 1976:18; Widmaier 1976:31; Ambrosius 1977; Abelshauser 1983; Bark and Gress 1989,1).

Three 'internal' developments in the British and American zones were crucial for the re-establishment of capitalism in West Germany: the hegemony of the forces of the United States; the position and composition of the economic council; and the money reform of 1948. The American dominance on the European continent expressed itself in the leading role of the United States and in their economic recovery plan for Europe, the Marshall plan. The hegemony of the United States became firmly established after the formation of the Bizone, which was economically decisive since the British zone included Germany's main industrial areas of the Ruhr, Lower Saxony, Hamburg and Schleswig-Holstein. The politics of the American occupying forces can be accurately described as the politics of prejudicing through the prohibition of all prejudicing (Hartwich 1970:66). This policy of the American military governor precipitated the preservation of the *status quo* and effectively blocked possible other models not principally committed to a restoration of the capitalist economy from becoming viable alternatives (Welteke 1976:25–8; Berghahn 1987:177). No measures would be taken that would deny the German people a real choice between a free and a socialist economy or that would impose 'external', American-style democracy on Germany (Welteke 1976:26; Hartwich 1970:68). On the strictest interpretation, any attempt to change the *status quo* would be an 'external form' being imposed on Germany. It was in this way that American foreign policy managed to organise a bias towards a free, capitalist market economy, without literally imposing their preferred economic and political order (see Hartwich 1970:68).

In practice, the United States were able to influence the economic policy of the Bizone substantially on the basis of their large resources. The completion of the development towards American hegemony in the western zones of occupied Germany was given by the expansion of the Marshall aid and its effects on the increasing integration of Germany into the Western European capitalist economic system. The motivation of these policies was fuelled by the American conviction that economic nationalism had caused the collapse of the system of international relations and that an open economy and a liberal democracy were institutional guarantees for integrating Germany into the global economy (Berghahn 1987:183; Hancock 1989:77–8; Widmaier 1976:33).

The economic council of the united British and American zones functioned in favour of the Christian democratic political ideology. Its legislation converged with the opinion of the Americans on economic structure and policy. In addition, the council was reorganised between 1947 and 1949 and came under Christian democratic domination (Hartwich 1970:95–101; Ambrosius 1977:148; Bark and Gress 1989,1:189). The American hegemony in the western part of Germany and the Christian democratic control of the economic council also explain the money reform, which reinforced the bias towards the social market. The effect of this reform was immediate to the extent that it normalised economic transactions rapidly and restored the relationship between the value and quantity of money. The reform, however, left property relations virtually untouched (Abelshauser 1983:46–50; Widmaier 1976:34).

The American theory of a freedom for the German people in the choice for the proper economic and social order was based upon a myth of historical contingency (Hartwich 1970:116). These reflections make plausible how in the period before the elections of 1949 and the inauguration of the 'basic law' a bias was mobilised. This bias regulated the restoration of capitalist economic relations and inhibited from the outset any radical experiment that drew upon propositions of societal transformation. It also explains the vitality of the neo-liberal facet of the Christian democratic ideology of the social market.

A significant further development – which is often overlooked but which was critical for the establishment of the social market – concerned the fragmentary incorporation and in part elimination of the demands of the left, labourite and Dominican wing of the Christian democratic movement. Initially these groups had articulated a vehemently anti-capitalist reformist ideology. One circle, consisting of the old Christian labour movement leaders and members of the Dominican order who had been active in the anti-Nazi resistance (Uertz 1981:23), mainly operative in the British zone, had formulated a social Christian programme for post-war Germany. This plan was partly based on the pre-Nazi designs and strategies of the Christian unions and partly on a revitalisation of Thomist social philosophy. The *Walberberger* circle, in fact, founded the first post-war Christian democratic party in occupied Germany. For the Christian socialists the economy should be based on the self-government of labour and capital. Among the goals of this group were a wider diffusion of private property among workers, a just tax system, a fair distribution of material wealth and comprehensive social legislation. The Christian socialists controlled the party political developments of Christian democracy in the British zone in 1947–8 (Uertz 1981), even if the concept of Christian socialism had already evaporated by that time.

This group of Christian socialists opted for a merger with other progressive forces in society in order to constitute a broadly based labour party similar to the 'breakthrough' movement in the Netherlands. They acknowledged their political kinship with the SPD and were perfectly willing to ally themselves with the social democrats in a reformist coalition (Heidenheimer 1960:46). Christian socialism was to be the vehicle for a realignment of the left to which other social layers, previously hesitant to be associated with socialism, could enter. Adenauer primarily countervailed the 'socialist agitation' from within his own ranks by formulating cautious compromises. Sufficient support for the more liberal economic recovery programme in the British zone in 1946 could only be won if the demands from the Christian socialist camp were incorporated. Adenauer's tactical skills were impressive and his political pragmatism was unmatched. In this sense, the political leader of the CDU and of Germany's resurrection was similar to his counterpart in Italy, the leader of the DC, Alcide de Gasperi (Corsini and Repgen 1979; Schwarz 1986). The compromises on socialisation and the manner in which the labourite demands were converted into a new social manifesto (the Ahlen programme) moderated if not rendered harmless the Christian socialist influence. The new programme was mainly designed to camouflage the near schism of the party into a group in favour of socialisation and a faction urging for a moderate reordering of large industries.

This is the background against which the notorious Ahlen programme must be interpreted, a programme – in rhetoric at least – anti-capitalist, but already interlarded with neo-liberal elements as a result of which both neo-liberals and Christian socialists could identify with it (Uertz 1981:103). Adenauer succeeded in integrating the labour wing into the party and thus tried to prevent the potential defection of workers to the socialist camp (Bark and Gress 1989,1:197). The Christian democratic left was so firmly convinced of the real substance of the compromise, that the union wing declared Adenauer the leader of the Christian workers (Uertz 1981:188)

The mobilisation of bias towards the restoration of capitalism through the money reform and similar economic measures expedited the downfall of the more positively reformist forces within German Christian democracy. The money reform in particular accorded the neo-liberal wing an advantage in the internal political struggle. The novel compromise between the increasingly strong neo-liberals and the social reformist wing consisted primarily of affirming the Ahlen programme as the determinant of the social face of free market capitalism, whereas economic policy would be based upon the neo-liberal theory of the benefits of a free market. The incorporation of the theory of the social market economy into the *Düsseldorfer Leitsätze* meant a shift from a predominantly social reformist Christian democracy to a movement that embraced free market capitalism as the foundation of social justice. Gradually, even the former adherents of Christian socialism committed themselves to liberal economic policies, provoking the demise of Christian socialism within the CDU (Uertz 1981).

The division of Germany effected changes in the political sociology of the western part of this nation and further sustained Christian democracy's road to power. The political development in the western zones and the emerging dominant position of Christian democracy was to a certain extent predetermined by the transformation of the religious structure. The ratio of Catholics to Protestants in the German *Reich* around 1925 had been 32.4:64.1, whereas this ratio in the Federal Republic (1950) amounted to 45.8:50.5 (Mintzel 1984:27; 1982:133). The division of Germany cut off the Soviet zone with its traditionally social democratic and communist strongholds. The predominantly Catholic areas of Bavaria, Rhineland–Palatinate and North Rhine–Westphalia gained prominence as a result.

The organised bias towards the reconstruction of capitalist economic relations constituted a power resource for Christian democracy to the extent that the social market economy flawlessly concurred with the constraints of the period. The complement of this development was the failure of social democracy to mobilise a bias towards the model of democratic socialism or at least to formulate its own 'flexible response' to the changing circumstances. The social democratic model was anachronistic given the structural bias towards private market capitalism. The SPD, however, was slow in adjusting to the emanating new configuration of the social structure in (West) Germany. The social democrats found it particularly difficult to find a feasible answer to the challenge of Christian democracy, especially since this new political movement managed to attract support from the working class as well. It took the social democrats until 1954 to adjust to the evolving and partly already institutionalised new relations of power (Drummond 1982; Crawley 1973:118–32) and to accept the competitive market as a regulating principle of the economy. This slow process of adaptation resulted in the revised party programme of 1959, in which the SPD broadened its appeal to the people of the federal republic as a whole rather than to the working class alone. The revision of the new programme was also most likely accelerated by the sweeping electoral triumph of Christian democracy in 1957. The SPD was facing such a powerful opponent that it would have been sheer suicide not to move into the direction of political power (Miller and Potthoff 1986; Hallett 1973:17; Schmidt 1985).

The first German elections after the war focused on the choice between Christian democracy and social democracy and their respective designs for post-war Germany. The choice was between a planned economy and a social market economy (Uertz 1981:201). Christian democracy won 31 per cent of the vote in the 1949 Bundestag elections, whereas social democracy received 29.2 per cent. Yet in 1953 the CDU/CSU managed to win 45.2 per cent as against a mere 28.8 per cent of the vote for the SPD. And in 1957 Christian democracy triumphed with 50.2 per cent of the vote, whereas the SPD succeeded in gaining an additional 3 per cent (31.8 per cent) (Mackie and Rose 1991:177–9). The Christian democratic model of the social market, therefore, had achieved clear legitimacy in the first three Bundestag elections.

The prestige, legitimacy, and consequently the political weight of Christian democracy was reinforced by the subsequent and unmatched economic success of the social market economy. Christian democrats claimed that their policies had generated Germany's miraculous economic recovery (the *Wirtschaftswunder*) (Abelshauser 1983:101). What mattered was that the social market economy did very well and that Christian democracy was declared to be its main architect. In addition, the social market was clearly superior to the socialist model as practised in East Germany. The 'systems competition' was therefore won by the West German path. Moreover, Christian democrats claimed that the values they defended were systematically violated in the German Democratic Republic (GDR). An effect of the 'systems competition' on all fronts was also that it became increasingly difficult for the social democrats to continue to make use of the very term 'socialism', which – given the experiences in the GDR – was subject to a dwindling respectability. The 'systems competition', especially strong within the context of the cold war, and the party's government record, particularly the success of the social market economy, established the CDU/CSU as the dominant force in the new polity of West Germany.

In Italy, too, the struggle over the Constitution clarifies the power accretion of Christian democracy. The DC gained already a plurality of the vote in the elections for the Constituent assembly in 1946. This assembly was to prepare the Constitution of a new republic rather than a monarchy, since at the same date a referendum was held which showed a narrow republican majority. In the constituent assembly the DC controlled 207 seats out of a total of 556 seats. The communists had won 104 and the socialists 115 seats. Alcide de Gasperi – as leader of the largest party of the assembly – was to make a government coalition with as its main assignments the preparation of the Constitution of the republic, the negotiations of the peace treaty and the commencement of the economic and social reconstruction of Italy. A four-party coalition, including the communists, the socialists (Partito Socialista Italiano, PSI) and the republicans (Partito Repubblicano Italiano, PRI) was the result. The DC's general view on the structure of the economy was entirely in line with the Christian democratic ideas elsewhere in Europe. Typical elements were the subordination of economic life to spiritual life, economic freedom conditioned by social justice and the reconciliation of capital and labour. The social function of private property was probably the clearest social Catholic proposal present during the time of the drafting of the Constitution. Private property was to be defended, but – similar to the early ideas of the CDU/CSU – the state had an obligation to intervene whenever monopolistic tendencies threatened the common good (Einaudi and Goguel 1952:36).

The initial phase of the political struggle over the Constitution was determined by the question whether the pre-fascist bourgeois liberal system had to be restored or whether a social order ought to be constructed in which there was room for the granting of social rights in addition to political liberty (Vercellone 1972:123). The central issue involved the extent of state intervention and the scope of social rights. The left opted for a 'socialist' constitution and proposed radical change of the societal order. Such a document was perhaps not to be a socialist blueprint but should at least facilitate the transition to socialism (de Grand 1989:109). The DC demanded reform according to a doctrine of gradual change and the 'social embeddedness of private property'.

The result of the political struggle around the Constitution was a – at points contradictory – compromise, in which on a majority of items Christian democracy was able to impose its views (Einaudi and Goguel 1952:39). The nucleus of the compromise consisted of formulations that did not exclude change, but did not demand the immediate transformation of society either. Both Christian democracy and the left – again analogous to developments in Germany – had an interest in a relatively open formulation of the important social and economic clauses, in the hope of future strength. The open Constitution was to provide a framework which would allow political power to decide substantial matters (Vercellone 1972:126). A telling change concerned the compromise on the first article, from 'Italy is a workers' republic' to 'Italy is a democratic republic founded on labour'. The Christian democratic influence is clearly discernable in articles 41, which limits private enterprise by the concept of social utility, and 42, which defines the right to limit private property according to social function. The social Catholic notion of the just wage is found in article 36 which states that 'a worker is entitled to a remuneration in proportion to the quantity and quality of his work, and in all cases this should be sufficient to ensure a free and dignified existence for himself and his family' (cited in Vercellone 1972:130). Christian democrats were also highly successful in reinforcing the strengthened position of the Church. Here the Constitution is most contradictory, since, on the one hand, it recognises that all religions are equally free before the law (article 8), but on the other hand it incorporates the Lateran treaties of 1929, which privilege Catholicism (article 7) (Einaudi and Goguel 1952:39–40; Vercellone 1972:125; Settembrini 1977: 130–85).

The first post-war governments had two main objectives: the continuation of economic reconstruction and the restoration of the public order. These aims were closely related, for restoring the public order implied constraining the potential effects of political strikes, stabilising the work ethic, finding a way to reduce the tensions between social classes, and establishing and reinforcing the authority of the state, particularly the monopoly of violence (Mammarella 1985:99). The policy of the 1946–7 coalition government (DC, PCI, PSI, PRI) was clearly to accord priority to economic recovery at the expense of social policies. Economic reconstruction was based on an economic policy similar to the neo-liberalism of German Christian democracy and constituted a mixed strategy of capital accumulation on the basis of low wages, deflationary monetary policy and the attempt to obtain and secure economic aid from the United States. And also in Italy the miracle happened and economic recovery was surprisingly fast (King 1987:42).

The main obstacle to development, however, was galloping inflation, which was partly due to the drastic decrease of production, but also caused by the presence of an exorbitant quantity of money. Deflationary policy (credit control) was entirely grounded in an 'almost religious belief in liberalism' (de Cecco 1972:161), but was successful to the extent that it deflated the economy considerably. An immediate negative impact of this policy, however, was that it caused a recession with increasing unemployment, while production actually declined. The deflationary policy pursued just before the decisive elections of 1948 can only be explained in political terms, i.e. in the government's attempt to obtain the support of small farmers and the *classe media* who had a clear interest in a control on rising prices (de Cecco 1972:174).

In the first elections under the new Constitution (1948) the DC won 48.5 per cent of valid votes, which gave the party the absolute majority in the parliament, i.e. 305 of a total of 574 seats. What were the conditions of this extraordinary electoral triumph? The Christian democrats had developed a political programme appealing to a cross-section of society. It could boast of a Constitution on which it had had momentous influence and for which it claimed recognition and credits. Moreover, the DC had shown remarkable political skill in letting liberals push through unpopular deflationary politics, so that the party would not have to do the dirty work, while still being able to profit from its stabilising effects (Einaudi and Goguel 1952:51). Other catalysts of the electoral victory concerned the mobilising effects of anti-communism, the financial support of Marshall aid, and the political interventions by the Church. In a specific sense they all worked in one direction: the isolation of Italy's left and the establishment of the DC in the centre of power.

The isolation of the Italian left (especially communism) found its origins already at the beginning of 1947 when a socialist group, which opposed the continuation of co-operation with the communists, left the party. This happened when de Gasperi had travelled to the United States in order to secure American economic aid (Harper 1986:108–16). The socialist schism and the resulting political crisis appeared to provide a unique opportunity for the increasingly anti-communist Christian democrats to provoke an end to the government participation of the communists and socialists. Upon his return in January, de Gasperi handed in the resignation of the government yet the left was not immediately expelled from governmental power.

There is some disagreement about the question whether the Americans made financial assistance directly contingent upon the expulsion of the left from the government or not. According to one observer the Americans had demanded precisely this and de Gasperi is reported to have confirmed the American pressure (Mammarella 1985:107). Another historian, however, claims that this hypothesis is implausible for this period and belongs to the mythology of the cold war (Ginsborg 1990:102–3). Nevertheless, it also seems implausible that the whole matter of communist government participation in Italy was not raised at all during de Gasperi's visit to the US. The way in which the American government phrased their conditions for financial support, for instance, left little doubt about its anti-communist intentions (Warner 1972:52).

De Gasperi probably was already looking for a way to shut out the communists and the American foreign-policy-makers did utilise their financial resources for exerting pressure on the leader of the DC. But why were the communists not immediately forced out of the new coalition that was formed after the crisis provoked by the socialist schism? There are several reasons for this. First of all, in order to form another coalition the DC had to find other partners. This was not easy since the small parties on the democratic left refused to co-operate (Mammarella 1985:107–8). A Christian democratic minority cabinet, furthermore, would likely stir up tensions in the nation which, in turn, might interfere with the concluding phase of the negotiations over the Constitution. At the time there was not yet agreement on the precarious – and for the DC vital – article 7 (the Lateran treaties), for which the communist vote was indispensable. Finally, there was still the peace treaty to sign and the DC leadership deemed it politically dangerous to bear sole responsibility for the expected unfavourable political aftermath of the treaty (Mammarella 1985:108).

The third de Gasperi Cabinet (first months of 1947) can best be interpreted as a Christian democratic attempt to gain time for the preparation of a government without the left (Mammarella 1985:109). The communist strategy was fueled by the conviction that continued collaboration with the DC was politically favourable. The communists argued that their support for article 7 would be rewarded by prolonged government participation (de Grand 1989:109). In effect, the opposite was true: the safeguarding of the interests of the Church in the Constitution reduced the Christian democratic dependence on the PCI and consequently intensified the anti-communist factions.

A worsening of the economic and social situation in Italy, increasing disparities between the PCI and the DC with regard to state intervention, the declining popularity of the DC at the regional and local level, and – in general – the intensification of the cold war in this period added to the DC's conviction that the communists did not belong in government. In addition, there was insistence from large industry and the employers' association, Confindustria, to break with the communists and reorient economic policy so as to favour large-scale rather than small businesses (Leonardi and Wertman 1989:57; Salvati 1982). Finally, the right wing of the DC had never been happy with the communist participation anyway and found itself now in a much stronger position to demand the expulsion of the PCI from government.

In May 1947 the historical anti-fascist coalition of Christian democracy and the left collapsed, culminating in a political crisis decisive for post-war Italian politics. The Italian political system was turned into an imperfect two-party system (Galli 1984) that combined a pluralist political system in which two parties dominate (the PCI and the DC) with the condition that only one (the DC) could assume power at the governmental level. The DC formed a minority government and an immediate effect of the exclusion of the left and the formation of the new government was a swing to the right of the DC itself. The government was supported by the liberals and the right, and the DC appeared to suspend its original programme of moderate reform. The solution of the political crisis of May 1947 was a costly victory, because it also blocked the potential for moderate yet necessary reform (Mammarella 1985:113). Another immediate effect of the expulsion of the communists and the growing atmosphere of anti-communism was a boosting polarisation, which forced other political movements to choose between the two camps.

Under these circumstances the elections of 1948 were held, which witnessed a desperate attempt of the left to counter the Christian democratic power advance. The PCI and the PSI combined their forces on one list, which had at least the unintended effect of highlighting the contrast between them and the DC and reinforced the fear for a communist uprising. This anxiety was exploited by the DC. The communist *coup d'état* in Czechoslovakia augmented the salience of the anti-communist issue and functioned as a formidable electoral catalyst for the DC vote. Anti-communism and the religious factor came to play a crucial role. The political struggle was transformed into one of 'apocalyptic proportions, and the vote was depicted as a telling climax in the battle between christ and antichrist, between Rome and Moscow' (Kogan 1983:39). The Church intervened politically at all levels of the hierarchy. It was proclaimed a mortal sin not to vote or to vote for those candidates who did not respect the rights of God and the Church. Parish priest more or less directly summoned parishioners to vote DC. Finally, numerous civic committees, the nucleus of which was formed by the various branches of Azione Cattolica, performed critical political tasks (Ginsborg 1990:117). These parochial committees were to persuade and to instruct hesitating, ill and even illiterate voters to elect Christian democratic candidates. The central organisation was sponsored by the Banca Vaticana, the American embassy and the employers' organisation, Confindustria (Settembrini 1977:209–10). Finally, the 'apocalyptic proportions' of the campaign virtually bestowed a devout aura on the efforts of religious women within the Catholic organisations to canvass votes and by this time the American government not only intervened by assisting the democratic parties financially and even mobilising the Americans of Italian descent (Kogan 1983:39) to instruct their kin in the home country, but now also made the Marshall aid to Italy directly contingent upon the election results (Mammarella 1985:140; Warner 1972:53). With this backing of American economic aid the DC stressed that only under its rule would prosperity arrive.

Immediately after the election, de Gasperi announced a programme of social reform (Ginsborg 1990:118). The government formula that was to initiate it consisted of a four-party coalition of the centre-right. It was a precarious balance between reformist and conservative political forces and was the result of a necessity: there simply was no alternative (Mammarella 1985:150). The coalition was sealed mainly as a consequence of shared anti-communism and much effort had to be put in to trying to keep the parties together (Kogan 1983:59). In addition, de Gasperi had to employ all his political skills and authority in order to keep the various factions within the Christian democratic party together. These factions ranged from the right (monarchists, allies of business and landowners' interests, clericalists), via the centre (supporters of de Gasperi), to the left (adherents of Gronchi, trade unionists, the group around Dossetti and later Fanfani (see Marlière forthcoming)) – and the Cronache Sociali (on factions see: Belloni 1972; Belloni and Beller 1978; Zuckerman 1979; Hine 1993:129–36; Furlong 1994:158–66).

One of the main Christian democratic promises during the electoral campaign had been the land reform. The agrarian issue became particularly pressing when at the end of 1949 peasants grew increasingly discontented and started to occupy lands in Sicily and other areas in the south. They claimed ownership of lots, which in many cases they were already cultivating anyway. These actions provoked harsh repression by the police and – what caused even more bitterness – by the hirelings of the landowners. After a series of tragic incidents (Ginsborg 1990:122–37; Galli 1978:129) and the protests this inflamed throughout the nation, the DC was finally instigated to action.

In favour of agrarian reform within the DC were the left-wing faction around Dossetti (Galli 1978:132) and some important industrialists who feared that disruption of social stability would interfere with their own interests. A series of laws was passed that authorised expropriations of land and its redistribution to day labourers, sharecropping farmers and other small peasants (King 1973; Grindrod 1977:200–3; Mammarella 1985:167–8; Ginsborg 1990:122–37). In addition, technical and financial assistance was offered for land improvement. In the Christian democratic view of power mobilisation the land reform was to serve an economic and a political goal (Mammarella 1985:170). Economically, it was expected to lead to an increase in agrarian production. However, the expected effect did not occur because the whole operation was of too small a scope and not adjusted to the demands of modern farming. Politically, it was to disengage large segments of the rural population from political extremism. This did not happen either because many beneficiaries of the reform hardly changed their opinions at all.

The land reform was characterised by a paternalistic approach (Grindrod 1977:203). Where traditional feudal bonds between landowners and day labourers were broken, 'rigid obligations to the reform's administrators' (King 1987:158) took their place. Social Catholic notions clearly came to the fore to the extent that land reform was to generate a class of small owner-farmers (King 1987:158–9). The amount of land falling under the reform bills, however, was not sufficient to satisfy the needs of the impoverished peasants. The scarcity of lots to be allocated and the weakness of impartial distributive mechanisms reinforced traditional clientelism. This, in turn, affirmed 'ritual ties between peasants and aspiring beneficiaries on the one hand and local political leaders and reform agency bureaucrats on the other' (King 1987:157). Party membership or at least party support became a prerequisite for obtaining a piece of land, which promised to strengthen the position of the DC in rural areas.

Land reform must be viewed in close association with other attempts to adjust regional, social and economic imbalances in Italy. There was an attempt at initiating a long-term development policy for the south (Allum 1972:119). Its main goal was to improve the infrastructural context of production (both agricultural and industrial) in the backward areas through public works. A somewhat effective employment policy was initiated in the form of a reforestation plan and a housing plan which was to construct low priced *case populari*. These years also witnessed an attempt to introduce in

Italy a modern taxation system, which it was hoped would reduce the huge tax evasion, but which entirely failed.

In sum, the balance between reformist forces (social democrats, the moderate and left wing of the DC) and conservatives was so precarious that it effectively blocked constructive reform policies. The price paid by the DC (and by Italian society) for the successful manoeuvering between the extremes was that 'the party's constituencies tended at times to checkmate one another to the point where agreement on policies was almost impossible to achieve. The original promises of social reforms had bit by bit to be abandoned' (Spotts and Wieser 1986:24). More resources and political skills were wasted in the political attempt to keep the coalition together than were actually used for undertaking reforms.

Three factors contributed to growing political and social tensions in Italian society and to a critique of the DC and its policies towards the end of the first legislature, and aggravated the political strain during the second legislation period: the accumulation of power by the DC and the growth of the *sottogoverno*; the attempt of the DC to change the electoral law to its own benefit; and the excessive influence of the Church on Christian democratic politics.

The Christian democrats had begun to use their power to expand their position throughout the state apparatus and the state-controlled corporations and banks (Donolo 1980; Marlière forthcoming). The DC annexed the state economic sector, a policy perfected during the second legislature. Rather than as a means for the accumulation of personal power, the colonisation of the (semi-) public sector – at least in the beginning – must be interpreted as a method for constructing new power resources and as a politically shrewd manner of appeasing intraparty struggles among factions. Such a strategy secured the DC a relatively autonomous position from the Church and other Catholic organisations, upon which the initial prosperity of the DC had depended so much, but for which a remuneration in terms of direct political control was now claimed by the clergy.

A modification of the electoral law was drafted by the DC in order to guarantee the government parties a workable majority in parliament. This 'swindle law', as it became known instantaneously, would accord 65 per cent the parliamentary seats to the combination of parties that would realise over 50 per cent of the vote. This manoeuvre provoked fierce political reactions for its undemocratic implications and was compared to the 'Acerbo law' of 1923 which had provided the fascists their 'democratic majority'. The 'swindle law' played a major role in the election campaign of 1953. The unseemly attempt to assure a parliamentary majority in such a way – next to the lesser role played by anti-communism and foreign policy in the electoral campaign – contributed to the notable electoral loss of the DC in 1953 (a decline from 48.5 per cent to 40.1 per cent). The more important and somewhat ironic fact, however, was that the governing parties gained only 49.85 per cent of the vote, rendering the 'swindle law' immediately ineffective in its anticipated consequences and locating the problem of finding a workable majority again in the centre of politics.

The Church and the Azione Cattolica had become 'increasingly aggressive in public life' (Kogan 1983:59) and intervened continuously in Italian politics on a large number of occasions (Settembrini 1977:458–91). Furthermore, in the summer of 1949 Pope Pius XII had excommunicated (or threatened to do so) members and adherents of the PCI. The civic committees of Azione Cattolica that had been instrumental in the victory of 1948 and had put severe constraints on the room to manoeuvre of the DC (Settembrini 1977:242–53), added to the urgency of the Christian democratic search for a more independent power basis in the *sottogoverno*.

The period 1953–8 is one of the most complex phases of Italian politics. The outcome of the elections impeded a smooth return of a four-party coalition and blocked what was left of the reformist zeal. In fact, political output was reduced to a minimum as a result of the continuous struggle over the creation of parliamentary majorities (Kogan 1983:68). The minority Cabinets of the DC continuously needed the support of the right, which rendered reforms recurrently difficult and generally impossible. This constituted the kernel of political immobilism at the level of state policies. Nevertheless, party politics flourished (Mammarella 1985:206), both to the extent that attempts were made within the DC to prepare a future deal with the socialists as a way out of the partisan deadlock and to the extent that the power of the party in the state and the semi-public agencies increased considerably.

Yet initiatives of social reforms were taken during this period such as the extension of pensions to farmers, which, however, was also 'an instrument for consolidating the control of the Christian democratic farm federation, the Coltivatori Diretti, over peasant proprietors' (Kogan 1983:80–1). The so called Vanoni plan represented the first shot at systematic intervention in the economy. Its principal aims were to increase investments, to stimulate economic growth, to raise the level of consumption, to create employment, and to redistribute wealth (Mammarella 1985:222–3; Kogan 1983:81–2). Although the plan was approved in the Italian parliament and despite its moderate inclination, the politics of parliamentary immobilism subsequently stripped it of its main – potentially effective (Mammarella 1985:223) – elements. In other words, Italian Christian democracy managed to accumulate considerable power resources, but never really was fully capable of employing them for purposes other than further power amassment.

The precondition for the establishment of the political power of Catholicism in the Netherlands and an initially strong influence of the Catholic left wing on policy consisted of a coalition between the KVP and the PvdA and the exclusion of the anti-interventionist orthodox Protestants and the free market liberals. It was a fundamental agreement over the need for social policy as a means to ease the pain of economic reconstruction, which functioned as the cement of the so-called 'Roman–red' coalitions in the first decade after the war. The likelihood of such a construction had already been greatly increased by abating resistance of the Catholic clergy against Catholic–socialist cooperation (Daudt 1980; Visser 1986). Moreover, during the economic crisis of the 1930s Catholic and socialist proposals on social and economic policy had rapidly converged. The cataclysmic *laissez faire* policy under the ruling ARP had already met increasing resistance from its partner in government, the Catholic party. One of the main conflicts over social and economic policy in the inter-war period concerned the Catholic demand to expand the budget for social policy. While the Catholic party tended to embrace pseudo-Keynesian ideas on demand management as unemployment policy (Blok 1978; de Rooy 1979), its Protestant coalition partner refused to consider any augmentation of state intervention. Finally, by the late 1940s the political projects of Catholicism and social democracy had considerably converged on two major areas: global Keynesian demand management and family policy, sealed by a broadly shared anti-communism. Both the KVP and the PvdA saw the family as the 'cornerstone' of society and attempted to shape the whole complex of incomes policies (taxation, social security, wages, prices) as far as possible according to this notion (ter Heide 1986).

Although there were some political conflicts over the precise formulation of economic and social policies as well as around the issues of the organisational forms of the implementation of these policies, a fundamental commitment to an export-led growth model and social policy constituted the political consensus between Catholicism and social democracy. What conditions were conducive in this process of political consensus-building? First of all, the experience of crisis, war and fascist oppression had contributed to a temporary radicalisation of societal forces, which, in turn, facilitated reforms. However, this radicalisation must not be exaggerated. Radicalisation did not have an immediate effect on reformist inclination, but it did fuel the anti-communism of the Catholic labour movement which consolidated the construction of a 'Roman–red' coalition (Righart 1985:89).

Anti-communism, strongly present within the social democratic labour movement as well, not only accelerated the integration of the non-communist labour movement into the institutional framework of corporatism, but also stimulated social policy as a means to cut the grass from under the feet of societal discontent fostered by the communist labour movement and party. Catholic demands for social policy reforms were frequently accompanied by anti-communist 'instruction'. Anti-communism functioned as a convenient catalyst in the reconstruction of Catholic unity and the solidity of the Catholic cross-class pillar. Oligarchical control in combination with mass obedience was crucial and the Church was an active force in this process of establishing Catholic political unity. The hierarchical structure of the Catholic Church assured the spread of the organic social doctrine throughout the Catholic segment of society. The clerical leadership frequently published pastoral letters, explaining the rights and duties of labour and capital and the need for organisation within the Catholic sub-culture. The ideological offensive not only concerned the Catholic workers, but equally addressed the Catholic *petit bourgeoisie* and the employers, who were summoned to support social reform. The KVP employed social Catholic conceptions, emphasising the emancipation of Catholic workers in particular. The influence of these conceptions was not merely confined to the Catholic pillar, but also reached the social democratic party via its Catholic workshops. Only against this background can one understand why in 1951 social democrats praised the encyclical letters *Rerum Novarum* and *Quadragesimo Anno* at a meeting organised by the Catholic union movement to commemorate these social documents of Roman Catholicism.

Successive Catholic–socialist governments developed an export-led growth model for the Dutch economy that relied on wage restraint in return for social policy and integration of labour into the social and political structures of policy-making. This scenario was placed in the context of a comprehensive attempt to stimulate industrial development in a predominantly rural and trading society (Böhl, Nekkers and Slot 1981; Fortuyn 1980, 1983; ter Heide 1986; de Wolff and Driehuis 1980) and to reconstruct Dutch labour relations further in democratic corporatist fashion (Windmuller 1969; Hemerijck 1993). The construction of a labour–capital accord largely consisted of a Catholic–social democratic compromise of corporatist reorganisation and the introduction of global, indicative or technocratic planning as the lubricant of the consensus machine.

The macroeconomic policies of the 'Roman–red' coalitions were dominated by the leading goal of export-led recovery (de Wolff and Driehuis 1980:37). The conditions for the export orientation of the Dutch economy were found in further economic integration into European markets, tax relief for entrepreneurs, a restrictive wage policy, the improvement of the infrastructure, an extensive regulatory socioeconomic framework (van Eijk 1980; ter Heide 1986) and compensatory social policies to be initiated by central government, but administered by semi-public institutions ruled by the organisations of labour and capital or other interest groups (Cox 1993).

By 1950 the tripartite institution of the Social Economic Council (SER) had assumed a central political role in the 'politics as business' practice of the politics of accommodation. Although Catholic politics and social democracy had found various fields of agreement, basic controversy over elementary ideological interpretations of social and economic policies re-mained potentially threatening to the stability of governments. The idea of 'technocratic planning' and the seemingly depoliticised role of economic experts within the SER reconciled in a typically consociational fashion political conflicts, while at the same time allowing labour and capital to realise some control over macroeconomic policy, thus reinforcing the very conditions of consensus. The SER had formulated the five official goals of economic policy that were to guide state intervention until the mid-1960s: full employment, economic growth, a reasonable income distribution, an equilibrium on the balance of payments, and price stability. Between the Catholic and social democratic forces agreement was reached on global steering of the economy. Catholicism moderated considerably its old cor-poratist heritage and social democracy tempered its plan socialism.

The export-oriented macroeconomic policy of industrialisation also originated in a Dutch conception of underdevelopment (Therborn 1989:209), activated by the demographic pressure of a fast-growing population and the international pressure to decolonise Holland's largest overseas colony, Indonesia. The (expected) economic loss of the Dutch Indies was feared to deprive Dutch capital of an important investment possibility. Released funds had to be reallocated and export-led industrialisation could provide an outlet by the opening up of new markets. At the same time, labour quiescence and wage restraint were seen as preconditions for profitable investment and a successful industrialisation strategy.

A tight income policy until the early 1960s, then, kept wages low and improved the international competitiveness of the Dutch economy. Both the Christian and the socialist unions accepted the restriction on wage development, mainly because of its favourable effect on employment, but also in exchange for the extension of social security. The goal of full employment, however, was a secondary target. The dominant theory was that an export-led growth founded on wage restraint in combination with global measures would automatically lead to an optimal allocation of labour power.

The predominance of the export-oriented growth scenario indicated a defeat of the reformism of the PvdA and a victory for the KVP, since between 1945 and the early 1950s the Dutch social democrats had to alter their conception of active Keynesianism substantially under Catholic pressure. Within the constellation of forces too much emphasis on 'plan socialist' policies ran the risk of directly confronting the still precarious consensus between social democracy and Catholic politics. Social democrats were conscious of the fact that it was the first time in history that they enjoyed real governmental power and that within the political system of co-existing minorities the Catholic party had always the opportunity to change coalition partners and shift the balance of power considerably to the right. This constraint on social democratic reformism led to a more passive orientation on global demand management and social policy, also within the PvdA.

A clear defeat of Dutch social democracy concerned the methodical dismantling of the ministry of social affairs, a department that was in the hands of the social democrats. The KVP and the PvdA fundamentally agreed on the institution of the family as the 'cornerstone' of society. Macroeconomic policy, and industrial policy in particular, corresponded to an attempt to prepare the population for industrial society without undermining the traditional family (Böhl, Nekkers and Slot 1981:239–73). The Catholics were particularly active on issues concerning family policy. In the semi-public pillarised organisation of social services Catholicism had been traditionally strong. The public control over this area, however, was in the hands of the ministry of social affairs. The period 1946–52 showed the successful attempt of Catholic politics to dissociate social services from this ministry and to relocate these to a new department of social work in 1952. This department became the embodiment of Catholic power in the Netherlands to the extent that it decentralised as far as possible the execution of policy to religious institutions and the 'private initiative', adding to the societal power accumulation of Catholicism. The predominance of a traditional ideology in the role of the family as a fundamental constituent of society came to dominate Dutch politics and reinforced the existing traditional patriarchal structure of Dutch society.

CONCLUSION

By the 1960s Christian democracy had indeed reached remarkable heights of power and had managed to exert a considerable influence on the constitution of the societies and polities in Germany, Italy and the Netherlands. The historical conditions under which the movements assumed their momentous political roles, however, differed considerably and, as a result, the character and position of Christian democracy in these nations varied to a substantial degree. Yet in all nations the parties managed to become predominant political forces. The preceding chapter already documented the one-party dominance of Christian democracy in Italy, Germany and the Netherlands in more general terms, although the question to what extent Christian democracy has been able to exercise power to the benefit of its own political project could not be answered.

The analysis presented here makes plausible that the final criterion of single-party dominance (the use of dominant power to pursue a specific political project, Pempel 1990) was satisfied in Germany, Italy and the Netherlands. First of all, the ideological sources that the various parties drew upon appear to warrant this. The Christian inspiration distinguished these parties from their main rivals. Christian values initially functioned in Germany and Italy as a major medium for defining a clear break with the fascist past and for highlighting the crucial contrast to socialism or communism. In the Netherlands the religious inspiration of politics equally had a profound impact to the extent that it larded national politics in general. The CDU/CSU, the DC and the KVP emerged as essentially non-ecclesiastical parties. Italian Christian democracy, however, was engaged in a difficult process of defining its independence from the Church on which its initial power mobilisation had hinged. The Dutch KVP was the most confessional party to the extent that it remained the political representative of the highly integrated yet segregated Catholic pillar.

Christian democracy did pursue the implementation of distinctive institutional projects that settled the distribution of power resources. In Germany the struggle over the 'basic law' and the social market economy in competition with social democracy established a form of capitalism that from the start had a clear neo-liberal leaning in terms of economic policies, but at the same time introduced a moderating social concern as a result of the inclusion of demands of the labour wing of the party. In Italy, the Christian democratic impact on the Constitution was equally forceful and in this nation, too, social policies were to compensate for the liberal economic policies that the successive DC-dominated governments pursued. However, the peculiarities of the Italian structure of political power inhibited the successful implementation of reforms. The Dutch KVP preferred a coalition with the social democrats precisely to be able to commit this alliance to an export-led growth model with compensatory social policy and to get control over social services. Therefore, there is some evidence that the various parties have tried to employ their powerful positions to carry through distinctive political projects.

The different historical conditions under which the Christian democratic movements came to power have had considerable effects on the character and political complexion of parties. National institutional and political legacies as well as the diverging political experiences of these nations in the period 1920–45 have been particularly crucial here. Fascism, the Second World War and the impact of American hegemony have caused a major rupture from the political past in Germany and Italy. In the latter nation, however, the persisting infrastructure of social Catholic power provided a weighty resource for political mobilisation of the Catholic sub-culture, whereas in Germany a continuation of the Zentrum was excluded by the conviction that the political divisions of the Weimar era had been harmful to democracy in general and to religiously inspired politics and the Catholic interest in particular. The course that historical events took in the Netherlands determined the return of pillarisation and with it the organic integration of a renewed political party as the elite of the Catholic pillar. In many senses pre- and post-war political Catholicism were identical, but the alliance of social democracy and Christian democracy, greatly facilitated by the religious or moral influences on Dutch social democracy, meant a crucial innovation of the logic of politics in the Netherlands.

The diverging roads of the post-war mobilisation of Christian democracy determined to a large extent the political complexion of the parties. Thus, the integration of right-wing liberals and conservative Protestants into the CDU/CSU, the dominance of neo-liberalism, the systems competition between East and West and the American hegemony in the western parts of Germany accorded a much more conservative character to Christian democracy in Germany, even though the labour wing of the CDU retained some influence. The integration of the southern ruling class into Italy's Christian democracy and the competition with communism tended to push the DC to the right as well. However, the characteristics of the Italian polarised political system and the difficulty of finding a balance both within the political system and within the party determined the dominance of centrism. In the Netherlands it was the influence of the organised labour wing and the exclusion of anti-interventionist Protestantism that accorded a more left-wing complexion to the KVP.

These considerations emphasise the conclusion of Chapter 2 that Christian democracy is a political movement which to a large extent varies historically and cross-nationally. Again, it has to be stressed that general accounts on the association between Christian democracy and welfare state development most likely underestimate cross-national variation and a caveat is therefore useful. The political entrenchment and the type of dominance of Christian democracy is now documented, as are the historical conditions that explain both similarities and differences between the various movements. The questions for the next chapters are whether and to what extent Christian democracy, despite these variations, nevertheless fosters a distinctive welfare state regime and whether and to what extent empirically observed differences between social systems in Christian democratic nations are in fact related to the different complexions and histories of Christian democracy.

5 Welfare state regimes and social spending

CROSS-NATIONAL COMPARISONS I: SOCIAL SECURITY SPENDING

Traditionally, the analysis of welfare state development has focused on 'welfare effort', i.e. the amount of money that a state is willing to devote to social expenditures. The justified criticism of this type of quantitative studies was that the concentration on spending data does not necessarily provide convincing information on the more qualitative differences between welfare state regimes. As an alternative, Esping-Andersen (1990) has argued that a crucial concept for understanding welfare state variations is 'decommodification'. This concept addresses the commodity form of labour under capitalist market conditions, where workers sell their labour power on the market. The extent to which workers depend on the market defines their degree of commodification (Esping-Andersen 1985a:31, 1990:37; Western 1989:202).

Decommodification is commonly viewed – as argued in the second chapter – as an exclusively social democratic social policy goal. A high level of decommodification is invariably contributed to social democratic power mobilisation, not only because social democracy defends the interests of workers, but also because intraclass solidarity and a low level of market dependence are preconditions for power mobilisation. The usual model holds that decommodification is a linear function of social democratic party strength and trade union power when socio-economic conditions and demographic pressures are controlled for.

Decommodification is a measure for the 'level and coverage of consumption derived from non-market sources in relation to wage-based consumption' (Western 1989:208). Among the top five decommodified nations in the 1980s, Belgium took the first place, followed by Sweden (2), the Netherlands (3), Germany (4) and France (5). Given this ranking of nations, one would have to problematise the anticipated importance of social democratic party incumbency and union power immediately, given the presence of nations with strong Christian democratic parties in this top five.

Decommodification may not be an exclusive property of social democratic politics. Perhaps there exist various forms of decommodification, one – the social democratic form – which attaches social rights to individuals as citizens, and another – the Christian democratic form – which ties social rights to other social units, particularly the family. The intent of these policies may not be identical, but their effects, particularly with respect to levels of social spending, may very well be similar. This could have given rise to the functional equivalence of social democracy and Christian democracy that the literature has frequently brought out. Both Christian democracy and social democracy can be equally decommodifying forces, although they may differ to the extent that they do not decommodify analogous units. In other words, even if one finds those nations with strong Christian democratic movements among the top most decommodified welfare states together with the social democratic nations, it does not necessarily imply that the quality of decommodification is similar. Such differences are hidden by the focus on spending alone.

Although decommodification appears an accurate concept in the context of welfare state research, there arise conceptual problems if the term is used in a too generalised fashion.[1] First, decommodification suggests that one can read the degree of market independence from the granting of social rights, without specifying the conditions under which market performance (i.e. commodification) is actually a condition for a rightful claim to a social benefit or service. This problem, however, can be overcome by taking into account, for instance, the variations in contribution periods, the replacement rates of benefits and the coverage ratio of social security schemes among the relevant population (Esping-Andersen 1990:49). In effect, one must conclude that real decommodifying social rights are only those that are granted on the basis of citizenship, i.e. on the basis of mere membership of a (national) community. Second, decommodification and its focus on market relations and waged labour cannot be a tool for understanding dependence of non-commodified labour, such as unpaid, non-marketised work in the household (see especially Daly forthcoming). Finally, there is the problem of how to understand active labour market policies that aim at 'commodifying' labour power, a characteristic of social democratic welfare states. Do these policies increase or decrease market-dependence? This is not to argue that the concept of decommodification should be avoided in welfare state research altogether, but that – given such possible conceptual confusion – it might make more sense to analyse welfare state development by looking at various indicators at lower levels of abstraction.

How to measure welfare state development? First of all and despite the above noted difficulties, it does make sense to look at social expenditures as a first step in identifying differences between welfare state regimes. Although solely referring to spending as a way of portraying attributes of welfare states may be misleading, it will certainly not be wholly uninformative either. Social expenditure tends to be determined by a variety of demographic, economic and political factors and may mean different things. At the same time, however, the granting of social rights (whether to citizens or families, or on the basis of performance on the labour market) will in one way or another be mirrored in social spending, since rightfully claimed social rights lead to higher spending (Korpi 1989:314).

The most frequently used measure of welfare state development and of the level of political rather than economic distribution concerns the social security expenditure of a nation. Table 5.1 provides an overview of expenditure of social security schemes as a percentage of GDP in 1960 and 1980. It is immediately clear that the nations scoring highest in 1960 are those where Christian democracy, but also social democracy were strong political actors. Austria, Germany and Belgium, in fact, all score one standard deviation above average in 1960. All nations that were identified in the preceding chapters as having strong Christian democratic movements (except Switzerland and Ireland) score above average, as do Denmark, Sweden and the United Kingdom. *Prima vista* this denotes that the traditional explanation of social democratic power mobilisation cannot convince, at least not for 1960. A political explanation that favours Christian democratic party strength would not suffice either, if one looks at the differences in the level of spending in 1960 between, for instance, Austria, Belgium and Germany (over 15 per cent of GDP), the Netherlands and Italy (over 11 per cent), and Ireland and Switzerland (less than 10 per cent).

The data suggest that Christian democracy and social democracy were perhaps functional equivalents in 1960 as far as spending was concerned. However, one might actually observe a spurious relationship, because other variables such as age structure, unemployment rates or the wealth of a nation, explain the observed levels of spending. The theoretically most satisfactory explanation, however, seems to be that – given other important factors such as an ageing population, economic wealth, and the level of unemployment and in addition to the functional equivalence of Christian democracy and social democracy – social expenditure in 1960 was particularly boosted under conditions of competition or interaction between Christian democracy and social democracy (see Castles and Mitchell 1993:119).

Table 5.1 Expenditure of social security schemes as a percentage of gross domestic product, 1960 and 1980

Country	% 1960	% 1980	Growth 1960–80 (% pts)	Rank order 1960	Rank order 1980
Australia	7.7	11.9	4.2	15	17
Austria	15.4	22.5	7.1	1	7
Belgium	15.3	25.9	10.6	3	5
Canada	9.2	13.7	4.5	13	14
Denmark	11.1	29.9	18.8	8	2
Finland	8.8	18.0	9.2	14	11
France	13.2	26.7	13.5	4	4
Germany	15.4	24.0	8.6	2	6
Ireland	9.3	20.1	10.8	12	10
Italy	11.7	21.5	9.8	5	8
Japan	4.9	10.8	5.9	18	18
Netherlands	11.1	28.3	17.2	7	3
New Zealand	11.5	16.6	5.1	6	13
Norway	9.4	20.2	10.8	11	9
Sweden	10.9	31.9	21.0	9	1
Switzerland	7.5	13.7	6.2	16	15
United Kingdom	10.8	17.3	6.5	10	12
United States	6.8	12.6	5.8	17	16
Average	10.6	20.3	9.8		
Standard deviation	2.9	6.5	5.0		

Source: ILO, *The Cost of Social Security*, various years.

Some researchers, however, have suggested that the demographic structure of a nation's population is the strongest predictor of social spending *per se* (Pampel and Williamson 1989). Older people simply need more care. However – as argued in the second chapter – it is not clear that older people get the care they need because they need it. Recent political debates on the financing of pension systems, the statutory retirement age and social security retrenchment policies in various nations make clear that social rights for the elderly may very well hinge on precarious cross-generational compromises and political trade-offs. The relevant question in the context of welfare state development is how needs are converted into effective social rights before social programmes were inaugurated or at a time that these schemes hardly had the time to 'mature'. In other words, the question of the mechanisms actually fulfilling the need has still to be answered. It is hard to image how 'needs' alone can explain their own fulfilment. It is politics that has to intermediate between need and fulfilment, between societal pressure and social solution. It can be expected, then, that the demographic structure of a society is related to social expenditure in 1960, but only in combination with political determinants, in particular the competition or interaction between social democracy and Christian democracy. The age effect on spending is most likely much greater in 1980, although the competition between political parties may still add to levels of spending above what can be explained by need.

A start model[2] was estimated for 1960, which states that social security expenditure (SSE) is a linear function of GDP per capita (GDPCAP), the unemployment rate (UERATE), the proportion aged in a nation (AGE), union density (UNION) and the strength of both Christian democracy and social democracy plus the interaction (competition) between these political forces (CDSD). The Ordinary Least Squares (OLS) regression results for 1960 are summarised in Table 5.2, panel a.

The finding is that in the start equation for 1960 the demographic and the political variables are statistically significant (model I). In the second model (Table 5.2, column 3) the insignificant variables were dropped. This model is clearly superior to the first and explains 71 per cent of the variance in the dependent variable. In addition, the proposed hypothesis on the relevance of politics (in this case the functional equivalence of social democracy and Christian democracy as well as the interaction between the two) in combination with demography cannot be rejected.[3] The analysis of the residuals, however, suggests – as could be expected – Switzerland to be an outlier, although an insignificant one according to the outlier test. Looking somewhat closer at the residuals of nations of interest reveals that Germany has a large positive residual, whereas Italy as well as the Netherlands had small positive residuals. This suggest that in 1960 there was still variation within the group of Christian democratic nations. The overall conclusion, however, is that it is plausible to assume that in terms of social spending both Christian democracy and social democracy equally promoted social spending in 1960, while – given a certain degree of demographic pressure – the 'competition' or interaction between the two particularly boosted spending. The results of this analysis suggest, furthermore, that – rather than accepting a functional explanation for social spending – a politically more sensitive account is quite feasible.

Do these arguments hold true for 1980, too? If one looks at the spending

Table 5.2 OLS regression, dependent variable = social security expenditure, 1960 and 1980

Variable name	Panel a (1960) Estimated coefficient (beta) I	Panel a (1960) Estimated coefficient (beta) II	Variable name	Panel b (1980) Estimated coefficient (beta) I	Panel b (1980) Estimated coefficient (beta) II
1. GDPCAP	-0.01		1. AGE	0.57	0.61
2. UERATE	0.04			(2.52, 0.007)	(3.15, 0.003)
3. AGE	0.49	0.44	2. CDSD	0.41	0.37
	(2.81, 0.007)	(3.08, 0.004)	R^2 (adj.)	0.33	
4. UNION	-0.09		F-test:		
5. CDSD	0.41	0.41	H_0:	$B2=0$	$B1=0$
	(3.44, 0.002)	(3.95, 0.0006)	$F =$	0.10	9.89
R^2 (adj.)	0.65	0.71	$Pr=$	76.20%	0.59%
F-test:					
H_0:	$B1=B2=B4=0$	$B3=B5=0$			
$F =$	0.14	21.14			
$Pr=$	93.31%	00.00%			

Note: numbers between brackets refer to significant t-statistics (first) and the probability that ($X >$ value of t) with X distributed as t(df) (second). Insignificant t-values are not reported.

data for 1980 (Table 5.1), the rank order of nations is Sweden (1), Denmark (2), the Netherlands (3), France (4), Belgium (5), Germany (6), Austria (7), Italy (8), Norway (9), and Ireland (10). These nations all spent above average and form a mix of social democratic and Christian democratic nations. Again, Switzerland (15) is a major exception with 13.7 per cent of GDP devoted to social security expenditure as is Finland (11) with 18.0 per cent. These data suggest that also in 1980 social democracy and Christian democracy do not have significantly different effects on the level of social spending. However, the picture is misleading as is shown in Table 5.2, panel b. Estimating similar models as for 1960 gave insignificant results for the economic (GDPCAP and UERATE) and social (UNION) variables in 1980. The same was true for the political variables, whether the strength of Christian democracy, the strength of social democracy or the competition between the two were entered into the equation,[4] indicating that for 1980 political explanations of variations in social spending are incorrect.

CROSS-NATIONAL COMPARISONS II: PENSIONS

Breaking down spending data and looking at pension expenditure makes sense, because pensions 'constitute a central link between work and leisure, between earned income and redistribution, between individualism and solidarity, between the cash nexus and social rights' (Esping-Andersen 1990:80). After the Second World War two types of state pension emerged, one with universal flat-rate benefits at a certain minimum level to be supplemented by private, occupational schemes (the Beveridge model), and another, social insurance type, relating benefits to contributions and employment experience. Here, the following hypothesis can be advanced. Because the issue of age concerns a risk of life rather than a risk of class, one can expect Christian democracy initially to be particularly active in the field of old age provision. Social policy is a means to establish cross-class support without having to rely on the political salience of class.

First, one can look at the differences in pension systems among developed welfare states in 1960 and 1980 in terms of spending. Table 5.3 summarises pension expenditure as a proportion of GDP in 1960 and in 1980 and gives the rank order of 18 OECD nations according to this criterion in 1960. It is not surprising to find a comparable rank order of nations as in Table 5.1 (Germany, Austria, France, Italy and the Netherlands all score above average, Sweden and Norway near the average and the Anglo-Saxon nations all below the average in 1960), since pensions do account for a large share of total social security spending. In the 1980s the Christian democratic nations still scored relatively high in terms of

Table 5.3 Pension expenditure as a percentage of GDP, 1960 and 1980 (descending rank order 1960)

Country	Expenditure	
	% 1960	% 1980
1. Germany	9.81	12.10 (2)
2. Austria	9.61	13.50 (1)
3. France	5.90	11.50 (5)
4. Italy	5.46	12.00 (3)
5. Netherlands	5.22	11.00 (6)
6. Denmark	4.63	9.10 (8)
7. Sweden	4.45	10.90 (7)
8. Norway	4.39	7.90 (10)
9. New Zealand	4.39	7.60 (11)
10. Belgium	4.35[a]	11.90 (4)
11. United States	4.20	6.90 (12)
12. United Kingdom	4.08	6.30 (14)
13. Australia	3.37	4.90 (15)
14. Finland	3.32	6.50 (13)
15. Canada	2.76	4.40 (18)
16. Ireland	2.52	4.50 (16)
17. Switzerland	2.30	8.00 (9)
18. Japan	1.39	4.40 (17)
Average	4.56	8.52
Standard deviation	2.14	2.97

Notes: numbers between brackets refer to rank order of 1980.
[a] 1964

Source: OECD (1985, Annex c, 79–97).

spending on pensions. Moreover, pension expenditure is remarkably stable to the extent that the rank order of countries in 1980 is extremely close to the rank order in 1960. Austria took over the lead from Germany. Italy, Belgium, France and the Netherlands still scored above average, as did Sweden and Denmark. The Anglo-Saxon countries all scored below average, indicating that these nations strongly rely on the provision of private rather than public pensions (see Esping-Andersen 1990:70).

However, these spending data might conceal real differences in coverage ratios of pension schemes among the total population. Table 5.4 shows

Table 5.4 Pension coverage ratios among population aged 15–65, 1960 and 1980 (descending rank order 1960)

Country	Coverage ratio	
	% 1960	% 1980
1. Canada	1.00	1.00
2. Denmark	1.00	1.00
3. Finland	1.00	1.00
4. Netherlands	1.00	1.00
5. New Zealand	1.00	1.00
6. Norway	1.00	1.00
7. Sweden	1.00	1.00
8. Switzerland	1.00	1.00
9. Austria	.63	.65
10. United Kingdom	.63	.63
11. Italy	.62	.60
12. France	.60	.60
13. Germany	.57	.63
14. United States	.56	.58
15. Belgium	.42	:54
16. Japan	.28	.76
17. Australia	.00	1.00
18. Ireland	.00	.43
Average	.68	.80
Standard deviation	.34	.21

Source: SSIB.

that the Scandinavian, social democratic nations already had universal coverage in 1960, as did Canada, the Netherlands, New Zealand and Switzerland. The Christian democratic nations Austria, Italy, Germany and Belgium had coverage ratios roughly between 40 and 60 per cent. This picture remains relatively stable over time, except for Australia which had reached universal coverage in 1980.

If one looks at the relative generosity of pensions (approximated by the net replacement rate for singles and couples, Table 5.5) in 1960, the Christian democratic nations were clearly in the lead, whereas the social democratic nations all scored below average. In 1980, Austria, Belgium, France, Italy and the Netherlands still scored above average, but so did Finland, Sweden and Norway.

Table 5.5 Net pension replacement rates for singles and couples (standard workers), 1960 and 1980 (descending rank order 1960 according to replacement rate for a single)

| Country | Replacement rate | | | |
| | 1960 | | 1980 | |
	single	couple	single	couple
1. Austria	.87	.87	.68	.71 (3)
2. Belgium	.64	.80	.65	.72 (4)
3. Germany	.52	.47	.53	.54 (11)
4. France	.46	.66	.62	.78 (6)
5. Italy	.44	.40	.70	.71 (2)
6. United States	.40	.57	.55	.78 (10)
7. New Zealand	.37	.63	.45	.76 (14)
8. Netherlands	.33	.50	.59	.78 (8)
9. Denmark	.33	.46	.47	.67 (12)
10. Finland	.29	.49	.64	.85 (5)
11. Sweden	.28	.42	.72	1.04 (1)
12. Australia	.25	.49	.35	.54 (18)
13. United Kingdom	.24	.36	.40	.60 (15)
14. Norway	.22	.32	.59	.75 (7)
15. Switzerland	.21	.34	.46	.67 (13)
16. Canada	.20	.38	.40	.53 (16)
17. Ireland	.19	.36	.36	.55 (17)
18. Japan	.17	.19	.58	.65 (9)
Average	.36	.48	.54	.69
Standard deviation	.18	.17	.12	.13

Note: numbers between brackets refer to rank order according to replacement rate for singles, 1980

Sources: SSIB.

Theoretically, it seems difficult to maintain that qualitative differences in coverage and replacement rates are explained by the 'need' of the aged or the number of old aged people in the population (see Table 5.6), because how can 'need' explain coverage and replacement? However, does the same argument hold for pension spending? Table 5.7 offers a summary of regression analyses with pension spending as the dependent variable (1960: panel a; 1980: panel b). The first estimated model states that pension spending is a function of economic wealth (GDPCAP), union density

(UNION), the demographic structure (AGE) and the strength of the left and of Christian democracy. The most interesting finding is that for 1960 the demographic variable is not significant. Model II[5] not only has a better fit but also clearly shows the significant effect of the political variables. Both social democracy and Christian democracy were related to pension spending in 1960, although the estimated coefficient for the latter is almost twice as high as the one for the former, indicating that the Christian democratic effect was stronger on spending. These results of cross-sectional analyses are consistent with recent findings of Huber and Stephens' (1993) pooled time-series and cross-sections analysis of public pensions. They found strong political effects of both social democracy and Christian democracy on public pension expenditure as well as economic effects, indicating that under conditions of economic prosperity nations are prepared to introduce more generous benefits. The Christian democratic effect was particularly strong on expenditure and less pronounced on the quality ('decommodification') of pension schemes. Their findings with respect to demography are less clear. The estimations of the models reported in Table 5.7, however, corroborate Huber and Stephens' (1993:317) conclusion that pension expenditure 'under a given set of entitlements is pushed up by an increase in the aged proportion of the population but that a large aged proportion of the population does not positively affect the level of pension entitlements'. Accordingly, they reject Pampel and Williamson's (1989) thesis that demography is the single largest determinant of social (pension) expenditure because the aged form a politically influential group. I fully agree with Huber and Stephens' (1993:323) thesis that 'just because there are a lot of elderly people does not mean that they are mobilized'.

The analysis of residuals of the regression for 1960 showed that Germany had a large positive residual, which cannot be explained by the model or by this nation's demographic structure (compare Table 5.6).

There may, however, be several reasons for the high levels of pension spending in the continental nations around 1960. First of all, Germany might score as high as it does because it was committed to pay pensions to war victims. A high level of pension expenditure may therefore partly reflect war experience, although political forces must, of course, grant such rights. In addition, some nations, such as Germany and Austria, for political reasons treat their government personnel generously in terms of pension rights, mainly as a means of rewarding the *Beamte* status. This may be due to the etatist legacy in these nations (Esping-Andersen 1990:122–24), but could perhaps also be explained in terms of status reproduction. The issue of old age protection is an opportunity for introducing reforms and attaching clearly defined groups to political projects without politicising

Table 5.6 Number of people over 65 years of age as a proportion of total population, 1960 and 1980

Country	1960	1980
Australia	0.08	0.10
Austria	0.12	0.15
Belgium	0.12	0.14
Canada	0.07	0.10
Denmark	0.11	0.14
Finland	0.07	0.12
France	0.12	0.15
Germany	0.11	0.16
Ireland	0.11	0.11
Italy	0.09	0.13
Japan	0.06	0.09
Netherlands	0.09	0.11
New Zealand	0.09	0.10
Norway	0.11	0.15
Sweden	0.12	0.16
Switzerland	0.10	0.14
United Kingdom	0.12	0.15
United States	0.09	0.12
Average	0.10	0.13
Standard deviation	0.02	0.02

Source: SSIB.

the issue of class, since all members of each class – so to speak – grow old. Upholding status or group positions after retirement age via earnings-related benefits – originally being the legacy of etatism – became a redefined non-class issue taken up by Christian democracy in the post-war period. Both in Germany and the Netherlands pension legislation or pension reform took place in the late 1950s under the leadership of Christian democracy (Germany) or under an alliance between social democracy and Catholic political forces and backed by a broadly shared consensus (Netherlands), whereas in Italy important changes took place only in the 1960s.

It would be a mistake to infer from the high levels of expenditure that the Christian democratic pension regimes in 1960 were remarkably generous systems in terms of both benefits and eligibility. The earnings-related,

Table 5.7 OLS regression, dependent variable = pension spending, 1960 and 1980

	Panel a (1960)			Panel b (1980)	
Variable name	Estimated coefficient (beta) I	Estimated coefficient (beta) II	Variable name	Estimated coefficient (beta) I	Estimated coefficient (beta) II
1. GDPCAP	0.37 (1.61, 0.07)	0.40 (1.98, 0.03)	1. GDPCAP	0.25 (1.42, 0.09)	0.25 (1.55, 0.07)
2. UNION	−0.07		2. UNION	−0.02	
3. AGE	0.12		3. AGE	1.54 (1.54, 0.07)	0.28 (1.60, 0.07)
4. LPS	0.40 (1.60, 0.07)	0.41 (2.26, 0.02)	4. LPS	0.37 (1.94, 0.03)	0.36 (2.12, 0.03)
5. CDS	0.74 (2.96, 0.006)	0.81 (4.18, 0.0004)	5. CDS	0.65 (3.78, 0.001)	0.66 (4.06, 0.0006)
R^2 (adj.)	0.45	0.51	R^2 (adj.)	0.68	0.70
F-test:			F-test:		
H_0:	B2=B3=0	B1=B2=B3=0	H_0:	B2=0	B1=B2=B3=B4=0
F =	0.14	6.61	F =	0.03	10.88
Pr=	87.30%	0.61%	Pr=	87.12%	0.03%
H_0:	B1=B4=B5=0		H_0:	B1=B3=B4=B5=0	
F =	8.85		F =	9.82	
Pr=	0.33%		Pr=	0.07%	

Note: numbers between brackets refer to significant t-statistics (first) and the probability that (X > value of t) with X distributed as t(df) (second). Insignificant t-values are not reported.

status-reproducing pension schemes, aside from being expensive, had fairly tough conditions tied to eligibility. So, if one looks at the conditions for receiving a state pension in 1960 (contribution period and reference period), one clearly finds that there existed indeed two pension regimes that coincide with the types identified above. The first regime had quite strong (Germany, Italy, Austria and France) or moderate (the Netherlands, Belgium and the United Kingdom) conditions attached to pension rights in terms of reference and contribution period[6] and the second had no conditions in this respect. On the other hand, in 1960 pensioners in countries like New Zealand, Canada and Ireland had to submit to a means test before being eligible to receive a pension.

In the 1980s, nations such as New Zealand and Australia had a 'basic' social security pensions scheme (conditional flat-rate benefits, financed out of general revenues). All Scandinavian countries had a mixed system (a combination of basic, needs-based and earnings-related benefits) as did Canada, Ireland and the United Kingdom. The Christian democratic nations (Austria, Belgium, France, Germany, the Netherlands and Switzerland) had a conditional system, covering the employed, where benefits were related to employment and where the system was primarily financed by contributions of the employed (OECD 1988:17). This last issue is particularly interesting, because it shows that social rights were granted on the basis of past contributions and may temper the possible impression that the Christian democratic nations were particularly beneficent to pensioners.

If one looks at Table 5.7, panel b, which reports on the regression results on pension spending in 1980, the finding – in line with the study by Huber and Stephens (1993) – is that at this point in time the demographic variable is significant, although only at the 0.1 level. The estimated model (I) again states that pension spending in 1980 was a function of economic wealth (GDPCAP), union density (UNION), the demographic structure (AGE) and the strength of the left and of Christian democracy. After dropping the insignificant UNION variable, the second model[7] indicates a better fit and shows the significant effect of the economic, demographic and political variables. And again, both social democracy and Christian democracy were significantly related to pension spending in 1980, and the estimated coefficient for the latter is almost twice as high as that for the former. In 1980, therefore, the Christian democratic effect was stronger than the social democratic effect. The significance of the age structure in 1980 makes sense, because – as argued – once pension programmes are introduced, an ageing population tends to lead automatically to higher social spending. Nevertheless, the more surprising finding is that the political variables remain significant.

But at this point one must ask precisely how politics matters for the establishment of social security schemes and under what conditions differences in legislated schemes emerged. Such questions cannot be answered fully by quantitative comparisons. In order to clarify Christian democracy's role in promoting social spending in general and expensive pension systems in particular a closer examination of the German case seems particularly relevant, because the quantitative analysis shows that Germany spent much more on pensions than could be expected on the basis of the models. A more detailed analysis of the German pension reform of 1957 will demonstrate that Christian democracy and social policy are actually related in a dual sense. Christian democracy influences social policy, but social policies affect the power of this political movement, too.

GERMANY: A CASE STUDY OF CHRISTIAN DEMOCRACY AND SOCIAL POLICY[8]

In the period until 1965 German economic liberalism left the economy virtually uncontrolled, but in social policy Germany was in the lead. Between the various social and political actors actively engaged in the formulation of the 'basic law' and the postulate of the social state (see Chapter 4) agreement had existed on two fundamental issues. First, the first freely elected democratic government of the Federal Republic would have a special obligation to initiate a reconstruction programme for solving the immense social and economic problems of the immediate post-war period. There were the acute needs of the mass of refugees, war victims and the so called 'displaced persons' (former slave labourers, prisoners and inmates of concentration camps). Official sources estimated that there were about 25 million such people on the move (Berghahn 1987:179). There were also the immense problems of the damaged cities and industrial plants, the shortage of houses, and the task of reconstruction through investment, employment policy and food supply. Second, the configuration of political power was such that it gradually generated consent as to a basic commitment to the tradition of German social policy, resulting in a return to traditional social laws (Hockerts 1980:21–106; Hentschel 1983:145–59; Abelshauser 1983:72; Alber 1989:58–67). Perhaps one can speak of restorative social policy (Widmaier 1976:23) to the extent that instruments of social policy of the Weimar Republic were implanted in the Federal Republic. Although the defeat of Germany had created the possibility of completely redesigning the social security system, traditional institutions survived the war. One reason for restoration could be institutional inertia (Alber 1989:66), but such an explanation of failed reform underestimates the importance of political struggles over social reform in the entire post-war period. The German social policy tradition is but one element in an account of a failed Allied attempt to force quasi-Beveridgean reforms upon occupied Germany.

The Allied Control Council's Manpower Directorate co-ordinated four plans of social reform that had been formulated by the occupation authorities. All designs turned out to be quite similar, since they were all largely based on the leading reformism of the unions, the social democrats and the communists as well as on recommendations by German social security experts who were highly critical of the fragmented traditional system (Hockerts 1980:23). A common design was therefore easily drafted and was presented in December 1946.

The Allied blueprint comprised a radical break with the German social policy tradition. It made provision for the unification of the schemes for sickness, accident and invalidity (to be administered at the level of the *Länder*), eliminating the fragmentation of the sickness scheme in a multiplicity of separate funds. The status-related differential between workers and employees was to be cancelled (Hockerts 1980:26–7). The unemployment insurance remained organisationally independent. Perhaps the single most important departure from the German tradition concerned the extension of compulsory insurance to all wage-earners, including the employees and the *Beamte*, and the self-employed, creating an *Einheitsversicherung*, i.e. one single insurance. There were several reasons for the proposed universalism: the introduction of comparable reforms in Berlin and the eastern zone; the affinity between the Allied reformists and the German labour movement; the attempt to subscribe to the reformist views elsewhere, especially in Britain; the conviction that fundamental reform would lead to rationalisation and – most significantly – to economisation (Hockerts 1980:28–32; but see Baldwin 1990:190–1). This latter aspect of austerity also fuelled the proposal to decrease the benefits and to emphasise the insurance character of reforms. The aim was to abolish state contributions in order to release funds for the reconstruction of the economy. The lowering of benefits aimed at equalising the replacement rates at the level of workers, which was in contrast to the policy of the socialists and the unions who wanted to equalise benefits at the (higher) level of employees.

The Allied design aroused considerable resistance from various groups for diverging reasons. 'The blueprint assaulted the traditional propertied classes (*Besitzstände*), utterly offended particularist interests and at the same time failed to satisfy long-cherished aspirations and empathically augmented demands of other interest groups' (Hentschel 1983:148, my translation). The unions' reaction was mixed. The organisational unification of the schemes was in line with their demands and in their interests: they gained a majority in the administration and the elimination of fragmentation and separatism enhanced the possibility of incorporating all wage-earners into one union (Hockerts 1980:37). The unions resisted, however, the discontinuation of state contributions, the increase in contributions and the reduction of benefits as obviously detrimental to their members' interests.

The outright opponents of reform were those organisations that existentially depended on the continuation of the traditional system such as private insurance companies, the sickness funds and the medical estate at large. The self-employed refused to give up their identity of independence by having to associate with workers in a compulsory scheme and feared, moreover, that they would not benefit from it, but rather bear a heavy burden. The organisations of employers primarily wanted to keep control over the accident funds and also feared an increase in their compulsory premiums. Employees had a stake in upholding their status as employees in the social security scheme. At the political party level the differences in appreciation of the Allied reformism were accurately mirrored (Hockerts 1980:50). The social democrats largely agreed with the labour movement whereas the Christian democrats and the liberals opted for a return to the traditional system and opposed universalism. Christian democracy particularly contested the idea of an *Einheitsversicherung* on the conjecture that such a system would shift the balance of power in the direction of the unions and the social democratic party (Hockerts 1980:50).

These various constraints articulated into an effective obstacle to fundamental reform and Christian democracy was committed to the restoration of the traditional edifice of social policy. Reforms along the line of the original Allied proposals, however, were implemented in the Russian zone in early 1947. A year later, the Americans voted against implementation of these reforms in their zone. After the *de facto* division of Germany into a western and an eastern zone, social reform and social policy in the western zone became the topic of the bizonal Economic Council, in which the opposition to reform had a majority and which simultaneously was preparing the constitutional reform. One sees here the relevance of the politics of prejudicing through the prohibition of all prejudicing (see Chapter 4). Structural revision was excluded, because 'such fundamental decisions were to be reserved to the parliament of the new West German state' (Hockerts 1981:320). Social policy should be provisional until the Constitution was drafted and elections had decided on the actual balance of parliamentary power. The same argument as with regard to the economic structure, therefore, seems plausible, namely that all parties had an interest in avoiding the predetermination of social policy in their hope of winning the first elections.

The provisional arrangements designated the *de facto* restoration of traditional structures and were therefore not simply the result of 'structural inertia'. Attention was shifted to improving the performance of the system through the Social Security Adjustment Act (*Sozialversicherungs-Anpassungsgesetz*, Hockerts 1980:85-106). The benefits were improved to cope with pressing needs of important segments of the population, particularly pensioners, who were suffering the effects of the money reform, because, although their pensions were exchanged at a 1:1 ratio, they were not price-indexed, nor were they particularly generous.

The final defeat of the reform came with the victory of Christian democracy at the 1949 elections. The social policy of the coalition between the liberals and the Christian democrats basically consisted in removing the structural reform from the political agenda, modifying the Nazi legislation, restoring the traditional structure of social security, introducing special measures for Germany's immense social problems (e.g. the *Lastenausgleichsgesetz* of 1952) and preparing a reform of the pension system.

What accounts for the attachment of the Christian democrats to the traditional organisational form of social security? In general, the heritage of a long tradition was 'virtually the only one with which Germany, defeated in war and deformed by national socialism, could still identify, which it could still refer to and be proud of' (Hockerts 1981:318). Affinity with a respectable legacy was a matter of prestige and a way of establishing some independence from the Allied occupation forces. More important, however, was the Christian democratic emphasis on the significance of subsidiarity for social policy. The principles of insurance, earnings-related contributions and benefits, and the minimal role of the state in administering the schemes as embodied in the social policy proposals flawlessly concurred with this foundational notion of Christian democracy and called for a restoration of the former Weimar institutions that had precisely these characteristics. Subsidiarity gained even more prominence in the ideological struggle against the competing proposals of social democracy as formulated in the SPD's social plan (1952), which had strong Beveridgean connotations in its universalism and its tax financing (Rimlinger 1971:158; Hockerts 1981:324). Moreover, the Christian democrats recognised the potentially negative feedbacks from their middle-class and employee constituencies if they were to opt for unification of separate schemes and universalism.

The 1957 pension reform in Germany is in many ways a fine example of the Christian democratic politics of mediation through social policy. This reform provided an alternative for the strictly market-oriented model of the liberals and for the social democratic universalist model. It embodied in every sense a unique formula for accommodating conflicting societal interests as it mixed stern eligibility criteria with benefit improvement and introduced a 'dynamic pension' that followed the general wage development in the private economy. In short, it represented a 'middle way' between social democratic reformism and liberal residualism (Manfred G. Schmidt 1987, 1988:75). And this 'middle way' found its foremost expression in the distributional intent and outcome of the scheme. The reform improved the material position of pensioners who until that time hardly had seen their rightful claims conceded. At the same time, strict eligibility and built-in differentials prevented large-scale redistribution of societal wealth from one social group to another, while still recognising their various claims. Existing status relations and inequality were reproduced in retirement without antagonizing any of the potential voter blocs. Redistribution became an inter- rather than intragenerational affair (Schmidt 1988:75) and social policy came to represent a distributional contract between generations rather than between classes. In effect, social policy moderated class as a basis for political identity because it addressed the general risk of age instead of class (Baldwin 1990:205). At the same time, the contract's built-in potential for expansion was considerable and the mediation and accommodation of differentiated interests could only be accomplished by relying heavily on the growing resources of the *Wirtschaftswunder*. The introduction of the dynamic element changed the political logic of development into a demographic and economic one. It established a link between the changing demographic composition of the German population, the growth of economic resources and social spending.

The critical element was that – in contrast to the Dutch reform at approximately the same time (see Chapter 6) – pensions were not to be flat-rate but earnings-related and dependent on former (earnings-related) contributions, while separate schemes for blue-collar workers and employees were preserved. The pension system 'projected the differentiation of earnings, and with it the distributive effects of market mechanisms, into pensions as well. It was consequently a non-levelling system, but one which put a premium on achievement and maintained individual status' (Hockerts 1980:330). Although the pension reform partly reflected the neo-liberalism of the social market faction of the CDU/CSU (Myles 1989:35), the implied generosity and particularly the status differentials do not fit easily with the idea of market conformity of neo-liberalism, but neatly concur with the social concern of social Catholicism.

The pension reform, and especially the timing of its introduction just prior to elections, clearly served purposes of power mobilisation. In fact, the reform was the main basis for the unparalleled electoral victory of Christian democracy in 1957. It

> not only had a material and socio-psychological effect on recipients of superannuation, disability and widow's pensions, but also on the attitudes and expectations of those still working, since it promised to prolong the benefits of economic growth into the retirement period and to provide more equitable norms for the distribution of the national product between generations.
>
> (Hockerts 1980:329)

Christian democracy was rewarded for the introduction of the pension reform by various groups in the electorate. This reform, as with other social policy measures, was capable of catering for a differentiated political clientele and therefore reinforced Christian democratic political power. The CDU/CSU consistently 'used the surplus of economic growth for mobilizing the poorer strata of the population, a calculation which proved to be successful' (von Beyme 1985:6; see also Lessmann 1985:238) and Hockerts has suggested (1981:332) that principal social reforms were frequently enacted just prior to general elections. Lessmann's study (1985) on electoral politics as determinants of policy output in West Germany has shown that electoral business cycles exist mainly in the domain of subsidies and social expenditures. Increases in social transfers have the general advantage that they positively affect the material position of voters immediately as well as the specific benefit of serving particular interest groups (Lessmann 1985:238).

The fate of German Christian democracy is associated with the pension reform in two diverging ways. In the short run it contributed to the unparalleled electoral victory of the CDU/CSU. Christian democracy used the pension reform as a major weapon in the electoral battle against the social democrats, who, by contrast, focused on foreign policy issues (Michalsky 1984:137). The 1957 elections were the first not to be dominated by hotly debated foreign policy issues (Baker, Dalton and Hildebrandt 1981:167). In the long run, however, Christian democratic complacency about the reform and the subsequent electoral victory led to a negligence of the potential for further power mobilisation through social reform. It immediately caused a certain relaxation of further social policy innovations (Alber 1989:61). A series of strategic errors inhibited a further institutionalisation of the Christian democratic presence in the field of social policy and made the movement – unlike for instance Italian Christian democracy (see Chapter 7) –

more dependent on contingent electoral behaviour. These considerations are important for understanding the failure of Christian democracy to continue to be the hegemonic force in German politics, as exemplified by the Erhard interlude (1963–6), the unsuccessful coalition with the social democrats (1966–9) and the long period of opposition (1969–82).

These considerations are exemplified by the fact that the Christian democratic government, formed after the elections of 1957, paradoxically opened with an austere warning as to further social reforms. The electoral slogan 'no experiments' was translated into an attack on the dangers of encompassing social policy (see Balfour 1982:193–5). Social reforms ought not to suffocate the possibilities of self-help and private initiative. Wage-earners were to be educated via social policy to behave as responsible citizens. The government wished to suppress the drift towards a 'total caring state' (*totalen Versorgungsstaat*) (Schmidt 1988:78; see Alber 1989:271). Although perhaps in line with the leading principles of social Catholicism, such criticism was ill-timed, for not only did it contradict the preceding reform efforts of Christian democracy, but it also tended to repudiate the subsidiary role of the state in areas where innovation was still needed. The Christian democratic position on social policy, therefore, ran the risk of exhausting the potential for societal accommodation by stressing too much the responsibility of the family and individuals to help themselves. Here, the neo-liberal leanings of the social market economy inhibited a fully developed social Catholic social policy in Germany and contributed to growing problems to maintain power.

The best illustration of this concerns the failure to appease and regulate the conflicting forces that were articulating around the issue of the sickness insurance (Alber 1989:271–4; Schmidt 1988:78–9; Michalsky 1984; Hentschel 1983:184–91). The proposed legislation coupled improvements in benefits to a decreasing public commitment to transfers. Patients were partly to pay directly for the services of doctors, who, in turn, would be remunerated on the basis of the number of patients they treated. The latter would accord patients a stronger control over medical services. The monopoly of the medical estate would be further moderated by the introduction of a state advisory council or service. One of the main goals was to free funds for the long-term ill and to reinforce the responsibility of the temporary sick. But the package deal was deliberately formulated so as to neutralise opposing interests (Alber 1989:272).

The design of a new sickness legislation and its accommodating and political intent, however, failed completely as a result of a strong coalition of opposing interests. In favour of the new law were only the employers' organisations and the private insurance companies, politically represented by the business wing of the CDU/CSU. The organisations of the medical estate were divided over the issues of 'self-responsibility' of patients, but feared a contraction of control over their own affairs. In order to defend their privileged status, the medical estate organised politically and even threatened a 'strike' (Alber 1989:273). The unions opposed the new legislation because of the potential detrimental effects on the financial position of their members and because of the outspoken moralising aspect that stated that wage-earners were to be educated as responsible citizens. This moral component and the financial threat facilitated a considerable readiness on the side of organised labour to act in resistance. The labour wing of Christian democracy and the social democrats represented the view of the unions in Parliament. The former were only ready to accept the proposals of direct financial efforts on the condition that wages for the sick would be fully replaced. The social democrats opposed the very idea of 'self-responsibility'.

The logic of electoral competition with regard to social policy took an intriguing turn. The SPD – supported by the extraparliamentary coalition of unions and the medical estate – attempted to delay the actual passing of the bill until just before the elections of 1961 (Alber 1989:275). It did so successfully and the government's reaction was to withdraw the proposal in the same year and to introduce a supplementary act that provided benefit improvements in line with the demands of the unions, the SPD and the labour wing of Christian democracy. However, at the elections of 1961 the Christian democracts lost their parliamentary majority. The position of the liberals was considerably strengthened; they jumped from 7.7 per cent in 1957 to 12.8 percent in 1961. The coalition between Christian democrats and liberals offered another attempt to reform the sickness insurance, by formulating a package deal between the reform, a proposal of wage continuation in case of sickness and a compensation for employers in the form of a transfer of the burdens for family allowances from the employers to the federal state. Again, however, it turned out to be impossible to accommodate the conflicting interests and the package deal disappeared from the agenda. In its stead came an improvement of family allowances, catering to the Catholic clientele in particular, and yet another supplementary act on sickness insurance.

The example of the sickness insurance illustrates the declining capacity of Christian democracy in Germany to provide feasible accommodation of societal conflicts through social reformism immediately following the pension reform. A specific problem facing Christian democracy in Germany concerned the absence of a Christian democratic labour union, which had the odd effect that the labour wing of the CDU/CSU in Parliament attempted to represent the Deutscher Gewerkschaftsbund (DGB), whose demands were also channelled through the social democratic party. At the same time, Christian democracy had to integrate the demands of the organisations of white-collar workers and the civil service union (Childs and Johnson 1981:67–71). The fact that unions were divided along status rather than confessional and ideological lines was a vital difference between Germany on the one hand and Italy and the Netherlands on the other, where organised labour was split into a Christian democratic and a left movement and where, consequently, Christian democracy found it easier to integrate labour demands within its own ranks, at least until the early 1970s. Religion here had significantly weakened class and status as sources of political articulation and facilitated a smoother cross-class integration through social policy.

The period preceding the grand coalition between Christian and social democracy was characterised by an attempt to contain rather than integrate the growing strength of the labour movement. Christian democracy faced a dual challenge in the first half of the 1960s. Social democracy had finally adapted to the presence and strength of the CDU/CSU and had modernised its programmatic outlook. As a result, and under conditions of growing secularisation – regular church attendance among Catholics declined from 60 per cent in 1953 to 48 per cent in 1969 and among Protestants from 19 per cent in 1953 to 7 percent in 1969 (Padgett and Burkett 1986:274) – the SPD became an acceptable alternative for religiously motivated workers (Baker, Dalton and Hildebrandt 1981:239–42). Besides, since the Bad Godesberg programme, the SPD recognised Christian ethics as one of its sources of inspiration, too (Paterson 1976:227). Christian democratic ideologues recognised the new emerging dilemma, but failed to formulate an alternative that would have had the disposition of a continued appeal to workers (Ute Schmidt 1983), thus leading to a declining capacity of integration.

A strategic miscalculation of Christian democracy in the 1960s in Germany concerned the tendency to stress autocratic solutions as an alternative for this loss of integrative capacity. The ideological innovation was based on a misunderstanding of the power base of the movement. Rather than an emphasis on the importance of the free market, the plurality of societal forces and the compensatory social side of the social market economy, the concept of the *formierte Gesellschaft* was launched in 1965 as an alternative for the social market economy. The *formierte Gesellschaft* provided what was understood as the Christian democratic blueprint of a society that represented the third phase in the development of the non-communist, industrialised world. In such a society, class, status and religious cleavages would have lost their political meaning and particularist interests would not have been able to constrain economic and political performance. It contained a critique of a welfare state that tended to develop an interest in itself and to expand in terms of spending and bureaucracy (Bark and Gress 1989, 2:39). The *formierte Gesellschaft* epitomised a peculiar mixture of free market liberalism and autocratic anti-pluralism, or in the words of Ute Schmidt (1983:548, my translation), 'an authoritarian variant of the social market economy'. Societal pluralism, rather than as a possibly rich source for Christian democratic power mobilisation and as a guarantee for plural democracy, was interpreted as a hindrance to economic prosperity and effective policies. Christian democracy appeared to offer an anti-democratic stance precisely at the moment that new (and old) social movements longed for more rather than less democracy. In this sense, German Christian democracy was badly equipped to face the new challenges and conditions of the second half of the 1960s, where democratisation was connected with every conceivable social and political issue.

Nevertheless, the elections of 1965 did not immediately reveal the weakened position of the CDU/CSU. Its main results pertained to the growing attractiveness of social democracy and the substantial losses of the liberals. Two conditions of the year after the elections were crucial for the political history of West Germany in general and for the fate of Christian democracy in particular. The first is the economic recession with rising inflation and unemployment, that eroded not only the trust in the stead-fastness of the social market economy and the miraculousness of the economic miracle, but also put the coalition between the weakened liberals and the Christian democrats under pressure. The electoral gift in the form of a tax reduction, granted just prior to the 1965 elections, made itself instantly felt through budgetary problems. The liberals opposed attempts to balance the budget by raising taxes, whereas the Christian democrats resisted a cut in public spending. A political crisis, the second condition provoked by the Christian democratic representatives in Parliament, forced Erhard to resign and a renewal of the liberal–Christian democratic coalition had thus become troublesome. Moreover, such a construction would again have had to rely on a narrow parliamentary majority, which was unstable because of the uncertainty as to the loyalty of the liberals' right wing (Balfour 1982:216).

The Christian democrats judged that a coalition with the SPD was a possible way of staying in office, for maintaining power at the govern-mental level and for recovering from the political problems of the Erhard period. The social democrats, on the other hand, interpreted the changing conditions as an opportunity to become a legitimate party of government. They were preparing their way out of the ghetto of opposition. In retro-spect, the grand coalition between the SPD and the CDU/CSU ended

Christian democratic domination and eventually pushed Christian democracy into opposition. Initially, social policy provided the main source of consensus between the former opponents, whereas the enthusiasm of the Christian democratic labour wing in particular cemented the new alliance of political forces. Paradoxically, social policy also sealed the fate of the grand coalition, when the balance of power within the CDU/CSU gradually shifted in favour of the representatives of business economic interests between 1966 and 1969 (Michalsky 1984:138).

Contrary to the rising expectations with regard to social democratic government participation and due to conditions of economic pressure and of increasing extraparliamentary opposition, social policy was driven towards austerity measures rather than reforms. The pension system was in financial trouble and the government's answer consisted of a reduction of public contributions and an increase of the premiums for the insured. An important innovation, however, concerned 'technical' reforms that *de facto* reduced the differentials between workers and employees (Schmidt 1988:80; Alber 1989:62). A further moderation of the privileged position of employees came about when workers, too, obtained the right to wage continuation for six weeks in case of sickness. The political conditions of the social democratic–Christian democratic coalition diminished the political capacity of employees to defend their privileges, because it was the combination of the CDU/CSU and the liberals that had been the protector of status differentials in social policy. Shifting power relations in Parliament and the assumption of government positions by social democrats weakened the political power base of the employees and social policy became much less differentiated according to status, as a result of which redistribution became feasible. The political support for these social policy innovations came from the labour wing of Christian democracy and from the SPD who had demanded a clearer representation of the interests of the working class in national politics (Schmidt 1988:81). These developments illustrate that the – moderate, yet crucial – 'social democratisation' of the German social system was largely an effect of piecemeal engineering. The transformation of some of the particularist features of social security was therefore not caused by a grand design of social democratic reformism, but by gradual policy changes under conditions of declining Christian democratic hegemony.

The initiative in social policy gradually went over into the hands of the social democrats. The integrative capacity of Christian democracy was further eroded during the period of the grand coalition, as exemplified in the electoral results of 1969 and 1972. The main problem for Christian democracy was its inability to attract voters from the increasingly important new middle class and at the same time to maintain the secularising Catholic workers within its own ranks. The support of the Catholic workers for Christian democracy declined from 58 per cent in 1965 to 52 per cent in 1969 and a mere 39 per cent in 1972 (Padgett and Burkett 1986:261). Simultaneously, the middle-class support for Christian democracy declined from 54 per cent in 1965 to 37 per cent in 1972, whereas the social democrats managed to increase the integration of substantial parts of this class (48 per cent in 1972) (Padgett and Burkett 1986:265). Christian democracy recaptured some of its Catholic worker support in the 1976 elections, because of a revitalisation of the religious dimension, mainly due to the social–liberal coalition's controversial legislation on divorce and abortion.

The coalition between the liberals and the social democrats was facilitated by a growing consensus between the two political movements around foreign policy issues (e.g. the recognition of the GDR), the 'new politics' (Baker, Dalton and Hildebrandt 1981) of democratisation, and by the 'cultural revolution' of the late 1960s. This coalition was formed in the autumn of 1969 and moved the Christian democrats into opposition until the *Machtwechsel* of 1982. It offered a break in the political history of Germany to the extent that the social–liberal alliance proved the possibility – absent in the Netherlands and Italy – of excluding Christian democracy from national power. The Brandt government, with its introduction of the concept of 'internal reforms', initially operated under favourable economic conditions and offered a mixture of social democratic and liberal social policy. The traditional social democratic goals of universalism were expressed in the plan of a people's insurance, but could only be partly implemented in the pension reform of 1972. The financial possibilities of the late 1960s were considerable. The growth rate of the German economy in 1968 was a high 7–8 per cent and the inflation rate was a low 1.5 per cent. The federal budget had a large surplus when the social–liberal coalition was installed and unemployment had already declined considerably. In fact, labour shortages intensified the presence of migrant labour in Germany (Bark and Gress 1989, 2:86). These favourable conditions offered the opportunity to correct the pension scheme. The Christian democrats in opposition wished to use the increased resources to improve benefits. The social democrats, however, proposed a 'flexible retirement age'. Because of the immense popularity of the latter proposal, the CDU/CSU adopted it quickly (Hentschel 1983:179). The pension reform of 1972 opened the scheme for independents and made entitlements partly independent of contributions. The main reforms of the SPD-dominated governments were supported by all parties in Parliament and social spending was boosted by what Schmidt (1988:84) has called the 'social policy race' under conditions of economic prosperity. Again, however, the implied universalism was not the result of a grand reform but an effect of gradual improvements.

The positive electoral effect of the reform of 1972 for social democracy was comparable to the one in 1957 for Christian democracy, but was further augmented by the SPD's success in foreign policy. Both coalition partners gained in support and the SPD surpassed the Christian democrats in electoral strength for the first time. The SPD now attempted to translate the electoral victory into a reinforcement of social reformism. Modern social policy was to create more social justice and to expand real freedom (Michalsky 1984:139). The conditions for such a novel stress on social reformism within the social democratic movement were given by a drastic change of attention from foreign policy to 'internal reforms', such as co-determination and tax reform, and by the radicalisation of a new generation of socialists and the rising demands for reform from societal organisations (the unions, the students). Prominent liberals, however, had already declared that there would be a liberal tax reform and liberal legislation on co-determination or no reforms at all (Michalsky 1984:139), which, of course, precisely clashed with the radicalisation within the social democratic camp. The reformist potential, therefore, was immediately obstructed by the declining willingness of the liberals to co-operate. Reforms became increasingly difficult as a result of the rapidly declining margins for expansive social policy under conditions of declining economic prosperity after the oil crisis and the recession of 1974.

In sum, Christian democracy gradually lost its grip on social policy after the pension reform of 1957. A slackening of social reformism coupled with the inability to view social policy as a medium of power mobilisation, made the strength of Christian democracy increasingly contingent upon electoral returns and therefore on structural changes within the electorate. Christian democracy failed to invest power resources in the social policy realm. The movement lost its integrative capacity at the moment when the social democrats successfully adjusted to such changing circumstances as class-structural transformations. Social policy as envisioned by Christian democracy, however, was not revolutionised as a result of social democratic reformism, but rather by the only partially intended effect of including formerly excluded groups into the edifice of social security and by the financial equalisation through 'technical' alterations of formerly distinguished status groups. Finally, a more daring social democratic reformism arrived at a time that political and economic conditions blocked a fundamental change in the relations of social security in Germany. Because of this, the institutional legacy of Christian democratic social policy provided the 'raw material' for new social and political struggles, but the social democratisation of the German system was only slow and imperfect. In other words, even if Christian democracy's power had declined since 1960, its impact on social policy could still be noticed in 1980.

6 The quality of welfare state regimes

CROSS-NATIONAL COMPARISONS I: QUALITATIVE INDICATORS OF WELFARE STATE REGIMES

What qualitative characteristics distinguish welfare states in general and the regime in Christian democratic nations in particular? What is the range and scope of social rights that lie behind the amount of money spent on welfare? To what extent can an individual or a family expect to preserve a level of income close to the level of or independent of the market wage in case of old age, sickness, accident or unemployment? The theoretically most satisfactory focus would be on income replacement schemes for unemployment, sickness, disability and old age. One can operationalise a measure for the quality of these schemes by looking at the average net (after tax) replacement rates of the schemes for unemployment, disability, sickness (average over the first 26 weeks, after waiting days) and old age, weighted by the appropriate coverage ratios. Table 6.1 gives the rank orders of welfare states in 1960 and 1980 according to this indicator as well as the average replacement and coverage ratios.

In agreement with other studies (Esping-Andersen 1990; Western 1989) the finding is that the Christian democratic countries Germany, Austria, the Netherlands, Belgium, Switzerland and Italy score above average on this measure in 1960 as do the Scandinavian countries Sweden, Denmark and Norway. The conclusion is that a clear difference between the social democratic and the Christian democratic nations did not exist in 1960. Again, there is some indication for the functional equivalence of social democracy and Christian democracy and for the relevance of the competition or interaction thesis. Using the information from Table 6.1 as a more detailed measure of the quality of schemes, the models as reported in Table 6.2 were estimated.

The models are similar to the ones as reported in Table 5.2. The second

Table 6.1 Weighted average net replacement rates, average net replacement rates and average coverage ratios of major social security schemes, 1960 and 1980 (descending rank order according to weighted average net replacement rates, 1960)

Country	Weighted average replacement rates		Average replacement rates		Average coverage	
	1960	1980	1960	1980	1960	1980
1. Sweden	.69	.88	.72	.93	.95	.95
2. Germany	.59	.77	.79	.89	.76	.87
3. Austria	.59	.77	.86	.89	.69	.86
4. Netherlands	.58	.75	.77	.88	.76	.85
5. Denmark	.53	.71	.68	.84	.79	.85
6. United Kingdom	.53	.66	.62	.77	.86	.86
7. Norway	.52	.84	.64	.88	.82	.96
8. Belgium	.51	.64	.84	.87	.61	.74
9. Switzerland	.45	.74	.64	.80	.71	.92
10. Italy	.45	.56	.73	.87	.62	.64
11. Finland	.40	.80	.89	.85	.45	.94
12. France	.39	.67	.74	.83	.53	.80
13. New Zealand	.37	.38	.75	.76	.50	.50
14. Canada	.34	.68	.64	.76	.53	.90
15. United States	.33	.43	.65	.74	.51	.58
16. Japan	.27	.58	.69	.83	.39	.70
17. Ireland	.27	.60	.63	.83	.43	.72
18. Australia	.13	.33	.64	.74	.20	.45
Average	.44	.65	.72	.83	.62	.78
Standard deviation	.14	.15	.08	.06	.19	.16

Source: SSIB.

estimated model (model II, column 3) with only the demographic and the political variables is superior and explains 71 per cent of the variance. Partly, the similarity between the two models results from the fact that both dependent variables use the same data on spending. Nevertheless, it shows that operationalising the dependent variable in a different yet more precise way does not lead to a change in the conclusions. The null-hypothesis that the model is correct cannot be rejected.[1] Estimating the model with only the

Table 6.2 OLS regression, dependent variable = weighted average net replacement rates of major social security schemes, 1960 and 1980

| | Panel a (1960) | | | Panel b (1980) | |
| | I | II | | I | II |
Variable name	Estimated coefficient (beta)	Estimated coefficient (beta)	Variable name	Estimated coefficient (beta)	Estimated coefficient (beta)
1. GDPCAP	0.03		1. GDPCAP	−0.09	
2. UERATE	−0.08		2. UERATE	−0.07	
3. AGE	0.44	0.48	3. AGE	0.62	0.60
	(2.50, 0.013)	(3.26, 0.003)		(2.70, 0.009)	(3.35, 0.002)
4. UNION	0.17		4. UNION	0.26	0.28
				(1.24, 0.12)	(1.58, 0.07)
5. CDSD	0.39	0.38	5. CDSD	0.02	
	(3.18, 0.004)	(3.60, 0.001)			
R^2 (adj.)	0.64	0.71	R^2 (adj.)	0.41	0.51
F-test:			F-test:		
H_0:	B1=B2=B4=0	B1=B2=0	H_0:	B1=B2=B5=0	B1=B2=0 B2=0
F =	0.16	20.04	F =	0.11	9.35 2.50
Pr=	92.12%	00.00%	Pr=	95.00%	00.20% 13.31%

Note: numbers between brackets refer to significant t-statistics (first) and the probability that (X > value of t) with X distributed as t(df) (second). Insignificant t-values are not reported.

left political variable gave insignificant results. The Christian democratic variable performed better, but less ($R^2 = 0.58$) than the 'competition' variable, which provided the best model. For 1980 the situation is different. In line with the findings on social security spending, the demographic structure of a nation has a strong impact on weighted average replacement rates, but the political variable is insignificant. However, the union density appears to have an effect, although the statistical significance occurs only at the 0.1 level. The F-test under the null-hypothesis that the beta-coefficient for union density is in fact zero has a 13 per cent probability to be true. Moreover, one of the tests for heteroskedasticity rejected the hypothesis that the residuals are homoskedastistic.[2] In addition, the model produced a large outlier, namely the Netherlands, which already had a large positive residual in the models for 1960 as well. This nation turns out to be much more generous in terms of coverage and replacement than the models predicted. These considerations show that the Dutch case might in certain respects indeed be exceptional. In order to be able to explain these considerable variations, the Dutch case needs to be analysed in more detail.

THE NETHERLANDS: A CASE STUDY OF CHRISTIAN DEMOCRACY AND SOCIAL POLICY[3]

The Dutch welfare state has posed a puzzle for comparative political sociology, the main mystery pertaining to the simultaneity of the dominance of confessional politics and generous social policy. The solution of this 'enigma' consists first of all in appreciating that Christian democracy does not *a priori* exclude extensive social policy. Second, the unique condition of a coalition between a religiously inclined reformist social democracy (see Zahn 1989) and a Catholic social and political movement unconstrained by Protestant anti-interventionism greatly favoured generous social policies. This concurrence of factors is largely responsible for an unparalleled consensus on social policy that emerged after the Second World War, except on one significant point.

Serious conflicts between social democracy and political Catholicism in the Netherlands existed only over the issue of the forms of organisation of social policy (Janssen and Berben 1982; Cox 1993). Subsidiarity and the remnants of corporatist notions on the Catholic side generated the opposite of Bismarckian social policy, namely the attempt to obstruct the attachment of workers to the state (Roebroek, Therborn and Berben forthcoming). The goal of social policy was to secure the existence of the sub-culture, not its transformation. It makes sense, therefore, to analyse briefly the conditions under which this issue was settled.

The Dutch government (in exile in London) had followed the example of Beveridge and had appointed a committee for the preparation of a renovation of social policy. Very much in agreement with the Allied plans for Germany, the Dutch version of the Beveridge report opted for a universal system of social security, largely administered by the state, that would not be confined to wage-earners and would end the privileging of specific status groups (see Cox 1993:101). The legal ground for this novelty was drafted in the following formula: 'the community, organised in the state, is responsible for the social security and freedom from want of all its residents, on the conditions that the residents will do everything within their reach to provide themselves with social security and freedom from want' (Commissie-van Rhijn 1945–6:10, my translation). The future social security system was to be a mixture of insurance-based legislation and direct state participation. A complete flat-rate benefit system, however, was rejected on the grounds that such a system completely denied existing income differentials. Benefits were confined by a maximum. In addition, the lowest benefits were to be linked to a minimum wage. The reforms as proposed by the van Rhijn committee, therefore, represented an attempt to preserve the earnings-related benefits and to introduce universalism in the sense of an extension of coverage and risks.

Employers' organisations as well as the unions – represented in the Foundation of Labour (Stichting van de Arbeid, StvdA) – contested the proposed control of the state over social security. The Catholic and Christian unions demanded a far-reaching decentralisation of administration in line with the leading theories of subsidiarity and sovereignty. The employers' organisations feared the projected state intervention (Hulsman 1981; Janssen and Berben 1982). The question was settled in 1952 via a foundational political compromise. The administration of the major insurance schemes was to be handed over to industrial associations (*bedrijfsverenigingen*). The control of the universal 'people's insurance schemes' was to be administered by public institutions and private funds. The execution of social assistance was to remain with local government (Braakman, Schendelen and Schotten 1984; Mannoury and Asscher-Vonk 1987; Veldkamp 1978; Cox 1993:118). Not surprisingly, this solution mirrored the pillarised organisation of society to a large extent and, in effect, reinforced the political significance of pillarised social associations.

Meanwhile, several other plans competed for a place on the political agenda in the immediate post-war period, whereas some revisions of the social system had already taken place during the period of occupation. First of all, the Nazis had initiated several measures that were improvements compared to the existing Dutch situation (Asselberghs 1982; Mannoury and Asscher-Vonk 1987; Veldkamp 1978). Some of the changes were accepted in the post-war legislation, such as the sickness insurance and modifications of the accident insurance (Mannoury and Asscher-Vonk 1987:58). As a reaction to these activities of the Nazis the Dutch government in exile had already started to broadcast its promises for social policy after the liberation of the nation in what might be called an ideological warfare (Mannoury 1985; Mannoury and Asscher-Vonk 1987; Van den Tempel 1946).

Civil servants, moreover, had kept the state bureaucracy running during the war and some of them had co-operated willingly with the Nazis, particularly with regard to social policy. There had been considerable resentment among the civil servants as to the policies pursued during the crisis of the 1930s, a resentment that contributed to their often autocratic views on the role of politics in social policy. The German proposals, therefore, had met scant opposition. The resistance movement, on the other hand, had already initiated negotiations over the post-war structure of labour relations in the Netherlands. Unions and employers' organisations agreed to opt for a bipartite institution (StvdA) that was to play an important role in the formulation and effectuation of social and economic policy (Windmuller 1969). Conflicts between social democratic central planning conceptions and Catholic corporatist proposals culminated in the foundation of a Social Economic Council (*Sociaal-Economische Raad*), which was both a tripartite bargaining institution and an advisory body of the government on macroeconomic policies. Remaining hopes of socialist planning in the form of a central planning bureau (Centraal Planbureau, CPB) were thwarted when Catholics got hold of the ministry of economic affairs (Wolinetz 1989:82; Griffiths 1980:137). The bargain between labour and capital and between social democracy and the Catholic movement consisted of full employment and the expansion of social policy in exchange for labour quiescence and wage restraint.

Two main social policy innovations characterise the first period after the war. The first is the introduction of the Unemployment Act of 1949 and the second the introduction of the first so-called 'people's insurance' for old age in 1957, which was preceded by an emergency act in 1947. Both measures illustrate the peculiar mixture of social Catholic and social democratic reformism. The Unemployment Act for all wage-earners combined a relatively generous replacement rate of 80 per cent with a typical element of differentiation. The 80 per cent replacement rate held exclusively for a breadwinner, i.e. a dependent worker earning a family wage. Other categories were entitled to 70 per cent (other persons older than 18 years who were not the breadwinner) or 60 per cent (others). Social democrats opposed

The quality of welfare state regimes 131

this differentiation, not because it would disproportionally disadvantage women, but because it was not in concordance with the idea of an insurance. The government argued that cancelling the distinction between replacement rates would necessitate the general curtailment of generosity. This met the resistance of the Catholic party, because 80 per cent was considered an indispensable rate for replacing a family wage. The KVP supported the plans for differentiation as a means to secure family income. Under favourable economic conditions, the differentiation was removed from the unemployment scheme in 1964 and benefits were upgraded, which under conditions of rising unemployment had the tendency to raise levels of spending.

The general old age act was the first law that transcended the idea of social insurance for wage-earners. This universal 'people's insurance' of 1957 came very close to the original proposals of the van Rhijn committee. It introduced a flat-rate minimum pension for all residents. It was carefully argued, however, that the scheme was not to be funded via taxation, but financed by special contributions. The benefits were linked to the general wage index. An intriguing aspect of the law concerned the fact that married women had no independent right to a benefit at the age of 65. Their entitlement was made contingent upon the retirement of their husband, to whom it was actually paid, thus clearly reflecting the traditional family conceptions of both the Catholic and the social democratic policy-makers (Therborn 1989:216).

The old age insurance was presented and defended by a social democratic minister of labour. This fact is sometimes taken as evidence of a strong social democratic influence on the Dutch welfare state. To be sure, the PvdA was active in the area of social policy. But the argument that social democracy was the real motor behind social legislation in the Netherlands is not convincing. Although the ministry of social affairs was frequently headed by a social democrat, no social policy legislation has ever been possible without the support of at least the Catholic party and of the interest groups organised in corporatist institutions (Cox 1993; Hemerijck 1993; Woldendorp 1993). And it was the combination of social democratic and Catholic forces which founded the organisational framework for social policy and the built-in mechanisms of expansion and generosity. In fact, recent research suggests that during the first period after the Second World War Catholics entirely dominated the politics of social and economic reconstruction (Roebroek 1993a, 1993b).

Under conditions of increasing pressure from economic liberalism – both from the conservative liberal party and the right wing of the confessional bloc – to withdraw from intervention in wage determination, social policy remained virtually the only theme of fundamental consensus between the social democrats and the Catholics (van Lier 1981; ter Heide 1986). Social policy had increasingly become an integral part of the political project of the 'Roman–red' coalitions and had clearly proven its feasibility. The favourable economic conditions of the late 1950s and early 1960s and the near full employment during this era, however, placed the strict wage policy of the government under pressure. Given the tight labour market, employers had already started to pay higher wages than those that were strictly permitted by law. One of the reasons for the collapse of the coalition between Catholicism and social democracy was that the latter consistently refused to give up wage policy as the last bastion of interventionism, while the former had started giving in on the demands of the employers and their representatives within the party to ease political control over wages and prices. The system broke down in 1964, under one of the confessional–liberal coalitions that ruled the Netherlands during 1958–72. Intervention in the wage determination, however, had become a policy routine to such an extent, that immediately after its termination – under the political insistence of a Catholic minister of social affairs – a minimum wage was agreed upon by unions and employers. When, in 1965, agreement could not be reached during the central wage bargaining, the Catholic minister intervened and one-sidedly determined the level. This set the stage for the introduction of the statutory minimum wage in 1968.

The loosening of the wage restriction in the late 1950s and its abolishment contributed to an economic boom in the 1960s which, in turn, resulted in a large scale reconstruction of the economy. Sudden, shock-wise wage increases caused a rationalisation of the labour-intensive industries. Employers started to invest in labour-saving techniques and massive lay-offs followed. The generous accident insurance, introduced in 1966 as a hallmark of Catholic social policy, provided the employers with a convenient opportunity to ease the pain of rationalisation for their workers. Rather than becoming unemployed, many older, less 'functional', i.e. economically redundant workers, could claim a right to a disability benefit, which secured them a level of income much higher and over a longer period than the unemployment benefit did. Releasing personnel via the disability scheme created a considerable pool of hidden unemployment which was accepted by workers and unions in exchange for the generosity of the scheme. This dramatically brought to the fore the passiveness of a transfer-oriented welfare system, which lacked any institutionalised set-up for active labour market policy (Braun 1988). However, the Netherlands could afford such generosity, partly as a result of favourable economic conditions, and partly because the nation reached a semi-OPEC status in the

1960s as a result of the discovery and profitable exploitation of natural gas resources in the northern province of Groningen (Lubbers and Lemckert 1980).

The further expansion of the welfare state mainly took place under Christian democratic–liberal hegemony in the 1960s, which makes the Dutch case perhaps even more enigmatic. The puzzle not only concerns the simultaneity of generous social spending and confessional dominance, but above all the fact that expansion took place while social democracy was in opposition. Major improvements concerned the substitution of the poor law of 1854 in 1964, additional schemes for unemployment (in 1964), and the introduction of the already mentioned accident insurance in 1966. The replacement of the archaic poor law grew out to be the general safety net for citizens who are not entitled to any of the other social security provisions. The lowest benefits (most importantly, the public pension) of all schemes were linked to the compulsory minimum wage. The minimum wage itself amounted to about 80 per cent of the average wage. The net–net linkage of benefits to the minimum wage guaranteed that no person would fall below what was considered to be a socially acceptable minimum. Ultimately, it accorded to the Dutch welfare state its generous remit at all levels.

Next to the factors already noted, two other conditions were critical for expansion, one of which was political and one economic, but, in effect, the two cannot be viewed separately. These conditions concern the unparalleled economic growth and prosperity of the Dutch economy in the 1960s and the initially gradual, but in the end quite sudden structural changes of society in the form of depillarisation, deconfessionalisation, culminating in a progressive political and cultural conjuncture (Braun and van Kersbergen 1986). Confessional politics did not escape the effects of depillarisation and deconfessionalisation, mainly exemplified by the radicalisation of anti-revolutionary politics and the gradual social democratisation of the Catholic labour movement. The Catholic party was forced to adopt more radical social policy demands in order not to lose its labour wing and the votes of Catholic workers altogether, which in the early 1970s facilitated the return of social democratic and Catholic co-operation at the national level.

In 1973, a coalition between social democracy and confessional forces was constructed, which had the parliamentary support of the PvdA and the smaller, radical parties, but which was merely tolerated by the KVP and the ARP. The CHU opposed the construction (Vis 1973). In spite of its fragile parliamentary base, the government expanded the social system considerably. Main events were the increase in the level of the minimum wage (and therefore of the benefits linked to it), and the introduction of a statutory minimum wage for young people.

Do these developments allow for the conclusion that social democracy had a lasting influence on the Dutch welfare state after all? This is not likely, because the logic of the parliamentary formation made social policy innovation contingent upon majorities that had to include the confessional bloc. Moreover, the minister responsible for social policy was an anti-revolutionary, Christian union leader. Major expansionary policies were already initiated during the period of confessional–liberal hegemony and social democracy simply followed the agenda set by the confessional parties. Finally, real radical changes proposed by the government domin-ated by social democracy (income redistribution, housing policy, profit sharing) time and again were blocked by the majority voting alliances of liberals and the confessional parties that also finally sealed the downfall of the government in 1977.

The short period of renewed confessional–social democratic co-operation was crucial for the construction of a cross-confessional Christian democracy and the mobilisation of power for the movement (van Kersbergen, Lucardie and ten Napel 1993). Both the Christian movements and the Catholic movement showed increasing signs of decomposition as a result of the fragmentation of infrastructural power. Secularisation and depillarisation tended to work in one direction: towards the disintegration of the traditional structure of political power in the Netherlands. The Catholic search for a realliance of Christian forces was driven not only by the dwindling control over the organisations of (Catholic) workers and the waning capacity to attract voters, but also by the lesser need for 'emanci-pation' of the sub-culture and by the changes within Catholicism at large after the second Vatican council.

Growing tensions between the KVP and the PvdA and successful ex-periments with cross-confessional co-operation at the local level (Kuiper 1988) prepared the way for the first joint Christian democratic list for the election of 1977. The social democrats won an additional 10 seats in parliament and the new Christian democratic alliance managed to stabilise its electoral strength. A combination of social democratic strategic errors and Christian democratic power play led to the exclusion of social demo-cracy from the government. The Christian democrats entered a coalition with the populist liberals and used the period until the 1980s to consolidate the reformation of Christian-inspired politics. These events reveal a con-siderable capacity to adapt on the side of the Catholic party in particular. However, the loss of the labour wing and the inclusion of Christian con-servative forces effected a Christian democracy in the Netherlands that is more conservative than the Catholic movement was in the 1950s and 1960s, especially with respect to social policy. The structuring of societal conflicts within the movement has become much more based on the demands of the new middle class and the employers than on the attempt to integrate workers. Crucial, however, was that a reorganisation of confessional politics at the governmental level not only strongly enhanced the competitive position of Christian democracy *vis-à-vis* social democracy, but also resulted in a continued capacity to maintain positions of power. The CDA occupied the centre of the political system and the logic of parliamentary majorities – as long as a social democratic–liberal coalition was excluded – determined further possibilities of Christian democratic power mobilisation.

The main foundation, therefore, of the idiosyncratic mixture of universalism, generosity and differentiation that characterises the Dutch welfare state and which has given rise to Dutch 'exceptionalism' is found in the concurrence of social democratic and Catholic reformism in the first decade after the Second World War. The construction was made viable through the barring of anti-interventionist orthodox Protestantism and free market liberalism in the 'Roman–red' coalitions that dominated Dutch politics until the late 1950s. The renewal of Dutch social democracy and the presence of a religiously inclined personalist-socialist doctrine facilitated a broadly shared pact on social policy.

The period of liberal–confessional dominance radically changed economic policy, but – under the leadership of Catholicism – not only kept the edifice of social policy intact, but considerably expanded its scope and performance in the 1960s. Once in place, the system gained momentum and developed its own logic of expansion. Confessionalism in social policy has an inherent expansionary potential under favourable conditions (Therborn 1989). Corporatism in combination with a pillarised structuring of labour relations expedited expansion to the extent that it generated a need for all organisations to develop their own designs for improvements. The fundamental agreement over the family as the nucleus of social life necessitated the generosity in replacement rates of the income of a 'breadwinner'. The prevailing high benefits later – under conditions of individualisation of society and the analogous decline of family ideology – became the norm when differentiation in the schemes was eliminated. Moreover, 'the liberal emphasis on economic incentives which, as far as social security is concerned, means disincentives to social generosity, is alien to confessional social thought' (Therborn 1989:212–13). The result was that the Catholic–social democratic majority effectively outweighed the resistance of liberalism and anti-revolutionary autonomy claims. Finally, the stress on 'private initiative', self-government and subsidiarity not only aimed at reinforcing the transfer character of state intervention, but also was 'financially open-ended' (Therborn 1989:213), so that 'once the expansionary potential of confessionalism had got started, it acquired a momentum which confessional politics was singularly inept at reining in' (Therborn 1989:215). The logic of expansion was given momentum because once established, relatively generous replacement rates of the major schemes were claimed as institutionalised social rights and were therefore difficult to curtail.

CROSS-NATIONAL COMPARISONS II: FAMILY- AND TRANSFER-BIAS IN WELFARE STATE REGIMES AND LABOUR MARKET PARTICIPATION

The cross-national comparisons have shown that there is some evidence to accept the view that both social democracy and Christian democracy are related to welfare state development. The competition between these two political actors in 1960 particularly promoted spending, whereas in 1980, these effects were much less pronounced or even insignificant. However, a distinctive Christian democratic welfare state regime could not be detected and the only conclusion so far is that social democracy and Christian democracy are 'welfare equivalents'. The Dutch case study, on the other hand, suggests that Christian democracy may make a difference with respect to how social rights are formulated and to whom they are granted.

Yet if one looks at the average net replacement rates for families with two children as a proportion of the net replacement rates for unmarried individuals, one finds that, first of all, some countries actually 'punish' families with two children to the extent that the net replacement rate of the major income replacement schemes is actually lower for a family than for a single individual. In addition, one does not find any systematic pattern in the family-bias of income maintenance schemes, which would indicate a clear difference between the Christian democratic nations and other regimes (source: SSIB). However, it may be the case that a family-bias is already present in the wage–tax structure of a nation, as a result of which differences in replacement rates between individuals and families in the social security system do not have to be reinforced in order to privilege the family. Table 6.3 shows the ratio between the net average production worker's wage (NAPW) for a family with two children where the husband earns the average production worker's wage and the NAPW of a single in 1960 and 1980.

In 1960, the NAPW in all nations was higher for a family than for a single. However, Denmark, Ireland, Australia, Canada and Japan are one (or close to one) standard deviation below average. Italy, Austria, France and the United Kingdom score more than a standard deviation above average, whereas the Netherlands and Belgium are above average as well.

Table 6.3 Privileging of families in net average production worker's wage, 1960 and 1980 (descending rank order 1960)

Country	Privileging			
	1960		1980	
1. Italy	1.31		1.15	(13)
2. Austria	1.25		1.35	(2)
3. United Kingdom	1.24		1.20	(6)
4. France	1.23		1.46	(1)
5. Netherlands	1.20		1.18	(8)
6. Norway	1.19		1.23	(3)
7. Belgium	1.18		1.22	(4)
8. New Zealand	1.16		1.18	(10)
9. Finland	1.16		1.19	(7)
10. Germany	1.15		1.22	(5)
11. Sweden	1.13		1.17	(11)
12. Switzerland	1.11		1.11	(15)
13. United States	1.11		1.12	(14)
14. Denmark	1.09		1.17	(12)
15. Ireland	1.08		1.18	(9)
16. Australia	1.08		1.11	(16)
17. Canada	1.08		1.10	(17)
18. Japan	1.02		1.07	(18)
Average	1.15		1.19	
Standard deviation	0.07		0.09	

Note: numbers between brackets refer to rank order of 1980.

Source: SSIB.

Germany appears to be an average case, while the case of Italy is exceptional. The latter nation is two standard deviations above average. There is, therefore, some confirmation for the thesis that privileging of families is present in the wage–tax structure of nations. And given the presence of Italy, Austria, France, the Netherlands and Belgium at the top of Table 6.3, this seems to be – although certainly not exclusively – a Christian democratic affair. As the data for 1980 show the privileging of families according to this indicator is not a stable characteristic of welfare state regimes. Italy, the leader in 1960, has considerably moderated the privileging of families, whereas France has reinforced it. The nations that scored below average in 1960, however, do so in 1980, too.

It is ultimately the interplay of taxation and social security that determines the actual distribution of income and the possible difference between individuals and families. It is difficult to estimate precisely how the various public programmes interact in terms of a final outcome. One way of getting some detail on these effects is by looking at disposable income as a proportion of gross earnings of an average production worker. Income tax is deducted from gross earnings as are social security contributions, whereas transfers are added. Taxes, contributions and transfers determine disposable income. In order to examine the possible privileging of families through tax–benefit regimes one can look at disposable income as a percentage of gross earnings and at the difference in disposable income between a family with two children and a single. The measure that was constructed was meant to cover both the absolute level of disposable income (as a proportion of gross earnings) and the relative position of a family *vis-à-vis* the single by multiplying the disposable income of a two-child family by the ratio of their income to the disposable income of a single. Unfortunately, there was no possibility of looking at this indicator for 1960 because of lack of data – the nearest date was 1976. The results for this year are shown in Table 6.4.

The most marked aspect concerns both the top and the bottom of the rank order of Table 6.4. Denmark and Sweden score as low as they do because the disposable income of a family as a percentage of gross earnings (71.2 per cent and 71.8 per cent) was the lowest in the OECD area. The bottom of the Table, therefore, also simply reflects the stern tax regimes in these nations. On the other hand, countries such as Australia, Canada and Japan are in the sub-top of the Table precisely because of their relatively lenient tax regimes. However, the top of Table 6.4 is made up of nations that did not have a particularly tolerant tax regime, but still scored more than one (Italy, Belgium and Austria) or even two (France) standard deviation(s) above average. The tax–benefit regimes of these nations apparently do favour the family over the single in a disproportional manner. The difference between disposable income of a family and a single is (in percentage points) 10.9 in Italy, 17.2 in France, and 17.9 in Belgium and Austria as, for instance, compared to 10.2 in Sweden, 9.9 in Norway, 9.6 in Denmark, and 5.3 in Japan. This has certainly to do with the fact that Italy, France, Belgium and Austria are welfare states that most strongly rely on cash benefits to families. These are the only nations that score more than one standard deviation above the average (5.16 per cent of gross earnings) of state transfers to families, with Belgium (13.0 per cent) leading, followed by Italy (9.6 per cent), France (9.2 per cent) and Austria (8.9 per cent) (source: OECD 1978:98).

Table 6.4 Privileging of families in disposable income in 1976
(descending rank order)

Country	Privileging 1976
1. France	120.1
2. Austria	117.6
3. Belgium	110.4
4. Italy	108.7
5. Australia	99.6
6. Canada	99.3
7. Japan	97.6
8. Ireland	96.7
9. Switzerland	95.6
10. Germany	91.9
11. United States	91.9
12. United Kingdom	88.9
13. Norway	88.8
14. Finland	88.6
15. New Zealand	87.6
16. Netherlands	86.4
17. Sweden	83.7
18. Denmark	82.3
Average	96.4
Standard deviation	11.2

Source: OECD (1978: 92, Table 2).

A measure of family-bias in the tax–benefit systems of advanced
capitalist nations is given by the difference between the take-home pay plus
cash transfers of a family with two children and the take-home pay plus
cash transfers of a single, expressed as a percentage of gross earnings
(take-home pay = gross earnings minus income tax and employee's social
security contributions, OECD 1986:53). The models that were estimated
with the family-bias in tax–benefit regimes as the dependent variable are
presented in Table 6.5.[4]

As expected, Christian democracy is positively related to the family-bias
in tax–benefit regimes, whereas social democracy is not. Unexpectedly, the

Table 6.5 OLS regression, dependent variable = family bias in tax–benefit regimes, 1980

Variable name	I Estimated coefficient (beta)	II Estimated coefficient (beta)
1. GDPCAP	0.03	
2. UNION	0.37	0.35
	(1.54, 0.07)	(1.94, 0.04)
3. LPS	−0.01	
4. CDS	0.65	0.63
	(3.18, 0.003)	(3.44, 0.002)
R^2 (adj.)	0.37	0.44
F-test:		
H_0:	B1=B3=0	B1=B2=0
F =	0.06	7.23
Pr=	94.45%	0.58%
H_0:	B2=B4=0	B1=0
F =	5.75	3.78
Pr=	1.50%	6.98%
H_0:	B2=0	
F =	2.37	
Pr=	14.62%	

Source: OECD (1986: 53, Table 4).

variable measuring union density is also related to family-bias, although the statistical significance is not very high. The F-test under the null-hypothesis that the estimated coefficient of UNION is in reality zero has a 15 per cent probability to be true in the first estimated model and a 7 per cent probability to be true in the second model. Given the 'borderline' statistical significance of the union variable and the comparatively poor fit of the model, no definite conclusions can be reached. The residual analysis of the model, however, shows a positive residual for France and negative residuals for Italy and the Netherlands, indicating perhaps that the latter two nations have far less family-biased tax–benefit systems than predicted by the model.

Christian democratic parties tend to promote social policies that rely on cash benefits rather than on benefits in kind (Huber and Stephens 1993) and are less ready to replace the logic of the labour market with active labour market policy. And as the Dutch case suggests, Christian democratic welfare state regimes can be characterised as transfer-oriented, passive welfare states (see Roebroek 1993a, 1993b). There may be differences in the role of the state in the redistribution of societal wealth and these discrepancies may cause distinct outcomes. Welfare regimes might redistribute equally large sums of money, but they may do so in fundamentally dissimilar ways.

> Societies can be divided into those that distribute their resources primarily through cash transfers and those whose spending patterns are concentrated on the provision of services. The latter is labour intensive, whereas the former is not because the income transfers that needy families receive from the state are more likely to be spent for basic necessities than for social welfare services. A service state, by contrast, constrains consumption into precisely those services which also require a high level of employment.
>
> (Rein 1985:96)

Christian democratic nations may be guided by different logics as to how transfers are spent. Transfer-oriented welfare states are focused on income replacement where the labour market fails to provide earnings, whereas service-oriented regimes are aimed either at creating jobs or facilitating re-entry into the labour market by a number of active policies (Rein 1985:96). It is incorrect to presume that a welfare state regime exclusively relies on cash transfers or on services in kind. It is a matter of bias. Christian democracy is expected to privilege transfers and to promote cash-benefit bias in social policy. In order to test this hypothesis one can operationalise the dependent variable as cash benefits as a proportion of total benefits of social security schemes. The OLS results are reported in Table 6.6.

In 1960, there was a clear, strong and highly significant positive relationship between the dependence on cash benefits of a welfare state regime and the strength of Christian democracy. The unemployment rate, the demographic structure and the strength of social democracy were not related to this characteristic of welfare states. Because of the collinearity between the union density variable and the social democratic variable, a second model was estimated that excluded LPS, but included UNION. The latter variable was statistically insignificant and was therefore excluded from the third model. Model III (panel a, column 3) underscores the plausibility of the hypothesis that Christian democracy tends to promote social policies that strongly rely on cash benefits, particularly – given the highly significant effect of the variable measuring wealth – under conditions of economic prosperity. If social democracy would foster welfare

Table 6.6 OLS regression, dependent variable = cash-benefit bias in welfare states, 1960 and 1980

Variable name	Panel a (1960) I Estimated coefficient (beta)	Panel a (1960) II Estimated coefficient (beta)	Panel a (1960) III Estimated coefficient (beta)	Panel b (1980) I Estimated coefficient (beta)	Panel b (1980) II Estimated coefficient (beta)	Panel b (1980) III Estimated coefficient (beta)
1. GDPCAP	0.83 (5.00, 0.0002)	0.73 (5.17, 0.0001)	0.74 (5.26, 0.00)	0.32 (1.23, 0.12)	0.34 (1.67, 0.06)	0.26 (1.39, 0.09)
2. UERATE	−0.34			−0.01		
3. AGE	0.04			−0.01		
4. UNION	−0.20 (1.08, 0.15)	0.11		−0.15		
5. LPS	0.13			0.29 (0.94, 0.2)	0.21	
6. CDS	0.96 (5.28, 0.001)	0.89 (6.22, 0.00)	0.90 (6.39, 0.00)	0.71 (2.81, 0.008)	0.72 (3.77, 0.0009)	0.69 (3.63, 0.001)
R^2 (adj.)	0.72	0.73	0.73	0.31	0.43	0.42

F-test:

Panel a (1960):
- Column I: H_0: B2=B3=B5=0, F= 0.78, Pr= 52.82%; H_0: B1=B4=B5=0, F= 9.54, Pr= 0.17%; H_0: B4=0, F= 1.17, Pr= 30.11%
- Column II: H_0: B1=B3=0, F= 22.80, Pr= 0.00%; H_0: B2=0, F= 0.73, Pr= 40.54%
- Column III: H_0: B1=B2=0, F= 23.90, Pr= 0.00%

Panel b (1980):
- Column I: H_0: B2=B3=B4=0, F= 7.29, Pr= 94.52%; H_0: B1=B5=B6, F= 2.68, Pr= 9.43%
- Column II: H_0: B1=B3=0, F= 6.70, Pr= 00.61%; H_0: B2=0, F= 1.18, Pr= 29.45%
- Column III: H_0: B1=B2=0, Pr= 0.77%; H_0: B1=0, F= 1.93, Pr= 18.93%

Note: numbers between brackets refer to significant t-statistics (first) and the probability that (X > value of t) with X distributed as t(df) (second). Insignificant t-values are not reported.

states that rely disproportionally on benefits in kind or services, one would have expected a statistically significant negative association between cash-benefit bias and strength of social democracy. This, however, was not the case in 1960. The third model has a good fit ($R^2 = 0.73$) for a cross-sectional regression with 18 cases and two independent variables. Model III, however, produced an outlier in Finland which actually had a moderating effect on the general fit.[5] The Finnish welfare state apparently relied much more on cash benefits than predicted by the model.[6] An interesting finding is that the Netherlands had a considerable positive residual, suggesting that this nation's regime relies even more on cash benefits than could be anticipated on the basis of the estimation. Estimation of similar models including the 'competition' variable reduced the fit of the model considerably. The situation in 1980 is roughly comparable to the one in 1960. Christian democracy is still significantly related to the cash-benefit bias of welfare states. An identical procedure of model reduction was followed for 1980. Model III[7] shows that on the basis of the F-test on the estimated coefficient of GDPCAP the significance of the economic variable should be rejected. It is also clear from Table 6.6, panel b that the fit of the model is much less in 1980 than in 1960. Italy had an unexpectedly large negative residual, whereas the Swiss welfare state relied much more on cash benefits than was predicted by the model. In sum, in both 1960 and 1980 Christian democracy explains to a considerable extent the variance in the cash-benefit bias of welfare states, although among the group of Christian democratic nations there was still considerable variation with respect to this characteristic of welfare state regimes.

The cash-benefit bias of Christian democratic welfare states indicates that the welfare regimes of these nations are indeed characterised by a certain passivity with respect to social policy. One could look at the relative importance of active labour market measures. There are, however, no data available for the 1960s. Data for the 1980s on the ratio of passive labour market expenditures (such as early retirement, income replacement) to active labour market expenditures (employment services, labour market training, measures for special groups) (source: OECD 1988:86, Table 3.1) generate mixed evidence. It is not the case that the Christian democratic nations only focus on passive labour market measures. What is unmistakable, however, is the 'activeness' of Sweden and Norway, the only two countries spending more on active than on passive measures in 1987. The data allow for the conclusion that the Christian democratic nations differ little from the liberal regimes in terms of labour market policy. However, Janoski's recent study (1994) of state intervention in the labour market between 1950 and 1988 shows that social democratic regimes are strongly directed towards replacing the logic of the labour market in case of market failure, whereas liberal welfare state regimes do precisely the opposite. One of the most interesting findings of Janoski's study, however, is the identification of the Christian democratic regimes in terms of ambiguity. Labour market policies in these nations can go both ways, depending on the political and economic conditions under which such policies are pursued.

Different types of configurations of market, state and family may create different types of employment patterns (Esping-Andersen 1990, 1993). One expectation is that labour market participation rates, especially female rates, are comparatively low in those welfare states that are characterised by transfer-bias and by passivity or, in general, by the dominance of a traditional family ideology. Clearly, the precise explanation of participation rates is much more complex than can be argued here (see Schmidt 1993). The assumption, however, is that different welfare regimes pattern employment in different ways. The focus is on the possible determinants of participation, which are assumed partly to be the effect of a particular regime, which – in turn – is assumed to be politically determined. If these theoretical considerations are correct, one can expect to find a fairly strong negative relationship between Christian democratic power and participation rates as well as a fairly strong positive relationship between the power of labour and participation on the labour market, even if one uses control data for the unemployment rate, age structure and the wealth of a nation.

Table 6.7 summarises the results of the regression analyses relating the total labour force as a percentage of total population as well as male and female labour force as a percentage of male and female total labour force in 1960 and 1980 to the economic and political variables of interest. First, it is quite surprising that every estimated model for 1960 gave entirely insignificant results (panel a), whereas the models for 1980 explain approximately 75 per cent of cross-national variation. In none of the estimated models did the strength of the left have any effect on labour market participation, although union density had a positive effect on female participation in 1980 (Table 6.7, panel b, column 7). The expected negative effect of the strength of Christian democracy is evident, consistent and considerable in 1980. The coefficients are not only quite high (for total labour force in 1980: –0.87; for male labour force in 1980: –0.46; and for female labour force in 1980: –0.77), but statistically also highly significant. This allows for the conclusion that Christian democratic welfare states do discourage women to enter the labour market or encourage female labour market exit. These findings corroborate the conclusion of a recent study that

Table 6.7 OLS regression, dependent variables = labour force participation rates: total, male and female, 1960 and 1980

Panel a: model I

Independent variables	Total labour force 1960	Total labour force 1980	Male labour force 1960	Male labour force 1980	Female labour force 1960	Female labour force 1980
	Estimated coefficient (beta)		Estimated coefficient (beta)		Estimated coefficient (beta)	
1. GDPCAP	-0.38 (1.22)	0.11 (0.78)	-0.39 (1.26)	-0.26 (1.00)	-0.23 (0.60)	0.24 (1.70)
2. UERATE	-0.34 (0.96)	-0.24 (1.86)	-0.44 (1.22)	-0.53 (2.24)	-0.19 (0.50)	-0.10 (0.78)
3. AGE	0.21 (0.63)	0.46 (2.97)	0.42 (1.27)	0.28 (1.02)	0.05 (0.14)	0.44 (2.92)
4. UNION	-0.21 (0.62)	0.33 (2.22)	0.11 (0.31)	-0.09 (0.33)	-0.27 (0.27)	0.43 (2.94)
5. LPS	-0.12 (0.28)	-0.24 (1.35)	-0.53 (1.18)	-0.41 (1.30)	0.09 (0.18)	-0.13 (0.75)
6. CDS	-0.48 (1.42)	-0.77 (5.34)	-0.48 (1.41)	-0.65 (2.52)	-0.23 (0.63)	-0.66 (4.71)
R^2 (adj.):	-0.003	0.78	-0.00	0.29	-0.19	0.79

Panel b: model II

Independent variables	Total labour force 1960	Total labour force 1980	Male labour force 1960	Male labour force 1980	Female labour force 1960	Female labour force 1980
	Estimated coefficient (beta)		Estimated coefficient (beta)		Estimated coefficient (beta)	
1. GDPCAP	...	...	...	...	...	...
2. UERATE	...	...	...	-0.40 (2.04, 0.03)	...	...
3. AGE	...	0.48 (4.29, 0.0003)	...	...	...	0.54 (3.92, 0.0007)
4. UNION	...	...	...	...	...	0.26 (2.00, 0.03)
5. LPS	...	...	...	...	...	...
6. CDS	...	-0.87 (6.43, 0.00)	...	-0.46 (2.33, 0.02)	...	-0.77 (5.84, 0.00)
R^2 (adj.):	...	0.73	...	0.35	...	0.76

Note: numbers between brackets refer to t-statistics. The probabilities that $(X >$ value of t) with X distributed as t(df) are only reported for the second estimated models (panel b).

Table 6.8 Growth of female labour force as a percentage of female population from 15 to 64 (percentage points), 1960–80

Country	Growth 1960–80
Australia	18.0
Austria	−3.4
Belgium	10.6
Canada	23.5
Denmark	27.9
Finland	4.5
France	8.3
Germany	3.6
Ireland	1.5
Italy	0.0
Japan	−5.2
Netherlands	9.3
New Zealand	13.2
Norway	26.0
Sweden	24.0
Switzerland	3.1
United Kingdom	12.2
United States	17.1
Average	10.8
Standard deviation	9.9

Source: OECD (1992: 38–9, Table 2.8).

centre parties in Catholic countries transform the conservative stance of Catholicism in gender-related issues into public policy, such as in family policy, taxation, education, social security and care for children, the elderly and other dependents. These governments thus place priority on the maintenance of traditional patterns of gender differentiation. . . . That policy, of course, creates powerful disincentives and obstacles to the incorporation of female labour into the economy.

(Schmidt 1993:204–5)

The explanation for the different effects of the models at two points in time can be explained by the fact that the growth of female labour market participation in most nations occurred precisely between 1960 and the

1980s. It was only in this period that the qualitative structures of the welfare systems and the political constellations in different nations encouraged or hindered the growth of female participation. Table 6.8 clearly indicates that the growth of the female labour force between 1960 and 1980 was below average in every Christian democratic nation.

One question remains when one looks at the results of the regression analyses reported in Table 6.7: why does the proportion of people over 65 have a positive effect on total labour force participation in 1980? First of all, it must be noted that this age effect is absent for the male labour force. It is therefore the effect on the female labour force which matters. *Prima facie*, one would expect an ageing population to have a negative impact on the female labour force, because of the gendered division of labour between men and women with respect to the care of the elderly. However, it might be that the larger the proportion of the aged in a society, the higher the dependency ratio, i.e. the ratio of social benefit recipients to employed persons. As a result of a high dependency ratio the pressure on women to enter the labour market might become higher and might override insti- tutional, cultural and political obstacles. In other words, the demographic pressure might lead governments to promote female labour market entry into the social service sector as a means to cope with a larger welfare demand. The capacity of women to enter the labour market successfully then depends – besides economic circumstances – on a range of institu- tional and political conditions, such as childcare facilities, the availability of part-time jobs and active labour market policies, in short, on the general willingness of governments to facilitate labour market entry of women.

7 The structure of welfare state regimes

CROSS-NATIONAL COMPARISONS I: ORGANISATION, FINANCING AND FRAGMENTATION OF WELFARE REGIMES

If Christian democracy does try to define its political place between free market liberalism and state-oriented socialism, between belief in the market and confidence in the state, then the impact of this movement should be discernable in the organisation and administration of the main welfare institutions. As the Dutch case suggests, a typical Christian democratic version of control over institutions would be private or semi-public organisations that are supervised and subsidised by the state. Ideally, one would anticipate a bi- or tripartite structure in the control of the main social security schemes. As an operationalisation of the dependent variable one might look at the level of bi- or tripartism in a nation by adding the number of central social security schemes (old age, disability and survivor programmes; sickness and maternity; work injury programmes; unemployment benefit programmes; family allowances) controlled by bi-or tripartism (BITRI). The focus is on 1980, because the reasonable expectation is that administrative and organisational characteristics of social security schemes in particular are slow to change since, once vested, institutions tend to be inert. It is important to stress that this measure cannot be taken as referring to 'corporatism' understood as a system of interest intermediation between the main societal interests. It may very well be the case that bi- or tripartite control over the social security system coincides with corporatist interest intermediation, but there is no necessary link (see Hemerijck 1993).

Christian democratic strength is indeed positively related to the number of social security schemes under bipartite or tripartite control, whereas social democracy is not related to this characteristic of welfare state regimes (see Table 7.1).[1]

Table 7.1 OLS regression, dependent variable = bi- and tripartism in social security administration, 1980

Variable name	I Estimated coefficient (beta)	II Estimated coefficient (beta)
1. LPS	0.15	
2. CDS	0.72	0.72
	(4.28, 0.0003)	(4.27, 0.0003)
R^2 (adj.)	0.51	0.52
F-test:		
H_0:	B1=0	B1=0
F =	0.83	18.20
Pr=	37.35%	00.05%

Note: numbers between brackets refer to significant t-statistics (first) and the probability that ($X >$ value of t) with X distributed as t(df) (second). Insignificant t-values are not reported.

Source: US Department of Health and Human Services (various years).

Estimating a similar model with union strength as an independent variable indicated its insignificance. In the present context this is interpreted to signify that as far as the administration of social security schemes is concerned it is Christian democracy that defines the co-operation between labour and capital (and the state). A speculation might be that unions, in turn, concentrate their efforts on economic bargaining in the market, an issue beyond the scope of this study. The most intriguing finding, however, came out of the analysis of the residuals. It reveals that France and the Netherlands had relatively large positive residuals, while Italy had a negative residual and Germany a modestly positive one. The case of France could perhaps be explained by the fact that Christian democracy (MRP), one of the major political forces of the fourth republic (1946–58), disappeared in the fifth republic. On the other hand, one might argue that Christian democracy is still present as one of the currents of the centre and centre-right of French politics (Irving 1979: 222–31). The data perhaps underestimate the strength of Christian democracy in France, given the inertia of institutional arrangements set in place in the first decade or so after the Second World War. Performing a brief counter-factual exercise by assuming that Christian democracy in France in 1980 had the momentum of the MRP in the 1950s, indeed exhibited a marked improvement of the model and reduced the positive residual of France considerably. A comparable manoeuvre, however, would not make sense with respect to the underestimation of the Netherlands. The explanation for this nation has to be sought in the system of pillarisation and consociationalism. The conclusion, taking into account these considerations, is that Christian democratic strength is associated with bi- or tripartism in the organisational structure of social security.

If one looks at the role of the state in the financing of the main social security systems, a mixed picture emerges. STATE in Table 7.2 is the average share of state financing in the schemes for unemployment and pensions.[2] Australia and New Zealand are the only nations in which the state in 1960 completely financed the unemployment and pension schemes. At the same time, it is clear that the role of the state in some of the Christian democratic nations was very modest in 1960, with Austria scoring only 0.09, Italy 0.12 and the Netherlands 0.16, whereas others score above average (Belgium, France). Looking at the share of the insured in 1960 one sees that Switzerland and the Netherlands score more than one standard deviation above average, indicating that in these nations the social security schemes were almost two-thirds financed by the contributions of the insured themselves. The Italian case is interesting to the extent that in 1960 employers financed 75 per cent of unemployment and pension benefits. Panel b of Table 7.2 shows that these distributions seem to be relatively stable over time, except that the state's involvement in France is much less in 1980 than in 1960, which brings this nation much more in line with the Christian democratic nations.

The expectation is reasonable that in nations where Christian democracy is strong the major schemes of social security are primarily formulated in such a way that the state's involvement is minimised. The bulk of the social security burden in the Christian democratic view ought to be carried by the employers and the insured. One way of measuring this is by taking the ratio of the share of employers and insured to the share of the state (Insured + Employer /State). Bivariate regressions did show a statistically significant effect of Christian democracy on this ratio, indicating that this movement does promote 'self-responsibility' in the financing of social security schemes. It must be stressed, however, that the data only expose the formal contribution shares as they are formulated in legislated social security laws. They are in no sense an indicator of the real financial burdens for the different categories. This is because where employers pay the bulk of social security contributions they are likely to shift the financial burdens to their employees via a lower paycheque, turning their contributions into a kind of deferred wage, whereas the state, of course, collects taxes.

Table 7.2 Financing of social security schemes (unemployment and pensions), shares of insured, employers and the state, 1960 (panel a) and 1980 (panel b) (descending rank order according to share of insured)

Country	Panel a (1960)			Country	Panel b (1980)		
	Insured	Employer	State		Insured	Employer	State
1. Switzerland	.66	.21	.14	1. Netherlands	.59	.25	.17 (2)
2. Netherlands	.60	.24	.16	2. Switzerland	.48	.44	.09 (1)
3. Austria	.45	.45	.09	3. Austria	.44	.46	.11 (3)
4. Sweden	.45	.00	.55	4. Japan	.42	.34	.25 (5)
5. Japan	.44	.44	.12	5. Germany	.40	.42	.18 (6)
6. Germany	.42	.41	.18	6. United Kingdom	.32	.47	.22 (8)
7. Norway	.40	.32	.29	7. Sweden	.28	.49	.24 (4)
8. United Kingdom	.38	.38	.25	8. Canada	.26	.21	.53 (13)
9. Finland	.33	.19	.48	9. United States	.26	.73	.02 (12)
10. Denmark	.30	.00	.71	10. France	.25	.60	.16 (16)
11. Belgium	.26	.28	.46	11. Belgium	.24	.25	.52 (11)
12. United States	.23	.71	.07	12. Norway	.22	.42	.37 (7)
13. Canada	.21	.21	.58	13. Italy	.19	.62	.20 (15)
14. Ireland	.14	.16	.71	14. Ireland	.17	.41	.43 (14)
15. Italy	.14	.75	.12	15. Finland	.11	.49	.41 (9)
16. France	.13	.28	.60	16. Denmark	.04	.05	.92 (10)
17. Australia	.00	.00	1.00	17. Australia	.00	.00	1.00 (17)
18. New Zealand	.00	.00	1.00	18. New Zealand	.00	.00	1.00 (18)
Average	.31	.28	.41	Average	.26	.37	.38
Standard deviation	.19	.22	.31	Standard deviation	.16	.21	.31

Note: numbers between brackets refer to rank order 1960.
Source: SSIB.

Social policy in Christian democratic nations can be expected to reproduce rather than overcome class and status differences. Benefits tend to be earnings-related rather than of the flat-rate type, so that they preserve rather than supersede social difference. One way of looking at the reproduction of status differentials is by studying benefit differentials, i.e. the ratio of the minimum benefit of a social insurance scheme to the maximum benefit (see Esping-Andersen 1990:69–78).

If one looks at the benefit structure of pensions (Table 7.3) it is clear that in 1960 there was a sharp difference between a group of nations with a

Table 7.3 Benefit structure and benefit inequality of pensions in 1960 and 1980 (descending rank order 1960 according to inequality or – in case of equality – according to highest replacement rate in 1960)

Country	Inequality		Minimum		Maximum	
	1960	*1980*	*1960*	*1980*	*1960*	*1980*
1. Germany	.81	.72	.26	.39	1.36	1.38
2. Austria	.79	.71	.42	.48	1.98	1.66
3. United States	.74	.77	.10	.15	.40	.63
4. Italy	.62	.76	.23	.31	.60	1.32
5. France	.59	.44	.19	.41	.46	.74
6. Switzerland	.55	.48	.12	.27	.26	.51
7. Belgium	.50	.48	.40	.55	.80	1.05
8. Japan	.39	.69	.13	.32	.22	1.05
9. New Zealand	.00	.00	.37	.45	.37	.45
10. Denmark	.00	.03	.33	.45	.33	.47
11. Netherlands	.00	.00	.33	.59	.33	.59
12. Finland	.00	.80	.29	.49	.29	2.50
13. Sweden	.00	.55	.28	.49	.28	1.07
14. Australia	.00	.00	.25	.35	.25	.35
15. United Kingdom	.00	.09	.24	.38	.24	.42
16. Norway	.00	.40	.22	.46	.22	.77
17. Canada	.00	.18	.20	.33	.20	.40
18. Ireland	.00	.08	.19	.33	.19	.36
Average	.28	.40	.25	.40	.49	.87
Standard deviation	.33	.31	.09	.11	.47	.57

Note: inequality is computed as 1 – (minimum/maximum).

Source: SSIB.

considerable inequality of benefits and a group of countries characterised by equality. Of the Christian democratic nations, only the Netherlands and Ireland fall within the latter group. As argued in the preceding chapter, the Netherlands adopted a flat-rate public pension scheme in the late 1950s and Ireland had a flat-rate retirement pension which was restricted to lower-paid employees until 1974 (Foster 1993:341). Although there is some reason to argue that benefit differentials are common in Christian democratic welfare states, the data for 1980 show a different picture. Certainly, the Christian democratic nations still had benefit differentials, but in 1980 they are joined by some of the Scandinavian countries as well. The reported benefit inequality in these nations is completely due to the very high maximum replacement rates in 1980. Definite conclusions with respect to benefit inequality of welfare state regimes are not warranted, however, because the data on replacement rates do not take into account income ceilings, private or occupational supplementary schemes and eligibility criteria such as work histories and means tests. Nevertheless, it is clear that in 1960 most Christian democratic nations had pension laws with inbuilt benefit differentials.

Another way of looking at the possible reproduction of status differentials is studying the fragmentation of welfare regimes in terms of the number of special schemes for distinct groups in society. Such fragmentation tells very little about benefit differentials, but may indicate the extent to which welfare state regimes attach importance to upholding the status of distinct occupational groups. The measure of fragmentation simply consists of the sum of special schemes within the major social security programmes. Because of a high probability of an outlier (Japan) a dummy variable for the outlier was entered into the regression equation which is reported in Table 7.4. The regression analysis shows that Christian democracy is indeed positively related to the fragmentation of social security schemes.[3]

The most interesting finding, however, came from the residual analysis. Whereas Germany and the Netherlands had small negative residuals, Italy had a notable positive residual, signifying that this nation's social security system is more fragmented than could be expected on the basis of the model. For this reason it is relevant to study the Italian welfare state and the role of Christian democracy in its development somewhat more closely.

ITALY: A CASE STUDY OF CHRISTIAN DEMOCRACY AND SOCIAL POLICY

In Italy the 1950s were characterised by political immobilism (see Chapter 4). However, this immobilism predominantly existed at the surface of party

Table 7.4 OLS regression, dependent variable = fragmentation in social security schemes in 1980

Variable name	I Estimated coefficient (beta)	II Estimated coefficient (beta)
1. DUMMY	0.69 (5.60, 0.00)	0.70 (5.59, 0.00)
2. LPS	0.13	
3. CDS	0.69 (5.55, 0.00)	0.68 (5.47, 0.00)
R^2 (adj.)	0.75	0.75
F-test:		
H_0:	B2=0	B1=B2=0
F =	1.21	25.44
Pr=	28.88%	0.00%
H_0:	B1=B3=0	
F =	25.90	
Pr=	0.00%	

Note: numbers between brackets refer to significant t-statistics (first) and the probability that (X > value of t) with X distributed as t(df) (second). Insignificant t-values are not reported.

Sources: Esping-Andersen (1990: 70, Table 3.1); US Department of Health and Human Services (various years) *Social Security Programs Throughout the World*.

politics. Simultaneously, Christian democracy had managed to build a new system of power in the state, establishing a new consensus in Italian society (Ginsborg 1990:181). It was the penetration of party, state and the semi-public sector by DC loyalists that came to characterise the welfare state in Italy.

Nevertheless, this pattern of state organisation was not simply the outcome of Christian democratic power politics. The state that Christian democracy inherited from the liberal and fascist period could already be identified as a centralised, inefficient, clientelist state, which had a disproportionate number of employees recruited from the south, and which was surrounded by a labyrinth of parallel bureaucracies of state corporations and other public agencies. These features were transplanted into the new republic and subsequently were modified and exploited by Christian democracy. They produced a peculiar form of latent corporatism (Donolo 1980). The doctrine of subsidiarity and comparable notions facilitated and sanctioned the assimilation of the parallel bureaucracies and public agencies (*enti pubblici*). And there was quite an array of agencies to absorb. In 1947, for instance, there existed already 841 of such agencies. The main sectors comprised, first of all, the railroads, post and telecommunications, as well as the state monopolies (tobacco, salt); second, the Istituto per la Ricostruzione Industriale (IRI, i.e. the state's nationalised industrial sector[4]), employing 216,000 people in 1948; third, the local governments; and fourth, the entire social welfare sector (Ginsborg 1990:150–1).

The *enti pubblici* of the welfare state have their origins in the fascist period. These institutions comprise the Istituto Nazionale della Previdenza Sociale (INPS) for old age, invalidity, unemployment, family allowances and tuberculosis; the Istituto Nazionale per le Assicurazioni contro gli Infortuni sul Lavoro (INAIL) for invalidity; and the Istituto Nazionale per l'Assicurazione contro le Malattie (INAM) for sickness. Fascism had accorded a preeminent position to social policy as an instrument of social consensus, parallel to its corporatist design (Paci 1989a:84; Ascoli 1984b:28). Fascism, however, had left the insurance bias of the Italian system intact and had given it a corporatist twirl. In spite of massive state intervention, the fascist strategy had been incapable of breaking the strength of Catholic action in the social assistance sector, a traditional bulwark of the church. In fact, the Lateran treaties of 1929 even implied a reinforcement of the control of Catholicism in this dominion (David 1984:189). The Italian republic inherited from fascism a social welfare system, which was characterised by a corporatist social security system, a para-statal organisation of social security administration and the predominant position of the Church in social assistance (Paci 1989a:85). In particular, the structuration of the administration of the welfare state through these *enti* prepared the road for the insertion of the welfare system into the emerging party and faction system of post-war Italian politics (Ascoli 1984b:29).

Immediately after the war social policy reform gained a prominent place on the political agenda (Ferrera 1984:36) and remained there during the entire post-war period. However, 'the history of social policy between 1945 and 1978 [the year of the establishment of the Servizio Sanitario Nazionale, SSN] has been a sequence of ambitious reform projects, tumultuous conflicts, delicate distributional compromises and incomplete (or distorted) achievements' (Ferrera 1993:233, my translation). In April 1947, for instance, a parliamentary commission was installed in order to prepare a reform of the social security system (Cherubini 1977:365–72; Ferrera 1993:233–46). A year later, but just before the new Constitution went into operation, this committee presented its report. In this way the government demonstrated its intention to recast profoundly the fascist heritage (Paci

1989a:85). The report's projected main innovations were: institutional centralisation, unification and, therefore, simplification, according to the suggestion that for every risk there should be only a single scheme; extension of social security to all employees and self-employed and their families for sickness, old age, invalidity, accident, and to all employees for unemployment; the introduction of a general old age pension system for employees, providing for a minimum pension to be complemented by private provisions; and the linking of benefits and income (Ferrera 1984:36–7, 1993:238; Paci 1989a:86). Perhaps not an Italian Beveridge plan, the blueprint would have implied a significant innovation of the highly fragmented and differentiated social security system of Italy (Ferrera 1984:37). 'Would have', because none of the proposals were implemented during the period of Christian democratic hegemony after the elections of 1948 (Cherubini 1977:372). Christian democracy, in the course of two legislatures, managed to live up to one principle with respect to reform: to give in as little and as late as possible and only when compelled by the logic of parliamentary majorities (Cherubini 1977:390). The difference between the Netherlands and Italy with respect to the introduction of more universal social policies can be contributed to the impossibility of Italian politics to follow the Dutch way of depoliticisation via a political alliance between reformist social Catholicism and the socialist left. As argued in Chapter 4, the coalition between Catholics and socialists (and communists) in Italy was short-lived and 'after the elections of 1948, with the arrival of polarised pluralism, universalism in social policy thus ceased to be (for a good fifteen years) an attractive political option for either the centre parties or the left' (Ferrera 1993:246, my translation). As a result, Italian Christian democracy started to defend and update the traditional system of social security.

The liberal and fascist particularist heritage of social policy was adopted by the centrist governments and made subordinate to the politics of consensus of Christian democracy in an attempt to substantiate and reinforce its middle-class support and to appease intraparty rivalry. Social policy improvements concerned extensions to small farmers, artisans, and shopkeepers and merchants (*commercianti*). The development of social security was largely incremental, and particularly the number of *enti* multiplied (Ascoli 1984b:31), i.e. a further fragmentation of the system through occupational differentiation. In contrast to Germany, in Italy Christian democracy hardly produced any social policy innovations. Just as the German Christian democrats successfully resisted allied attempts to break with the particularist social security tradition in Germany, Italian Christian democracy mobilised its resources to block universalist reforms and used the social security heritage to further its own power resources.

Italian social scientists have come to view the Italian welfare state as a peculiar mixture of particularism and clientelism (Ascoli 1984a; Ferrera 1984, 1993; Paci 1984, 1989a, 1989b). The particularism of the Italian system is first of all present at the institutional level where occupational status defines the granting of social rights and where there is a close link between performance and services or benefits (Paci 1989b:217). This particularism, however, is not only prevailing in the labyrinth of differentiated schemes and benefits, but also in the way in which social security is financed. In this system certain groups, especially public employees and the self-employed benefit disproportionally (Paci 1984:307). Pensions, however, are a peculiar case. Of the developed welfare states, Italy had (in 1980) the largest number of occupationally distinct public pension schemes in combination with the lowest spending on private pensions (about 2 per cent of total pension spending) (Esping-Andersen 1990:70). Even the Italian expert on pensions, Castellino (1976) found it difficult to construct an inventory of the numerous *enti*, institutions, *casse*, etc., that make up the maze of the pension system. 'To whom, for instance, must one turn', he complained, 'to get information about this "Social Security Fund for Supervisors of Bookshops in Railway Stations" that around 1960 counted . . . about 200 insured? (Castellino 1976: 10, my translation.)'

Selectivity, status reproduction and representation of sectoral interests do not necessarily lead to the distortion of impartial administrative principles. On the contrary, one might expect that interest representation and autonomy of control produce a particularist-meritocratic type of welfare state (Paci 1989b:219). However, the Italian welfare state is rather an assistential-clientelist type. It is the 'extensive clientelist character that the provision of services has taken on, in both its "corporate" and its "assistance" components' (Paci 1989b: 222), which makes the Italian welfare state peculiar.

Now, what is actually meant by clientelism? Here Walston's (1988:8) definition of interventionist state clientelism is adopted, precisely because it emphasises the role of state agencies in the political pathology of the Italian system. This type of clientelism is characterised by formal bureaucratic rule but allowing for 'personal interpretations' of these rules. Clientelism depends on failing public regulations that do not guarantee a distribution of resources according to rights. Under these conditions patrons assume their role as collectors and distributors of public resources. Two criteria need to be fulfilled for welfare clientelism to take effect. First, clientelism must concern a public resource to which – in principle – individual citizens have a right and equal access. Second, the actual distribution of resources on the basis of these rights contradicts official morality (Walston 1988:28). Clientelism with respect to the welfare state refers to the distribution of benefits and services based on an exchange between a patron in the welfare agency and a client under conditions of failing bureaucratic regime. The principles of distribution are political and personal and are not part of public morality and 'since the controllers and mediators of public resources are the members of the bureaucracy and/or of representative institutions both of whom depend upon and are in contact with the whole of society, this type of clientelism is a mass phenomenon' (Walston 1988:23). The patron gets repaid for his 'service' in money or in a remuneration which is political, where the political compensation can be a vote or a financial gift to the party.

This is the quintessence of the clientelism of the Italian welfare state. It clarifies the critical position of the public agencies in the system and conjectures their failure as a precondition for welfare clientelism. The welfare agencies were quickly recognised by Christian democrats as potentially rich sources for political power (Cazzola 1979). It was through the establishment and the diffusion of clientelist relationships that the DC created a power base in the semi-public welfare sector and at the same time reproduced and reinforced the traditional, insurance-based, particularist social system. Social security benefits in general have been important if not the main sources for clientelist exchange. This held for pensions in particular, simply because of the number of people involved (Ferrera 1984). Moreover, the welfare agencies were turned into an important 'job machine' where thousands of jobs were distributed to party loyalists. Both the *sottogoverno* and the Italian welfare state became large pools of political party patronage and party membership virtually became a necessary condition for effecting social rights and obtaining a job in the large public sector (Spotts and Wieser 1986:144).

The political history of Italy in the 1960s is primarily characterised by the transformation of the centrist formula of government of the 1950s and the gradual development towards and realisation of an alliance between Christian democracy and socialism. This realliance of political actors would in principle have been able to broaden the possibilities for social reform. In reality, however, this period witnessed an almost complete standstill of political efficacy. The political stalemate was only briefly broken by the unsurpassed mass mobilisation of students and workers in the late 1960s (see extensively Lumley 1990). At the same time, Christian democracy managed to expand its power outside the strictly electoral realm, whereas the socialists were seized by the power virus, too, and demanded (and collected) their share of resources. As a result, the particularist-clientelist welfare state was not only consolidated between 1950 and 1966, but in fact expanded rapidly (Ferrera 1993:246).

A number of political and social changes provided the pre-conditions for the opening to the left (*apertura alla sinistra*) on the side of the DC and the increasing legitimacy of the socialists as a party of government. At the local level (Florence, Milan, Genoa, Venice) experiments with the new centre-left formula had already proven their viability before 1962. At the international level, with a Democratic president in the White House, US resistance against the inclusion of the socialists declined and was transformed into support for the construction. The PSI, in its turn, renounced its anti-Atlanticism in early 1962, started to support NATO as a defensive alliance and thus removed a major obstacle for the centre-left experiment (Platt and Leonardi 1979).

An unanticipated yet vital change concerned the metamorphosis of Vatican policy towards Italian politics. Pope Pius XII, who had so often directly intervened in Italian politics, died in 1958 and was succeeded by John XXIII. The Church had been against any experiment with a coalition between Christian democracy and socialism and had not hesitated to make this point of view well known. The Church's position, however, was moderated in 1961. The opposition against the co-operation between Catholics and socialists withered away. The DC thus obtained more room to manoeuvre (Mammarella 1985:271) in its search for a workable and productive parliamentary majority. More important, however, was the fact that the ecclesiastic hierarchy decided to cancel the practice of continuous and direct intervention in political matters. The civic committees of Catholic action, that had been instrumental in channelling the Vatican political message to the people and that had constituted the bulwark of Catholic conservatism, gradually lost their political significance and almost instantaneously vanished (Ginsborg 1990:260). The Vatican urged Catholic action to concentrate on spiritual matters only. The publication of *Mater et Magister* (1961) marked a break in official Vatican ideology and further undermined conservative Catholic resistance against the *apertura*, because this encyclical contained all the elements of a more progressive social Catholicism, such as the acceptance of social policy and a call for social justice (Kogan 1983:166–7). The second Vatican council and the publication of *Pacem in Terris* (1963), with its stress on human rights, even facilitated the beginning of a *rapprochement* of Catholics and communists.

Another obstacle for the centre-left was removed when big business (Fiat, Pirelli, Olivetti) and the corporations of the public sector started to support the idea of Christian–socialist co-operation (Ginsborg 1990:264). Planning at the national level was thought to be in their economic interest and the incorporation of socialists in the government was expected to have a moderating effect on labour unrest. Confindustria, however, opposed a possible realliance at the political level vehemently, for a centre-left government threatened to nationalise the electric power industries, whose interests it in fact mainly represented. Christian democrats supported the plan for nationalisation also because of the expected political effect of weakening Confindustria, which since the second half of the 1950s had started to back the liberals politically and financially (Kogan 1983:175).

There were three distinctive reformist forces actively engaged in the construction of the centre-left alliance (Ginsborg 1990:265–67). There were those within the DC and outside the party who represented social Catholic ideas most clearly. They opted for social and political corrections of the failure of the market, especially with respect to the southern question, agriculture, and the large scale drift from the land and the accompanying, uncontrolled urbanisation. Such reforms would also have to serve the purpose of increasing the efficiency of the state bureaucracies and diminishing corruption. The socialists (and the communists) opted for structural reforms in agriculture, education, and construction. Substantial alterations of the structure were to facilitate the transition towards socialism. Rather than to correct the market system, these forces opted for its transformation. Finally, there were those within the Christian democratic movement, who were most interested in keeping the unity of the party and who wanted to use reforms strategically for power maintenance.

The first centre-left government (1962) consisted of the DC, the republicans and the social democrats, and still excluded the socialists. The government presented an extensive reform programme (Mammarella 1985:291–2; Kogan 1983:172), of which the main elements were the nationalisation of the electric power industry, school reform, agricultural innovation (abolition of the sharecropping phenomenon), urban reforms, and the installment of regional governments for which the Constitution had already made provisions. The socialists, hampered by the anarcho-syndicalists (Kogan 1983:173), abstained rather than support the government and made their future support contingent upon the successful nationalisation of the electric power industry, the reform of the schools and the creation of regions with substantial executive authority.

The government stayed in power for about a year and was to a certain extent effective in carrying out some of the proposals (Mammarella 1985:293), in spite of unfavourable conditions such as the election of the rightist and anti-reformist Christian democrat, Antonio Segni, as president of the republic, and the commotion within business circles and the press that predicted economic catastrophe. The five monopolies of the electric power industry were united under state control in the Ente Nazionale di Energia Elettrica (ENEL), while substantial financial compensations were offered. The economic motives for nationalisation pertained to the stabilisation of prices, the control over investments and the development of the south (Kogan 1983:175). The political rationale was to destroy the hard core of conservative resistance against reforms, concentrated in this part of the monopoly sector of Italian capitalism. The creation of the ENEL was immediately used by the DC to enlarge its influence by stationing party members in the top positions of the ENEL. The 'unequal' distribution of posts, however, contributed to the tensions between the DC and the PSI (Kogan 1983:177).

The reformist zeal, although still successful with regard to education, was interrupted by increasing economic problems, which were caused partly by scarcity of labour power and rising labour costs and partly by political sabotage through investment strikes. Within the DC ground was lost for reformism and the 'minimalists' argued that the DC risked losing the backing of the *classe media*. Both the introduction of the regional governments (which would have allowed the socialists and communists to govern the 'red belt' of Italy) and urban planning perished as a result of the 'minimalist' power play.

The first centre-left experiment, in spite of its moderateness, had aroused resistance from many sides. The right accused the Christian democrats of undermining traditional values (for instance private property), whereas the communists denounced the socialists for betraying the working class by supporting the DC. The elections of 1963 put DC support for the first time under the 40 per cent (38.3), while the PSI lost slightly, too. Both the liberals and the communists gained in strength. These results were taken as a sign that the first experiment had failed. A return to centrism, however, had become difficult, if not impossible and a renovation of the centre-left formula by including the socialists in government remained the only feasible solution.

The centre-left governments under Aldo Moro (1963–8) – with direct socialist participation – retained a rhetoric of reformist commitment, but gradually returned to an almost complete immobilism in the domain of social policy in practice. The socialists lost a part of their left wing as a result of government participation (1964), but temporarily reunited with the social democrats (1966). Economic conditions declined (inflation, unemployment) which led to Moro's strategy of *due tempi*: stabilisation first, reforms later (Ginsborg 1990:377). The socialists consented to the postponement of reforms as the best guarantee to stay in power and to provide a counter-weight against reactionary forces. The latter had become urgent since the coalition and, in fact, Italian democracy were threatened by right wing attempts to prepare a *colpo di stato* under the leadership of the head of the para-military *Carabinieri*.

Few reforms, then, were carried out and the ones that could pass the barrier of immobilism were formulated in such a way that their potential was mitigated. The overall achievements of the period of centre-left coalitions was substandard. The nationalisation of the electric power industry had been carried out, but was accompanied by a compensation that allowed the former monopolies to maintain much of their immense financial power. The absence of necessary urban planning did not only lead to unconstrained and chaotic expansion of major cities, but was also largely responsible for the disastrous effects of the floods of Florence and Venice in 1966. Legislation in general had been contradictory and was usually delayed and finally rendered ineffective. The extension of compulsory primary education had indeed been an accomplishment, but secondary and higher education had been left untouched. A readjustment of the tax system had not even been attempted and the rationalisation of the bureaucracy, although hotly debated, had not been able to claim a firm place on the political agenda. The transfer of power to the regions was blocked and had to wait until the early 1970s before it could be effected. In terms of the struggle between the three currents of reformism, the 'minimalist' power-searching direction had therefore clearly won the battle.

The isolation of the gradualist reformers within Christian democracy and the socialist movement, the refusal of the communists to support gradual change, the transformation of socialist power politics and the incorporation of the socialists into the system of clientelist distribution of power, the incapacity of large industries to counter-balance Confindustria and the financial power of the former monopolies, and the economic sabotage of industry (capital flight, investment strike), were the elements that explain the incapacity to perform a more coherent and effective social and political correction of capitalism in Italy. Nevertheless, the fate of Christian democracy as the hegemonic actor in Italian politics was linked with the success of the minimalist strategy. On the one hand, minimalism in social policy initially inhibited clear and efficacious reforms, but on the other hand led to a further institutionalisation of the political power of the DC and to the reproduction of the traditional structure of social policy. The semi-public sector was made instrumental for power accumulation and faction politics. The consequence was that its initial efficiency was completely eroded by the appointment of politicians who were not selected on the basis of their managerial competence so that political decisions not only came to regulate careers but also investments (Bianchi 1987:279), whereas the absence of bureaucratic reform led to a paralysis of public administration (Ginsborg 1990:286).

Special attention should be paid to the systematic refinement – especially in the south – of the system of clientelism, which distorted the actual attempts to develop the region. This renewed clientelism was particularly beneficial to a new generation of Christian democratic leaders, who – affiliated with leaders of the older generation – prepared their careers on the national level. Four resources were exploited for the accumulation of power: the construction boom, the southern development fund, the financial resources of the local *enti* and those funds that derived immediately from the national government and national legislation. As argued, pensions have been a major currency in clientelist exchanges, as exemplified by their distorted distribution between the north and south in comparison with the number of inhabitants of the respective regions. In 1975 the southern region received approximately twice the amount of pensions that it should have received on the basis of its labour force (Ginsborg 1990:290).

With respect to social policy reforms, it has to be stressed that under the conditions of the *apertura*, Christian democracy came up with few initiatives. Instead, a new plan was launched by the Consiglio Nazionale dell'Economia e del Lavoro (CNEL) to reform the structure of the particularist-clientelist welfare state. The main proposals concerned the introduction of a basic, non-particularist, flat-rate, unconditional and national pension system as well as an extension of health services to the entire population as the initiation of a national health system financed by the state. The CNEL, in effect, proposed to introduce Scandinavian-type welfare arrangements (Ferrera 1993:248). On the one hand, the conditions in the 1960s for introducing universalism in the Italian system appeared more favourable than in the early years after the war. Piecemeal extensions of social rights already appeared to inaugurate universalism, whereas the Italian Constitution, in fact, guaranteed some social rights on the basis of citizenship. Universalism, moreover, had come to symbolise progressive politics more generally. The economic growth of the 1960s not only nourished rising expectations on the part of previously excluded groups, but could also weaken the resistance of particularist interests to the extent that the extra financial burdens would not have to be carried by these groups. Most importantly, universalism appeared to provide the possible cement for the centre-left coalition, very much similar to the Dutch experience of the 1950s, and promised to be an effective political instrument for political integration and democratic consolidation (Ferrera 1993:248–51).

This ambitious reform – as in the other areas described above – was blocked in several respects. Although a social pension was introduced in the late 1960s as a step towards a universal system, the original proposal of the CNEL was never completed, and the labyrinth of occupationally distinct pensions not only remained unchallenged, but was, in fact, reinforced and improved. This turned the social pension into a last and minimal resort for aged citizens without accumulated pension rights and reinforced the 'Balcanisation' of the Italian pension system (Ferrera 1993:252).

The health reform was more successful to the extent that – although at a slow pace – a general health insurance was introduced with universal coverage that replaced the former, highly differentiated system. The diverging paths of the pension reform and the health reform can by and large be explained by a combination of historical legacies, ideological, constitutional and institutional conflicts, varying coalitions between particularist interests, and the logic of parliamentary politics that worked in different directions (Ferrera 1993:248–72).

As pointed out, the Italian Constitution had already made a distinction between social rights attached to citizenship (as in the case of health) and social rights attached to performance on the labour market (as in the case of pensions). This was also reflected in the distinction in the Italian welfare system between social assistance (*assistenza sociale*) and social security (*previdenza sociale*). In fact, article 32 of the Italian Constitution defines health as a basic, individual right and health care as a public duty (Bernardi-Schenkluhn 1992:428; Ferrera 1993:249), which explains the uninterrupted debate on how to implement this universalism of the Constitution. The interesting fact is that the Italian left was not in favour of universalism in the pension scheme because it considered pensions as a workers' right, a kind of deferred wage, rather than as a citizenship right. Accordingly, the left defended the continuing distinction between social assistance and social security, whereas the Christian democrats were in favour of an extension of pension rights, while leaving the occupational rights intact. With respect to health, however, both the left and the centre had little trouble in accepting some form of universalism, although the DC had an interest in maintaining the system as it was, because of its strong position of power in this sector.

In the struggle over greater regional autonomy, the institution of a national health service, controlled by the central state, but executed at the local level, appeared to provide a compromise that not only satisfied the regions' striving after more competence, but also gave the socialists an opportunity to increase their power in the Italian welfare state at the cost of the Christian democrats who defended their established positions in the health sector. In fact, the local organisations that were to control the health system (Unità Socio-sanitarie locali, USL) 'were immediately colonised by the political parties, who filled them with individuals with little managerial competence, expertise, or understanding of cost controls, but a voracious appetite for the exercise of political patronage in purchasing and job-creation'

(Hine 1993:249). Comparable opportunities did not exist in the field of the pension system, where positions were long taken and firmly established. The vested interests in the differentiated pension system defended their positions, since they would clearly lose if the occupational logic of the system with its distinct privileges for specific groups was to be transformed into a universal system without such distinctions. The reason for these divergent developments is found in the favourable economic conditions (e.g. near full employment) of the late 1950s and 1960s which caused an accumulation of resources in the pension funds. This condition was conspicuously absent in the realm of health services, where expenditure rose faster than revenue. In fact, the unification of health care provided the opportunity to shift the burden of deficit spending on to the state (Ferrera 1993:260). As a result, a variety of particularist interests united to defend the traditional pension system and effectively blocked the envisioned reform (see also Castellino 1976), whereas precisely the opposite happened with respect to the health system.

The compromise on pensions in the late 1960s introduced the social pension as the remnant of universalism, but at the same time sanctioned existing privileges and differentiations, satisfying most interests, but reinforcing 'one of the most chaotic and financially unbalanced pension systems of the West' (Ferrera 1993:264, my translation). It is unlikely, however, that the introduction of a national, universal pension system would have guaranteed a less costly and squandering system, as the experience with the universal health system and its open-ended financial basis perhaps indicates (see Hine 1993:249–51). The USL have large deficits and public health expenditure has increased by an average of 16 per cent per year between 1980 and 1987 (Bernardi-Schenkluhn 1992:465).

What was the role of Christian democracy in the health reform? The DC, in fact, managed to delay the introduction of the SSN until 1978, but could not block it. The medical estate, traditionally an adherent of Christian democracy, feared nationalisation in general. The introduction of a national health service, therefore, involved a risk of declining support for the DC. More important, however, was that the health reform threatened the established Christian democratic power resources in this part of the *sottogoverno*, particularly because the new health system was to be decentralised, of which the effects were incalculable. The DC then redefined the laws time and again to serve its own interests. These attempts eventually failed as a result of the successful introduction of regional governments in the 1970s (see Leonardi, Manetti and Putnam 1987; Putnam 1993), which accorded a strong incentive to the health reform and at the same time broke the anti-reformist resistance (Ferrera 1993:268–9).

It was eventually the extra-parliamentary pressure of societal forces, the pressure from the organisations affiliated with the DC and a range of institutional conditions, which temporarily forced the Christian democratic minimalists to take action in the field of social policy. It was only in 1969 that – under pressure from the mass mobilisation of the labour movement – the pension system was altered, although not transformed. In 1968 the financing and administration of hospitals was reformed, while the transfer of authority to the regions caused the introduction of the national health service. The health reform can be seen as a major setback to Christian democratic social policy to the extent that this revision transcended the traditional, particularist and differentiated welfare system. The pension reform, however, was a success of Christian democratic politics, since it effectively obstructed a universal transformation and reinforced extreme particularism and differentiation.

Other political events, such as the outcome of the referenda on divorce law and abortion, also meant a defeat for traditional Catholicism and for the DC. However, neither these political defeats nor the bad results of the elections of 1975, where the support for the DC dropped to 35.5 per cent, decisively reduced its power. Unlike Christian democracy in Germany, the DC was much less sensitive to electoral fluctuations, partly because the movement managed to control electoral outcomes to some extent through its central position in the web of clientelist exchanges. In a recent paper, Sidney Tarrow (1990) has posed the question why Christian democracy in Italy managed to survive a series of crises that in other nations most likely would have decomposed a political movement completely. The clue for the tenacity of Christian democratic power, for its immense capacity for survival even under conditions of serious challenges, lay in the fact that the movement was 'softly hegemonic'. It never dominated society completely and its power was based on a variety of resources, such as the Catholic sub-culture, cross-class support, political patronage, anti-communism, American support and the establishment of independent power moments in the para-statal organisations and the welfare state. Soft hegemony greatly enhanced the capacity to adapt. 'Hard' hegemony would have excluded a flexible response to changing conditions as it did in Germany in the wake of the 1957 pension reform and the absolute majority won in the same year. Christian democracy's strength and survival depended on the movement's ability to nourish a plurality of power resources, especially in the *sottogoverno*, in the course of continuous crises. Since the traditional, insurance-based system inherited from fascism, with its distinction between social assistance and social security was already fairly close to what Christian democrats preferred, an activist reform policy was not necessary. On the contrary, Christian democracy in Italy has tried to defend the particularist-clientelist welfare state against the universalist, reformist zeal of the left, as a result of which fragmentation was reproduced and reinforced.

The conclusion on the Italian welfare state and the role of Christian democracy must be one of ambiguity. The ambiguity stems from the combination of unparalleled power mobilisation at the level of state apparatuses and para-statal agencies and an almost paralysing constellation of power on the governmental level. The development of the Italian welfare state seems to have been more an effect of the incapacity to act and to reform than the result of intentional intervention. The restoration of the traditional framework of social policy with its latent corporatism as inherited from fascism and the extreme fragmentation can be interpreted against this background. The dominance of the minimalist reformist strategy was mainly an attempt to secure Christian democratic unity and hegemony under conditions of increasing competition from the socialists and the communists.

CROSS-NATIONAL COMPARISONS II: WELFARE STATES AND THE FAMILY

As argued in the context of the transfer-bias of welfare state regimes (Chapter 6), Christian democracy appears to be particularly beneficial to families if one looks at the interplay of the tax, wage and benefits system. In addition, the thesis that Christian democratic welfare states discourage labour market participation of women was found to be plausible. Christian democrats attach special importance to traditional family structures when they implement social policies. It makes sense, therefore, to elaborate further the possible role of Christian democracy in configuring the relationship between state, market and family so as to reinforce family structures. If these hypotheses are valid, the effects of Christian democratic policies should still be discernable in the 1970s and 1980s and the focus of the analyses is therefore on this period.[5]

The cash transfers to families as a percentage of gross earnings at the level of an average production worker (APW) are a first indicator to look at. Table 7.5 demonstrates that the gross wage of an average married production worker, whose spouse does not receive a salary, consisted in considerable part of transfers in Austria, France, Italy and Belgium. These are the nations all scoring more than (or close to) one standard deviation above average. Germany and the Netherlands, as well as Sweden and New Zealand are also above average, whereas the majority of the Anglo-Saxon

Table 7.5 Cash transfers as a percentage of gross earnings of a married couple with two children at the level of an average production worker, 1972–6 (descending rank order)

Country	%1972–6
1. Belgium	13.3
2. Italy	10.7
3. France	10.5
4. Austria	8.9
5. Sweden	7.3
6. Netherlands	6.9
7. Germany	6.0[a]
8. New Zealand	6.0
9. Norway	5.1
10. Denmark	4.9
11. Switzerland	4.1
12. Finland	3.7
13. Canada	3.6
14. United Kingdom	2.3
15. Ireland	2.2
16. Australia	1.9
17. Japan	0.0
18. United States	0.0
Average	5.4
Standard deviation	3.7

Note: [a] Only 1975 and 1976.

Source: OECD (1978: 98, Table 8).

countries are considerably below average. This gives some more support to the hypothesis that the structure of Christian democratic welfare states is characterised by a transfer-bias and that especially families with children tend to benefit from this in terms of cash transfers.

To have a closer look at the family-bias in the social systems of OECD nations it makes sense to study again the differences in disposable income between various household compositions, because disposable income is the income that remains when tax and social security contributions have been paid and transfers have been received. Table 7.6 gives disposable income as a percentage of gross earnings at the level of an APW in 1978, according to different household compositions. Looking at the first column of Table 7.6 it is clear that the disposable income for singles as a percentage of gross earnings in the Scandinavian countries is comparatively low. Germany and

Table 7.6 Disposable income as a percentage of gross earnings at the level of an average production worker in 1978, selected household compositions

Column:	1	2	3	4	5
Household composition:					
Number of adults	1	2	2	2	2
Number of incomes	1	1	2	1	2
Number of children	0	0	0	2	2
Country					
Australia	78	84	81	87	83
Austria	76	78	78	93	87
Belgium	74	75	72	90	82
Canada	79	83	81	91	87
Denmark	61	67	64	71	66
Finland	68	71	71	80	77
France	71	86	83	98	89
Germany	67	74	70	79	73
Ireland	72	79	71	84	75
Italy	83	86	84	91	87
Japan	85	87	86	90	88
Netherlands	65	67	66	75	71
New Zealand	72	74	75	80	77
Norway	68	74	70	80	75
Sweden	64	67	67	75	73
Switzerland	78	81	77	86	80
United Kingdom	69	73	75	81	80
United States	75	79	73	82	76
Average	73.1	76.9	74.7	84.1	79.2
Standard deviation	6.9	6.7	6.5	7.2	6.7

Source: OECD (1980: 13–22, Tables 32–6).

the Netherlands score relatively low as well (67 and 65 per cent respectively), i.e. about a standard deviation below average. Comparing the first and the second column shows that in all nations disposable income for a one-earner couple without children as a proportion of gross earnings is higher than for singles. A remarkable result appears when one compares the first and the third column, i.e. disposable income of a single and a two-earner married couple without children. In most nations the disposable income of the latter as a percentage of gross earnings is higher than for singles, except in Belgium, Ireland and Switzerland. These nations, then, appear to disfavour household compositions where both spouses earn an income. In addition – comparing columns 2 and 3 – one notices that in most nations disposable income as a percentage of gross earning for a two-earner married couple without children is lower than for a comparable couple where only one income is earned. However, in some nations (Austria, Finland and Sweden) there is no difference, whereas in New Zealand and in the United Kingdom disposable income for a two-earner married couple as a percentage of gross earnings is actually higher than in the one-earner case. Furthermore, it is clear (from column 4) that disposable income is highest for a one-earner married couple with children, with France scoring an exceptional 98 per cent of gross earnings for a one-earner married couple with children, Austria 93 per cent, Italy 91 per cent and Belgium 90 per cent of gross earnings. At the same time, this is not exclusively a Christian democratic attribute, with Canada scoring 91 per cent, Japan 90 per cent, the Netherlands 75 per cent and Germany 79 per cent. Finally, all nations appear to disfavour paid work for women with children (comparing columns 4 and 5).

Table 7.7 gives more detailed information on the relative position of various households in the tax–benefit structure of a welfare state. The first column of Table 7.7 shows the increase in disposable income (as a percentage of the disposable income of a single man) as the household composition changes from a single man to marriage without children, where the wife has no income. It reveals that in Germany the positive change is the largest (10.5 per cent), immediately followed by Denmark (9.8 per cent) and Ireland (9.7 per cent). The second column shows the increase in disposable income (as a percentage of the disposable income of a single man) as the household composition changes from a single man to marriage with two children, where the wife has no income. All nations score positively, indicating that all tax–benefit systems do favour families with children. Austria (22.4 per cent), Belgium (21.6 per cent) and France (21 per cent) – being one standard deviation above average – do so disproportionally, whereas Germany, Finland, Norway and Sweden are above average as well. Italy is the one Christian democratic nation that does not appear to favour families with children very strongly and is, with 9.6 per cent, more in line with Japan and the United States.

Column 3 displays the effect (as a percentage of disposable income of a two-person household where the wife has no income) on disposable income as the household composition moves from a one- to a two-income household without children. What is remarkable is that in most nations the effect

Table 7.7 Percentage change in disposable income as percentage of
gross earnings, moving from one household composition to another, at
the level of an average production worker in 1978

Column: Country	1	2	3	4	5	6
Australia	7.69	11.54	-3.57	-4.60	6.41	5.13
Austria	2.63	22.37	0.00	-6.45	14.47	7.19
Belgium	1.35	21.62	-4.00	-8.89	10.81	10.81
Canada	5.06	15.19	-2.41	-4.40	10.13	5.06
Denmark	9.84	16.39	-4.48	-7.04	8.20	8.19
Finland	4.41	17.65	0.00	-3.75	13.24	4.41
France	6.17	20.99	-3.49	-9.18	9.88	11.11
Germany	10.45	17.91	-5.41	-7.57	8.96	8.95
Ireland	9.72	16.67	-10.13	-10.71	4.17	12.50
Italy	3.61	9.64	-2.33	-4.40	4.82	4.82
Japan	2.35	5.88	-1.55	-2.22	3.53	2.35
Netherlands	3.08	15.38	-1.49	-5.33	9.23	6.15
New Zealand	2.78	11.11	1.35	-3.75	6.94	4.17
Norway	8.82	17.65	-5.41	-6.25	10.29	7.36
Sweden	4.69	17.19	0.00	-2.67	14.06	3.13
Switzerland	3.85	10.26	-4.94	-6.98	2.56	7.70
United Kingdom	5.80	17.39	2.74	-1.23	15.94	1.45
United States	5.33	9.33	-7.59	-7.32	1.33	8.00
Average	5.42	15.23	-2.93	-5.71	8.61	6.62
Standard deviation	2.81	4.63	3.21	2.56	4.26	3.08

Source: OECD (1980: 13-22, Tables 32-6).

is negative, that the largest negative effect takes place in Ireland (-10.1 per cent) and that New Zealand and Britain show a moderately positive effect. In column 4 – the most relevant for the present purposes – the same effect is presented for the case of moving from a family with two children where the wife does not have an income to the situation where she does (as a percentage of the disposable income of a two-child, one-earner family). The negative effect is largest in Belgium, France and Ireland (all one standard deviation under average), while Austria, Germany and Switzerland score above average, too, as do Denmark, Norway and the United States.

One could also look – as in column 5 – at the 'jump' from a single household to a situation where the household consists of two children and both spouses are earning an income. As can be expected, there is an increase in all nations of disposable income (as a percentage of the disposable income of a single man), with Austria, Finland, Sweden and the United Kingdom clearly in the top. The changes are, however, less dramatic than in the case of the increase in disposable income (as a percentage of the disposable income of a single man) as the household composition changes from a single man to marriage with two children, where the wife has no income. To give an idea of the effect of the fact that a married wife earns an income, too, the difference between column 2 and column 5 is displayed in column 6 of Table 7.7. The smaller the number the less difference it makes whether a married wife with children earns an income or not in terms of disposable income. The larger the number, the more difference it makes and the less disposable income as a percentage of a single man remains. This number, then, can be interpreted as the relative disadvantaging of women with children as a result of the tax-benefit structure of a welfare regime. Again, the finding is that the Belgian, French and Irish welfare states appear to be especially disadvantageous for married women, in particular when they have children. Austria, Denmark, Germany, Norway, Switzerland and the United States score relatively high, too. Italy and the Netherlands are the Christian democratic countries that do not appear to disadvantage women (or benefit the family) in this sense.

Table 7.8 OLS regression, dependent variable = absolute values of column 4, Table 7.7

Variable name	Estimated coefficient (beta)
1. LPS	−0.38
	(1.96, 0.03)
2 CDS	0.49
	(2.53, 0.01)
R^2 (adj.)	0.37
F-test:	
H_0:	B1=B2=0
F =	5.38
Pr=	1.64%

Note: numbers between brackets refer to significant t-statistics (first) and the probability that (X > value of t) with X distributed as t(df) (second).

Source: Table 7.7, column 4.

A look at Table 7.8, which makes use of the information from Table 7.7 (column 4), shows that both the strength of the left and of Christian democracy are related to the effect on disposable income of a working wife with two children, but in different directions. Christian democracy appears to enhance the negative impact on total disposable income when a married mother of two children enters the labour market, while the variable representing left strength tends to diminish this effect.[6] The information from the residuals showed that the nations of interest all had negative residuals, which in this case indicates that in these countries the negative impact of Christian democracy and the positive impact of the left variable was less than anticipated.

8 Social capitalism and Christian democracy

SIMILARITIES AND DIFFERENCES: FINDINGS

The cross-national comparisons and the German case study (Chapter 5) clarified not only the extent to which social democracy and Christian democracy were functional equivalents with respect to social spending, but also how this functional equivalence came about. The findings of the quantitative analyses, that the competition or interaction between social democracy and Christian democracy particularly encouraged spending and that Germany had a disproportionly high level of pension spending, could be understood better in the context of the political struggles over social policy reforms in Germany. The German case shows that Christian democracy was successful in its attempt to uphold the traditional system of social security and that the 1957 pension reform was, in fact, the conclusion of a long political struggle against forces opting for a more universal, Beveridge type of welfare state. This means that in terms of social spending the social democratic and Christian democratic welfare states were not dissimilar, although comparable levels of spending perhaps camouflaged real qualitative differences.

However, going beyond the simple indicator of social spending and looking at more qualitative features of welfare states, such as coverage ratios and replacement rates, Christian democratic welfare states did not emerge as particularly distinctive regimes either, as the analyses in Chapter 6 demonstrated. With respect to spending, coverage and replacement, social democracy and Christian democracy still appear to be functional equivalents. And again, the competition between these movements had a positive effect on the quality of welfare state regimes in this sense.

The Dutch case study, however, documents that political competition takes various forms and results in dissimilar outcomes. In the Netherlands the 'social policy race' between social democracy and Christian democracy was qualitatively different from the competition between the SPD and the CDU/CSU in Germany. The coalition between the KVP and the PvdA explained why the Dutch welfare state came to be characterised by a mixture of universalism, particularism and benefit differentiation. The pension scheme, for instance, was defined as a universal flat-rate programme, whereas the replacement rates of the unemployment insurance were differentiated according to position in the household. The Catholic interest in such differentiation was explained by the fact that benefits were to replace the income of a family via the head of the household, under the assumption that women would not enter the labour market. The Dutch welfare system became a 'breadwinner' system *par excellence*.

Moreover, it was the resistance of employers, Christian democracy and the Catholic unions that effectively blocked a universalist reform of the entire social system in the Netherlands. The relationship between confessional and social democratic forces took another shape when the Catholics allied with the liberals. Competition between Catholicism and social democracy in opposition, however, inhibited the more conservative stance in social policy that the CDU in Germany gradually took. And the expansion of the Dutch welfare state took place when social democracy did not assume any role at the level of government in the 1960s. Passive yet generous social policies became a means to safeguard the support of the Catholic working class and to ease the social costs of economic reconstruction in the 1960s.

The Dutch welfare state became a prototypical, transfer-oriented, passive welfare state. Further cross-national comparisons indicate that this transfer-orientation is a general (despite variations) and distinctive characteristic of Christian democratic welfare state regimes. Not only were these regimes highly oriented towards replacing incomes rather than protecting or creating jobs (as their cash-benefit bias indicated), but they also strongly privileged the traditional family structure through their tax–benefit policies. These differences were found to have a considerable impact on labour market participation, especially on the opportunities for women to enter the labour market. The power of Christian democracy has been a major obstacle to the economic emancipation of women. The distinctiveness of Christian democratic welfare states, therefore, did not appear when examining variations in social spending and studying slightly more detailed data on coverage and replacement. The effect of the power of the movement on the family-bias of welfare state regimes and on the labour force participation of women, however, did distinguish Christian democratic regimes clearly from the social democratic type.

The final question that was addressed (in Chapter 7) was whether and to what extent Christian democracy fosters a distinctive welfare state structure. The Dutch case study reveals that Christian democrats appeared to attach special value to semi-public control over major social security schemes and that this was virtually the only political issue that weakened the consensus between social democracy and Christian democracy in this nation. It seems plausible that there was a noticeable impact of Christian democracy on the structure of social security, particularly when looking at the organisation, financing and administration of major schemes. The Christian democratic movement appeared to favour 'self-responsibility' in both administration and financing. In other words, Christian democratic politics was not directed at politicising the field of social policy, but rather – so to speak – attempted to minimalise the state's control over the administration and execution of policies. Moreover, status reproduction via earnings-related social insurance rather than equality through universal flat-rate systems seems to belong to the typical Christian democratic package of welfare policies. Status reproduction was also found to be strongly related to the power of Christian democracy when examining the differentiation of social security schemes according to occupational status.

The Italian case explains one peculiar way in which Christian democracy influenced these characteristics of welfare state regimes. The political history of social policy reforms in Italy is in some aspects similar to, but in other respects quite different from, the evolution of the welfare state in Germany and the Netherlands. In Italy, too, the immediate post-war period witnessed an attempt to reform the particularist, highly fragmented and differentiated welfare arrangements inherited by fascism, according to designs similar to the Beveridge plan. As in Germany, the reform failed under conditions of a political constellation that excluded a possibly fruitful co-operation between reform-minded social and Christian democrats. As a result of the failed reform and the particular Italian conditions, where Christian democracy not only faced the competition of social democracy but of a strong communist movement, too, the fragmentation, status reproduction and differentiation of the traditional structures of social policy were reproduced and reinforced.

The Italian case demonstrates that the competition between Christian democracy and the communist movement and the resulting immobilism of parliamentary politics turned social policy even more into a central instrument of power mobilisation and accumulation than was the case in the Netherlands or Germany. The Italian welfare state remained highly fragmented in the course of the struggles over reforms. The particularity of the Italian welfare state lies in the combination of two factors: the reinforcement of fragmented particularism in social policy and the intensification of clientelism as a form of power maintenance, which is especially clear when looking at Italy's chaotic pension system. The welfare state became subject to clientelist and factionalised party politics and was gradually integrated into the power struggle of the *sottogoverno*, which, in effect, tended to reinforce fragmented particularism even more. The universalism of the national health service, on the other hand, was the effect of a peculiar and highly complex sequence of events under conditions that favoured health reform but frustrated the pension reform. Although Christian democracy managed to postpone the health reform, it was incapable of avoiding its final implementation. The conclusion is that fragmentation, status reproduction and benefit differentiation are characteristics of Christian democratic welfare states, but that the degree of fragmentation and differentiation of the Italian welfare state can only be explained with reference to the particular political history of this nation.

SOCIAL CAPITALISM AND THE CHRISTIAN DEMOCRATIC PROJECT: AN EXPLANATION

The conclusion is that there is – despite variations – a core of social policies that is distinctively Christian democratic. This core will be defined as *social capitalism*. This finding further substantiates the thesis that Christian democratic parties have used their dominant position of power to pursue a specific political project through public policy (Pempel 1990; see Chapters 3 and 4). This model of social capitalism significantly and systematically differs from both the liberal and the social democratic conceptions of social citizenship, although real differences between social democratic and Christian democratic welfare state regimes are concealed behind a veil of comparable levels of social spending.

The argument to be pursued here and in the following chapters is that social capitalism is intimately affiliated with the European tradition of social Catholicism and comprises one of the main 'little traditions' of Roman Catholicism as opposed to the 'grand tradition' of the established hierarchy of the Church. The claim is that there is a distinctive Catholic path to welfare capitalism. Although it seems feasible to defend this generalisation of Catholic idiosyncrasy with respect to welfare statism, the empirical finding was that there is nevertheless considerable variation in social policy performance among those nations of continental Europe where Christian democracy has been crucial for the shaping of the configuration of market, state and family. This variation was anticipated in the discussion of Christian democracy (Chapter 2) and the empirical analyses indicate that Christian democracy is indeed first and foremost characterised by an unremitting endeavour to realise compromises between possibly opposed societal interests and that the political identity of national Christian democratic movements varies according to the structuring of these interests under disparate historical conditions. Therefore, the actual social policies pursued by Christian democratic movements were found to be contingent upon, on the one hand, the balance of power within the movement and – as far as the movement mirrors society – within the national community, and on the other hand, upon the structuring of power relations and coalitions within the political system in which the movements operate. As a result, competition between political forces has had diverging consequences across political contexts. In short, there is an association between Catholicism and welfare capitalism, between Christian democracy and social capitalism. The relation is not a simple linear association, but can be better appreciated as variations around a common kernel of social capitalism. This explains both cross-national resemblances and contrasts.

Given the seemingly functional equivalence of social and Christian democracy, a first step in the clarification of social capitalism would consist in highlighting the central ideological precepts of Christian democratic political thought and practice by contrasting these with social democratic political theory. The second step would involve a synopsis of the distinctiveness of social capitalism in a set of coherent propositions. The concluding stage of the analysis would incorporate (Chapters 9 and 10) the analysis of the historical development of the theory of social capitalism.

Christian democracy nourishes an ideal concept of social citizenship that departs significantly from the individualist, yet solidarist connotations of the Marshallian notion. Christian democrats stress duties rather than rights, the family and the social group rather than the individual, society rather than the state, and distributional justice rather than social justice. T.H. Marshall conceptualised citizenship as

> a status bestowed on those who are full members of a community. All who posses the status are equal with respect to the rights and duties with which the status is endowed. There is no universal principle that determines what those rights and duties shall be, but societies in which citizenship is a developing institution create an image of an ideal citizenship against which achievement can be measured and towards which aspiration can be directed.
>
> (Marshall 1964:84)

The developmental idea of citizenship stresses that inequality of class is compatible with the equality of individual citizenship rights, that the logic of the market can and has been altered by the extension of social citizenship, that the development of citizenship is characterised by a decisive shift from duties to individual rights, and that social citizenship is itself an instrument of social stratification. Marshall argued that citizenship consists of civil, political and social components that correspond to successive phases of the history of capitalist democracies. Eighteenth-century civil rights established individual freedom, nineteenth-century political rights inaugurated political freedom, and twentieth-century social rights provided the foundation for social welfare, or – as one might say – for freedom from want. The social principle of citizenship embodied 'the whole range from the right to a modicum of economic welfare and security to the right to share to the full in the social heritage and to live the life of a civilised being according to the standards prevailing in the society' (Marshall 1964:72).

Looking closely at the idea of the accumulation of rights one might infer that this notion of citizenship primarily deals with the possibly tense relations between the individual (or individual rights) and the state (or public authority). The theory of citizenship is – to borrow a phrase – a theory of politics against markets that focuses on the politically guaranteed rights of individuals to be free and the possibility of equality among citizens in a society that is dominated by capitalist market relations. Citizenship links the private market economy to the public authority of the state, the individual to the collectivity and freedom to equality. Civil rights emerged as the rights of the individual to be free, particularly in the economic realm. Political rights are conceptualised as strengthened individual civil rights that both permit groups to perform as legal individuals (as the recognition of the right of collective bargaining demonstrates) and establish universal suffrage that 'treats the vote as the voice of the individual' (Marshall 1964:94). Civil rights are linked to the idea of freedom and equality before the law; political rights to the notion of (formal) equality. The development of social rights, however, is mainly understood as the consequence of trying to make rights actually work, i.e. of removing the barriers that block the full and equal exercise of civil and political rights. Capitalist market relations, poverty and inadequate education tended to reduce the social meaning of these rights to mere formal capacities, a contradiction that created the foundations of and necessity for social policy. Hence, the conclusion that 'although citizenship, even by the end of the nineteenth century, had done little to reduce social inequality, it had helped to guide progress into the path which led directly to the egalitarian policies of the twentieth century' (Marshall 1964:92). And these egalitarian policies were grounded upon 'the conception of equal social worth, not merely of equal natural rights' (Marshall 1964:92), i.e. on an equality of substance rather than opportunity. The development of the welfare state on this account is, therefore, the historical unfolding of individual rights of members of a national community who – as citizens – became inclusively entitled to the material promises of civil freedom and political equality.

One might argue that the concept of citizenship is fundamentally about the reconciliation of liberty and equality, about the egalitarian possibilities of politics in correcting the inequalities produced by the market without decisively disrupting the freedom of the individual, and about the necessary correspondence between individual social rights and the duties of citizenship. Liberal and social democratic principles come together in engendering a better life for both the community at large and its individual citizens.

The social Catholic notion of citizenship that underlies the theory of social capitalism provides distinctive ideological alternatives for the Marshallian trinities of 'market–citizen–state' and 'civil–political–social'. Understanding Christian democracy and social capitalism crucially involves other strings, those of 'market–state–family', 'charity–distributive justice–subsidiarity' and 'class–religion–reconciliation', that have strong religious connotations. It has to be emphasised, however, that in Christian democratic ideology faith or belief in God and politics do not coincide. Forms of political Christianity are excluded. There exists no linear, direct and compulsive link between Christianity (or Christian principles) and practical choices in the realm of politics. At first sight, this seems to exclude the very possibility of Christian democracy. However, this is an essential and logical condition for any form of Christian-inspired politics that views itself as democratic, since political Christianity would be intolerant. A church that claims to possess absolute and comprehensive knowledge of Divine revelation would be unable to accept other churches or ways of thought as fundamentally equal. Therefore, a commitment to democracy would be excluded, since democracy implies (at least ideally) religious liberty, liberty of conscience, freedom of thought, speech, assembly and of the press, and freedom of action.

Like Christian faith and politics, state and society do not coincide in Christian democratic doctrine. The political institutions of a society have a separate identity. State and society make up an organic unity. The state furthers this unity and maintains the legal framework of social action. The political and legal framework sets the conditions under which the parts of the organic unity can best perform their functions. Direct state intervention in social and economic relations is permitted only to the extent that the organic and natural order of society is restored by providing relief for poverty or by recreating solidarity – or rather harmony – between various social groups. When this organic unity revitalises with the help of political intermediation, the limits of intervention are reached. State interference is always transient to the extent that it cannot absorb social functions, since this would lead to an unbalanced organic whole. The realm of political action is in principle unlimited, whereas the span of intervention depends on the point of time at which lower social organs are once again able to perform their organic duties. States in the Christian democratic view enforce – so to speak – organic assignments. The ideal state is a welfare state and 'its responsibility consists in defining and enforcing the responsibility of others – individuals or social groups – rather than providing services itself' (Fogarty 1957:91). This is an important point and makes clear why public services in Christian democratic welfare states do not assume a comparable importance as for instance social insurance and public assistance. An institutional commitment to full employment, for instance, is at odds with the tenet of the enforcement of 'self-responsibility'.

The central role of the state in the enforcement of social responsibilities accords a distinctive place to politics within the organic totality, but does not signify that politics in one way or another occupies the top position in the social hierarchy of various organs. All parts of the natural order of society have specific tasks that are necessary for the stability of the larger whole. According to the theory of 'subsidiarity' it is nevertheless the state's function to guarantee and facilitate the steady and orderly proficiency of the lower social organs up to a point where these components can operate independently of political arbitration. 'Subsidiarity' is in this sense open-ended and the actual likelihood and boundaries of politicisation are historically contingent (on the contemporary relevance of 'subsidiarity', see van Kersbergen and Verbeek 1994). The Protestant notion of 'sovereignty' is much stricter than 'subsidiarity' and confines state intervention even more. In this context one can find two other concepts, which cover both mentioned principles: autonomisation and horizontal pluralism. The doctrine of 'horizontal pluralism' both delineates the autonomy of the 'life circles' and encourages these 'circles' not to neglect their own capacity of recuperation, as a result of which the state is at the same time protected against overburdening.

Vertical pluralism is another disposition of Christian democracy and it refers to the way in which ideologies cut vertically across all layers and groups in society. It can be understood as the Christian democratic way of defining tolerance and the Dutch system of pillarisation is the prototype of such vertical pluralism.

Different 'spiritual families' . . . – Catholics, Protestants, Marxists, 'humanists', or whoever they may be – should on the principle of 'vertical' pluralism be permitted and enabled to follow their own way of life, even when they are in a minority in a nation or groups as a whole. . . . It reduces conflict, since it allows everyone, without discrimination or loss to himself, to build up a set of associations which fits his own ideals.

(Fogarty 1957:42)

Christian democrats stress the relative autonomy of social organisations in the context of a plural society, glued together by a morality that is supposed to provide harmony or solidarity between the various groups and organisations of a society and which is assisted by a 'caring' state.

A first tentative conclusion on the differences between the ideologies of Christian democracy and social democracy can thus be formulated. For social democracy state intervention is not limited by a principle comparable to 'subsidiarity'. The emphasis on the primacy of politics is much stronger here. The goal of intervention is social reform according to the norms of equality, freedom and solidarity. Social democracy instrumentalises the state in order to eliminate inequality, which is seen as an inherent characteristic of the capitalist system of production. The function of the state is perceived as a permanent capacity for reform. There is a general conviction of the possibilities of politics (Ringen 1987). Social democracy recognises the limits to state intervention only so far as the idea of market conformity of Keynesian economics is concerned. Intervention ought not to rule out the market yet the state should intervene where the market shows imperfections and violates the principles of equality, freedom and solidarity. Ultimately, markets should be replaced whenever they generate unfavourable distributional outcomes.

Christian democratic politics is antithetical to the historical materialist view of man and society, where class struggle propels the progress of society. Christian democratic politics is always founded upon some notion of harmony between all members, groups or classes of society, illustrated by the concepts of integration, class compromise, accommodation and pluralism. Christian democrats define capitalism (or 'the system of production through private firms') as an organic division of labour. Various social groups and classes have their own specific and indispensable role in the division of labour. Mellifluous co-operation between classes is not only possible, but also necessary and 'natural'. Property relations are founded upon natural right and, therefore, not only ought not be changed but cannot be altered without devastating effects. In *Rerum Novarum* (1891), for instance, four interrelated arguments are provided in favour of the natural right of private property: man is rational, therefore he saves for the future;

man has a right to the fruits of his labour. These fruits become his private property; private property has always existed; and man needs private property to be able to look after his family in his function as *pater familias*.

In *Quadragesimo Anno* (1931) a distinction is elaborated between private property and its use. It is the function of the state to control how and where private property is used. If, and only if, necessity demands intervention can it be argued to be legitimate. Natural right, furthermore, implies the obligation of co-operation between labour and capital. The organic character of the economic order should reflect itself in the integration of labour and capital in public affairs through the so-called 'industrial groups' or 'statutory industry councils'. These councils are supposed to contribute to the abolition of class struggle. If labour is to be integrated into society the working class needs organisations, because in order to be able to perform the 'natural functions' within the organic body of society it is necessary to organise as a class. The 'respect' of employers for the working class must be enforced by the strength of organisation.

The 'redemption' of the proletariat must follow the path of private property acquisition, of fighting unemployment, of developing labour law and of co-determination in firms. Christian democratic unions, although appreciating that industrial collaboration is often difficult, have always emphasised shared interests and the joint responsibility of management and workers for economic well-being. Ultimately, this should be reflected in joint control over firms: 'for only full industrial democracy, with not merely a consultative but a decisive voice for all, can provide full opportunity for the "promotion of the working class", the widest chance for workers to take their responsibility and develop their power to lead' (Fogarty 1957:65). Christian democratic parties initiated and implemented laws regulating co-determination in firms in the late 1940s and early 1950s all over Western Europe (Irving 1979:43–51).[1] This *Weltanschauung* in terms of a possible and necessary 'fellowship' in a well-ordered society has contributed to the view that Christian democracy is nothing but the middle of the road between socialism and liberalism.

There is a certain ambiguity in basic Christian democratic ideology here. The principle of subsidiarity regulates in abstract and general terms the possibilities and limits of state intervention. The requirements of distributive justice dictate the duty of social policy. In practice, principles of market efficiency and the idea of justice produce a perennial dilemma of agency. This runs the risk of a friction between the insistence on subsidiarity and the principle of social justice as a moral obligation.

A second tentative conclusion on the difference between social democratic and Christian democratic ideology can be formulated here. Social democracy views existing property relations as the root cause of inequality, injustice and class struggle. The property relations themselves might be the object of change. Unlike the Christian democrats the social democrats strive for a shift in power from capital to labour, resulting in a shift from profit to labour income. The economic relationship between various social groups is a permanent societal struggle. Property rights are not defined by natural law, but are considered to be the result of a historical development. Therefore property relations can, in principle, be transformed by political action. The end of a 'good' economic order is the 'good society' in which every individual has an equal opportunity to a reasonable existence and to work and welfare. Unions are central rather because of their ability to promote working-class power than because of their function within the organic totality. Solidarity is a central notion of social democratic ideology. Solidarity between people is emphasised as founded upon material and formal equality. Asymmetrical power relations require intervention by the state.

The notion of solidarity as harmony is an intrinsic component of the Christian democratic tradition and is alternately paraphrased as 'integration', compromise, accommodation and pluralism. It symbolises the idea of personalism. Men and women as individuals can only unfold their potentiality in an incomplete manner. Men and women, therefore, are compelled to co-operate and hence they are principally social beings, although with social roles differentiated according to gender. 'Personalism', a term recently enjoying a remarkable revitalisation among Flemish Christian democrats and at the European level (see Dierickx 1994), entails a particular theory of social justice, that – rather than balancing rights and duties – fundamentally underscores a moral obligation to help the 'weak', 'poor', 'lower strata' or whoever may be in need of help. Furthermore, social justice does not refer to the relations between individuals (as a liberal concept would), but instead to the relations between social groups and organisations.

Personalism accords the *Weltanschauung* of Christian democracy its specificity and has the definite consequences for practical policy. All social action should be oriented to enable personalities (rather than individuals) to develop along ideal lines, to acquire certain basic characteristics and social and technical skills. These ideal personalities should be grouped in a plural social structure, in which room is left for the free, though socially responsible, development of groups of all shapes and sizes, from the family as the cornerstone of society to the international community of nations. The social structure should be glued together by and function through sanctions (political, economic or social) and mechanisms (competition, direction, consultation) combined as to maintain its personalist and pluralist character (see Fogarty 1957:29).

The family in this theory is the authentic and pre-eminent social unit in which individuals evolve into complete persons. Without the social bonds of family life, individuals remain incomplete persons. Like the state, the family exists by natural necessity. The germ of society at large is present in this elementary social unit. The role division between men and women is a natural one. Christian democrats see themselves as the special upholders of the family's needs and rights and of the natural order of society in general. With respect to social policy the results of the empirical analyses clearly reveal the special position of the family within Christian democratic ideology. It is therefore correct to emphasise that

> Christian democrats think in terms not so much of providing families with services, particularly state services, as of ensuring them, through a modification of the wage system, the income with which to provide services for themselves, on their own or through co-operation with others. All of them support strongly the idea of a family living wage.
>
> (Fogarty 1957:49).

Family allowances, then, became a means to supplement the possibly inadequate family living wages, and relatively high replacement rates in the benefit structure of a society are to assist families in times of misfortune. This stress on providing income rather than services to the family is a function of the Christian democratic ideology of the family and its role in the organic division of the societal body. Christian democrats do not merely try 'to ensure the family justice but to increase its responsibility and independence. The family is by all means "the cornerstone of society"' (Fogarty 1957:50).

A final tentative conclusion on the difference between Christian democratic and social democratic ideology addresses these topics. The performance of work (the application of labour power) is for social democrats the manner in which individuals unfold their personalities. Individuals are rational and solidarity springs from an individual yet reciprocal responsibility towards mankind. Social democracy has a philosophy that strongly suggests social action: existing social inequality implies a commitment to change in order to arrive at the state of equality and freedom for all. This search for change, this commitment to reform, establishes human beings as political rather than purely social beings. As political beings they need organisation in order to be able to (co-)decide at various levels (parliamentary democracy and political participation).

PROPOSITIONS ON SOCIAL CAPITALISM: AN IDEAL-TYPE

The model of social capitalism is related to the distinctive features of Christian democracy identified in the previous chapters, particularly to the politics of mediation, defined (in Chapter 2) as the religiously motivated, ideologically precipitated and politically practised doctrine that conflicts of interests can and must be appeased politically in order to maintain or restore the natural and organic order of society. The establishment of social capitalism can be seen as the means by which Christian democracy has tried to establish cross-class accommodation. Religiously induced politics is crucial here, because it invites all people sharing a common religion or confession to take part in mediation. Religion cuts across class and acts to unite social groups. Christian democracy's theory of social capitalism deviates from the Marshallian notion of citizenship to the extent that it is not a theory of politics against markets, but of how the fundamental elements of the organic society at large cohere and harmonise; it is an organic theory of society. Christian democracy emphasises a variety of sub-systems of society: the market (private property in particular), the state and the wide array of organisations and institutions within society, such as the Church, the organisations or capital and labour, and the family.

As to the state and the social infrastructure, Christian democracy does not acknowledge the primacy of politics. All societal organs have their own autonomy. There can be no fundamental change of property relations in the name of equality; there can only be compensation of social costs. The state is not characterised by a permanent reform capacity, but at most by a temporary correction of the inadequacies produced by the market or elsewhere. In general, inequality is regarded as a natural phenomenon and is and should be reproduced at other levels.

As to private property, Christian democracy does not aim at changing its place and function, but rather embeds it in a moral framework. Reform is possible with regard to its use, not to its existence, except in extreme circumstances and when everything else fails. Property relations in society do not give rise to a permanent struggle between classes, but are the foundation of the capacity of a permanent accommodation of conflicting interests. As such they produce harmony rather than conflict. Neither unions, nor employers nor parties are class agents, but instruments in the establishment of society as an organism, as are all other social institutions. Each has its place, each is indispensable, and all contribute to the public good. Intraclass solidarity, though useful in itself, is not what really matters; only interclass harmony may establish the happiness of all. Solidarity on this account is equivalent to harmony.

Christian democracy sees the family and the social infrastructure as a precondition of the person. The human self is not primarily a political, but a social being. Man (in this case the male) through his labour is the centre of public life. Woman, through her work as mother and through her natural facility to care, is the centre (but not the head) of the family and the neighbourhood. The family is the cornerstone of society. The state is the completion of the societal body to the extent that it assists the lower organs to assist themselves and the Church is the moral authority which accords the whole construction its stability.

The identification of the source of social misery and poverty in the functioning of the capitalist market linked with a fundamental yet conditional acceptance of capitalism represents a first element of social capitalism. Initially, the 'social question' was seen as an effect of religious failure and moral decadence on the part of the poor themselves. Therefore, it was the task of the Church and of the Christian-inspired social actors to provide relief through charity and pastoral care. The solution consisted in a regeneration of Christianity. Vital for social capitalism was the development away from charity and neighbourly love towards an embrace of the state as an institution which could channel the necessary funds to families in need. It is precisely at this point that the 'little tradition' of social Catholicism and the 'grand tradition' of the Church started to go separate ways. Under conditions of failing Christian love on the side of the employers, the causal chain of analysis in social Catholic theory was reversed. It was capitalism that created social misery. Misery, in turn, generated moral decadence and apostasy. Using the state as a mechanism of subsidy would enhance the capacity of families to regenerate. Consequently, the Christian faith would re-enter the hearts of the grateful poor and the poor would return to the mother Church. As will be shown below, this determining reversal was never made by the Vatican.

For this causal analysis to take practical effect, however, capitalism had to be recognised as a nearly 'just' economic system in principle. Acceptance of capitalism on the condition of social policy established the stipulation of social capitalism. Charity, therefore, could not be but a part of the solution of the social question. The problem of justice under capitalist conditions was intensified where secularisation had rendered charity ineffective. Social Catholicism, therefore, was forced to accept capitalism because it aimed at its reform. Social Catholics loathed the treatment of workers as commodities. A rudimentary idea of decommodification – so to speak – emerged with the conditional acceptance of capitalism. Since the family is the unit of society, which cannot be broken down into further smaller components, its dependence on the commodity form of the labour power of a husband was made contingent upon his remuneration being sufficient to allow his wife to perform her natural function at home.

A second element of social capitalism concerns the scope and limits of state intervention, which became problematic as a result of the ineffectiveness of charity. If religious fear was not enough to induce employers to act in charity and to give alms, another mechanism was to take the place of the queen of all virtues. The more social policy became conceivable as an alternative for failing Christian love, the more the problem of the extent of state intervention was raised. Consequently, Catholics developed a peculiar theory of state intervention which constitutes the nucleus of social capitalism.

Its peculiarity lies in the emphasis on the duty of the state to act as a subsidiser in case of inadequate lower social organs. State intervention is limited to the extent that it must not absorb the smaller social units, but should help these to such an extent that they can again take over themselves. The theory of 'subsidiarity' – such a well-chosen term – defines the range and boundaries of public intervention. Subsidiarity is also a crucial parameter of what might be called community production; it is a way of generating Christian citizens rather than citizens. Subsidiarity allows organised religion still to appear as the generous donator and upholder of decent lives. Social capitalism does not generate social citizenship in terms of individual rights, but accords the state a special duty in upholding the capacities of persons and social or status groups in their social environment. It is a clever, but perhaps still ambiguous solution for the problem of defining social justice as a correlation between public duties and social rights. Most probably because of the ambivalence of the concept, 'subsidiarity' did make it to the 'grand tradition'. The doctrine of subsidiarity can already be found in *Rerum Novarum*, but found its clearest expression in *Quadragesimo Anno* (see McOustra 1990:45–6; see also Chapter 10).

Christian democracy promotes what has been identified empirically as passive or reactive social policies. Such a practice typically moderates the outcome of the logic of the imperfect market by transferring considerable sums of money to families and other social institutions in need, but is hesitant in changing this logic itself. In this sense, social capitalism is the perfect middle way between socialist collectivism and liberal individualism. Christian democratic reformism is therefore basically 'repair work'. A fundamental commitment to full employment has never been a central goal of social capitalist arrangements. This presupposes too farreaching a level of interference. Full employment policy is not an intrinsic element of social capitalism; compensation for unemployment, of course, is.

Another effect of subsidiarity concerns the reluctance to transfer authority and control over policies entirely to the state. Privately governed, but publicly financed welfare arrangements are the ideal. Such institutions are intermediary organs with a function of their own. They ought not to be absorbed by the state, nor should they themselves absorb any lower organ. The corollary of self-government is self-responsibility. Financing through taxation seems contrary to the social capitalist project, except in those cases where the ability of families is entirely exhausted.

A third proposition on social capitalism concerns the specific theory of class and the idea of society as an organic whole of functionally differentiated members. Crucial is the implicit theory of inequality. In the organic view of society, classes are not antagonistic forces, but mutually dependent entities. They are different, but equally important for the organic society as a whole. Inequality is a natural phenomenon that cannot and should not be altered. An extensive redistribution of societal wealth from one class to another disrupts the organism. With a typical Catholic metaphor one could say that one cannot transfer part of the brain, which thinks, plans and directs, to the hands that do the work, whether via the market or in the home. Social policy, therefore, does not aim at establishing a more equal distribution of societal resources.

A fourth element of social capitalism follows from the theory of limited state intervention and the philosophy of natural inequality. It concerns the distinctively Catholic conception of justice, or better, the peculiar theory of distributive justice. Distributive justice on the Catholic account accords to each and every class what is its due. On this part, there appears to be no ambiguity as to rights and duties. Classes and vocational groups have a claim to what they are entitled to. Members of a class and of vocational groups, therefore, have a right to be treated in accordance with their status. The state has the duty to enforce these rightful claims. Social policy is not to alter status, but to reproduce it. Nevertheless, such a theory lacks a conception of individual rights of citizens as full members of a society. In Christian democratic theory individuals are first and foremost full members of lower social organs that make up society as a whole, not citizens of the national community. Their rightful claim to assistance is therefore not an absolute right derived from their status as citizens, but from their status as members of indispensable classes and other bodies.

A fifth element and the final proposition of social capitalism concerns the idea of private property as social policy. It primarily functions in opposition to the socialist solution of socialisation or nationalisation. Although the theory of private property did initially play a role in the discussion on social policy, the theory of the just wage (or family wage) gradually replaced it. A money income ought to be sufficient for a man and his family. In addition, the acquisition of private property presupposes a money wage. Such a wage should not only be sufficient for a worker to provide for himself and for the needs of his family, but it should also allow him to put something aside. This is the background of the theory of the just wage. It addresses the family as well as the propensity to save. In other words, it stresses the need for the family to provide for the present and future of its members.

Benefits for adult male employees, therefore, are typically characterised by a capacity to replace the family income at the level of the present status. As an unintended consequence of this, social capitalist regimes become generous in their benefit structure, especially with regard to families. Benefits for women, on the other hand, are either dependent on the income of the husband or at least lower than for an adult worker. In its extreme form, social security is projected to be sexually differentiated, not as the result of an implicit theory about the lesser worth of women, but stemming from the explicit theory about the natural gender roles of men and women. The very idea of social capitalism assumes women to be only marginally present on the labour market and the family to be the prime provider of care. It comprises a set a of hypotheses on the division of labour according to gender: paid jobs for men, unpaid domestic and community labour for women.

Social capitalism is committed to capitalist market relations, but encourages social and economic policies that counter socially unacceptable effects of uncontrolled markets. The state cannot assume an extended role in the economy, nor can citizenship be recognised as the foundation of social rights. Social rights are attached to family or status groups, and the state only provides the conditions under which the family and social groups can continue to function according to their natural and organic roles. Intervention into market relations is excluded, compensation for market failure is crucial.

Social capitalism is a distinctive arrangement between market, state, society and family by which resources produced in the private economy are channelled into social institutions that fail to secure their means of income themselves. The state assists those who fail to help themselves in the performance of their natural duty. In sum, Christian democracy is a distinctive political phenomenon and its distinctiveness concerns a religiously inspired model of social reform which is both social and capitalist. Social capitalism provided the kernel of social and economic policies pursued by Christian democratic parties that characterises the Christian democratisation of capitalism in continental Western Europe, although the politics of mediation and its implied integration and reconciliation of interests has also produced considerable cross-national variation among this common core. The questions for the remainder of this book are the following. How did the theory of social capitalism come about? And how is Christianity in general and Catholicism in particular related to welfare state development?

9 Catholicism and social citizenship
From charity to social justice?

The strongest argument against hypothesising any historical relation between Christianity and social citizenship is that Christianity, and Catholicism in particular, has always stressed the centrality of charity. Charity, given its one-sided emphasis on the Christian obligation to give, is opposed to the distinguishing feature of the modern welfare state: the granting of social rights.

> Solidaristic policies have become accepted, legitimate and uncontroversial only to the extent that they are regarded as a right rather than as charity or altruism. This was the point of Marshall's trinity of rights and the concept of social citizenship. This has been the basis of the claim made for the superiority of Scandinavian welfare.
>
> (Baldwin 1990:19)

The justice of today is the charity of yesterday. Solidarity marks the true welfare state and the granting of social rights liberates the individual from the humiliating position of having to beg for alms. Catholicism had no part in the development of the true welfare state, because it had no concept of social citizenship and could not view a need as the foundation of a right. Those who received help were indeed needy, but had no right to be helped (Marshall 1964:87). Charity inhibited social justice, Christian obligations thwarted the development of social rights, and compassion as a Christian virtue hampered solidarity. Religiously inspired actors have had little to do with the transition from charity to social justice. On the contrary, the conversion was accomplished by those who managed to shake off the religious heritage of charity.

Love and charity are the essential moral principles of Christianity and these values constitute the heart of contemporary 'bourgeois religion', because they 'reflect bourgeois interests' (Shoenfeld 1992:124). Their place within the system of Christian morality is currently even more prominent than within pre-capitalist Christianity, because 'both love and charity support the ideals of private property and the maintenance of the *status quo*' (Schoenfeld 1992:124). Poverty is a problem of unfortunate individuals, and charity – by supporting the poor – reinforces the *status quo*, because it represses a critical analysis of the causes of poverty. It also functions as a defence of private property and personal freedom

> by stressing that it is the right of an individual because of his own choice to give or not to give, to control one's own property even when such giving or withdrawal can affect another's life. Charity reinforces the bourgeois values of personal freedom in that it is an act of the free will: it cannot be legislated, it must be an act of love.
>
> (Schoenfeld 1992:125)

Charity, in sum, is a bourgeois religious value that legitimates rather than criticises social inequality. Justice is directed towards change. Charity is not, because it does not question the underlying causes of inequality.

These considerations are valid to the extent that they address the relation between organised religion and private charities. The critical argument on charity loses some of its bite, however, if one poses the question of how religiously inspired social and political actors have tried to come to terms with rightful claims to assistance, i.e. if one shifts one's attention away from religious practice and private charities towards the development of the social and political movements of the 'little' tradition of Roman Catholicism in particular. The main argument to be elaborated here is that the social Catholic movements of Western Europe have managed to transcend the 'bourgeois' values of love and charity by formulating a distinctive social critique of capitalism, but that Vatican social teaching has never made a comparable breakthrough and still stresses charity as a fundamental moral concept. In other words, it is crucial to make a distinction between religion (as a possibly conservative institution) and religiously inspired social and political movements that have considerably moved beyond religion in their attempts to formulate a positive yet critical theory of contemporary capitalism.

This leaves one other problem unresolved. Welfare state research has cherished the claim that secularisation (as a correlate of industrialisation and urbanisation or as a phenomenon of modernisation in general) rather than religion lies at the heart of the development of the welfare state. Studying the transition from charity to a distinctive social Catholic notion of justice would not make sense, because it was rather the decline of religion, the impact of Protestantism and the rise of the secular nation-state – as a consequence of the 'surrender' of the Church to the state or as a result of the retreat of the church into the 'private' realm – that have governed welfare state development.

Secularisation is taken to refer to the decline of the categorical impact of religion on human conduct (Chadwick 1975) and points to the increasing powerlessness of organised religion in temporal affairs coupled with the decreasing plausibility of the religious interpretation of the world (Martin 1978). Religious institutions lost their dominance over society and culture and Protestantism 'served as the historically decisive prelude to secularization' (Berger 1990:113).

Christianity is related to welfare capitalism only so far as Protestantism involved a first step in the process of secularisation and individualisation, because this belief caused 'an immense shrinkage in the scope of the sacred in reality' (Berger 1990:111). Protestantism qualitatively changed church–state relationships which, in turn, facilitated the construction of the welfare state. Protestantism and secularisation have influenced the transformation of traditional societies into mass democracies and this process affected the institutional arrangements of modern welfare states. Flora's generalisation of the Rokkan macro model of European history, for instance, asserts that

> the Protestant nationalization of the territorial culture in the North favored the mobilization of voice 'from below': the early development of literacy encouraged the mobilization of lower strata into mass politics, and the incorporation of the church into the state apparatus reduced one potential source of conflict and produced a clear-cut focus for the opposition of the dominated population. By contrast, the supra-territorial influence of the Catholic church favored a mobilization 'from above': the late development of literacy retarded spontaneous mass mobilization and the conflicts over the control over the educational system led to efforts by the church to mobilize against the state.
>
> (Flora 1983:22)

In nations in which the Reformation had a lasting impact and in which state–church relations gradually developed, the conditions for collective welfare services were most favourable, the more so as the decline of religion facilitated the growing political salience of class (but see Stephens 1979b). In those nations where Catholicism continued to shape culture and politics, the conflict between state and church inhibited or at least retarded the emergence of a welfare state. This contrast between the Protestant and the Catholic nations explains the qualitative differences between their welfare states. These differences concern the degree of 'stateness' (the level of centralisation; the level of state–church integration; the degree of state intervention in the economy) and the degree of institutional coherence (universalism versus fragmentation).[1] The ideal-type of the welfare state refers to a historical combination of universalism and stateness and is taken to comprise the following characteristics: political centralisation, nationalisation of the Church, cultural homogeneity, advanced (democratic) agriculture, lack of, or at least limited, absolutism, smooth democratisation and a limited division of state and society. The ideal type of welfare state development is found in Europe's periphery, i.e. in Scandinavia, where the physical distance from Rome is greatest.

In an important article Heidenheimer (1983) focused on the relationship between religion and secularisation patterns on the one hand and the westward spread of the welfare state on the other. His article is in the form of two imaginary dialogues, the first between Max Weber and Ernst Troeltsch, taking place in 1904, and the second between Ernst Reweb and Max Schroeltt, the modern impersonations of the two great sociologists. The birth of the welfare state is dated at 1883, the year of the introduction of the first workers' insurance in Bismarckian Germany. The question, to Weber and Troeltsch, is 'whether the spread of social insurance is at all related to the religious ethos prevalent in different countries and if so, how do the different branches of Christianity compare in the degree to which they have welcomed or opposed this trend?' (Heidenheimer 1983:6). In the Weberian perspective it could be expected that adoption of social insurance occurred in an early stage because both doctrine and the intimate relationship between the state and the Church were favourable to paternalist types of social policies. Catholic countries are expected to be laggards because Catholicism inhibits economic development. On the account of Troeltsch, on the other hand, there is a crucial difference between Calvinist and Lutheran countries, the latter probably more willing to accept social insurance as a tolerable intervention; the former, because of the association with liberal capitalism, probably even more slow in their adaptations than the Catholic nations.

Secularisation patterns affect national experiences by altering the velocity with which social insurance schemes are introduced. In the Weberian perspective secularisation is assumed to accelerate the development of the welfare state because it is viewed as a concluding phase of Western rationalisation. On the Troeltschian interpretation, however, secularisation is a multidimensional process by which in some domains religion loses its influence entirely, whereas in others traditional values are transplanted to secular structures and processes (Heidenheimer 1983:9).

The manner in which this causal link between Protestantism, secularisation and the development of the welfare state is interpreted, is perhaps largely convincing, but nevertheless leaves unanswered the question of how the social and political movements in the Catholic belt of Europe have adjusted to capitalism and the striving after equality and social justice. Charity is routinely viewed as antithetical to the welfare state, both by critical sociology of religion and by mainstream welfare state theories. Surely, charity refers to a religiously inspired obligation to give, whereas the welfare state is essentially a matter of secular rights. Yet there is a way in which charity as a Christian canon became crystallised in a distinctive version of the welfare state, namely through the social Catholic reformulation of charity as social (distributive) justice and through Catholic politics, although again it has to be stressed that Vatican social teaching has never moved beyond the traditional view on charity.

ON THE SPIRIT OF SOCIAL CAPITALISM

To clarify these points a distinction has to be made first between Catholicism and ascetic Protestantism. In his *pièce de résistance* of classical sociology, *The Protestant Ethic and the Spirit of Capitalism*, Weber (1976) argued that Catholics and Protestants differ systematically through their belief systems in their respective attitudes towards economic life in general and towards capitalism in particular. Appreciating the insights of the early debate on the Weber thesis (see Brodrick 1934; Fanfani 1935; Sombart 1959; Tawney 1975; Robertson 1973), the main point was that for Calvinists salvation could never, as in Catholicism, be attained by the accumulation of good works. The Calvinist thesis of proof of grace was, in fact, the reverse of the doctrine of salvation by good works. Both creeds adapted to capitalism, but did so in divergent manners. Unlike ascetic Protestantism, which has adopted its theology to capitalism gradually in such a way that this religion eventually became its prime moral apologist, Catholicism has systematically refused to accept capitalism unconditionally. Worldly economic activity on the Catholic account became the object of a social and religious critique rather than the appropriate place to seek proof of grace. Catholic social theory has always been strongly infused with anti-capitalist ingredients. However, one should make a distinction between traditionalist Catholicism and modern social Catholicism, because only the latter managed to develop a positive critique of capitalism and a Catholic version of reformist policies under capitalist conditions.

Protestantism's choice in favour of capitalism was facilitated by the fact that it originated as an anti-traditionalist force. It was fundamentally opposing Catholic traditional power. Catholicism, as a result, was forced to defend traditionalism and this religion became so firmly associated with the old order that it remained for a long time a vigorous anti-modernist church.

It struggled well into the twentieth century against all varieties of modernism, be it the Enlightenment, capitalism, liberalism, democracy or socialism. The battle against capitalism was just one, albeit central, element in this struggle against modernity. The Roman Catholic church eventually had no choice other than to accommodate to capitalism, which it only gradually and conditionally accepted. At the same time Catholicism's medieval social ideas were revitalised as a strategy for formulating a solution for the social question, which capitalism was producing next to its material gains.

Weber's distinction between Catholicism and ascetic Protestantism is useful here, because it clarifies the decidedly divergent manners in which these religions control what has been called the 'salvation panic'. This 'panic' established a permanent feature of the life of the Calvinist believer for which no relief was possible. As a consequence of predestination and the complete transcendence of God, there existed no course or conduct to secure salvation. Psychologically induced, diffused through pastoral work and with distinct practical effects, the salvation panic did not lead to the logical conclusion of fatalism, but – mediated through the idea of the possibility of proof of grace in a worldly calling – to the unintended consequence of inner-worldly asceticism. This inner-worldly asceticism, in turn, was directly associated with what Weber called the spirit of capitalism. The complete elimination of salvation through the Church and the sacraments constituted the determining difference between ascetic protestantism and Catholicism.

The Catholic had many more possibilities of dealing with and acting upon uncertainty over personal destiny. The Catholic believer could always try to seek compensation for imperfection or for sinful behaviour through the Church and the priest. Surely, in order to correct imperfection something had to be done in order to show repentance and goodwill. The pious believer in his weakest moments could at least show the intention of improving upon imperfection, of bettering the sinful life, of correcting weakness and of compensating for shortcomings. Forgiveness of sins, absolution and even eternal salvation could be reached by an accumulation of good works. The Catholic creed allowed the salvation panic to be transformed from a permanent distressing feature of daily life into a momentary discomfort of religious practice. In Catholicism a number of different ways of dealing with the crisis of Divine recognition could be found.

The accumulation of good works as a medium of personal religious relief by means of the material relief of others constitutes the core of what may be designated as 'the spirit of *social* capitalism'. The early Catholic teaching on private property illustrates this point. Private property as such was never condemned. Only certain forms of its anti-social use could be seen as sinful. Any form of surplus lawfully gained, for instance, gave the proprietor the opportunity to do good. The surplus enabled the rich man to give alms as a Christian duty. The problem of private property was not of an economic nature at all, but 'there was an ethico-religious problem, which fluctuated between the radicalism of the claims of love and the natural claims of the necessity of earning a living' (Troeltsch 1931:116). The glorification of the poor has to be interpreted along these lines. The poor were special because they – so to speak – had the disposition to increase the rich man's ability to do good and consequently through the accumulation of good works to attain salvation. Catholics have fundamentally different views on poverty than Protestants. Whereas the latter regard being poor as a state to be avoided because it is taken as proving damnation, the former consider poverty as an opportunity to do good, and the act itself of doing good is 'infused' by the duties of neighbourly love. The poor themselves, however, even occupy a special place in the Gospel, for Jesus' message was that poverty facilitates salvation. Charity assumed its importance in this context of achieving forgiveness of committed sins through the accumulation of good works to the benefit of those privileged to suffer (the poor). These are the central components of the spirit of social capitalism and this spirit addresses the rich and the poor alike.

From the outset, charity was an intracommunal affair, an aspect of communism of love, i.e. 'a communism which regarded the pooling of possessions as a proof of love and of the religious spirit of sacrifice' (Troeltsch 1931:62). As a result of the differentiation of society, however, charity's function and place rapidly changed. Relations of charity soon lost their personal character. Almsgiving was regulated by institutions, mediated by the religious hierarchy and turned into one of the prime penances for sin (Troeltsch 1931:136). Charity lost its original meaning and the idea of making sacrifices for the sake of love disappeared. Alms could not assume the status of a right or a claim. They were fundamentally 'a gift of love, to be received in love and humility' (Troeltsch 1931:137). The religious duty or the religious means to discharge sin on the part of those who had a surplus was not matched by a rightful claim on the part of those who lacked a minimum of subsistence. Such was the position of charity at the eve of the industrial and political revolutions of the late eighteenth and early nineteenth centuries. By that time charity had materialised in a large number of charities. It grew out to be a church-funded systematic relief arrangement for the poor, bereft of its personal and intracommunal character and with no systematic or coherent view on the relationship between duties and rights. Instead of the early communism of love evolved the institutionalisation of impersonal gifts. The theory behind charity and almsgiving concerned the idea that the wealthy must buy their place in heaven by alms. Almsgiving had become a means to salvation for the rich.

The meaning and contents of charity and almsgiving in the period immediately preceding the Industrial Revolution is clarified in the enlightened critique of traditional charity. Christian charity had a denominational and sectarian character and was directed to the spiritual rather than the material or physical well-being of the poor. And what is more, the salvation of the benefactor dominated the relations of charity: 'almsgiving was a method of easing the charitable donor's soul through the after life and the recipient was merely an incidental means to a lofty end' (Jones 1982:2).

Charity, then, was completely dependent upon the goodwill and fear of the benefactors and not subject to methodical conduct. It did not posses the instruments for adequately reacting to the continuously changing conditions of the eighteenth century (Groethuysen 1968; Jones 1982). The institutions of charity were unable to make a distinction between the 'deserving' and the 'undeserving' poor. There existed no clear definition of the object of charity. From the handouts at the gate of the convent both groups could equally profit. The object of charity included the 'undeserving' vagrants as well as the sick, the disabled, widows, orphans and other 'deserving' poor. Finally, charity was too much confined to the relief of the urban poor, whereas the agrarian areas were hardly reached (Fairchilds 1976).

Charity as a perennial characteristic of Christianity and as a means for poor relief out of love was in serious crisis precisely when industrial capitalism was producing a new, even further alienated class of poor, the proletariat, and a secularised class of rich entrepreneurs. Unlike the attempts of social Catholicism, the 'little' tradition, the first attempts to deal with the new situation led the Vatican ideologues to search for a revitalisation of the idea of charity. This is one of the reasons for the re-emergence of Thomist philosophy as the official metaphysics of Catholicism and of Thomas Aquinas as the undisputed authority and official exponent of Catholic teaching (Kenny 1976, 1980). An important reason for this revival is that Thomist philosophy was particularly apt to face modernity and the Enlightenment because of its central concept of reason. In this sense, it was possible to encounter enlightened philosophy on its own grounds.

On the basis of these considerations the following argument seems plausible: the 'buying' of salvation through almsgiving as charity was an important element of Christian social thought at the eve of the social, economic and political revolutions of the eighteenth and nineteenth centuries.

Charity is the crucial concept for understanding the accommodation of Catholicism's medieval heritage to industrial capitalism. The Catholic Church and the Catholic social and political movements, however, have differed considerably in the way they accomplished this adaptation. In particular, the manner in which the religious inspiration behind the theory of almsgiving and charity became modernised outside the traditional institutions of the Church is fundamental for understanding the emergence of a coherent view on the possibilities and limits of social policy within capitalist constraints.

Vatican social teaching has not been particularly flexible nor for that matter quick, in its conditional acceptance of industrial capitalism – and one can take the dates of publication of the two most important social encyclical letters as indicative for this: *Rerum Novarum* (1891) and *Quadragesimo Anno* (1931). The prevalence and revitalisation of the theory of charity in official Catholic social ideology thwarted and frustrated the transition to a more moderate and workable view on modernity and industrial capitalism. The lack of a conception of rights corresponding with the duties of charity resulted in an imperfect Catholic version of justice. Vatican ideologues never solved the philosophical, conceptual and ethical problems of charity.

This is corroborated by the fact that it was Thomas Aquinas' theory of charity that was adopted in the late nineteenth century as the official guideline for Catholic philosophy. Scholastic philosophy became the foundation of the social teaching of the church since Leo XIII. According to this Pope, the philosophy of Aquinas provided Catholics with powerful arguments in defence of religious dogma, because the scholastics in particular 'demonstrate the firm foundations of the faith, its Divine origin, its certain truth, the arguments that sustain it, the benefits it has conferred on the human race, and its perfect accord with reason' (*Aeterni Patris* [1879], in Gilson 1954:48). As a result, the philosophical problems of charity were not solved by adopting Thomist philosophy as the foundation of social teaching, since this in fact reinforced the conservative or negative connotations of charity.

The emphasis on the Thomist conception of charity has delayed, if not obstructed, a complete modernisation of Catholic doctrine. Aquinas stressed the so-called external acts of charity: beneficence, almsgiving and fraternal correction. Beneficence simply meant doing good to others. Almsdeeds was of more practical relevance. One motive for almsgiving was to relieve one who is in need. Strictly speaking, almsgiving was an act of mercy. There existed seven corporal almsdeeds: to feed the hungry, to give drink to the thirsty, to clothe the naked, to harbour the homeless, to visit the sick, to ransom the captive, to bury the dead. Likewise, there were seven spiritual almsdeeds: to instruct the ignorant, to counsel the doubtful, to comfort the sorrowful, to reprove the sinner, to forgive injuries, to bear with those who trouble and annoy us, and to pray for all. Which type of alms was to be preferred depended on the circumstances. In general, the spiritual alms were considered to be of higher quality. On the other hand, Aquinas straightforwardly argued, that 'a man in hunger is to be fed rather than instructed' (Aquinas 1978: Question 32, article 3:543).

However, the decisive point was that corporal almsdeeds had spiritual effects. The physical and therefore spiritual well-being of the one who was the object of the almsdeeds was a direct, favourable effect. More important, however, was that benefactors themselves profited indirectly through God's grace and because those who received would pray for their benefactors. But personal almsgiving had given way to forms of public provision of relief and institutional rather than personal arrangements co-ordinated fund-raising and distribution. The difficulty of updating the contents of charity lay in the formidable task of designing and establishing new forms for the organisation, regulation, co-ordination and eventually normalisation of alternative ways of fundraising. Catholic philosophers have struggled over the question of how to replace personal almsgiving by taxation. They were problematising the function of the state as a collector and distributor of funds, but argued that this tended to diminish the role of the Church. Nevertheless, the decline of almsgiving as the principal instrument of financing the assistance of the poor ultimately led to the necessity of questioning the role of the state and the best form of government. It called for a theory of state intervention and the proper object of social policy. And precisely at this point, Catholic philosophy failed to come up with con-vincing answers. Who were the needy? Who had the power to define needs? What was the amount to be given to the poor? Was there a way of discriminating between deserving and undeserving poor? The philosoph-ical heritage of Aquinas handicapped the solution for the problems of arbitration, accountability and responsibility.

The historical critique on charity has always focused on the act of charity as the granting of a favour rather than the fulfilment of a right, and on the act of charity as patronage. Charity had the unpleasant effect of placing the recipient in a humble, submissive and obedient relationship to the bene-factor. The recipient was dependent upon the benevolence of the one who had decided to give and in addition had to show gratitude. The decisive point was the lack of a right to charity on the part of the recipient; the recipient was passive. He or she could not be considered to be a rightful claimant, i.e. he or she could not actively seek the fulfilment of a right to a benefit. Patronage is the reflection of the Thomist patriarchal and organic idea (Troeltsch 1931:285). The notion of patriarchy was implied in the idea of organicism, because organicism stressed the multiplicity and inequality of the bodily parts. Mutual adjustment, therefore, was not given but became problematic. Higher members had the authority and the obligation to provide order and harmony. The model for this was the order of the family with a dominant father and the willingly subordinated members of the family subject to his authority. The responsible father sacrificed himself for the care of his family, whereas the members of the family were obedient, hard-working, full of admiration and thankful.

There existed a tension between the need of the needy (who could not claim a share of someone else's surplus) and the obligation to give on the part of the rich (who did or did not decide to give to one rather than to another individual). In charity the emphasis was on the duty to give. In abstract terms this was identified earlier as a means to deal with salvation panic. Through almsgiving a place in heaven could be bought. This one-sided emphasis on the obligation to donate was matched by a minimalisation of the right to receive. Ultimately charity lacked a concept of rights. From this stemmed the difficulty of including a conception of rights in the reformulation of Catholic social thought along the lines of charity.

Moreover, charity, as in the saying 'charity begins at home', expresses the prior claims of the ties of the family, friendships and the neighbourhood to a man's consideration. The fundamental issue in this case is the tension between the private and public provision of assistance, i.e. between social care and public welfare. If it was the case that charity began at home, what then could be defined as the role of the public sector (the state) in providing assistance to the poor? The primacy of politics seemed to be excluded if it was assumed that the family or the neighbourhood was the first and foremost responsible provider of care. The question was what happened if such a social unit was unable to take care of its members? What if the family did not neatly behave along the lines of a sexual division of labour? What appeared to be the issue was the need of redefining the precise configuration of the relationship between the market, the family and the state under the changing conditions of industrial capitalism. The official Roman Catholic ideological concepts coming out of this struggle for modernisation typically reflected this abstract tension between the public and the private. This is exactly what one finds if one looks at such concepts as the just wage (tailored to the need of providing an income to a family) and subsidiarity (the very concept expressing the tension between private and public, or for that matter, between the social and the political).

If it was the case – as Thomas Aquinas argued – that charity belongs to the realm of virtues, and if it was the case that there existed the obligation to give which was not matched by a right to receive, then the fundamental issue that Catholics had to address was the following: charity as a vehicle for social solidarity or harmony under industrial capitalist conditions lacked the fundamental concept of rights. Charity contrasted with justice, because justice was fundamentally a matter of rights (but see Buchanan 1987). Consequently, the central difficulty for Catholic social thought resulted from the attempt to go from charity to justice. But the modernisation of the medieval heritage of Catholic social doctrine was a failed attempt to move away from the emphasis on the obligation to give to the incorporation of the idea that the poor or the helpless had a right to be assisted.

CONCLUSION

Charity was religious rather than social policy. Its aim was not the relief of poverty nor the improvement of a social order which caused suffering. Instead, charity increasingly derived its prominence from its function as provider of salvation. The theory behind charity and almsgiving concerned primarily the idea that the wealthy must buy their place in heaven with alms taken from their worldly surplus. But precisely because it was religious rather than social policy the concept was rendered problematic outside the religious context. Charity's unbalanced reliance on the Christian-inspired obligation to give ultimately ended in futility under conditions of a secul-arising, industrial capitalist world. The religio-psychological mechanism of almsgiving was powerless when not fuelled by insecurity as to one's eternal fate. The lack of a conception of rights, corresponding to the duties of charity, resulted in a period of transition in which a new Catholic con-ception of social justice was sought. Specifically, it was necessary to consider other mechanisms that could assure funds to be raised to assist the poor. Where the fear of damnation had ceased to be psychologically compelling, and hence 'voluntary' solutions failed to be an alternative, compulsion arose as an alternative to religious obligation. However, public coercion posed several problems, of which the most important were: the problem of the (best) institution for enforcing the obligation to give, the proper objects of taxation and relief, and the difficulty of legitimising coercion of obligations which were not matched by correlative rights.

The main problems of formulating a Catholic theory of social policy concerned the role of the state and the incorporation of a notion of rights. Vatican ideologues never succeeded in reformulating and updating the notion of charity, as a reading of a recent encyclical letter (*Centesimus Annus*) still illustrates:

In order to overcome today's widespread individualistic mentality, what is required is a concrete commitment to solidarity and charity, beginning in the family with the mutual support of husband and wife and the care which the different generations give to one another'.

(*Centesimus Annus*)

As will be shown in the next chapter, social Catholics throughout Europe (and in Germany in particular) did manage to solve these problems by according a prominent, yet peculiar role to the state in the relief of poverty and by formulating a conception of social justice and social citizenship which significantly departs from the conception of charity. This conception is still quite different from liberal and social democratic ideas of justice and accords distinctiveness to social capitalism, a point which is sometimes overlooked if a distinction is not made between social Catholicism (the 'little' tradition) and official Vatican social teaching (the 'grand tradition') or between religion and the social and political practice of religiously inspired political actors.

10 The intellectual origins of Christian democracy and s[...] capitalism

Modern Christian democracy springs from two main sources: political Catholicism, which addresses the changing role and status of the Church in nineteenth-century Europe after the French revolution, and social Catholicism, which confronts the rise of industrial capitalism and the integration of the proletariat as Christian citizens into modern industrial society. Social Catholicism was politically indifferent to the extent that it did not address the constitutional state, but rather a changing society. And because social Catholicism explored the possibilities of societal power, it initially denied (democratic) politics. To a large extent it constituted a strategy to 'conserve' workers as religious workers, thus diluting the social and political meaning of class and introducing religion as a basis for the articulation of political identity.[1]

Christian democracy is the result of a historical coincidence of liberal political Catholicism and social Catholicism (Maier 1969:22). Consequently, it is useful to analyse the conditions and contents of this historical coincidence, concentrating on the manner in which Catholics have come to terms with democracy and clarifying the manner in which a social critique of capitalism was successfully defined and refined, leaving room for social policy and state intervention.

THE ACCEPTANCE OF DEMOCRACY AND THE INTEGRATION OF THE WORKING CLASS

It should be self-evident that the unconditional acceptance of democracy as the chief mechanism to organise, mediate and moderate social and political conflict is a prerequisite for any political movement claiming the adjective 'democratic' in any legitimate manner. The acceptance of democratic principles by the Catholic church has been a long and laborious struggle with considerable variance across different regions and states in Europe and elsewhere (Moody 1953b:10; Martin 1978).

ere are roughly four views on the relationship between the Catholic adition and democracy (see Sigmund 1987). The first, uncritical view holds that Catholicism is indifferent as to the form of government, the only condition being that it promote the common good. The second, more critical analysis argues that the Church has always bolstered the regime which protected the Church's interests. The third argument states that a church that itself is authoritarian is hardly able to favour non-authoritarian forms of government. Those sympathetic to the Catholic cause nowadays typically argue that indifference as to the technique of government has led to the acceptance of democracy (Sigmund 1987:547).

The liberal, laic and individualistic spirit of the French Revolution was the original foe of the Church in the modern era (Irving 1979). The Popes stood for order, that is they stood for the order of the old regime. This 'link with order, and stance against "liberalism", was the curse which the revolution bequeathed to the Popes' (Chadwick 1981:610). Democracy and the arrogation of possessing the absolute truth do not go together very well. Liberal freedom included the freedom of press and in the eyes of the Popes this invited and sanctioned immoral and false publications. The Catholic Church was therefore perfectly ready to range itself on the side of anti-liberal or anti-democratic governments (Chadwick 1981:610).

In *Immortali Dei* (1885) Leo XIII did not exclude democracy as a possible form of government, and it may be read, therefore, as paving the way for the acceptance of democracy (Moody 1953c:69). One has to be a very sympathetic reader of the encyclical to accept this, for no more is said than 'no one of the several forms of government is in itself condemned, inasmuch as none of them contains anything contrary to Catholic doctrine, and all of them are capable, if wisely and justly managed, to insure the welfare of the state' (*Immortali Dei*, in Gilson 1954:177). It was not until 1944 that a more positive acceptance of democracy was proclaimed. In his Christmas message of 1944, Pius XII argued that state intervention had assumed such large proportions that democratisation had become a logical corollary of this increased presence of the state (see Moody 1953c:70; Maier 1969:24). The central tenets of natural law, on the basis of which a certain endurance in time accords legitimacy to institutions, facilitated the acceptance of democracy. The general background was given by the experience of war and fascism in Europe and was deepened by the geo-political dimension of allying the Church to the West and the 'free world' (Dorr 1983:78), rather than to the atheist communist regimes.

Although corporatism is rightly viewed as an intrinsic component of the Catholic tradition, its importance for the post-war development of Christian democracy must not be overstated. In fact, one could argue that deliberately subduing the importance of corporatism (under Pius XII) was a precondition for the acceptance of democracy and for Christian democracy as a democratic political movement. Historically, the Church's plea for a reconstruction of capitalist society in corporatist fashion (other than the earlier Romantic and conservative vision) came at a time when practical experiments were taking place very near the holy see, namely in Italy under fascist rule. In fact, *Quadragesimo Anno* (1931: sections 91–4) gives a fairly detailed description of the Italian system in practice. The encyclical is articulate as to why the experiment is to be judged positively. It facilitates the harmonious co-operation between classes, suppresses socialism and accords regulating power to corporatist institutions. The listed advantages of the system, however, are immediately followed by its likely drawbacks: the risk of the omnipresence of the state, the stifling of private initiative and the gradual development of a politicised bureaucracy, which would benefit particularist political interest rather than the public good. Moreover, the successor of the 'corporatist' Pope, Pius XII, hardly paid any attention to this aspect of *Quadragesimo Anno*. In 1949 the official view was changed and corporatism was defined as an 'opportunity missed' (Dorr 1983:81). In the post-war period it had become an anachronism and even politically dangerous to be associated with the idea of a corporate society. Therefore, the official sanction of corporatism died as soon as its implemented versions in Italy, Austria and Germany had proven to be so disastrous. 'In large measure, its cause was guilt by association' (Williamson 1985:23). Remnants or echoes, however, remained operative, although under different terms.

Equally important, yet almost never appreciated as such, for Christian democracy to come into being, is the *rapprochement* of the Church and the workers. The criterion of democracy is rather obvious and straightforward. However, whether (and to what extent) the working class is integrated into and organised within the Christian democratic movement determines not only its nature, but the very existence of Christian democracy, as the first part of this book demonstrates. Without the working class – or perhaps formulated more accurately – without substantial working-class support, there can exist no Christian democracy. It was Pius XI (1922–39) who very well understood the importance of this point when he argued that 'the greatest scandal of the nineteenth century was the fact that the Church lost the working class' (cited in Camp 1969:77). It may very well have been Christian democracy's greatest triumph that it managed to attach again parts of the working class, if not to the Church, then at least to a political movement based upon Christian principles.

Summarising the argument, one can begin to speak of Christian democracy when the criteria of democracy and (attempted) class reconciliation and integration are met. Christian democracy comes into being where liberal political and social Catholicism meet. The accommodation to capitalism and democracy has not been an easy road because there has been a long and uneasy controversy between liberal political Catholicism which came to adhere political democracy, and social Catholicism which had difficulties embracing democratic principles because of its ideology of the organic society and its corporatist rather than democratic stance.

TRADITIONALISM

Christian democracy's first historical source is the French Revolution. The effects of this revolution upon the status and position of the Church – or Christianity in general – in modern society were tremendous. 'The entire Church had been profoundly shaken by the traumatic experience of the revolution in which, for the first time in modern history, one of the greatest states in Europe had attempted to wipe out the influence of Christianity' (Camp 1969:5). The ultramontane and anti-individualistic counter-revolutionaries developed their own systematic social, political and historical critique of the revolution. This critique is known as traditionalism. The core of the theory of traditionalism consists of the thesis that Divine truth is revealed in history. Institutions prove themselves as being willed by God because of their capacity to endure. To replace institutions with this capacity by revolution is to deny the will of God. Time is an important element in the evaluation of human institutions and both the French Revolution and the Enlightenment were the targets of the traditionalist attacks because they denied Divine truth in tradition.

The growing trend towards the type of political conservatism characteristic for traditionalism after 1815 was facilitated by the fact that both the monarchy and the Church had been the main victims of the revolution (Moody 1953d:119). Monarchists thus became the natural allies of the Catholics. Moreover, those were no secure times for the clergy. Clerics argued that only the strong state of the regime could protect them from further persecution. The Bourbons, in turn, deliberately used religion in their attempts to strengthen their position, whereas many of the aristocrats became (again) Catholics, because they felt that the Church would be supporting their cause. Traditionalism shares with Romanticism a longing for the past.

The political programme of traditionalism was defined as the 'contrary to revolution' (de Maistre 1971). Traditionalism mixed to a large extent ecclesiastical elements with political stances. Religion and the model of the

Church provided the basis for a reconstitution of a Christian society ruined by revolution (Maier 1969:146). In Lamennais' famous words: 'Réconstituer la société politique á l'aide de la société religieuse'. The revolution itself, however, could be reinterpreted as a satanic and messianic event at the same time. Revolt was seen as a human passion dictated by the devil. The revolution was therefore satanic. However, since the revolution was also the judgement of providence, it was also Divine and one could therefore have faith in it. Moreover, the confiscation of the properties of the Church, the abolition of privileges and the imposition of the oath to the Civil Constitution on the clergy in 1790 provided the foundation for the renewal and regeneration of the Church. The traditionalists readily admitted that the clergy had been in need of reform and that the revolution had at least a purifying effect on the perverted part of the clergy and was therefore welcomed. Viewed in this way it might have been that 'political revolution is only a secondary object of the great plan which is developing before our eyes with such terrible majesty' (de Maistre 1971:59), but which perhaps could not be entirely understood by mortals.

The next object of traditionalist criticism was the type of fanatical individualism which had been linked with a total belief in reason and the correlate denial of the Divine plan (Lively 1971:5). Traditionalism developed its own concept of reason which was not individualistic, but a reason of the group. Reason is good for nothing and outside the realm of needs, knowledge becomes useless or doubtful. 'Wherever the individual reason dominates, there can be nothing great, for everything great rests on a belief' (de Maistre 1971:110). According to traditionalist theory, reason derives from a 'superindividual being', the Roman Catholic Church, and reveals itself in tradition. The authority of the Church is absolute (Boas 1967:154). There is only one truth and this truth is eternal. And because it is eternal, it must be true. And because it is embodied in the Church, the Church is a Divine institution.

Papal infallibility was even defended before it became official Vatican doctrine. Furthermore, the power of the papacy was considered sovereign over any temporal power (Maier 1969:155). This ultramontanism was therefore not only a theological construction but – more importantly – also a political one. It was not a matter of solely restoring the position and the status of the Pope; it equally referred to the demarcation of absolute power. The spiritual power of the Church, headed by the infallible pope, was interpreted as a counterweight to the political pervasiveness of the revolutionary state.

Paradoxically, the logical completion of the traditionalist argument (carried out by Lamennais) implied an approbation of a peculiar democratic point of view. It is this odd effect of extreme traditionalism which led to its eventual condemnation by the Church and marks the birth of liberal political Catholicism.[2] Two elements can be distinguished which led to the espousal of a bizarre democratic point of view. First of all, the premise was that the Pope is the ruler of the Church and the Church is superior to the state. Therefore, the Church is greater than the state. And if the state blocks the obedience to tradition, revolt is not only legitimate but a duty. To be able to rise up against the state's violation of the Church's eternal truth, however, freedom of speech, of the press and of education became mandatory (Boas 1967:155; Buchheim 1963:46). The second element pertains to the revolution interpreted as a Divine judgement. If the revolution was indeed such a Divine judgement one had to admit that the political forms that emerged from it, notably democracy, deserved a theological justification, too. Furthermore, the typical traditionalist argument that 'every good government is good when it has been established and has existed for a long time without being disputed' (de Maistre 1971:142) could in a certain sense and in the long run be transformed into an argument in defence of some of the results of the revolution, notably the liberal value of political freedom.

The struggle over traditionalism was a struggle over the reorientation of the Church. It created the need for a theological justification of a new position of the Church in modern, i.e. post-revolutionary society. And this society was somewhere halfway between Christian and secular. Hence, the attempt to reconcile the Church and revolution and even to promote an alliance between the Church and democracy. The liberal political Catholicism produced in the wake of this transition was of a specific kind. It did not aim at political freedom as such, but on *religious* freedom. The Catholic Church had to be free from the state. For this reason French Catholicism in its traditionalist version eventually opted for a strengthening of the Church and a break with the Bourbons (Moody 1953d:122). To free the Church from the state, all bonds between the two had to be relaxed if not entirely broken. Most importantly, the *Concordat* with Napoleon had to be abolished. It was in the strive for a complete separation of the Church and state that 'liberal Catholicism for the first time announces the claims of the Church community in defiance of the state: demands for freedom of conscience, freedom of teaching, freedom of the press, and freedom of association' (Maier 1969:193).

The traditionalists, centred around the periodical of French liberal Catholicism, *Avenir*, gradually came to adopt a more progressive liberalism, where the rights of the people were considered human rights and where the democratic principle of self-determination was fully accepted

(Spencer 1973:44). Criticism and attempts to silence the journal came from within France as well as from abroad. Liberal Catholicism's stance in political matters was, no doubt, a thorn in the side of the conservative governments in Europe. The liberal Catholics, however, were so confident as to the rightness of their crusade that they decided to submit their views to the Pope for an evaluation (Spencer 1973:46). The reaction of the Pope was negative (Woodward 1963:265) and in the encyclical *Mirari Vos* (1832) liberalism was condemned and with it liberal democratic freedoms (Spencer 1973:47).

In sum, the traditionalist argument finally resulted in an espousal of democracy, but was followed by the condemnation of the holy see. Liberal political Catholicism, then, marked the point where Catholic traditionalism became radical. The paradoxical twist of traditionalism consists of a reversal in the interpretation of the French Revolution which it came to accept, because time had proven the durability of democracy (Maier 1969:198).

ROMANTICISM

The Romantic critique of capitalism constitutes the second historical root of contemporary Christian democracy. Romanticism started off as a literary reaction against the rationalist, eighteenth-century, neo-classicist aesthetics. Although perhaps prepared and anticipated by the works of Jean Jacques Rousseau (1712–78), Romanticism's centre of gravity became Germany. The term 'Romanticism' was launched by Friedrich Schlegel (1772–1823) and was at first and foremost an aesthetic critique of modernity (see Jones 1974).

On a more general level it was Romanticism's anti-modernity which made it politically relevant, too. As a political critique it attacked the Enlightenment on its central assumptions and beliefs, in particular the ideas of rational solutions for human problems and the unshakable trust in progress. Yet Romanticism cannot simply be equated with a reactionary stance in political matters. It had many varieties, although anti-modernity certainly was Romanticism's basic strain (Berlin 1979:20).

The conservative Romantic critique of the emerging industrial society was the starting point for social Catholicism. Like its aesthetic ancestor, political conservatism found its foremost Romantic expression in Germany. Although the main period of conservative Romanticism in Germany was somewhere between 1820 and 1848, its influence on the ideas and practice of social policy reaches well into the nineteenth and twentieth centuries (Alexander 1953; Görner 1986). Conservative Romanticism can be defined as the movement which strove for the restoration of the social order of the Middle Ages as an answer to the uncertainty, instability and vulnerability of modern times. The Romantic social critique was the first doctrine to pay attention to the problems related to the societal and economic change of the nineteenth century in a more or less systematic fashion. Its object was the impoverished, although not yet quite proletarian, masses.

Romanticism wished to replace the contemporary 'atomised society' by *ständische Gliederung*, i.e. by a society classified, arranged and divided by 'estate' in order to restore the supposed unity of feudal society (Bowen 1971; Görner 1986). This basic conviction resulted in an attempt to force upon the newly establishing industrial and social reality the order of bygone times (Stegmann 1969:336). In the Romantic's eyes the new spirit of rationalist individualism, the erosion of traditional bonds and the predominance of the pursuit of self-interest constituted the root cause of what gradually became known under the name 'social question' or the 'workers question'.

The contents of political Romanticism varied considerably. There existed no such thing as a coherent set of ideas constituting a doctrine, because the single great mistake of the Romantics was that they reduced politics to aesthetics. The emphasis on aesthetics inhibited political activity (Schmitt 1986:158–9). Nevertheless, some binding elements can be distinguished. The Romantics were in favour of an organic order of society in which the estates would be orderly arranged and in which they would function as equally vital parts of a body, i.e. as if they were part of a larger whole, a living organism, to whose survival they would all contribute. In such an ideal organic society, the corporation and the *Gemeinschaft* would alter the fate of the individual who was threatened in his very existence by free competition. Social problems would find a social, or rather communal, solution without risking the power of the state to become omnipresent.

Romanticism – however contradictory this may sound – tended to be a mixture of reactionary and revolutionary ingredients. Any feasible and viable solution to the social question could only be achieved by transforming or revolutionising the basic structures of society (Weiss 1977:42). This central idea of radically transforming the foundations of modern society as a means to establish the idealised social and political bonds patterned upon the medieval example was upheld throughout the nineteenth century. Reactionary radicalism, however, alienated itself eventually from the more liberal and progressive, if not 'enlightened', social Catholics of the second half of the nineteenth century with their most prominent representative, the later bishop of Mainz, Wilhelm Emmanuel von Ketteler (1811–77).

Before the 1860s, however, mainstream social thinking within Catholic circles in Germany was deeply conservative. These conservatives opposed all types of experiments with social policy to moderate the excesses of developing capitalism. The hard-core conservatives – unlike von Ketteler and his followers, who had objections of a more religious character – had rather peculiar reasons for opposing social policy within the boundaries of capitalism. Since the goal was the replacement of the economic and social order of liberal capitalism by an organic society, social policy organised and implemented by the state within the limits of liberal society could not but strengthen this objectionable order. The conservatives argued that social policy simply obstructed the smooth transition to an organic society (Stegmann 1969:387).

The reactionary critique of capitalism loathed the evolving class struggle. Capitalism degenerated into a society in which two classes bitterly fought each other. Thus, Karl Frhr. von Vogelsang recognised 'exploiting employers, who strangle each other economically as a result of the raging international competition, and exploited workers, at whose material and moral expense this competition is being fought out' (as cited in Stegmann 1969:387, my translation). The conservative reaction to capitalism consisted of attacking it as a revolting social system. Capitalism, moreover, had brought about the equally appalling and objectionable idea of socialism. As an alternative, the reorganisation of the estates could produce the capacity to transcend the chaos of capitalism and could provide a viable barrier to the luring socialism. The conservatives were both anti-socialist and anti-liberal (Stegmann 1969:388). The political ideal still prevalent among conservatives in the 1880s in Germany was to return to the moral foundation of the early-Christian era. At that time, however, mainstream Catholic thinking and practice was already based on a more progressive analysis of the 'social question' as a religious and moral problem and on a better understanding of capitalism.

RELIGIOUS CONSERVATISM

Thus, the third historical inspiration of Christian democracy is rooted in the tradition of conservative Catholicism. Well into the second half of the nineteenth century German Catholics analysed the social effects of modernisation and industrialisation as a problem of religion and morality. The disruption brought about by capitalism was seen as an effect of a society that had given up its Christian values and had let 'egotism' rule (see Görner 1986:159). The 'social question' was essentially a religious question. Since moral decadence and the de-Christianisation of the masses were the cause of social misery it was the task of the Church to provide the solution through charity and pastoral care. This solution should consist in the renewal and deepening of the religious spirit, because the suffering of the masses was caused by the absence of the right religious spirit and conviction.

Typical for the account of the social question in religious and moral terms were the so-called journeymen's societies (*Gesellenvereine*), which were viewed as a kind of family in which the wandering and socially detached journeymen could feel at home, be morally uplifted, and enjoy some education. Originally, these organisations were so strongly tailored at moral and religious tasks, that they discouraged attention for strictly economic matters (Bowen 1971:87). Although a strong patriarchal or paternalist constitution characterised the societies – they were headed by a priest, who was assisted by a council of honour (*Ehrenrat*) consisting of prominent citizens (*achtbare Bürger*) – the journeymen's societies became successful (70,000 members in 1879; Görner 1986:162).

The social question was mainly analysed with the help of a religious and moral vocabulary: it was seen as the result of apostasy and moral decadence. The proposed solution naturally reflected this perception. Only a return to Christianity could lead to improvement. The various alternative and competing solutions offered by politicians and economists were evaluated as of little value for curing social evil. In fact, the more impotent these 'worldly' solutions proved themselves, the more powerful the doctrine of Christianity appeared. Social misery did not stem from outer needs, but from the inner spirit. Things could be easily solved if only the religious persuasion were different. Two aberrations of the spirit caused the illness of social relations: insatiable hedonism and greed, and the narcissism which smashed up the love of one's neighbour. These illnesses had infected the rich and the poor alike. Christianity was aiming at the root of the problem: the spiritual betterment of man (Stegmann 1969:344).

The endurance of this religious and moral conceptual framework in Germany can perhaps be explained by the following reasons. First of all, up until the 1860s the Industrial Revolution in Germany was occurring at a rather slow pace. The social question was hardly a problem of the prole-tarianised industrial workers. It was rather a rural problem. Second, when the Industrial Revolution accelerated, German Catholics found themselves in the middle of the *Kulturkampf*. The *Kulturkampf* seriously weakened the position of the Catholic Church within German society. The defensive position into which many Catholic politicians and ideologues were forced did not permit straightforward substantial alterations of the basic doctrines, however outworn the old dogma might have been. For any such substantial change would have been interpreted by the adherents of Bismarck as a sign of indulgence. Social doctrine became, in a sense, even an important weapon in the *Kulturkampf* (Görner 1986:164). After all, if the social question was a religious and moral problem which demanded religious solutions, then the Church would be the natural institution to take up this enormous task. The Church should not be weakened, but strengthened. In fact, the Church should be granted a monopoly in social care.

However, by repeating this claim time and again during the *Kulturkampf*, it became increasingly difficult to get rid of this point of view – even when the religious definition of the social question was no longer politically useful nor theoretically tenable. Thus, the early social Catholic movement was accused of being a movement which instrumentally employed social concern as a religious strategy to lure workers back to the Church, and which had no genuine concern for the proletariat (Görner 1986:164). It was only when the momentum of the *Kulturkampf* was relaxed that a social Catholic reorientation became feasible.

The third reason for the endurance of the religious overtones in the conceptual framework and in practical social action may be found in the fact that the Church as well as political and early social Catholicism became increasingly involved in the competition with and struggle against socialism. Although conservative social Catholicism and socialism shared a basic anti-liberal and anti-capitalist attitude which could have facilitated a coalition between the two, this did not occur for the obvious reason that they had opposing views concerning the constitution of the future society and the role of religion in it. The theoretical elements with which the social question was analysed were no grounds for agreement either. In particular the ardent anti-religious attitude of the socialists – the resignation of Church membership was a condition for party membership – could not possibly be reconciled with a movement which saw in de-Christianisation and anti-clericalism the root cause of social misery (Görner 1986:162). Collectivist solutions had too much of a socialist connotation.

It was von Ketteler, however, who began to analyse the social question increasingly in terms of reformist social policies. Paradoxically, this re-orientation presupposed the recognition of capitalism as an efficient and in principle 'just' economic system, or at least as a *fait accompli*, and the role of the state in social policy as at least a possibility. Von Ketteler is in many senses the personification of the attempt to modernise the Catholic social movement. He embodies through his life and works the whole spectrum from charity and neighbourly love to the embrace of state aid and social policy as the means to moderate capitalism. In fact, von Ketteler 'represents the pivot not only of contemporary social and political Catholicism, but of integral Catholic Germany of the 19th century' (Alexander 1953:412).

SOCIAL CATHOLICISM

In a letter (January 1864) to Lasalle, von Ketteler acknowledged for the first time that the social question was an economic question, too (see Hogan 1946:100), and he took over Lasalle's wage theory to analyse it as such. In the same year von Ketteler published his famous *Christianity and the Labour Question*, in which he rejected both socialism and liberalism. He argued that the material existence of the worker depended upon his wage. The wage was determined by the minimal necessities of life, that is, the minimal amount of food, clothes and shelter which are necessary for survival. The wage of the worker was a commodity, whose price was determined by supply and demand. Von Ketteler, no doubt, echoed Lasalle (Hogan 1946) in arguing that economic efficiency and capitalist competition threatened the material position of wage-labourers and led to malnutrition and starvation of workers and their families (Stegmann 1969:354).

Co-operative productive associations provided the solution for the labour problem. They could abolish the detachment of capital and labour and accordingly lead to the deproletarisation of the workers. The worker in such a productive association would also be employer. He could therefore receive a double income: a wage and a share in the profit. If the wage would not suffice, the share in the profit could make up any shortcoming. Apparently, the causes of the social misery and abuses were increasingly interpreted in socio-economic terms, although religious overtones were not completely absent. Most importantly, the argument was still that the state had no significant role in solving the social question.

The idea of productive associations is remarkable to the extent that it went much further than the dominant practice of charity of the conservative or Romantic Catholics. The concept of productive associations presupposed the acceptance of industrial production and was therefore a major step towards the recognition of capitalism as an economic system (Görner 1986:162). There existed, however, a tremendous problem with the feasibility of the productive associations. These simply lacked capital to get started. In addition, on the Catholic account the state was not accorded a function in providing capital for the associations. The Christian spirit was expected to be strong enough to provide the necessary resources. Still convinced of the force of charity and neighbourly love, social Catholics hoped for the generosity of the faithful, rich Catholics to raise the capital.

The almost complete failure of the productive associations in practice – the faithful rich Catholic capitalists turned out to be not that generous and 'moved' by Christian love after all – plus the implication that upon such miscarrying organisations a corporative society could not be built, were the elements contributing to a fundamental change within German social Catholicism around 1866. The majority of the social Catholic movements abandoned their anti-capitalism because it became more urgent to moderate capitalism's defects and provide workers with a share of the revenues of the new system of production (Stegmann 1969:383).

There are a number of reasons for this reorientation. One reason was already pointed to, namely the impossibility of building a corporative social order upon the co-operative productive associations that were doomed to fail. Second, natural law tends to prohibit the glorification of a historic- ally developed social and economic order as if it were the only possible, God-given, societal order. The idealised pre-capitalist society was left behind as soon as it became clear that capitalism was a new historical order with a capacity to endure and feudalism and the guild system were not supra-historical forms. Third, it became increasingly clear to German Catholics that they simply lacked the power to put a halt to the capitalist advance. Eventually, one could not afford to pursue utopian ideals at a time when things increasingly got worse. Adaptation was called for if Catholicism was to remain a power in the land.

The main result of the reorientation was that the causal relationship between religious and moral degeneration and the Industrial Revolution was redefined. It became clear that 'the miserable social relationships are the cause of the alienation of the workers from the Church, and not quite the reverse' (von Ketteler, cited in Görner 1986:168, my translation). As a result, a new role for the state became feasible. The Church was to support public social policy, since Catholicism was not opposed to social and material progress.

As Kaufmann (1988:82) argues, the demand for public social policy was characteristic for the Catholic party (Zentrum) ever since its foundation, whereas von Ketteler's design for the political programme of 1871 already contained a systematic – although mainly corporatist – proposal for social policy. In 1874 von Ketteler was president of the national convention of Catholics (*Katholikentag*) which was primarily devoted to the formulation of demands for state intervention. The following proposals were formu-lated: legal protection against physical and financial exploitation; state administration of welfare arrangements for all classes of society; legislation to improve the industrial codes; labour legislation; self-help; cherishing of the moral and religious life of the families of workers; and finally Christian charity (see Hogan 1946:208). The mix of modern and pre-modern ele-ments in this programme is striking. If one would read this list in reverse, i.e. by starting with the proposal of Christian charity, one can almost see the history of Catholic social thought in a nutshell, coming from charity, moralising and self-help to labour legislation and social policy.

The German Zentrum took over this programme and proposed what is known as the 'labour protection bill' of Clement von Galen (19 March 1877). This proposal was almost identical with what von Ketteler had defended some years before. German political and social Catholicism, therefore, had adopted quite an active position with regard to social policy already in the 1870s. In fact, the eagerness to remedy capitalism through public social policy was such that factions within the Zentrum arose that wanted a discussion on 'the limits to which the state should be restricted in framing new legislation for the workers' (Hogan 1946:214). The more social policy became conceivable, the more the problem of the extent of state interference was raised.

Von Ketteler's influence was considerable, not only on the political practice of German political Catholicism, but also on papal social ideology. *Rerum Novarum*, in particular, was inspired by him and Leo XIII mentioned this more than once (see Bowen 1971:79). The Pope, in fact, called von Ketteler his great predecessor. For Germans who were familiar with von Ketteler's *Christianity and the Labour Question* nothing original or new could be found in *Rerum Novarum* (Hogan 1946:237), because the similarity between the two documents – even in the use of words – was conspicuous (Hogan 1946:238). However, the crucial difference between the two is that *Rerum Novarum* completely failed to formulate a positive action programme.

In the gradual development to the acceptability of social policy lies an interesting parallel to the social democratic debate on parliamentarism and reformism. If it was agreed that moral and religious decay were not the cause but an effect of the excesses of capitalism, then social policy could come in to provide material relief. This, in turn, could have the beneficial effect of restoring the relationship between the Church and the workers. However, in order to be able to accept practical social policy through the parliamentary vehicle as a means to improve the material position of the working class, capitalism itself had to be recognised as a more or less 'just' economic system. In order to improve morality and religion through social policy one had to accept the very system which had caused the misery in the first place. As a consequence, religiously inspired charity, for instance, could not be but a minor part of the solution of the social question. The problem of social justice under capitalist conditions and of social policy was thus raised and the 'revolutionary' corporatist theory was rendered problematic.

Gradually, and in spite of the resistance of conservative Catholics (Stegmann 1969:390–2), reformist social Catholicism became the dominant current of German Catholicism. In Bowen's (1971:118) words: 'Meliorism, within the existing capitalist-individualist scheme of things, became the order of the day. Only a minority of social Catholics and a still smaller proportion of the Centre continued to demand radical institutional changes', i.e. a reconstruction along corporative lines. In fact, the conservative, Romanticist corporatism never assumed a prominent position in the Zentrum's political programme, although it kept functioning as the utopian ideal, as a point of reference for the critique of liberal individualism and socialist collectivism.

PAPAL DOCUMENTS

The final historical source for contemporary Christian democracy concerns the extensive body of Roman Catholic social teaching. The 'social doctrine' or 'social teaching' of the Catholic Church is a relatively recent phenomenon. It did not exist as a separate body of theory before 1878. Since then it has gained an important place among official Vatican ideology and has functioned as a source of inspiration for social Catholics and Christian democracy throughout Europe and elsewhere. The first question is why the papacy became increasingly interested and active in formulating a social doctrine which could be distinguished from other dogma?

It might be that the Church after an era of complete negation of the social question until the 1880s was badly in need of a 'leader in the Vatican who could detect the disease and prescribe an effective remedy' (Camp 1969:7) and that it was Pope Leo XIII who led the Church into the modern era. But most probably, it was the economic crisis of the 1880s which not only worsened the conditions of the working class but also led to the greater magnetism of the radical, Marxist socialist movement. The socialist movement was for the main part anti-Christian and in the eyes of the clerics constituted a threat to the very existence of the Church. Consequently, the pressure on the papacy to pay attention to the social question was greatly increased. The circumstances were – so to speak – begging for a gesture from the Church. *Rerum Novarum* (1891) was a main attempt to keep workers as Catholics within the Church. Social Catholics in Germany under the leadership of Bishop von Ketteler had paved the way for the official papal social ideology. The decisive difference between Leo XIII and his predecessors, who merely rejected all phenomena of modernism, was that this Pope believed that industrial society and Catholicism could be reconciled (Camp 1969:13). In addition, the Thomist revival within the Catholic 'intelligentsia' stimulated the formulation of a new and modernised social doctrine.

Social doctrine originated as a new branch of Catholic doctrine as the result of the decline of the temporal power of the Church (Burns 1990). The Church started to centralise its control over morality and the moral dimensions of the economic realm in particular. Rome became the oracle of the moral dimension of social, economic and political life. The 'neo-feudalism' of social doctrine was essentially an attempt to provide an alternative for liberal individualism and socialist collectivism (Burns 1990:1126).

These reasons contributed to the appearance of a new body of doctrine, social doctrine. The Industrial Revolution and the victory of industrial capitalism constitute the incentive as a reaction to which this new doctrine was formulated. The timing of the emergence of the new branch of ideology can be explained by the economic crisis of the late 1870s and 1880s, which made the social question all the more imperative, as well as by the success of the socialist movement, which posed a political challenge with its anti-clericalism. The already available philosophy of Thomas Aquinas could be drawn upon precisely because of the emphasis on reason as a foundation of faith, which provided the Church with theoretical weapons to defend the faith against the attacks of rationalist philosophies.

Throughout the first social encyclical explicitly addressing the conditions of the working class one can find clear signs of what might be defined as a theoretical endeavour to go from the basic contents of old ideas on the centrality of charity and neighbourly love to a new conception of justice. In *Rerum Novarum* (1891), however, the emphasis remains on charity. It is not until the reign of Pius XI that the movement of modern Catholic social theory away from the dominance of charity was further developed, although never entirely completed. By that time, however, Catholic political parties had already an extended experience with social policy. Leo XIII argued:

> True, no one is commanded to distribute to others that which is required for his own needs and those of his household; nor even to give away which is reasonably required to keep up becomingly his condition in life. . . . But, when what necessity demands has been supplied and one's standing fairly taken thought for, it becomes a duty to give to the indigent out of what remains over. . . . It is a duty, not of justice (save in extreme cases), but of Christian charity, a duty not enforced by human law.
>
> (*Rerum Novarum*, in Gilson 1954:217–18)

And further:

The common mother of rich and poor has aroused everywhere the heroism of charity, and has established congregations of religious and many other useful institutions for help and mercy, so that hardly any kind of suffering could exist which was not afforded relief. At the present day many there are who . . . seek to blame and condemn the Church for such eminent charity. They would substitute in its stead a system of relief organized by the state. But no human expedients will ever make up for the devotedness and self-sacrifice of Christian charity.

(*Rerum Novarum*, in Gilson 1954:221–2)

Now, compare these statements with the words of Pius XI 46 years later in his encyclical against communism:

A charity which deprives the working man of the salary to which he has strict title in justice is not charity at all, but only its empty name and hollow semblance. The wage-earner is not to receive as alms what is his due in justice. And let no one attempt with trifling charitable donations to exempt himself from the great duties imposed by justice.

(*Divini Redemptoris*, in Camp 1969:100)

Rerum Novarum is the first papal document attempting to introduce other means than the duties of charity as relief for social misery. Apparently, Pope Leo XIII took sides against such Catholics as the Belgian economist Périn and his followers, some of whom rather cynically argued that poverty was a necessary condition for charity (Camp 1969:79). The question is whether the Pope offered a real alternative.

The first modification of charity was that instead of continuing to stress the duty to give, Leo XIII started to emphasise the duty of employers to treat workers as fellow Christians by improving the conditions of work. At the same time the working class had to be obedient and show respect for the employers. Careful reading of the encyclical reveals that the emphasis remains on obligations rather than rights. Ultimately, the great social encyclical lacks a clear conception of rights, except where the right to private property is concerned.

The main fear that the first social encyclical deals with concerns the danger of socialism. The papal programme of social reform can be defined as the opposite of socialism. The generalisation of private property rather than its socialisation is proposed as the solution to the social question. Increasing wages and savings could improve the material position of workers and lead to a more equal distribution of resources. As a result, workers would empathise with their employers and turn away from the errors of socialism. The lengthy rejection of socialism facilitates a critique of capitalism that avoids the risk of an association of the Catholic social view with socialism (Dorr 1983:14). The object of *Rerum Novarum* is the condition of the working class. Its real subject matter, however, is not the one-sided attention to labour but rather the 'relative rights and mutual duties of the rich and of the poor, of capital and labor' (*Rerum Novarum*, in Gilson 1954:206).

The encyclical argues that the misery of the working class is caused by the erosion of the traditional bonds of religion and of the guild society. Nothing that could protect the workers had come in their place. This class lost all means of protection and security and was subject to 'the hard-heartedness of employers and the greed of unchecked competition' (*Rerum Novarum*, in Gilson 1954:206). Greed and usury of employers deepened this social crisis as a result of which 'a small number of very rich men have been able to lay upon the teeming masses of the laboring poor a yoke little better than that of slavery itself' (*Rerum Novarum*, in Gilson 1954:207).

The socialist solution of socialising private property was not a tenable solution. In the first place, the workers themselves would be the main victims of such a policy, because private property can be seen as wages in another form. In his defence of private property, Leo XIII developed some elements of a Catholic conception of justice. Socialising is against justice, because every man has by nature the right to possess property as his own. Man is a rational being who through private property tries to take care for the future; private property is in accordance with natural law.

Private property was at the same time the adequate means for bettering the condition of the working class. This theory of private property as social policy must above all be interpreted as anti-socialist in its propensity, because any attempt to pursue social reform had to start with the recognition of the inviolability of private property (*Rerum Novarum*, in Gilson 1954:213). This view of private property is atypical and is possibly the weakest part of this encyclical (Camp 1969). It was unusual because it did not seem to correspond with Thomist theory. The scholastics typically argued that needs be provided for through the common labour of all. They never implied that it should be guaranteed that each could provide enough for himself (and his family). The scholastic version of the theory of private property implicitly leaves room for charity by stressing the fruits of common labour instead of individual effort. The Pope's version, on the other hand, seems to limit the possible role of charity. The basic weakness of this theory of property stems from the fact that it is hardly applicable to modern industrial society, and is rather based on a view of society which was primarily agrarian, i.e. a society where proletarians could buy a piece of land and become small farmers and thus diminish the status of their labour power as a commodity on the market.

Rerum Novarum argues that the best approach to the betterment of the position of the proletariat consists in the recognition of inequality as the normal and natural condition of society. Suffering, furthermore, is the lot of humanity. This type of reasoning must be interpreted as an attempt to justify inequality and the resulting social misery rather than as a well-reasoned account of the necessity of change. In fact, the Pope goes so far as to argue that only because inequality exists can society function properly. A puzzling sentence, furthermore, holds that 'nothing is more useful than to look upon the world as it really is, and at the same time to seek elsewhere . . . for the solace to its troubles' (*Rerum Novarum*, in Gilson 1954:214). This means that society cannot be changed fundamentally. It basically contains a call for escapism.[3] As such it shows the Pope's deeply conservative view on the constitution of society and the possibilities of reform. Relief of worldly misery should above all be sought in the comfort religion provides and in the hope of a better life hereafter. The cryptic sentence cited above may be taken to mean that one has to look upon the world

> as inhabited by men whose natural inequalities necessarily beget social inequalities; it is to accept the fact that, ever since original sin, work has ceased to be a freely chosen delight; it is to become reconciled to the idea that, for the same reason, hardships, sufferings, and death will have no cessation or end so long as the world and mankind continue to exist; in short, it is not to turn the world into the fool's paradise imagined by so many social reformers.
>
> (Gilson 1954:200)

This theory of inequality originates in the theory of society as an organism. On the organic view of society, hands do the work and the heads provide direction. The classes that perform manual labour are the poor and the classes that control are the rich. This division of society into classes was considered to be permanent and, by implication, inequality was seen as a permanent feature and quality of human society. Such a theory of inequality as a perennial characteristic of society brings in the concept of charity, because it excludes the rightful claim of the poor to a larger share of societal wealth (see Agócs 1988:41).

If inequality was natural and therefore good and just, it was a mistake to think in terms of class struggle, because how can the members of one and the same body be at war among themselves? The idea of class struggle was the greatest fallacy of socialism. The truth of the organic society is that the relations between classes are harmonious and that these classes co-operate simply because they are mutually dependent (*Rerum Novarum*, in Gilson 1954:214). Surely, there is always a certain extent of friction and it was only religion that had the ability to hold the two classes firmly and harmoniously together. Religion pointed to the mutual duties of justice.

On the Catholic interpretation of justice, however, duties have no corresponding rights. The basic contradiction in *Rerum Novarum* as the expression of Catholic social theory, therefore, is found in the attempt to define a conception of justice while omitting a theory of correlative rights. In other words, the first social encyclical acknowledges only the right to private property. Only the duties of justice are clearly defined. Among these the following bind the workers: work according to the agreed conditions of the contract; respect private property and the employer; abstain from violent revolt; and avoid 'evil' men (socialists) (*Rerum Novarum*, in Gilson 1954:215). The duties of justice prescribed for a capitalist are: respect workers as fellow Christians; respect labour as honourable; do not look on workers as commodities, but as Christians; therefore, make sure that workers can perform their religious duties, protect them; have the worker respect his family; provide suitable work, fairly paid, because 'his great and principal duty is to give every one what is just' (*Rerum Novarum*, in Gilson 1954:215). Reading this fragment more than 100 years after publication it strikes the reader that what now for the most part would be identified as rights of workers are formulated here as duties of capital and vice versa. Furthermore, the cause for the commodification of labour power (man as a thing) was found in the misuse the employer made of the physical powers of workers rather than in the structural features of anonymous markets.

What is just, however, remains obscure, and the question remains: what is to be done when those who have the obligation to provide a just wage (however defined) fail to do so and those who are to receive such a wage have no rightful claim to it? The answer is charity. Employers are expected to obey the duties of charity, while the proletariat is not given any right to action to get that to which it is 'entitled'. The fear of revolution or the disruption of societal stability excluded such a possibility. The Pope 'set up an ideal of harmony in society that was so exalted and perfect that it remained abstract and unreal' (Dorr 1983:23). The conclusion, therefore, is that – unlike in the social theory and practice of German social Catholics in particular – no progress was made in the attempt to update charity as a workable concept for reform and political action. Whenever the Pope used the vocabulary of 'rights and duties' of capital and labour, he had only a vaguely modernised version of the duties of charity in mind and in fact only one right: the right to private property.

In trying to formulate a positive action programme the relative roles of Church and state are underlined. Although the Church is defined as primarily interested in the spiritual well-being of the workers, the Catholic theory holds that 'Christian morality, when adequately and completely practiced, leads of itself to temporal prosperity' (*Rerum Novarum*, in Gilson 1954:220). The Church is said to have intervened with great success on behalf of the poor by organising and supporting the organisations of charity. The claim is that in order to spare the poor the shame of begging the Church has arranged for their relief.

Why, then, did the Pope find it necessary to write an encyclical on the misery of the working class if charity were indeed so successful? This contradiction plainly shows the failure of the Vatican ideologues to fully recognise the fact that charity under conditions of a secularising capitalist society had become an anachronism. In this sense, the Pope in 1891 was theoretically at the level of German social Catholicism in the 1860s. He failed to integrate the major insights with regard to social policy and the rights of workers that von Ketteler had already formulated in the early 1870s.

Surely, the social question is partly interpreted as the result of the failure of the obligations of charity. It is for this reason that the relative roles of state and Church are being analysed. The state's role in the relief of the poor, however, could only be understood as derived from the imperfect obligation of the conception of justice. It is only because duties turn out to be not so binding as the Church would want that the state acquires a role in the solution of the social question. Nevertheless, in a typical manner the function of the state is defined as the obligation to govern society by allowing the institutions of society to prosper (*Rerum Novarum*, in Gilson 1954:222). The only reason the state should work for the benefit of the poor is because it should work for the benefit of all classes of society.

The argument is continued with an often misinterpreted sentence: 'among the many and grave duties of rulers who would do their best for the people, the first and chief is to act with strict justice – with that justice which is called distributive – towards each and every class alike' (*Rerum Novarum*, in Gilson 1954:223). *Prima facie*, distributive justice could be mistakenly taken to imply an important function of the state in the redistribution of wealth of society, let us say, a conception that is very near the social democratic one. However, the fact that distribution has to be just to 'every class alike' does not imply redistribution. On the contrary, it puts strict limits to the extent to which wealth can be transferred from one class to another. The doctrine of the natural inequality of society defines that redistribution may never go so far as to mitigate class differences because this would be unjust. Justice, therefore, does not demand more than that the state takes care that workers are clothed, housed and fed 'so that they find their life less hard and more endurable' (*Rerum Novarum*, in Gilson 1954:224). Again, it has to be stressed that this role of the state is defined as a duty of the body politic, not as the right on the side of the working class. Poverty, then, becomes the effect of a double failure to perform a duty: of the rich to give alms and of the state to provide relief; poverty is not the lack of guarantees for the fulfilment of a right. There is no such thing as a rightful claim to relief.

State intervention is even further limited to the extent that the smaller social units such as the family are not to be absorbed. The state should only come in 'whenever the general interest or any particular class suffers, or is threatened with harm, which can in no other way be met or prevented' (*Rerum Novarum*, in Gilson 1954:224–5), as in the case of strikes, the relaxation of family ties, the lack of time for the performance of religious duties, moral decay through the mixing of the sexes, too high burdens upon workers and dangers for health. But the limits are strict, albeit dependent on concrete cases; a successful mediation of the state should immediately be followed by abstaining from further intervention (*Rerum Novarum*, in Gilson 1954:225). This is of course the doctrine of 'subsidiarity' in its embryonic form, which has come to play such a central role in Christian democratic political theory. Forty years later the theory of subsidiarity was more clearly defined in *Quadragesimo Anno*:

> It is indeed true, as history clearly shows, that owing to the change in social conditions, much that was formerly done by small bodies can nowadays be accomplished only by large organizations. Nevertheless, it is a fundamental principle of social philosophy, fixed and unchangeable, that one should not withdraw from individuals and commit to the community what they can accomplish by their own enterprise and industry. So, too, it is an injustice and at the same time a great evil and a disturbance of right order to transfer to the larger and higher collectivity functions which can be performed and provided for by lesser and subordinate bodies.
>
> (*Quadragesimo Anno*, in O'Brian and Shannon 1992:60)

With respect to the conception of rights and correlative duties there is a further ambiguity. Rights are to be defended religiously and the state has the duty to protect rights. In fact, Leo XIII argues that the poor and the badly off have a 'claim' for special consideration, because the poor have less to protect themselves and, accordingly, depend on assistance offered by the state. 'And it is for this reason that wage-earners, since they mostly belong in the mass of the needy, should be specially cared for and protected by the government' (*Rerum Novarum*, in Gilson 1954:225–6). Although the word 'claim' suggests that a right to assistance exists, corresponding with a duty on the side of the state, such a right is nowhere defined.

This ambiguity is increased by the analysis of exploitation in terms of the passion of greed. Paradoxically, where this passion is intense, the first duty is to control the poor. Relief is of lesser importance, because a redistribution of wealth cannot but violate private property (*Rerum Novarum*, in Gilson 1954:226). In case of a conflict between capital and labour, even if the cause of the conflict is exploitation, the first thing to make sure is that capital be protected by guaranteeing private property. The Church feared most of all the revolutionary forces of society. The state had the obligation – so to speak – to protect the workers from themselves, so that they would not engage in unjust, radical political activity (*Rerum Novarum*, in Gilson 1954:226). There is no option for the poor left but 'to put up with their sad situation' (Dorr 1983:20).

There are, however, some positive rights for workers, such as the right to rest one day a week (Sunday) in order to pray, and certainly not to spend in idleness or worse, in 'vicious indulgence' (*Rerum Novarum*, in Gilson 1954:227). This right to Sunday rest is mainly motivated by the fact that religious practice can make a man forget the daily sorrow and pay attention to God. The worker, moreover, ought to receive a just wage (the vocabulary of rights is again avoided here). The free market wage-setting procedures of supply and demand were not accepted. Wages should not go beyond the level of the just wage, i.e. a wage sufficient to provide for the needs of the worker and his family.[4] The anti-liberal doctrine on the just wage is one of the clearer statements of *Rerum Novarum*. Wage policy should come in as a rudimentary means of making wage-labour less dependent upon market relations. It is implied that the just wage should even be slightly more than just enough for the worker and his family to the extent that it should also allow for some saving. Saving was seen as the proper means to acquire property and property was the suitable means to solve the social question. The role of the state, then, was not only to protect the private property of the capitalists, but also to promote deproletarisation by stimulating workers to save.

The solution of the social question on the Pope's account, therefore, consists in making everybody a small proprietor. It reveals the Pope's naive worldview which was basically still agrarian and feudal in outlook. It explained poverty in terms of the lack of morality. There is no account of the structural conditions of modern society, let alone a view on the difference between feudal and industrial society (Camp 1969:56). More specifically, the great social encyclical letter of Leo XIII lacks a theory of capitalism and therefore fails to offer a workable solution to the social question. The third way between capitalism and socialism is neither simply reform nor revolution. The basic mistake concerns the inability to understand the fundamental difference between private property as such and the private ownership of or control over the means of production, since the fundamental characteristic of capitalism is the separation of producers from their means of production. The section on the great and excellent things that will follow from the spread of private property shows the inability of the Catholic Church 'to see the capitalist world as it really was'. If only workers would have the prospect of acquiring a privately owned plot, 'the consequence will be that the gulf between vast wealth and sheer poverty will be bridged over, and the respective classes will be brought nearer to one another' (*Rerum Novarum*, in Gilson 1954:230–1).

CONCLUSION

Christian democracy is intimately affiliated with the European tradition of political and social Catholicism and comprises the main 'little tradition' of Roman Catholicism as opposed to the 'grand tradition' of the established hierarchy of the Church. The 'grand tradition' of official Vatican social teaching has accorded the European Christian democratic movement a body of ambiguous doctrine which could be used and translated for practical purposes. It was, however, the 'little' tradition of social Catholicism that has provided the Christian democratic movements of Western Europe with a social concern and with a more practical theory of social policy and modern politics. Social Catholicism has managed to go beyond Medieval ideas on charity in spite of rather than thanks to the social teaching of the Church.

11 Conclusion

There seem to be two paths in providing an answer to the question whether, to what extent and under what conditions Christian democracy fosters a distinctive welfare state regime. A first answer is that it is not so much politics or politically generated institutional settings that matter in explaining cross-national qualitative differences between welfare state regimes, but rather it is cultural variables that are of consequence. This idea comes very close to the reasoning behind the families of nations hypothesis (Castles 1993). Families of nations are defined in terms of 'shared geographical, linguistic, cultural and/or historical attributes and leading to distinctive patterns of public policy outcomes' (Castles 1993:xiii). The conjecture then would be that nations that (partly) fall within the Catholic belt of continental Europe and that share the common cultural heritage of Catholicism will most likely be quite similar in their configuration of market, state and family. *Prima facie*, the analysis presented here provides evidence that this is empirically plausible. Catholicism furnishes a common core of social policy characteristics around which various regimes within the Catholic group tend to converge.

Theoretically, however, there are three complications arising with respect to the families of nations argument. The first concerns the question to what extent 'sharing a common cultural heritage or experience' matches requirements of comparability. If the distinction between 'little' and 'grand' traditions makes sense, then to share the common cultural heritage of Catholicism means different things across nations as well as within nations. For instance, does Catholicism as a cultural variable mean the same thing in France and in Italy? And has the impact of the second Vatican Council been the same in the Netherlands and in Germany? Second, there are only a few nations that are homogeneously Catholic and the question must be how different cultural traditions (such as Calvinism and Catholicism in the Netherlands and Catholicism and Lutheranism in Germany) interact in producing a 'common culture'. Third, how does one operationalise a common cultural heritage. How to measure the impact of Catholicism? As argued in Chapter 3, one cannot simply take the number of Catholics in a nation as an approximation and one needs to check carefully the number of people who actually attend church services. But even in the latter case, the question remains whether 'going to church' means the same thing across nations.

Culture, conceptualised as the whole of beliefs, morals, habits and laws that routinely shape everyday life, engenders the structural context for political culture, understood as the norms and values that pattern political behaviour. The political culture of a nation consists of 'a set of orientations toward a special set of social objects and processes', as one classical statement holds (Almond and Verba 1963:13). Catholicism as a cultural variable influences such orientations, but not necessarily in an identical way across national contexts. A cultural tradition, as far as it can be identified, still needs to be translated into politics and policies. In this sense, the path followed in this book is complementary to the cultural argument yet necessary for an answer to the question whether and to what extent Christian democracy fosters a distinctive form of welfare capitalism. It is difficult to understand how culture shapes politics and policies directly. Social policy was shown to be produced by political movements in the context of the norms and values that shape political life and to be dependent on the prevalent relations of power in a nation and on the coalitional behaviour of parties. At the same time, Christian democracy had to be understood as a variable, too. The character of this movement, particularly with respect to social policy conceptions, could not simply be identified in general terms, precisely because the movement is characterised by a ceaseless attempt to accomplish a settlement between possibly opposed societal interests. And because the contents of such a possible accord vary historically and cross-nationally, the question whether Christian democracy fosters a distinctive welfare state regime is answered by a qualified 'yes'. The 'little' tradition of social Catholicism has provided the Christian democratic movements of Western Europe with a distinctive social theory of capitalism, a common core that all movements share. But the manner and extent of its crystallisation in the social policy performance of nations in the Catholic belt of Europe was only established by documenting the conditions under which social and political actors actually have tried to concretise and implement social policy on the basis of the teachings of social capitalism.

If Christian democracy can be argued to represent a middle way between capitalism and socialism, between a blunt commitment to the market and a confident trust in the possibilities of politics, one still must acknowledge that such a stance is founded upon a set of foundational concepts and on a specific social and political practice. Christian democracy is a distinctive political phenomenon that – despite variations – nourishes a distinctive welfare state regime. The study of Christian democratic ambiguity in terms of political programme and ideology leads to the conclusion that distinctiveness arises out of the indeterminacy as to the concrete profile of the central political concepts of pluralism, accommodation and reconciliation. Christian democracy appears to be more about method than about substance. Nevertheless, the continuous attempt to harmonise conflicting interests has given rise to a specific and empirically identifiable mix of social policies that mitigates the political salience of cleavages but does not aim at a transcendence of their social reality.

Christian democracy's seemingly open-ended ideology has yielded a marked capacity to adapt. Its central concepts mirror and facilitate this unique capacity. Christian democracy is therefore defined as fundamentally the embodiment of societal accommodation. Religion or religious appeal can be identified as the mechanism for producing cross-cleavage appeal. Integration of a plurality of societal interests is not only a basic feature of the movement, it is its reason for existence.

The recognition of class differences and the supposition of class and cleavage reconciliation induces the necessity to reproduce the salience of class and other social cleavages and deny their political thrust at the same time. Social capitalism can be interpreted as the common core and solution of the eternal search for what is in this specific sense a 'middle way'. Social capitalism aims at the perpetuation of societal differences and transformation of their political effect. Social capitalism is indeed both capitalist and social. It allows virtually every class and social status group to organise and to exist without allowing conflicts between them to become politically dominant and threaten the stability of the construction. Christian democracy interferes when fundamental social units fail to secure their own existence, whether this be the family, vocational entities or the market itself.

A corollary of this type of distinctiveness is that the precise configurations of social capitalism become historically contingent, although societal accommodation and the integration of demands of the working class are always at the heart of the package. There is no predetermined plan, there is only a predetermined mechanism. This is why social capitalist nations vary among themselves and yet, taken as a group, can be distinguished from other models of affiliating the market, the state and the family. It has mainly been the 'little' Catholic tradition which has accorded social capitalism its unity around the specific theory of state intervention. Subsidiarity's peculiarity lies not only in the prominence that it accords to the lower social organs, but also in the emphasis on the duty of the state to act as a subsidiser in case of inadequate functioning of organic parts. The state steps in to abet and to restore self-responsibility and the capacity of lower members of the body politic to help themselves. While social misery was originally the effect of the failure on the side of the rich to perform their duties of charity, persisting poverty would now be the failure of the duty of the state to provide relief. Public authority on the Christian democratic account has largely taken over the failing psychological mechanism of salvation panic.

There are two ways of viewing the relationship between Protestantism and welfare statism. The first stresses the Protestant revolution of religion as a major step towards secularisation. In those nations in which the reformation had a lasting impact and in which an intimate state–church relationship gradually developed, the conditions for the collectivisation and nationalisation of welfare services were most favourable. Protestant secularisation prepared the way for social democratic welfare statism. The second interpretation does not accord any direct relationship between protestantism and social capitalism either. Protestant social movements have had little to do with the development of this regime. In the Netherlands, for instance, it was the exclusion of the anti-interventionist Protestant politics that was crucial for a Catholic–socialist coalition (but see Therborn 1994). In Germany, Protestant liberalism became an integral part of Catholic-dominated Christian democracy, which – in turn – facilitated an alliance with the secular liberals. In Italy, Protestantism did not play any role for the obvious reason that in this nation the reformation had little impact on popular religion.

Such ideas of historical contingency and the theory of structural dependency allowed for the appreciation of three variants of social capitalism and Christian democracy and for divergence in the historical fate of social capitalism and Christian democracy in different nations. In Germany, Christian democracy relied more on an accommodation of the centre and the moderate right without having to disengage itself from working-class support. Nevertheless, founded upon unique historical conditions and constraints, the balance of forces within society and within the movement accorded German Christian democracy a more conservative silhouette. Compared with the Netherlands social capitalism in Germany was less generous and more particularist. German political discourse hardly allows for the *Wohlfahrtsstaat*, but nourishes the *Sozialstaat*. In the Netherlands the conditions of an alliance between social democratic reformism and social Catholic 'correctivism' under the exclusion of anti-state Protestant-ism yielded an exceptional form of generous, yet passive interventionism. Nevertheless, the dominance of traditional structures and ideologies – particularly with respect to the role of the family – made the Dutch opt for a strong gender differentiation in social policy. The welfare state regime in this nation mirrors this facet in that the state almost became a *pater societas*. The Dutch speak of a *verzorgingsstaat*, that is a 'caring state' which not only transfers large amounts of cash benefits, but – according to the connotation of the Dutch word – has a heart for its people, too. Italian Christian democracy has allowed its integrative capacity to distort its version of social capitalism as a form of unparalleled power accumulation. The effect of the peculiar conditions in this nation in the early period after the war was parliamentary inertness and socio-political incrementalism. In Italy, too, pre-war structures were reinstalled in many fields as a result of Christian democratic politics to prevent universalism. The physical pre-sence of the Roman Catholic Church in the nation produced a formidable support for the Christian democratic movement, but ultimately led to a search for alternative power resources. The historical legacy of a plurality of semi-public institutions provided an opportunity to build a momentous double public power: the authority of the state and an intermediary level where Christian democracy ruled. In Italy, Christian democracy does not appear to constitute societal accommodation, but the capacious field of semi-public institutions facilitated the reconciliation of dissension within the movement itself. The Italians rather use the terms *stato assistenziale* and *stato previdenziale* to reflect the fragmentation of rights attached to citizenship as in the health sector and those attached to performance on the labour market.

In all three nations social policy has constituted a resource for power mobilisation. Christian democratic parties have managed to establish cross-cleavage co-operation without diluting social status and identities. In the course of their policies they have moderated the political salience of class and have forced the left into a defensive position. In the Netherlands, social democracy was quick to adapt and consequently enjoyed the power to govern for a decade or so after the war and in the 1970s. German social democracy was much slower in understanding the political presence and effect of an immensely integrative Christian-inspired cross-confessional movement. As a result, social democratic reformism had to wait until conditions changed and a modernisation of the movement itself had taken place. The transformed communist party in Italy still awaits the opportunity to enter national governments. However, governmental power in Italy mattered less than in the other nations and conflicts have piled up in the *sottogoverno* to such an extent that Italy's permanent crisis of government is presently turning into a crisis of the political system at large.

The historical fate of Christian democracy is associated with the development of social capitalism. Failure to provide feasible accommodations for conflicting interests endangers the survival of Christian democracy. Difficulties in providing cross-cleavage appeasement tend to reinforce class as a basis for political articulation and consequently weakens the appeal to workers through the vehicle of religion. In addition, the reliance on electoral appeal alone tends to threaten the possibilities for power mobilisation. German Christian democracy is the example of a movement which failed to become the embodiment of societal accommodation in the 1960s and which consequently lost the initiative in societal consensus building. Dutch Christian democracy successfully surmounted the confessional differences under pressure of electoral and infrastructural disintegration. Only because it managed to re-ally forces in a renewed attempt to provide an integration of interests (including those of workers) did it manage to survive and increase in strength until very recently. Italian Christian democracy seemed to have been most successful in investing power resources. It created a plurality of resources that it employed not only to accommodate societal difference, but also to provide an outlet for intraparty rivalry. The difference between Italy on the one hand and Germany and the Netherlands on the other lies in the fact that in Italy the method of reconciliation became the means of power accumulation rather than an end of politics. Paradoxically, it is this characteristic of Italian Christian democracy which is also related to the recent and surprisingly fast decomposition of the movement, as will be argued below.

In general, the structural characteristics of social capitalist nations have first facilitated but may now render problematic the continued reproduction of the power of Christian democracy. Social capitalism may continue to provide a medium and outcome of Christian democratic power only to the extent that the movement manages to compose a plurality of resources throughout society and the state, continues to foster cleavages in the social realm and dilutes their political salience through accommodation at the same time, and gradually replaces an outspoken religious appeal with a more soft-spoken and general enchantment of Christian morality. But the prospects of doing precisely this are dim, as the decomposition of Christian democracy in Western Europe in the 1990s indicates.

THE DECOMPOSITION OF CHRISTIAN DEMOCRACY AND SOCIAL CAPITALISM?

If one adopts an elementary political-sociological view and believes that there exists a direct link between changes in the social structure and the transformation of contemporary party politics, predicting the decomposition of Christian democracy should be a safe bet. The movement is likely to wither away as religious cleavages cease to control the articulation of political identities. Christian democracy is rapidly becoming a political anachronism in the secular world we live in at *fin de siècle*.

However, if one rightly assumes that secularisation is a long-term historical process that has accelerated since the 1960s and that has negatively affected the capacity of religiously inspired political movements to continue to attract support, it is actually surprising that – perhaps with the exception of Italy – Christian democracy has not yet disappeared entirely. In fact, in the perspective of a 'naive' political sociology, the very survival of the movement in the 1970s, its revival in the 1980s and its tenacity in the 1990s seems to constitute a paradox. The analysis presented in this book, however, may substantiate the claim that no direct, linear and immediate relation between politics and the social structure can be assumed. The political fate of Christian democracy is not solely determined by the declining impact of religion on social and political attitudes. Although changes in the social structure most likely affect the power of political movements, they do not do so linearly. Specifically, it is not so much – or at least not only – the transformation of the religious cleavage structure of continental Western Europe, but rather – or primarily – the exhaustion of the post-war Christian democratic model of welfare capitalism which is presently modifying the capacity of enduring power mobilisation.

An implication of the very argument elaborated above is that if one speaks of the contemporary fate of Christian democracy, one is simultaneously talking about the destiny of a distinctive political economy. If 'social democracy has a double meaning, at once denoting a political movement and its purported achievements' (Esping-Andersen and van Kersbergen 1992:187), so does Christian democracy. It indicates both a distinctive political movement and an equally idiosyncratic political economy. Throughout this study the term Christian democracy was used for the political actor and the notion of social capitalism for the movement's alleged achievements. The present argument is that social capitalism has been both the outcome and medium of Christian democratic power mobilisation and that the exhaustion of social capitalist arrangements is currently draining the movement's power resources.

It has to be stressed that this argument is necessarily somewhat specula-tive, since it deals with contemporary developments. Nevertheless, in order to make plausible that the depletion of social capitalism is causing the decomposition of Christian democracy, one has to accept that once politics, policies and policy outcomes were causally connected, but that now the severance of such causal links is producing feedback effects that are detri-mental to the power of the political movement. The prospects for contem-porary Christian democracy cannot be appreciated adequately unless its historical distinctiveness in terms of ideology, power resources, politics and policies is taken into account. The analysis of distinctiveness and of the dilemmas that the contemporary movements face will then also prove valuable for understanding the current development of the politics and political economies of Christian democratic nations.

This study has attempted to correct a theoretical and empirical short-coming of comparative political sociology and economy and to provide more satisfactory interpretations of Christian democracy in various con-texts of analysis and of the political economy that the movement has fostered. Perhaps it can also contribute to a comprehension of the move-ment's current dilemmas and prospects.

As argued, it appeared particularly difficult to appreciate fully the political distinctiveness of Christian democracy. Many approaches to the comparative study of political movements have started from the assump-tion that Christian democratic parties do not possess an elaborate ideology,[1] cannot boast of a definite political practice and have had no specific impact on the political economies of the nations in which they operate (e.g. Bingham Powell 1982; Steiner 1986; Mény 1990; Lane and Ersson 1991; Gallagher, Laver and Mair 1992; Therborn 1994; see van Kersbergen 1994:31–5). In general, there has been a tendency among social and political scientists to either 'forget' Christian democracy or to treat the movement in a 'stepmotherly fashion'.

As a result, Christian democracy was commonly but inaccurately under-stood – depending on the context of analysis – as functionally equivalent to social democracy, particularly when dealing with the expansion of the welfare state. The risk is that now the movement will be equated with conservatism, particularly when dealing with welfare retrenchment or moral issues. This assumed functional equivalence, i.e. the idea that Christian democracy does more or less what other movements under comparable conditions would have done, has nourished the conviction that compre-hensive, comparative studies of Christian democratic politics and policies are by and large irrelevant for understanding the contemporary politics of advanced capitalist democracies. Many a study of the impact of politics on society, which include the Christian democratic nations, have produced incorrect accounts, not just because they underestimated or wrongly appreciated the distinctiveness of Christian democracy, but mainly because they generated partial, and therefore inaccurate, accounts of the political systems and political economies upon which the Christian democratic movements have had considerable influence.

The justification for rejecting a simple theory of functional equivalence and for allowing at least some notion of distinctiveness started from the observation that Christian democracy has nurtured and profited from the salient religious cleavage in Western Europe. This cleavage has not only changed the logic of political conflict in general by transforming and moderating the political significance of class, but has also provided the terms of a qualitatively distinctive post-war path to welfare capitalism.

If post-war advanced capitalist democracies have generally been characterised by economic prosperity, stable polities and relatively fixed political alignments, politically recognised systems of interest intermediation, the institutionalisation of the welfare state and international economic integration, the Christian democratic nations were no exception in these respects. However, these nations do exhibit historically specific economic and political-institutional qualities that have governed a distinctive path of post-war economic growth and modernisation, that have likely constrained their adaptation to the economic stagnation and the crises of the 1970s and 1980s in a particular manner and that are currently structuring a characteristic response to the globalisation of the international economy and to the transformation of capitalism into what we are still compelled to call post-industrial society.

Christian democratic parties in power have neither opted fully for the social democratic project of maintaining full employment nor for the neo-liberal market-based accommodation to changes in the international economic order. Instead, they have continued to uphold what they view as a socially acceptable capitalism. Post-war Christian democracy in power has indeed fostered a distinctive political economy, social capitalism. And the contemporary movements, although increasingly compelled to follow policies of retrenchment and austerity, have consistently attempted to preserve some form of social compensation that could ease the pain of economic adjustment.

The extent to which Christian democracy has managed to uphold a specific form of welfare capitalism even under worsening economic conditions and changing structural constraints hinged upon its capacity to preserve and reinforce social and political power resources that were capable of countering various forces of transformation, whether these arose from domestic social and political contexts or stemmed from transnational, 'systemic' constraints. And it is precisely the increasing difficulty of defending a distinctive political heritage that is seriously hampering the capacity of continued power mobilisation.

As Christian democratic politics and policies become increasingly contradictory, the movement is heading for double trouble. The declining political significance of religion is not only sapping the potential electorate of Christian democracy, but – most importantly – is causing the decay of what was identified as the politics of mediation, defined as the religiously inspired, ideologically condensed and politically practised conviction that conflicts of social interests can and must be reconciled politically in order to restore the natural and organic harmony of society. It was this feature that stained the distinction between Christian democracy and conservatism. The perennial search for societal accommodation was one of the movement's major electoral assets and determined its 'natural' position in the centre of the political system. This, however, is now rapidly losing its pronounced ideological significance and is blurring the distinction between conservatism and Christian democracy. The golden age of the politics of mediation is coming to an end as the general sources that used to provide the cement for social capitalist arrangements are drying up. The passive, corporatist, transfer-oriented political economies of Christian democratic nations increasingly fail to deliver the goods that provided the currency for the kind of beneficial political exchanges that Christian democracy nurtured in the attempt to mediate opposed societal interests.

In sum, Christian democracy's trouble is double. On the one hand, it consists of the declining significance of religion which is decreasing the ideological importance of the politics of mediation. On the other hand, the politics of mediation is losing its potential for success in any case as the terms and goods upon which a stable accommodation of conflicts of interests could be based are increasingly becoming scarce. This defines the contemporary political position of Christian democracy and of social capitalism.

The politics of mediation has historically distinguished Christian democracy. This religiously motivated politics determined Christian democracy's social policy. Under expedient economic circumstances possibly opposed interests were accommodated with beneficial effects on the position of political power. Christian democracy has indeed fostered – despite variations – a distinctive welfare state regime.

Social capitalism was crucial for generating cross-class support. The religiously inspired political theory functioned as an important electoral asset to the extent that it was capable of subduing the political significance of class and facilitated cross-class accommodation. Consequently, the electoral class dilemmas that tend to emerge from any attempt to widen the social substructure of electoral support were relaxed. However, although religious appeal facilitated cross-class support, it did so only at the risk of losing a clientele of non-religious groups. In other words, there was the continuous threat that an emphasis on Christian principles deterred secular voters. Nevertheless, Christian democracy continuously benefited from the ability to politicise at certain times the religious cleavage and, at other times, to use social and economic contrasts in an attempt to become a catch-all party of specific type (Schmidt 1985).

The constraints of electoral competition affected policy. Social capitalist bargains were to moderate the political effects of class cleavages, but not to temper the political and ideological influence of religious cleavages or other conflicts. It was to accommodate social, economic and cultural contrasts, not to transform occupational, economic and social status differentials. Christian democracy's model was in no sense an attempt to create universal solidarity. Rather it was a procedure for moderating societal cleavages while reinforcing social groups and group identities in an attempt to gain as broad a social support as it could possibly obtain.

This is how social capitalism became both a medium and outcome of Christian democratic power. In other words, the typical patterns of electoral mobilisation (as identified in Chapters 3 and 4) forced Christian democracy to follow a politics of mediation. At the same time, however, successful cross-class mobilisation depended on the material promises of the movement's distinctive political project as the case studies of social policy in Germany, Italy and the Netherlands have documented.

These case studies, moreover, not only illustrate how the politics of mediation and social policy were once positively associated, but also how Christian democratic social contracts and the political trade-offs they embody are vulnerable and difficult to reinforce if the infrastructure of ever-growing resources is falling apart. If Christian democracy has successfully harmonised conflicting interests in the past by relying on the integrative capacity of religion and social capitalism, the declining political salience of religion might have undermined the possibility of upholding social capitalist arrangements. But then secularisation should have led to the disintegration of Christian democracy already in the 1980s. Surely, the Christian democratic movements of Western Europe did lose support in this period, but they were also capable of regenerating politically. How can this be explained? There are two explanations that refer to secularisation and that may clarify that the thaw of the 'frozen' cleavage structures of Western Europe is not sufficient to appreciate the political fortune of contemporary Christian democracy.

First, Europe is still far from being an entirely secularised society. Inglehart (1990) has shown that – although regular church attendance has declined considerably in the post-war period – 35 to 50 per cent of the population of Germany, Italy and the Netherlands still regularly attend religious services. Particularly interesting is the fact that still about a quarter of the 18–24 age group in West Germany attend religious services at least once a month. In the Netherlands this percentage was 37 per cent and in Italy 40 per cent. Moreover, atheists constitute a minority of the population in every European nation. In the Netherlands 71 per cent, in West Germany 80 per cent and in Italy 88 per cent of the population answered positively to the question whether they believed in God. And the percentages of the people considering themselves religious were 69 for the Netherlands, 65 for West Germany and 84 for Italy. In fact, in the most secular nation of continental Western Europe, France, 65 per cent of the population reports to believe in God and 53 per cent of the population is religious. 56 per cent of the French youth (15–24) believe in God and 42 per cent are religious, although only 11 per cent go to church regularly. These data appear to indicate that the opportunity for Christian democracy to continue to appeal to religiosity as an electoral asset has by no means necessarily disappeared entirely.

But one might argue that the political significance of religion has changed considerably and that being religious means something entirely different now than it did some 20–40 years ago. Secularisation cannot be read from data on church attendance or by asking such vague questions as 'Do you believe in God?' People might go to church as often as they did in former days, but they now refuse to accept the message from the pulpit as having a necessary impact on their social and political attitudes. Secularisation may be a multidimensional process of which declining church attendance is but an imperfect indicator.

If one studies recent party manifestos it is clear that Christian democrats themselves sense that their clientele still potentially exists. Rather than fearing the transformation of traditional religion as a threat to political power, they have increasingly analysed the transformation of the religious cleavage structure as indeed changing, but not eliminating the capacity of power mobilisation. The adaptability of Christian democracy in their view remains unaffected, because Christian morality has not disappeared, but is now more generally diffused outside the traditional institutions of religion. Moreover, a political project of trying to accommodate social conflicts is still relevant to the extent that the *raison d'être* of politics continues to be rooted in societal contradictions.

Christian democrats seem to have a point here. Recent research on the

Dutch case, for instance, indicates that about 25 per cent of the Christian democratic electorate is secular, that 31 per cent attends religious services regularly, and that 46 per cent of those who vote for Christian democracy are indeed religious, but rarely ever go to church (Pijnenburg 1993). The conclusion is that the continuing electoral appeal of Christian democracy under conditions of secularisation of the 1980s might indeed have been a paradox (i.e. a seeming contradiction), because the degree of secularisation is either overestimated or wrongly interpreted.

Unless one adopts the view that secularisation suddenly is causing the decomposition of Christian democracy in the 1990s, the current position of Christian democracy cannot be explained by looking at the declining influence of religion alone. Yet there are signs of the decline of Christian democracy. The Dutch have recently witnessed a historic political event. For the first time since the introduction of universal suffrage and proportional representation in 1917 a government coalition was inaugurated (in August 1994) in which Christian democracy did not take part. Dutch Christian democrats have lost their long-established political dominance. Their electoral defeat of May 1994, the ideological *rapprochement* of social democracy and conservative liberalism, and the consistent anti-Christian democratic politics of the liberal democrats, particularly during the coalition negotiations of the summer of 1994, have effectively blocked a return of a usual government dominated by the Christian democratic party.

Although Christian democracy in the Netherlands has experienced a considerable loss of political power, it still manages to attract about 20 per cent of the vote. Italian Christian democracy, on the other hand, seems to have been marginalised entirely. At the national elections of 1992 the DC attracted a historic low 29.7 per cent of votes (see Pasquino and McCarthy 1993). A full-scale electoral collapse, however, occurred at the local elections of 1993, where Christian democracy was decimated. The party's share of the vote fell to about 11 per cent. In effect, the DC no longer exists, although in an attempt to modernise, stifle the scent of corruption, suggest a radical break with the past and maximise the chance of rebirth, the centrist and right-wing factions of the DC (or what was left of these) have established a new party. Because until the early 1990s democracy and Christian democracy in Italy were virtually synonymous, the decomposition of the DC symbolises the disintegration of the entire post-war Italian political system.

By contrast, Christian democracy in Germany shows less signs of decomposition. But this may be an illusion. The 43.8 per cent of the vote that the CDU/CSU managed to win at the federal elections of 1990 was 6 to 10 per cent above the party's support that the polls were anticipating before the collapse of the communist regime in East Germany (Hancock *et al.* 1993). The favourable unification effect seems to be played out now as a western post-unification tax backlash and eastern popular discontent are taking over. The downward electoral trend that can be observed since the early 1980s is likely to be confirmed at future elections when the unification surplus of Christian democracy will be undone, although appealing to anti-communism may gain some electoral potential again as the 1994 electoral campaign of the CDU/CSU emphasised the threat of a coalition between the former East German communists and the social democrats.

In other continental European nations the electoral appeal of Christian democracy is decreasing, too. Whereas in 1978 Belgian Christian democracy still attracted about 36 per cent of the vote, by the early 1990s its electoral support had dropped to about 24 per cent. And whereas the ÖVP consistently won 42–5 per cent of the vote in the 1970s, the 1990 elections signified a considerable loss for Christian democracy in Austria, too: Christian democracy scored a historic low 32 per cent of votes.

Again, patterns of secularisation alone cannot account for these diverging developments and the exhaustion of the politics of mediation is what matters, too. The success of the politics of mediation, social capitalism, and cross-class accommodation, and with it the potential for Christian democratic power mobilisation, have crucially depended on the extent to which religion moderated class as a ground for the articulation of political identity and on the resources available for making beneficial political exchanges between various social interests. And it is the exhaustion of resources that now tends to hinder the politics of mediation through social policy, because it is increasingly difficult to satisfy opposed social interests in terms of a political pay-off if the political process increasingly resembles a zero-sum game.

One of the main difficulties that governments dominated by Christian democracy in the Netherlands have faced in the period 1982–9, for example, concerned the inability to contain increasing claims on the extensive system of social security. An increasing number of people are becoming dependent on the welfare state, while a decreasing number of people are contributing to the resources of the system. This has led to a 'crisis of inactivity', exemplified by the dependency ratio: the ratio of social benefit recipients to employed persons, still only 45.9 per cent in 1970, increased to 68.4 per cent in 1980 and to 86.4 per cent in 1985. In 1990 it was 85.6 per cent and it has been this high ever since.

It is precisely the burden of 'inactivity' which is exhausting the capacity of the politics of mediation, blocks the continuation of cross-class and cross-generational contracts and causes electoral decline. The 1994 electoral campaign of Dutch Christian democracy was overshadowed by internal frictions between a faction that opted for a greater stress on neo-liberal adjustment policies and a faction trying to uphold social compensation. The party's leader increasingly represented the former faction. This, however, impeded the ability to keep the support of key electoral groups. Farmers were already resisting cut-backs of subsidies, the raising of taxes and the increasing financial burdens of environmental pollution. But the powerful farmers' union explicitly refused to lend support to the Christian democratic cause, when a secret note of the Christian democratic minister of agriculture filtered through, in which for electoral reasons he proposed to postpone a major increase in the price of natural gas[2] until after the elections. The Christian democrats also lost the support of considerable sections of the elderly population when they announced that they would not be able to guarantee the current level of public pension benefits. In fact, this issue has led to the establishment of two new parties exclusively for the aged that primarily draw their support from the core Christian democratic areas in the south and that managed to win 7 seats in the parliament in May 1994. Similarly, Christian union leaders have become increasingly reluctant to instruct their members to vote for Christian democracy. Surely, neither the Dutch workers, nor the farmers, nor the elderly have suddenly lost their religious faith; they have lost their faith in Christian democracy.

In Italy, too, voters have lost their confidence in Christian democracy. But in Italy too the fall of Christian democracy cannot be explained by a sudden drop in the religiosity of the core Catholic constituencies (see Cartocci 1993). There is no way in which an answer can be provided here to the question why the post-war Italian political system has collapsed. But the exhaustion of resources that used to grease the politics of mediation 'Italian style' has most certainly played an important role.

The breakdown of the DC has come as a surprise. As argued in Chapter 7, in 1990 Tarrow still explained the DC's amazing capacity to survive under conditions of continuous crises in terms of the movement's 'soft hegemony'. Christian democracy's strength and survival depended on the movement's ability to nourish a plurality of power resources in the course of continuous crises, without ever dominating Italian society entirely. But the soft hegemony of the DC, the highly factionalised organisation of the party and the ineffective and clientelist welfare state have now proven to be both strong and weak elements in the power accumulation of the movement. As public deficits spiralled and the crisis of the welfare system became undeniable in the late 1980s, the clientelist welfare state increasingly failed to deliver the currency for politically advantageous exchanges. Anti-communism dwindled as a major electoral asset for the DC after the disintegration of the communist regimes. The economic integration of the European Union and the completion of the single market pressured the Italian state to take retrenchment policies seriously. As a result of these developments, the DC's capacity to adapt and to survive through the usual politics of faction reconciliation by means of the costly allotment of money and jobs decreased spectacularly.

Clientelism and corruption have always been recognised as major problems of Italian post-war politics, but it was only when the resources for political exchanges dried out that the critique of the *partitocrazia* and *sottogoverno* took practical effect. Explanations of the collapse of clientelist politics in terms of public outrage are not convincing, because – as the saying goes – those who live in glass houses should not throw stones. The politics of mediation *all' italiana*, i.e. political clientelism with a strong inclination toward political corruption, was not just a phenomenon of corrupt politicians, but presupposed a corrupt society (Maraffi 1993). The clientelist mechanism was a means by which 'political parties channel policies and resources towards individuals and groups and, in return, are guaranteed continual electoral support' (Waters 1994:174). Therefore, if patrons fail to deliver the goods (e.g. a job or a benefit) to their clients, there is no reason for the clients to return a non-existent favour.

In conclusion, the fate of a political movement may very well be associated with its historical record in terms of policies and policy outcomes. The original conditions for Christian democratic power mobilisation seem to have deteriorated considerably and the characteristic political mechanisms that belonged to the post-war period roughly until the 1980s now seem to have lost much of their capacity to generate support. Although changes in the social structure have always presented political movements with a necessity to adapt, such adaptation has become increasingly difficult. Current constraints and pressures are now harder to assimilate and seem to exclude the possibility of continuing 'politics as usual'.

Christian democratic governments since the late 1970s have attempted to adjust to new demands and constraints by adopting a very moderate course of neo-liberal, supply-side policies, without entirely abandoning the post-war model of compensatory social policies. The political project of Christian democracy in the 1980s was different from, for instance, the monetarist project of Thatcherite Britain to the extent that the process of gradual adaptation did not result in a shift in the policy paradigm. Instead, Christian democratic policies in the 1980s very much resembled normal policy-making – i.e. 'a process that adjusts policy without challenging the overall terms of a given policy paradigm' (Hall 1993:279) – that attempted to avoid a zero-sum logic by refusing to shift resources from one group to another or from one programme to another. For instance, retrenchment in the field of social policy has tended to be characterised by general benefit cuts rather than by attempts to restructure programmes entirely (see e.g. Alber 1986). However, the opportunity for such 'salami tactics' seems to decline and the legitimacy and acceptance of such policies may have reached their limits. Adjustment policies that do not alter the policy paradigm may have worked for a certain period of time, but may also have produced feedbacks that currently bridle their continuation, with negative effects on the electoral appeal of Christian democracy.

The current difficult situation of Christian democracy may have other, deeper roots, too. Perhaps it is not only the depletion of a specific type of political economy which is causing the decomposition of the political movement, but also a much broader social process that is affecting traditional politics in general and Christian democracy in particular. The attempt to accommodate possibly opposed interests has characterised Christian democracy. The politics of mediation, however, presupposed the existence of groups with distinct identities. Processes of differentiation and individualisation, however, have eroded groups and group identities to such an extent that it is now virtually impossible to identify them as in any sense politically distinct. Christian democracy's political practice has always been infused by the conviction that society consists of socially embedded persons rather than individuals and that group loyalties are stronger than individual choices. Accordingly, Christian democrats have found it very difficult ideologically and politically to cope with the erosion of traditional bonds and particularly with the transformation of the family. The ideological innovation of Christian democracy in the 1980s in the Low Countries and elsewhere has primarily consisted of an attempt to redefine group identities and to revitalise the theory of social personalism as an alternative for liberal individualism (Dierickx 1994). But this has caused Christian democratic political theory gradually to develop into nothing but a normative theory of society, which increasingly lost its capacity to understand the condition of modern, individualised capitalism empirically. As a result, it has lost much of its capacity to appeal, not because it speaks in religious terms, but because it addresses the modern world with superseded concepts.

Christian democracy is also affected by the general disintegration of traditional politics. As a result of changing cleavage structures and the transformation of political contexts, we might currently be witnessing both the dealignment and realignment of voter blocs, accompanied by a general disorientation among voters and policy-makers. Contrary to what some observers have claimed (e.g. Gallagher, Laver and Mair 1992), the frozen party systems of continental Western Europe may indeed have entered a phase of thaw. The political superstructure of capitalist democracies has long since ceased to reflect the social base upon which it originally rested. Although the effect of this discrepancy on party identification and political configurations has lagged behind, it might currently cause an alteration of traditional democratic politics. This transformation is exemplified by a collapse of the functions of political parties and the decline of conventional political participation (declining party membership, an increasing incapacity to find and nominate candidates for public office and a declining capacity to aggregate, articulate and accommodate conflicting societal demands in coherent political programmes), but is at the same time matched by a rise of other forms of political participation (Lawson and Merkl 1988; Dalton and Kuechler 1990).

Similarly, the current transformation of democratic politics seems to be characterised by a 'crisis of representation'. Contemporary political parties not only find it difficult to explain who they represent, but are increasingly – so to speak – socially indifferent in this respect. This is not only (if at all) an effect of changing cleavage structures and eroding political (group) identities, but also (or more critically) the consequence of the changing function of political parties as the very intermediary between society and the state. It is not so much the party which is in decline, but the party as we knew it in the twentieth century, i.e. the party that represented civil society at the level of the state. Political parties now have lost their rooting in society and increasingly depend on the resources of the state. As a result, it seems to make sense to abandon entirely a political-sociological view that assumes a link between society, institutions, policies and policy outcomes, and adopt a conception that emphasises that 'the state and its resources are used by the parties in order to ensure their own survival and persistence, and in order to make themselves more self-sufficient' (Mair 1994:18). If this is correct, the days are numbered for the politics of mediation and for social capitalism, and Christian democracy may not live to see the twenty-first century.

Appendix

A SOURCES AND SUMMARY STATISTICS OF THE VARIABLES USED IN THE REGRESSION EQUATIONS (CHAPTERS 5–7)

1. Expenditure of social security schemes as percentage of gross domestic product, 1960

Source: ILO *The Cost of Social Security, Basic Tables*, various years

Arithmetic Mean =	10.6	Geometric Mean =	10.1
Variance =	8.4	Standard Dev. =	2.9
Minimum =	4.9	Maximum =	15.4
Number of values =	18		

2. Expenditure of social security schemes as percentage of gross domestic product, 1980

Source: ILO *The Cost of Social Security, Basic Tables*, various years

Arithmetic Mean =	20.3	Geometric Mean =	19.3
Variance =	39.9	Standard Dev. =	6.5
Minimum =	10.8	Maximum =	31.9
Number of values =	18		

3. Gross domestic product per capita at current prices and current exchange rates in US dollars, 1960

Source: OECD *National Accounts*, various years

Arithmetic Mean =	1366.9	Geometric Mean =	1256.6
Variance =	307710.6	Standard Dev. =	554.7
Minimum =	477.0	Maximum =	2841.0
Number of values =	18		

4. Gross domestic product per capita at current prices and current purchasing power parities, 1980

Source: OECD *National Accounts*, various years

Arithmetic Mean =	8597.7	Geometric Mean =	8465.1
Variance =	2170398.5	Standard Dev. =	1473.2
Minimum =	4978.0	Maximum =	11794.0
Number of values =	18		

5. Proportion of aged (65 or older) as a proportion of total population, 1960

Source: SSIB

Arithmetic Mean =	0.10	Geometric Mean =	0.10
Variance =	0.00	Standard Dev. =	0.02
Minimum =	0.06	Maximum =	0.12
Number of values =	18		

6. Proportion of aged (65 or older) as a proportion of total population, 1980

Source: SSIB

Arithmetic Mean =	0.13	Geometric Mean =	0.13
Variance =	0.00	Standard Dev. =	0.02
Minimum =	0.09	Maximum =	0.16
Number of values =	18		

7. Unemployed as percentage of total labour force, 1960

Source: OECD *Historical Statistics*

Arithmetic Mean =	2.45	Geometric Mean =	1.81
Variance =	3.55	Standard Dev. =	1.88
Minimum =	0.40	Maximum =	6.40
Number of values =	18		

8. Unemployed as percentage of total labour force, 1980

Source: OECD *Historical Statistics*

Arithmetic Mean =	4.71	Geometric Mean =	3.64
Variance =	6.02	Standard Dev. =	2.45
Minimum =	0.20	Maximum =	7.70
Number of values =	18		

9. Number of union members as a proportion of the total labour force, 1960

Source: SSIB

Arithmetic Mean =	0.39	Geometric Mean =	0.37
Variance =	0.02	Standard Dev. =	0.14

Minimum =	0.17	Maximum =	0.66
Number of values =	18		

10. Number of union members as a proportion of the total labour force, 1980

Source: SSIB

Arithmetic Mean =	0.46	Geometric Mean =	0.42
Variance =	0.03	Standard Dev. =	0.18
Minimum =	0.20	Maximum =	0.81
Number of values =	18		

11. Left parliamentary seats as a proportion of total parliamentary seats, average 1946–60

Source: Thomas T. Mackie and Richard Rose *The International Almanac of Electoral History*

Arithmetic Mean =	0.37	Geometric Mean =	0.29
Variance =	0.02	Standard Dev. =	0.15
Minimum =	0.01	Maximum =	0.52
Number of values =	18		

12. Left parliamentary seats as a proportion of total parliamentary seats, average 1946–80

Source: Thomas T. Mackie and Richard Rose *The International Almanac of Electoral History*

Arithmetic Mean =	0.37	Geometric Mean =	0.29
Variance =	0.02	Standard Dev. =	0.14
Minimum =	0.00	Maximum =	0.51
Number of values =	18		

13. Parliamentary seats of Christian democracy as a proportion of total parliamentary seats, average 1946–60

Source: Thomas T. Mackie and Richard Rose *The International Almanac of Electoral History*

Arithmetic Mean =	0.17	Geometric Mean =	0.77
Variance =	0.04	Standard Dev. =	0.19
Minimum =	0.00	Maximum =	0.48
Number of values =	18		

14. Parliamentary seats of Christian democracy as a proportion of total parliamentary seats, average 1946–80

Source: Thomas T. Mackie and Richard Rose *The International Almanac of Electoral History*

Arithmetic Mean =	0.16	Geometric Mean =	0.74
Variance =	0.03	Standard Dev. =	0.18

Minimum =	0.00	Maximum =	0.47
Number of values =	18		

15. *Pension expenditure as a percentage of gross domestic product, 1960*

Source: OECD *Social Expenditure, 1960–1990. Problems of Growth and Control*

Arithmetic Mean =	4.56	Geometric Mean =	4.12
Variance =	4.56	Standard Dev. =	2.14
Minimum =	1.39	Maximum =	9.81
Number of values =	18		

16. *Pension expenditure as a percentage of gross domestic product, 1980*

Source: OECD *Social Expenditure, 1960–1990. Problems of Growth and Control*

Arithmetic Mean =	8.52	Geometric Mean =	7.97
Variance =	8.81	Standard Dev. =	2.97
Minimum =	4.40	Maximum =	13.50
Number of values =	18		

17. *Weighted average net replacements rates, 1960*

Source: SSIB

Arithmetic Mean =	0.44	Geometric Mean =	0.41
Variance =	0.02	Standard Dev. =	0.14
Minimum =	0.13	Maximum =	0.69
Number of values =	18		

18. *Weighted average net replacements rates, 1980*

Source: SSIB

Arithmetic Mean =	0.65	Geometric Mean =	0.63
Variance =	0.02	Standard Dev. =	0.15
Minimum =	0.33	Maximum =	0.88
Number of values =	18		

19. *The difference between the take-home pay plus cash transfers of a family with two children and the take-home pay plus cash transfers of a single (expressed as a percentage of gross earnings) in 1980 (take-home pay = gross earnings minus income tax and employee's social security contributions)*

Source: OECD *The Tax/Benefit Position of Production Workers, 1981–1985*

Arithmetic Mean =	11.67	Geometric Mean =	11.25
Variance =	9.75	Standard Dev. =	3.12
Minimum =	5.60	Maximum =	18.20
Number of values =	18		

20. Cash benefits as a proportion of total benefits of social security schemes, 1960

Source: ILO *The Cost of Social Security*, various years

Arithmetic Mean =	0.75	Geometric Mean =	0.75
Variance =	0.01	Standard Dev. =	0.09
Minimum =	0.53	Maximum =	0.87
Number of values =	18		

21. Cash benefits as a proportion of total benefits of social security schemes, 1980

Source: ILO *The Cost of Social Security*, various years

Arithmetic Mean =	0.68	Geometric Mean =	0.67
Variance =	0.01	Standard Dev. =	0.10
Minimum =	0.52	Maximum =	0.86
Number of values =	18		

22. Total labour force as percentage of population 15–65, 1960

Source: OECD *Economic Outlook, Historical Statistics 1960–1990*

Arithmetic Mean =	68.73	Geometric Mean =	68.54
Variance =	25.51	Standard Dev. =	5.05
Minimum =	60.70	Maximum =	78.00
Number of values =	18		

23. Total labour force as percentage of population 15–65, 1980

Source: OECD *Economic Outlook, Historical Statistics 1960–1990*

Arithmetic Mean =	69.90	Geometric Mean =	69.60
Variance =	41.32	Standard Dev. =	6.43
Minimum =	57.70	Maximum =	81.00
Number of values =	18		

24. Male labour force as percentage of male population 15–65, 1960

Source: OECD *Economic Outlook, Historical Statistics 1960–1990*

Arithmetic Mean =	94.69	Geometric Mean =	94.61
Variance =	15.04	Standard Dev. =	3.88
Minimum =	85.50	Maximum =	100.00
Number of values =	18		

25. Male labour force as percentage of male population 15–65, 1980

Source: OECD *Economic Outlook, Historical Statistics 1960–1990*

Arithmetic Mean =	85.71	Geometric Mean =	85.62
Variance =	15.65	Standard Dev. =	3.96
Minimum =	78.90	Maximum =	94.50
Number of values =	18		

26. *Female labour force as percentage of male population 15–65, 1960*

Source: OECD *Economic Outlook, Historical Statistics 1960–1990*

Arithmetic Mean =	43.27	Geometric Mean =	42.13
Variance =	100.51	Standard Dev. =	10.03
Minimum =	26.20	Maximum =	65.60
Number of values =	18		

27. *Female labour force as percentage of male population 15–65, 1980*

Source: OECD *Economic Outlook, Historical Statistics 1960–1990*

Arithmetic Mean =	54.06	Geometric Mean =	52.93
Variance =	118.46	Standard Dev. =	10.88
Minimum =	35.50	Maximum =	74.10
Number of values =	18		

28. *Number of central social security schemes controlled by bi- or tripartism, 1980*

Source: US Department of Health and Human Services *Social Security Throughout the World*, various years

Arithmetic Mean =	1.22	Geometric Mean =	1.26
Variance =	1.62	Standard Dev. =	1.27
Minimum =	0.00	Maximum =	4.00
Number of values =	18		

29. *Fragmentation as the sum of special occupational schemes within major social security schemes, 1980*

Source: SSIB; Esping-Andersen (1990: 70)

Arithmetic Mean =	6.28	Geometric Mean =	4.69
Variance =	20.76	Standard Dev. =	4.56
Minimum =	1.00	Maximum =	15.00
Number of values =	18		

B A SHORT DESCRIPTION OF ECONOMETRIC TESTS (SEE IAS 1990)

1. F-test for significance of estimated coefficients

General form:

H_0: $B^i = 0$;

H_1 = At least one of the restrictions is not valid.

2. Jarque-Bera test for normality of residuals

General form:

H_0: residuals are normally distributed;

H_1: residuals are not normally distributed.

3. White's test for general heteroskedasticity

General form:
H_0: residuals are homoskedastistic;
H_1: residuals are heteroskedastistic.

4. Goldfield-Quandt test for general heteroskedasticity

General form:
H_0: residuals are homoskedastistic;
H_1: residuals are heteroskedastistic.

5. Outlier test for structural change induced by a one-time shift in the mean of the dependent variable (mean shift outlier model)

General form:
H_0: there is no outlier;
H_1: there is an outlier (if test-statistic exceeds critical value).

6. Regression specification error test

H_0: standard assumptions of OLS-regression apply;
H_1: model specification is incorrect.

7. Residual analysis (a) and sensitivity analysis (b)

a) detection of outliers and structural break;
b) detection of influential data.

Notes

2 THE WELFARE STATE AND CHRISTIAN DEMOCRACY: AN INTRODUCTION

1 Reviews are offered by Alber (1982), Shalev (1983), Uusitalo (1984), Wilensky *et al.* (1985), Therborn (1986b), Skocpol and Amenta (1986), Henriksen (1987), Olsson (1987) and Pierson (1991).

2 For stylistic reasons, I use the terms 'capitalist democracies', 'industrial democracies', 'industrialised democracies', 'advanced industrial nations' and the like interchangeably. Capitalist democracies are those democracies that have combined a capitalist economy with a continuous democratic political system since 1945.

3 Accordingly, I largely ignore the otherwise significant body of literature that is concerned with the effects of welfare state development in terms of employment trajectories and economic growth (see Esping-Andersen and van Kersbergen 1992; Esping-Andersen 1993).

4 This point can perhaps be elaborated more generally. Many welfare state studies examine the extent to which states rather than markets provide welfare, and therefore analytically neglect the role of families and semi-public or voluntary associations in the provision of care and welfare. In addition, although Esping-Andersen's emphasis on decommodification rightly draws attention to the development of social rights attached to wage labour, the concept is analytically less sensitive to claims and rights based on needs (social assistance) and to those on the basis of gender (marriage, motherhood) (Orloff 1993:317; see also Bussemaker and van Kersbergen 1994; Daly 1994).

3 THE POLITICAL ENTRENCHMENT OF CHRISTIAN DEMOCRACY IN WESTERN EUROPE, 1870–1960

1 Protestantism has contributed little to the European tradition of Christian democracy. Historically oriented studies have suggested that one can safely speak of the 'minimal contribution of European Protestantism to the formation of Christian democracy. . . . It is . . . no exaggeration to say that before 1945 the idea and the movement of Christian democracy in continental Europe were limited to regions of Catholic prevalence' (Maier 1969:5–6). The German

Protestants, for instance, were much more preoccupied by the *Kulturkampf* than with the misery of the masses at the same time that German Catholics were already proposing social policy (see Chapters 9 and 10). Although Bismarck's social laws may have followed flawlessly from the ideal of the Christian state founded on the identification of the Prussian state with (Lutheran) Protestantism, in Germany, too, Protestants hardly developed a workable social idea and their social movements remained relatively weak (Kaufmann 1988:80). Within Protestant circles 'social reform failed to become a serious ecclesiastical issue either for orthodox, church-going Protestants or for those of more liberal persuasion' and the uncertainty 'about the delicate balance between civil and ecclesiastical power effectively postponed the German Protestant effort to reach an understanding of modern social issues' (Shanahan 1954:416). Moreover, in predominantly Protestant nations, there are no Christian democratic parties. The Christian parties of Scandinavia are parties of moral protest as are the minor Protestant parties in the Netherlands (Karvonen 1994; Madeley 1982, 1994).

2 In the definition of Kossmann (1978:304) 'the system of institutionalised segmentation according to which each religious or quasi-religious group . . . was encouraged and subsidised by the state to create its own social world, comprising the entire existence of an individual from nursery school via sporting club, trade union, university, hospital, broadcasting and television corporation, to the burial society'.

3 Note that the 'instability' of government in Switzerland is in fact an effect of the peculiarities of this nation's system. Government leadership is rotated among the major coalition parties in a one-year cycle. In addition, once appointed a government cannot be dismissed during the entire electoral period.

4 The sad estimation is that of the 140,000 people that the Nazi's had 'classified' as '*Volljuden*', 100,000 did not survive the concentration camps.

5 WELFARE STATE REGIMES AND SOCIAL SPENDING

1 I am indebted to Olli Kangas for pointing out some of these problems.

2 This model and all other regression models reported in Chapters 5–7 were tested for violation of regression assumptions, using the Interactive Simulation System (IAS), developed at the Institute for Advanced Studies, Vienna, Austria. All variables in each estimation reported in this and the following chapters are standardised. The Appendix offers the summary statistics of the variables and a short description of the econometric tests (see IAS 1990, which contains an explanation of the mathematical properties of the tests).

3 Further second-order testing of the second model showed that there appeared to be no problems with the main regression assumptions. Jarque-Bera test: 0.21, Pr: 89.9%; White's test: 4.91, Pr: 29.71%; Goldfield-Quandt: 1.46, Pr: 31.49%; Outlier-test: 2.095 (insignificant). In addition, none of the various specifications of tests for functional form indicated problems.

4 Test results for model II (1980): Jarque-Bera test: 0.60, Pr: 73.96%; White's test: 1.23, Pr: 54.72%; Goldfield-Quandt: 3.36, Pr: 5.29%; Outlier-test: 2.55 (insignificant). In addition, none of the various specifications of tests for functional form indicated problems.

5 Jarque-Bera test: 0.51, Pr: 77.30 %; White's test: 9.31, Pr: 23.13 %; Goldfield-Quandt: 0.33, Pr: 90.01 %; Outlier-test: 2.59 (insignificant). In addition, none of the various specifications of tests for functional form indicated problems.

6 Computed by adding reference period and contribution period for state pensions (social security and government employee pensions) in 1960 (source: SSIB).

7 Jarque-Bera test: 1.47, Pr: 47.91 %; White's test: 8.82, Pr: 63.86 %; Goldfield-Quandt: 4.10, Pr: 7.39 %; Outlier-test: 1.71 (insignificant). In addition, none of the various specifications of tests for functional form indicated problems. However, the Goldfield-Quandt test indicates that this model might have a problem of heteroskedasticity, although the other tests fail to reject the nul-hypotheses that the residuals are homoskedastic.

8 This section is mainly based on the outstanding study by Hockerts (1980) on social policy in Germany in the period 1945–57. In addition, I consulted Hockerts (1981), Hentschel (1983), and Baldwin (1990).

6 THE QUALITY OF WELFARE STATE REGIMES

1 Further second order testing of model II showed that there appeared to be no problems with the main regression assumptions. Jarque-Bera test: 0.74, Pr: 69.09 %; White's test: 2.39, Pr: 66.42 %; Goldfield-Quandt: 0.53, Pr: 79.00 %; Outlier-test: 2.26 (insignificant). In addition, none of the various specifications of tests for functional form indicated problems, neither did the analysis on the externally studentised residuals.

2 Jarque-Bera test: 3.45, Pr: 17.39 %; White's test: 1.00, Pr: 90.92 %; Goldfield-Quandt: 4.56, Pr: 3.12 %; Outlier-test: 3.49 (insignificant). None of the various specifications of tests for functional form indicated problems.

3 This section partly draws on earlier work done in collaboration with Uwe Becker (Becker and van Kersbergen 1986; van Kersbergen and Becker 1988; van Kersbergen 1991).

4 Jarque-Bera test: 1.29, Pr: 52.55 %; White's test: 2.27, Pr: 68.62 %; Goldfield-Quandt: 0.84, Pr: 58.94 %; Outlier-test: 2.10 (insignificant). In addition, none of the various specifications of tests for functional form indicated problems.

5 Using different estimation techniques to neutralise the outlier effect (both least absolute deviation which minimises the sum of absolute values of the residuals and robust estimation, using bi-weighted least squares, see Dietz, Scott and Kalof 1987), however, did not change the estimated parameters dramatically. As a result I decided to stay with OLS.

6 As far as the econometric tests are concerned, there were no problems with the main regression assumptions. Jarque-Bera test: 3.11, Pr: 21.15 %; White's test: 3.87, Pr: 42.41 %; Goldfield-Quandt: 0.56, Pr: 77.06%; Outlier-test: 3.10 (insignificant). In addition, none of the various specifications of tests for functional form indicated problems.

7 Jarque-Bera test: 1.47, Pr: 47.88 %; White's test: 4.41, Pr: 35.35 %; Goldfield-Quandt: 1.96, Pr: 19.74%; Outlier-test: 2.08 (insignificant). In addition, none of the various specifications of tests for functional form indicated problems.

7 THE STRUCTURE OF WELFARE STATE REGIMES

1 Jarque-Bera test: 0.77, Pr: 67.96 %; White's test: 2.12, Pr: 34.84 %; Goldfield-Quandt: 0.86, Pr: 58.52 %; Outlier-test: 2.95 (insignificant). None of the null-hypotheses that the standard assumptions of the regression-model do not apply could be rejected on the basis of tests for functional form.
2 These were chosen because of incomplete data on sickness and disability.
3 Jarque-Bera test: 1.69, Pr: 42.99 %; White's test: 2.54, Pr: 63.68 %; Goldfield-Quandt: 0.86, Pr: 57.51%; Outlier-test: 2.8 (insignificant). In addition, none of the various specifications of tests for functional form indicated problems. Estimating similar models with other techniques that give less weight to outliers indicated that Japan was an insignificant outlier to the extent that the estimated parameter of the CDS variable did not change.
4 The IRI construction involved the public ownership of private firms and established a powerful interpenetration of political and economic interests. It grew eventually into a brood-cell of 'a new ruling class of public managers promoted by and supporting the emerging groups of DC politicians' (Bianchi 1987:287).
5 Data constraints, moreover, made analyses of earlier points in time impossible.
6 Jarque-Bera test: 0.53, Pr: 76.53 %; White's test: 2.37, Pr: 66.84 %; Goldfield-Quandt: 0.86, Pr: 57.78 %; Outlier-test: 2.26 (insignificant). Various specifications of tests for functional form did not lead to the rejection of the null-hypothesis that the standard assumptions of the regression model apply.

8 SOCIAL CAPITALISM AND CHRISTIAN DEMOCRACY

1 Glasman (forthcoming) offers a highly original comparison between German post-war reconstruction and Poland's transition towards democratic capitalism. His argument is that post-war Germany could have provided a model for Poland's transition and that a 'Polish social market economy' could have prevented this nation's current 'unnecessary suffering'.

9 CATHOLICISM AND SOCIAL CITIZENSHIP: FROM CHARITY TO SOCIAL JUSTICE?

1 These reflections are taken from a lecture by Peter Flora to the second European School of Historical and Comparative Sociological Research on Social Policy, Sociological Institute, University of Amsterdam, November 1990. My notes may not be accurate and therefore may not precisely reflect the views of Flora.

10 THE INTELLECTUAL ORIGINS OF CHRISTIAN DEMOCRACY AND SOCIAL CAPITALISM

1 The social Catholic attention for the situation of the working class sometimes leads to a confusion of social Catholicism with Christian socialism. For reasons of substantive and conceptual clarity the term Christian socialism should be reserved to denote those approaches within Catholicism which attempt to formulate some sort of compromise between socialism (or Marxism) and the

Christian faith, as for instance 'liberation theology' (Gutiérrez 1971; see Berryman 1987; Levine 1988; Nitsch 1986). Christian socialism cannot be taken to refer to all Catholics who increasingly came to believe in social policy as a means to 'elevate' the working class.

The crucial difference between social Catholicism and Christian socialism is illustrated by the vehement anti-socialism of the former. Murchland (1982) fails to recognise this when he argues that the German bishop and social thinker Wilhelm von Ketteler was the major figure among the Christian socialists in Germany. To be sure, von Ketteler abhorred liberalism, but he saw socialism as its heir and rejected both (Hogan 1946:182). Von Ketteler was a social thinker, but not a socialist. Social Catholicism, then, denotes those attempts of Catholics to define and pursue policies that aim at the improvement of the position of the working class or the poor, while in principle accepting the capitalist mode of production.

2 Gregory XVI in his encyclical letter *Mirari Vos* (1832) enjoined silence on Lamennais. In the encyclical *Singulari Nos* (1834) Lamennais was explicitly condemned (see Woodward 1963:248–76).

3 In evaluating the differences between *Rerum Novarum* and *Quadragesimo Anno*, Dorr (1983:59) argues that 'there is a slight but noticeable shift in emphasis from a more "escapist" to a more "worldly" spirituality'.

4 *Quadragesimo Anno* defines more clearly the concept of a family wage, while at the same time holding that it is a disgrace if a woman is forced to work because of the inadequate income of her husband. As a result, she would only neglect her natural duty of caring for her children (*Quadragesimo Anno*, section 71).

11 CONCLUSION

1 A recent survey of contemporary political ideologies (Eatwell and Wright 1993), for instance, defines liberalism, conservatism, social democracy and democratic socialism, Marxism and communism, anarchism, nationalism, fascism, feminism and ecologism as the key twentieth-century ideologies. Apparently, Christian democracy is not such a key twentieth-century ideology. In fact, Christian democracy's elaborate political doctrines are treated as nothing but a conservative compromise between moderate socialism, authoritarianism and traditionalism, which supposedly lost its appeal in the 1960s and 1970s, but gained prominence again in the 1980s (O'Sullivan 1993:63).

2 Comparatively cheap natural gas has been an important means by which green-house farming was supported by Christian democrats who controlled the Ministry of Agriculture since 1958.

References

Abelshauser, W. (1983) *Wirtschaftsgeschichte der Bundesrepublik Deutschland (1945–1980)*, Frankfurt: Suhrkamp.

Agócs, S. (1988) *The Troubled Origin of the Italian Catholic Labor Movement, 1878–1914*, Detroit: Wayne State University Press.

Alber, J. (1982) *Vom Armenhaus zum Wohlfahrtsstaat. Analysen zur Entwicklung der Sozialversicherung in Westeuropa*, Frankfurt and New York: Campus.

—— (1986) 'Der Wohlfahrtsstaat in der Wirtschaftskrise. Eine Bilanz der Sozialpolitik in der Bundesrepublik seit den frühen siebziger Jahren', *Politische Vierteljahresschrift* 27:28–60.

—— (1989) *Der Sozialstaat in der Bundesrepublik, 1950–1983*, Frankfurt and New York: Campus.

Alexander, E. (1953) 'Church and society in Germany. Social and political movements and ideas in German and Austrian Catholicism (1789–1950)', in J.N. Moody (ed.) *Church and Society. Catholic Social and Political Thought and Movements, 1789–1950*, New York: Arts.

Allum, P.A. (1972) 'The south and national politics', in S.J. Woolf (ed.) *The Rebirth of Italy, 1943–1950*, London: Longman.

—— (1990) 'Uniformity undone: aspects of Catholic culture in postwar Italy', in Z.G. Baransky and R. Lumley (eds) *Culture and Conflict in Postwar Italy. Essays on Mass and Popular Culture*, Houndmills and London: Macmillan.

Almond, G. (1948) 'The Christian parties of Western Europe', *World Politics* 1:31–58.

Almond, G. and Verba, S.(1963) *The Civic Culture. Political Attitudes and Democracy in Five Nations*, Princeton: Princeton University Press.

Alvarez, R.M., Garret, G. and Lange, P. (1991) 'Government partisanship, labor organization, and macroeconomic performance', *American Political Science Review* 85:539–56.

Ambrosius, G. (1977) *Die Durchsetzung der sozialen Marktwirtschaft in Westdeutschland, 1945–1949*, Stuttgart: Deutsche Verlags-Anstalt.

Amenta, E. (1993) 'The state of the art in welfare state research on social spending efforts in capitalist democracies', *American Journal of Sociology* 99:750–63.

Andeweg, R.B. and Irwin, G.A. (1993) *Dutch Government and Politics*, Houndmills and London: Macmillan.

Aquinas, T. (1978) *Summa Theologica*, Chicago: William Benton (Encyclopedia Britannica, series: Great Books of the Western World).

Ascoli, U. (ed.) (1984a) *Welfare State All'Italiana*, Bari: Laterza.
—— (1984b) 'Il sistema Italiano di welfare', in U. Ascoli (ed.) *Welfare State All'Italiana*, Bari: Laterza.
Asselberghs, K. (1981) 'De sociale verzekering tijdens de bezetting', *Sociologisch Tijdschrift* 7:5–40.
Baker, K.L., Dalton, R.J. and Hildebrandt, K. (1981) *Germany Transformed. Political Culture and the New Politics*, Cambridge and London: Harvard University Press.
Bakvis, H. (1981) *Catholic Power in the Netherlands*, Kingston and Montreal: McGill-Queen's University Press.
Baldwin, P. (1990) *The Politics of Social Solidarity. Class Bases of the European Welfare State 1875–1975*, Cambridge: Cambridge University Press.
Balfour, M. (1982) *West Germany. A Contemporary History*, London and Canberra: Croom Helm.
Bank, J. (1978) *Opkomst en Ondergang van de Nederlandse Volks Beweging (NVB)*, Deventer: Kluwer.
Bark, D.L. and Gress, D.R. (1989) *A History of West Germany, Vol. 1, From Shadow to Substance, 1945–1963*, Oxford: Basil Blackwell.
—— (1989) *A History of West Germany, Vol. 2, Democracy and its Discontents, 1963–1988*, Oxford: Basil Blackwell.
Becker, U. (1986) *Kapitalistische Dynamik und politisches Kräftespiel. Zur Kritik des klassentheoretischen Ansatzes*, Frankfurt: Campus.
Becker, U. and van Kersbergen, K. (1986) 'Der christliche Wohlfahrtsstaat der Niederlande. Ein kritischer Beitrag zur vergleichenden Politikforschung', *Politische Vierteljahresschrift* 27: 61–78.
Belloni, F.P. (1972) 'Politics in a faction-dominated system: analysis of the Christian democratic party in Italy', unpublished Ph.D. thesis, University of California.
Belloni, F.P. and Beller, D.C. (eds) (1978) *Faction Politics: Political Parties and Factionalism in Comparative Perspective*, Santa Barbara: ABC-Clio.
Berger, P.L. (1990) *The Sacred Canopy. Elements of a Sociological Theory of Religion*, New York: Doubleday.
Berghahn, V.R. (1987) *Modern Germany. Society, Economy and Politics in the Twentieth Century*, Cambridge: Cambridge University Press (second edition).
Berlin, I. (1979) *Against the Current. Essays in the History of Ideas*, London: Hogarth.
Bernardi-Schenkluhn, B (1992) 'Italien', in J. Alber and B. Bernardi-Schenkluhn *Westeuropäische Gesundheitssysteme im Vergleich: Bundesrepublik Deutschland, Schweiz, Frankreich, Italien, Großbrittannien*, Frankfurt and New York: Campus.
Berryman, P. (1987) *Liberation Theology*, New York: Pantheon.
Bianchi, P. (1987) 'The IRI in Italy: strategic role and political constraints', *West European Politics* 10:269–90.
Bingham Powell, G. (1982) *Contemporary Democracies. Participation, Stability, and Violence*, Cambridge and London: Harvard University Press.
Bjorn, L. (1979) 'Labor parties, economic growth, and redistribution in five capitalist countries', *Comparative Social Research* 2:93–128.
Blackbourn, D. (1980) *Class, Religion and Local Politics in Wilhelmine Germany. The Centre Party in Württemberg before 1914*, New Haven and London: Yale University Press.

—— (1987) *Populists and Patricians. Essays in Modern German History*, London: Allen and Unwin.

Blok, E. (1978) *Loonarbeid van Vrouwen in Nederland, 1945–1955*, Nijmegen: SUN.

Blom, J.C.H. (1977) 'The Second World War and Dutch society: continuity and change', in A.A. Duke and C.A. Tamse (eds) *Britain and the Netherlands, Vol. 6, War and Society*, Den Haag: Nijhoff.

—— (1982) 'Nederland onder Duitse bezetting, 10 Mei 1940–5 Mei 1945', *Algemene Geschiedenis der Nederlanden, 15, Nieuwste Tijd*, Haarlem: Fibula-Van Dishoeck.

Boas, G. (1967) 'Traditionalism', *The Encyclopedia of Philosophy*, New York and London: Macmillan, 154–5.

Böhl, H. de Liagre and Meershoek, G. (1989) *De Bevrijding van Amsterdam. Een Strijd om Macht en Moraal*, Zwolle: Waanders.

Böhl, H. de Liagre, Nekkers, J. and Slot, L. (eds) (1981) *Nederland Industrialiseert! Politieke en Ideologische Strijd rondom het Naoorlogse Industrialisatiebeleid 1945–1955*, Nijmegen: SUN.

Bosmans, J. (1982) 'Het maatschappelijk-politieke leven in Nederland 1945–1980', *Algemene Geschiedenis der Nederlanden, 15, Nieuwste Tijd*, Haarlem: Fibula-Van Dishoeck.

Bowen, R.H. (1971) *German Theories of the Corporatist State, with Special Reference to the Period 1870–1919*, New York: Russell and Russell.

Braakman, T., van Schendelen, M.P.C.M. and Schotten, R.Ph. (1984) *Sociale Zekerheid in Nederland*, Utrecht and Antwerpen: Spectrum.

Braun, D. (1988) 'Der niederlandische Weg in die Massenarbeitslosigkeit (1973–1981). Eine politisch-institutionelle Analyse', unpublished Ph.D. thesis, Universiteit van Amsterdam.

Braun, D. and van Kersbergen, K. (1986) 'Wendepolitik und politische Kräfteverhältnisse in den Niederlanden', *Blätter für deutsche und internationale Politik* 31:857–69.

Brodrick, J. (1934) *The Economic Morals of the Jesuits: An Answer to Dr H.M. Robertson*, London: Oxford University Press.

Broughton, D. (1994) 'The CDU-CSU in Germany: is there any alternative?', in D. Hanley (ed.) *Christian Democracy in Europe. A Comparative Perspective*, London and New York: Pinter.

Buchanan, A. (1987) 'Justice and charity', *Ethics* 97:559–76.

Buchhaas, D. (1981) *Die Volkspartei. Programmatische Entwicklung der CDU, 1950–1973*, Düsseldorf: Droste.

Buchheim, K. (1963) *Ultramontanismus und Demokratie. Der Weg der deutschen Katholiken im 19. Jahrhundert*, München: Kösel.

Burns, G. (1990) 'The politics of ideology: the papal struggle with liberalism', *American Journal of Sociology* 95:1123–52.

Bussemaker, J. and van Kersbergen, K. (1994) 'Gender and welfare states: some theoretical reflections', in D. Sainsbury (ed.) *Gendering Welfare States*, London: Sage.

Cameron, D.R. (1978) 'The expansion of the public economy: a comparative analysis', *American Political Science Review* 72: 1243–61.

—— (1984) 'Social democracy, corporatism, labor quiescence and the representation of economic interests in advanced capitalist society', in J.H. Goldthorpe (ed.) *Order and Conflict in Contemporary Capitalism*, Oxford: Oxford University Press.

Camp, R.L. (1969) *The Papal Ideology of Social Reform: A Study in Historical Development*, Leiden: Brill.

Candeloro, G. (1982) *Il Movimento Cattolico in Italia*, Roma: Editori Riuniti.

Cartocci, R. (1993) 'Rilevare la secolarizzazione: indicatori a geometria variabile', *Rivista Italiana di Scienza Politica* 23:119–52.

Casella, M. (1987) *Cattolici e Costituente. Orientamenti e Iniziative del Cattolicesimo Organizzato (1945–1947)*, Perugia: Edizioni Scientifiche Italiane.

Castellino, O. (1976) *Il Labirinto delle Pensioni*, Bologna: Il Mulino.

Castles, F.G. (1978) *The Social Democratic Image of Society. A Study of the Achievements and Origins of Scandinavian Social Democracy in Comparative Perspective*, London: Routledge and Kegan Paul.

—— (1985) *The Working Class and Welfare: Reflections on the Political Development of the Welfare State in Australia and New Zealand, 1890–1980*, London: Allen and Unwin.

—— (1993) 'Introduction', in F.G. Castles (ed.) *Families of Nations. Patterns of Public Policy in Western Democracies*, Dartmouth: Aldershot.

—— (1994) 'On religion and public policy: does Catholicism make a difference?', *European Journal of Political Research* 25:19–40.

Castles, F.G. and Mitchell, D. (1993) 'Worlds of welfare and families of nations', in F.G. Castles (ed.) *Families of Nations. Patterns of Public Policy in Western Democracies*, Dartmouth: Aldershot.

Catalano, F. (1972) 'The rebirth of the party system, 1944–48', in S.J. Woolf (ed.) *The Rebirth of Italy, 1943–1950*, London: Longman.

Cazzola, F. (ed.) (1979) *Anatomia del Potere DC: Enti Pubblici e 'Centralità Democristiana'*, Bari: de Donato.

Chadwick, O. (1975) *The Secularization of the European Mind in the Nineteenth Century*, Cambridge: Cambridge University Press.

—— (1981) *The Popes and European Revolution*, Oxford: Clarendon.

Cherubini, A. (1977) *Storia della Previdenza Sociale in Italia (1860–1960)*, Roma: Editori Riuniti.

Childs, D. and Johnson, J. (1981) *West Germany: Politics and Society*, London: Croom Helm.

Clark, M. (1984) *Modern Italy, 1871–1982*, London and New York: Longman.

Cohan, P. (1983) 'Ireland', in V.E. MacHale and S. Skowronski (eds) *Political Parties of Europe*, Westport: Greenwood Press.

Commissie-van Rhijn (1945–6), *Sociale Zekerheid. Rapport van de Commissie, Ingesteld bij Beschikking van den Minister van Sociale Zaken van 26 maart 1943, met de Opdracht Algemeene Richtlijnen Vast te Stellen voor de Toekomstige Ontwikkeling van de Sociale Zekerheid*, 's-Gravenhage.

Conradt, D.P. (1989) *The German Polity*, New York and London: Longman (fourth edition).

Corsini, U. and Repgen, K. (eds) (1979) *Konrad Adenauer e Alcide De Gasperi: Due Esperienze di Rifondazione della Democrazia*, Bologna: Il Mulino.

Cox, R.H. (1993) *The Development of the Dutch Welfare State. From Workers' Insurance to Universal Entitlement*, Pittsburgh and London: University of Pittsburgh Press.

Crawley, A. (1973) *The Rise of West Germany, 1945–1972*, London: Collins.

Cutright, P. (1965) 'Political structure, economic development and national social security programs', *American Journal of Sociology* 60:539–55.

Daalder, H. (1966) 'The Netherlands: opposition in a segmented society', in R.A. Dahl (ed.) *Political Opposition in Western Democracies*, New Haven and London: Yale University Press.

—— (1989) 'The mould of Dutch politics: themes for comparative inquiry', in H. Daalder and G.A. Irwin (eds) *Politics in the Netherlands. How Much Change?*, London: Frank Cass.

—— (1990) 'Ancient and modern pluralism in the Netherlands. The 1989 Erasmus lectures at Harvard University', *Centre for European Studies Working Papers* 22.

Daalder, H. and Irwin G.A. (eds) (1989) *Politics in the Netherlands. How Much Change?*, London: Frank Cass.

Dalton, R.J. and Kuechler, M. (eds) (1990) *Challenging the Political Order: New Social and Political Movements in Western Democracies*, Cambridge: Polity.

Daly, M. (1994) 'Comparing welfare states: towards a gender friendly approach', in: D. Sainsbury (ed.) *Gendering Welfare States*, London: Sage.

Daudt, H. (1980) 'De ontwikkeling van de politieke machtsverhoudingen in Nederland sinds 1945', in G.A. Kooy, J.H. de Ru and H.J. Scheffers (eds) *Nederland na 1945. Beschouwingen over Ontwikkeling en Beleid*, Deventer: van Loghum Slaterus.

David, P. (1984) 'Il sistema assistenziale in Italia', in U. Ascoli (ed.) *Welfare State All'Italiana*, Bari: Laterza.

de Antonellis, G. (1987) *Storia dell'Azione Cattolica*, Milano: Rizzoli.

de Cecco, M. (1972) 'Economic policy in the reconstruction period, 1945–51', in S.J. Woolf (ed.) *The Rebirth of Italy, 1943–1950*, London: Longman.

de Grand, A. (1989) *The Italian Left in the Twentieth Century. A History of the Socialist and Communist Parties*, Bloomington and Indianapolis: Indiana University Press.

de Keizer, M. (1979) *De Gijzelaars van Sint Michielsgestel. Een Elite-Beraad in Oorlogstijd*, Alphen aan den Rijn: Sijthoff.

de Maistre, J. (1971) (see Lively 1971).

de Rooy, P. (1979) *Werklozenzorg en Werkloosheidsbestrijding 1917–1940*, Amsterdam: van Gennep.

de Rosa, G. (1953–4) *Storia Politica dell'Azione Cattolica in Italia*, 2 vols, Bari: Laterza.

—— (1988) *Il Partito Popolare Italiano*, Bari: Laterza.

de Swaan, A. (1988) *In Care of the State. Health Care, Education and Welfare in Europe and the USA in the Modern Era*, Cambridge: Polity.

de Winter, L. (1992) 'Christian democratic parties in Belgium', in M. Caciagli (ed.) *Christian Democracy in Europe*, Barcelona: ICPS.

de Wolff, P. and Driehuis, W. (1980) 'A description of post war economic developments and economic policy in the Netherlands', in R.T. Griffiths (ed.) *The Economy and Politics of the Netherlands since 1945*, The Hague: Nijhoff.

Diamant, A. (1960) *Die Österreichischen Katholiken und die erste Republik. Demokratie, Kapitalismus und Soziale Ordnung 1918–1934*, Wien: Verlag der Wiener Volksbuchhandlung.

Dierickx, G. (1994) 'Christian democracy and its ideological rivals', in D. Hanley (ed.) *Christian Democracy in Europe. A Comparative Perspective*, London and New York: Pinter.

264   *References*

Dietz, T., Scott, R. and Kalof, L. (1987) 'Estimation with cross-national data: robust and nonparametric methods', *American Sociological Review* 52:380–90.

di Loreto, P. (1991) *Togliatti e la "Doppiezza". Il Pci tra Democrazia e Insurrezione*, Bologna: Il Mulino.

Donolo, C. (1980) 'Social change and transformation of the state in Italy', in R. Scase (ed.) *The State in Western Europe*, London: Croom Helm.

Donovan, M. (1994) 'Democrazia cristiana: party of government', in D. Hanley (ed.) *Christian Democracy in Europe. A Comparative Perspective*, London and New York: Pinter.

Dorr, D. (1983) *Option for the Poor. A Hundred Years of Vatican Social Teaching*, Dublin: Gill and McMillan.

Drummond, G.D. (1982) *The German Social Democrats in Opposition, 1949–1960. The Case Against Rearmament*, Norman: University of Oklahoma Press.

Dunn, J.A. (1983) 'Belgium', in V.E. MacHale and S. Skowronski (eds) *Political Parties of Europe*, Westport: Greenwood Press.

Eatwell, R. and Wright, A. (eds) (1993) *Contemporary Political Ideologies*, London: Pinter.

Ebbinghaus, B. (1993) 'Labour unity in union diversity. Trade unions and social cleavages in Western Europe, 1890–1989', unpublished Ph.D. thesis, European University Institute.

Einaudi, M. and Goguel, F. (1952) *Christian Democracy in Italy and France*, Notre Dame: University of Notre Dame Press.

Elster, J. (1989) *Nuts and Bolts for the Social Sciences*, Cambridge: Cambridge University Press.

Esping-Andersen, G. (1985a) *Politics Against Markets. The Social Democratic Road to Power*, Princeton: Princeton University Press.

—— (1985b) 'Power and distributional regimes', *Politics and Society* 14:223–56.

—— (1987) 'The comparison of policy regimes: an introduction', in M. Rein, G. Esping-Andersen and L. Rainwater (eds) *Stagnation and Renewal. The Rise and Fall of Policy Regimes*, Armonk and New York: Sharpe.

—— (1990) *The Three Worlds of Welfare Capitalism*, Cambridge: Polity.

—— (ed.) (1993) *Changing Classes. Stratification and Mobility in Post-Industrial Societies*, London, Sage.

—— (forthcoming) 'Welfare states and the economy', in N. Smelser and R. Swedberg (eds) *Handbook of Economic Sociology*, Princeton: Princeton University Press.

Esping-Andersen, G. and Korpi, W. (1984) 'Social policy as class politics in post-war capitalism: Scandinavia, Austria and Germany', in J.H. Goldthorpe (ed.) *Order and Conflict in Contemporary Capitalism*, Oxford: Clarendon.

—— (1986) 'From poor relief to institutional welfare states: the development of scandinavian social policy', in R. Erikson *et al.* (eds) *The Scandinavian Model: Welfare States and Welfare Research*, Armonk: Sharpe.

Esping-Andersen, G. and van Kersbergen, K. (1992) 'Contemporary research on social democracy', *Annual Review of Sociology*, 18:187–208.

Fairchilds, C.C. (1976) *Poverty and Charity in Aix-en-Provence, 1640–1789*, Baltimore and London: Johns Hopkins University Press.

Fanfani, A. (1935) *Catholicism, Protestantism and Capitalism*, London: Sheed and Ward.

Ferrera, M. (1984) *Il Welfare State in Italia. Sviluppo e Crisi in Prospettiva Comparata*, Bologna: Il Mulino.
—— (1993) *Modelli di Solidarietà. Politica e Riforme Sociali nelle Democrazie*, Bologna: Il Mulino.
Flora, P. (ed.) (1983) *State, Economy and Society in Western Europe, 1815–1975*, Chicago: St. James, 2 vols.
—— (ed.) (1986) *Growth to Limits. The Western European Welfare States since World War II*, Berlin: de Gruyter, 4 vols.
Flora, P. and Alber, J. (1981) 'Modernization, democratization, and the development of the welfare states in Western Europe', in P. Flora and A.J. Heidenheimer (eds) *The Development of Welfare States in Europe and America*, New Brunswick and London: Transaction.
Flora, P. and Heidenheimer, A.J. (eds) (1981a) *The Development of Welfare States in Europe and America*, New Brunswick and London: Transaction.
—— (1981b) 'Introduction', in P. Flora and A.J. Heidenheimer (eds) *The Development of Welfare States in Europe and America*, New Brunswick and London: Transaction.
—— (1981c) 'The historical core and changing boundaries of the welfare state', in P. Flora and A.J. Heidenheimer (eds) *The Development of Welfare States in Europe and America*, New Brunswick and London: Transaction.
Fogarty, M.P. (1957) *Christian Democracy in Western Europe, 1820–1953*, London: Routledge and Kegan Paul.
Fortuyn, W.S.P. (1980) 'Sociaal-economische politiek in Nederland', unpublished Ph.D. thesis, University of Groningen.
—— (1983) *Kerncijfers 1945–1983 van de Sociaal-Economische Ontwikkeling in Nederland. Expansie en Stagnatie*, Deventer: Kluwer.
Foster, H. (ed.) (1993) *Employee Benefits in Europe and USA*, London: Longman.
Furlong, P. (1994) *Modern Italy. Representation and Reform*, London and New York: Routledge.
Furniss, N. and Tilton, T. (1977) *The Case for the Welfare State. From Social Security to Social Equality*, Bloomington: Indiana University Press.
Gallagher, M., Laver, M. and Mair, P. (1992) *Representative Government in Western Europe*, New York: McGraw-Hill.
Galli, G. (1978) *Storia della Democrazia Cristiana*, Roma and Bari: Laterza.
—— (1984) *Il Bipartitismo Imperfetto. Comunisti e Democristiani in Italia*, Milano: Mondadori.
Gilson, E. (1954) *The Church Speaks to the Modern World. The Social Teachings of Leo XIII*, New York: Image Books.
Ginsborg, P. (1990) *A History of Contemporary Italy. Society and Politics, 1943–1988*, London: Penguin.
Ginsburg, N. (1979) *Class, Capital and Social Policy*, London and Basingstoke: Macmillan.
Gladdish, K. (1991) *Governing from the Centre. Politics and Policy-Making in the Netherlands*, London: Hurst/The Hague: SDU.
Glasman, M. (forthcoming) *Unnecessary Suffering*, London: Verso.
Goodin, R.E. and LeGrand, J. (1987) *Not Only the Poor: The Middle Classes and the Welfare State*, London: Allen and Unwin.
Görner, R. (1986) 'Die deutsche Katholiken und die soziale Frage im 19. Jarhundert', in G. Rüther (ed.) *Geschichte der christlich-sozialen Bewegungen in Deutschland*, Köln: Verlag Wissenschaft und Politik.

Gough, I. (1979) *The Political Economy of the Welfare State*, London and Basingstoke: Macmillan.

Griffin, L.J., O'Connell, P.J. and McCammon, H.J. (1989) 'National variation in the context of struggle: postwar class conflict and market distribution in the capitalist democracies', *Canadian Review of Sociology and Anthropology* 26:37–68.

Griffin, L.J., Walters, P.B., O'Connell, P.J. and Moor, E. (1986) 'Methodological innovations in the analysis of welfare-state development: pooling cross sections and time series', in N. Furniss (ed.) *Futures for the Welfare State*, Bloomington: Indiana University Press.

Griffiths, R.T. (1980) 'The Netherlands Central Planning Bureau', in R.T. Griffiths (ed.) *The Economy and Politics of the Netherlands since 1945*, The Hague: Nijhoff.

Grindrod, M. (1977) *The Rebuilding of Italy. Politics and Economics 1945–1955*, Westport: Greenwood.

Groethuysen, B. (1968) *The Bourgeois. Catholicism vs. Capitalism in Eighteenth-Century France*, London: Barrie and Rockliff/The Cresset Press.

Guttiérrez, G. (1971) *Teología de la Liberacíon*, Lima: CEP.

Hage, J., Hanneman, R. and Gargan, E.T. (1989) *State Responsiveness and State Activism. An Examination of the Social Forces and State Strategies that Explain the Rise in Social Expenditure in Britain, France, Germany and Italy 1870–1968*, London: Unwin Hyman.

Hall, P. (1993) 'Policy paradigms, social learning, and the state. The case of economic policymaking in Britain', *Comparative Politics* 25:275–96.

Hallet, G. (1973) *The Social Economy of West Germany*, London and Basingstoke: Macmillan.

Hancock, M.D. (1989) *West Germany. The Politics of Democratic Corporatism*, Chatham: Chatham House.

Hancock, M.D., Conradt, D.P., Peters, B.G., Safran, W. and Zariski, R. (1993) *Politics in Western Europe. An Introduction to the Politics of the United Kingdom, France, Germany, Italy, Sweden, and the European Community*, Houndmills, Basingstoke and London: Macmillan.

Hanley, D. (1994a) 'Introduction: Christian democracy as a political phenomenon', in D. Hanley (ed.) *Christian Democracy in Europe. A Comparative Perspective*, London and New York: Pinter.

—— (ed.) (1994b) *Christian Democracy in Europe. A Comparative Perspective*, London and New York: Pinter.

Harper, J.L. (1986) *America and the Reconstruction of Italy, 1945–1948*, Cambridge: Cambridge University Press.

Hartwich, H.-H. (1970) *Sozialstaatspostulat und gesellschaftlicher Status Quo*, Köln and Opladen: Westdeutscher Verlag.

Heclo, H. (1974) *Modern Social Policies in Britain and Sweden*, New Haven: Yale University Press.

Heclo, H. and Madsen, H.J. (1986) *Policy and Politics in Sweden*, Philadelphia: Temple University Press.

Heidenheimer, A.J. (1960) *Adenauer and the CDU. The Rise and Fall of the Leader and the Integration of the Party*, The Hague: Nijhoff.

—— (1983) 'Secularization patterns and the westward spread of the welfare state, 1883–1983. Two dialogues about how and why Britain, the Netherlands, and the

United States have differed', in R.F. Tomasson (ed.) *The Welfare State, 1883–1983. Comparative Social Research* 6, Greenwich and London: Jai Press.

Hemerijck, A. (1993) 'The historical contingencies of Dutch corporatism', unpublished Ph.D. thesis, University of Oxford.

Henriksen, J.P. (1987) 'Some perspectives on Scandinavian welfare research', *Acta Sociologica* 30:379–92.

Hentschel, V. (1983) *Geschichte der deutschen Sozialpolitik (1880–1980). Soziale Sicherung und kollektives Arbeitsrecht*, Frankfurt: Suhrkamp.

Hewitt, C. (1977) 'The effect of political democracy and social democracy on equality in industrial societies: a cross-national comparison', *American Sociological Review* 42:450–64.

Hicks, A. and Misra, J. (1993) 'Political resources and the growth of welfare in affluent capitalist democracies, 1960–1982', *American Journal of Sociology* 99:668–710.

Hicks, A. and Swank, D.H. (1984) 'On the political economy of welfare expansion', *Comparative Political Studies* 17:81–119.

—— (1992) 'Politics, institutions, and welfare spending in industrialised democracies, 1960–82, *American Political Science Review* 86:658–74.

Hicks, A., Swank, D.H. and Ambuhl, M. (1989) 'Welfare expansion revisited: policy routines and their mediation by party, class and crisis, 1957–1982', *European Journal of Political Research* 17:401–30.

Higgins, W. and Apple, N. (1981) *Class Mobilization and Economic Policy: Struggles over Full Employment in Britain and Sweden*, Stockholm: Arbetslivcentrum.

Hine, D. (1993) *Governing Italy: The Politics of Bargained Pluralism*, Oxford: Clarendon.

Hockerts, H.G. (1980) *Sozialpolitische Entscheidungen im Nachkriegsdeutschland. Alliierte und deutsche Sozialversicherungspolitik, 1945 bis 1957*, Stuttgart: Klett-Cotta.

—— (1981) 'German post-war social policies against the background of the Beveridge plan. Some observation preparatory to a comparative analysis', in W.J. Mommsen (ed.) *The Emergence of the Welfare State in Britain and Germany, 1850–1950*, London: Croom Helm.

Hogan, W.E. (1946) *The Development of Bishop Wilhelm Emmanuel von Ketteler's Interpretation of the Social Problem*, Washington: Catholic University of America Press.

Huber, E. and Stephens, J.D. (1993) 'Political parties and public pensions: a quantitative analysis', *Acta Sociologica* 36:309–25.

Huber, E., Ragin, C. and Stephens, J.D. (1993) 'Social democracy, Christian democracy, constitutional structure, and the welfare state', *American Journal of Sociology* 99:711–49.

Hulsman, T. (1981) 'Het Nederlandse sociale zekerheidsstelsel. De rol van de overheid in ontstaan, groei, krisis', unpublished M.Phil. thesis, University of Groningen.

ILO (various years) *The Cost of Social Security*, Geneva: ILO.

Immergut, E.M. (1992) *Health Politics: Interests and Institutions in Western Europe*, Cambridge: Cambridge University Press.

Inglehart, R. (1990) *Culture Shift in Advanced Industrial Society*, Princeton: Princeton University Press.

268   References

Institute for Advanced Studies (IAS) (1990) *Inter-Active Simulation System, Level Ias-3.8, User Reference Manual*, Vienna: IAS.

Irving, R.E.M. (1979) *The Christian Democratic Parties of Western Europe*, London: Allen and Unwin.

Irwin, G.A. (1989) 'Parties having achieved representation in parliament since 1946', in H. Daalder and G.A. Irwin (eds) *Politics in the Netherlands. How Much Change?*, London: Frank Cass.

Jackman, R.W. (1975) *Politics and Social Equality: A Comparative Analysis*, New York: Wiley.

—— (1986) 'Elections and the democratic class struggle', *World Politics* 39:123–46.

Jacobs, F. (ed.) (1989) *Western European Political Parties: A Comprehensive Guide*, Harlow: Longman.

Janoski, T. (1994) 'Direct state intervention in the labor market: the explanation of active labor market policy from 1950 to 1988 in social democratic, conservative, and liberal regimes', in T. Janoski and A.M. Hicks (eds) *The Comparative Political Economy of the Welfare State*, Cambridge: Cambridge University Press.

Janoski, T. and Hicks, A.M. (eds) (1994) *The Comparative Political Economy of the Welfare State*, Cambridge: Cambridge University Press.

Janowitz, M. (1976) *Social Control of the Welfare State*, New York: Elsevier.

Janssen, G. and Berben, T. (1982) 'De vakbeweging en sociale zekerheid in Nederland na 1945', unpublished M.Phil. thesis, University of Nijmegen.

Johnson, E.A. (1983) 'Historical Germany', in V.E. MacHale and S. Skowronski (eds) *Political Parties of Europe*, Westport: Greenwood Press.

Jones, C. (1982) *Charity and Bienfaisance. The Treatment of the Poor in the Montpellier Region, 1740–1815*, Cambridge: Cambridge University Press.

Jones, H.M. (1974) *Revolution and Romanticism*, Cambridge: Harvard University Press.

Kangas, O. (1991) *The Politics of Social Rights. Studies on the Dimensions of Sickness Insurance in OECD Countries*, Stockholm: Swedish Institute for Social Research.

Karvonen, L. (1994) 'Christian parties in Scandinavia: victory over the windmills?', in D. Hanley (ed.) *Christian Democracy in Europe. A Comparative Perspective*, London and New York: Pinter.

Katz, R.S. and Mair, P. (1992) (eds) *Party Organizations: A Data Handbook on Party Organizations in Western Democracies, 1960–90*, London: Sage.

Katzenstein, P.J. (1985) *Small States in World Markets: Industrial Policy in Europe*, Ithaca: Cornell University Press.

Kaufmann, F.-X. (1988) 'Christentum und Wohlfahrtsstaat', *Zeitschrift für Sozialreform* 34:65–89.

—— (1989) *Religion und Modernität. Sozialwissenschaftliche Perspektiven*, Tübingen: J.C.B. Mohr (Paul Siebeck).

Keman, H. (1988) *The Development Toward Surplus Welfare: Social Democratic Politics and Policies in Advanced Capitalist Democracies (1965–1984)*, Amsterdam: CT Press.

Kenny, A. (1976) *Aquinas: A Collection of Critical Essays*, Notre Dame: University of Notre Dame Press.

—— (1980) *Aquinas*, Oxford: Oxford University Press.

Kerr, C., Dunlop, J.T., Harbison, F.H. and Myers, C.A. (1973) *Industrialism and Industrial Man*, London: Penguin.

King, R. (1973) *Land Reform: The Italian Experience*, London: Butterworth.

—— (1987) *Italy*, London: Harper and Row.

Klein, P.W. (1980) 'The foundations of Dutch prosperity', in R.T. Griffiths (ed.) *The Economy and Politics of the Netherlands since 1945*, The Hague: Nijhoff.

Kogan, N. (1983) *A Political History of Italy. The Postwar Years*, New York: Praeger.

Kohl, J. (1983) *Staatsausgaben in Westeuropa. Analysen zur langfristigen Entwicklung der öffentlichen Finanzen*, Frankfurt and New York: Campus.

Korpi, W. (1978) *The Working Class in Welfare Capitalism: Work, Unions and Politics in Sweden*, London: Routledge and Kegan Paul.

—— (1983) *The Democratic Class Struggle*, London: Routledge and Kegan Paul.

—— (1989) 'Power, politics, and state autonomy in the development of social citizenship: social rights during sickness in eighteen OECD countries since 1930', *American Sociological Review* 54:309–28.

Kossmann, E.H. (1978) *The Low Countries, 1780–1940*, Oxford: Oxford University Press.

Král, M.J.E. (1983) 'Austria', in V.E. MacHale and S.Skowronski (eds) *Political Parties of Europe*, Westport: Greenwood Press.

Kuiper, D.Th. (1988) *Christen-Democratie*, Leiden: Stichting Burgerschapskunde.

Kuyper, A. (1898), *Het Calvinisme. Zes Stone-Lezingen in October 1898 te Princeton (N.J.) Gehouden*, Kampen: Kok.

Lane, J.-E. and Ersson, S.O. (1991) *Politics and Society in Western Europe*, London: Sage.

Lane, J.-E., McKay, D. and Newton, K. (1991) *Political Data Handbook OECD Countries*, Oxford: Oxford University Press.

Lawson, K. and Merkl, P. (eds) (1988) *When Parties Fail: Emerging Alternative Organizations*, Princeton: Princeton University Press.

Leaman, J. (1988) *The Political Economy of West Germany, 1945–85: an Introduction*, Houndmills: Macmillan.

LeGrand, J. (1982) *The Strategy of Equality*, London: Allen and Unwin.

Lenhardt, G. and Offe, C. (1984) 'Social Policy and the Theory of the State', in C. Offe *Contradictions of the Welfare State*, London: Hutchinson.

Leonardi, R. and Wertman, D.A. (1989) *Italian Christian Democracy. The Politics of Dominance*, Houndmills: Macmillan.

Leonardi, R., Manetti, R.Y. and Putnam, R.D. (1987) 'Italy. Territorial politics in the post-war years: the case of regional reform', *West European Politics* 10:88–107.

Lessman, S. (1985) 'Electoral politics as determinants of policy outputs: an empirical investigation of the West German case', unpublished Ph.D. thesis, European University Institute.

Levine, D.H. (1988) 'Assessing the impacts of liberation theory in Latin America', *The Review of Politics* 50:241–63.

Lijphart, A. (1974) 'The Netherlands: continuity and change in voting behavior', in R. Rose (ed.) *Electoral Behavior: A Comparative Handbook*, New York: Free Press.

—— (1975) *The Politics of Accommodation. Pluralism and Democracy in the Netherlands*, Berkeley: University of California Press (second edition).

Linz, J.J. (1967) 'Cleavage and consensus in West German politics: the early fifties', in S.M. Lipset and S. Rokkan (eds) *Party Systems and Voter Alignments. Cross-National Perspectives*, New York: Free Press.

Lively, J. (1971) *The Works of Joseph de Maistre*, New York: Schocken.

Lubbers, R. and Lemckert, C. (1980) 'The influence of natural gas on the Dutch economy', in R.T. Griffiths (ed.) *The Economy and Politics of the Netherlands since 1945*, The Hague: Nijhoff.

Lucardie, P. and ten Napel, H.-M. (1994) 'Between confessionalism and liberal conservatism: the Christian democratic parties of Belgium and the Netherlands', in D. Hanley (ed.) *Christian Democracy in Europe. A Comparative Perspective*, London and New York: Pinter.

Lumley, R. (1990) *States of Emergency. Cultures of Revolt in Italy from 1968 to 1978*, London and New York: Verso.

MacHale, V.E. and Skowronski, S. (eds) (1983) *Political Parties in Europe*, Westport: Greenwood Press.

McOustra, C. (1990) *Love in the Economy: Catholic Social Doctrine for the Individual*, Slough: St. Paul.

Mackie, T.T. and Rose, R. (1991) *The International Almanac of Electoral History*, Houndmills and London: Macmillan.

Madeley, J. (1982) 'Politics and the pulpit: the case of protestant Europe', in S. Berger (ed.) *Religion in West European Politics*, London: Frank Cass.

—— (1994) 'The antinomies of Lutheran politics: the case of Norway's Christian People's Party', in D. Hanley (ed.) *Christian Democracy in Europe. A Comparative Perspective*, London and New York: Pinter.

Maier, H. (1969) *Revolution and Church. The Early History of Christian Democracy, 1789–1901*, Notre Dame and London: University of Notre Dame Press.

Mair, P. (1994) 'Party democracies and their difficulties', Inaugural address, Rijks Universiteit Leiden.

Mammarella, G. (1985) *L'Italia Contemporanea (1943–1985)*, Bologna: Il Mulino.

Mannoury, J. (1985) 'De ontwikkeling van het sociale verzekeringsstelsel', in F. Holthoorn (ed.) *De Nederlandse Samenleving sinds 1815. Wording en Samenhang*, Assen and Maastricht: van Gorcum.

Mannoury, J. and Asscher-Vonk, I.P. (1987) *Hoofdtrekken van de Sociale Verzekering*, Alphen aan den Rijn: Samsom and Tjeenk Willink.

Maraffi, M. (1993) 'Politica corrotta o società corrotta?', *Polis* 7:503–17.

Marlière, P. (forthcoming) 'Du spirituel dans la république: histoire de la démocratie chrétienne Italienne', *La Revue Politique*.

Marshall, T.H. (1964) *Class, Citizenship and Social Development*, Garden City and New York: Doubleday.

Martin, D. (1978) *A General Theory of Secularization*, Oxford: Basil Blackwell.

Mead, L.M. (1983) 'Religion and the welfare state', in R.F. Tomasson (ed.) *The Welfare State, 1883–1983. Comparative Social Research* 6, Greenwich and London: Jai Press.

Mény, Y. (1990) *Government and Politics in Western Europe. Britain, France, Italy, West Germany*, Oxford: Oxford University Press.

Michalsky, H. (1984) 'Parteien und Sozialpolitik in der Bundesrepublik Deutschland', *Sozialer Fortschritt* 6:134–42.

Miller, S. and Potthoff, H. (1986) *A History of German Social Democracy: from 1848 to the Present*, New York: Berg.

Milner, H. (1989) *Sweden: Social Democracy in Practice*, Oxford: Oxford University Press.

Mintzel, A. (1982) 'Conservatism and Christian democracy in the Federal Republic of Germany', in Z. Layton-Henry (ed.) *Conservative Politics in Western Europe*, London and Basingstoke: Macmillan.

—— (1984) *Die Volkspartei. Type und Wirklichkeit*, Opladen: Westdeutscher Verlag.

Mishra, R. (1984) *The Welfare State in Crisis. Social Thought and Social Change*, Brighton: Wheatsheaf.

Mitchell, D. (1990) 'Income transfer systems: a comparative study using microdata', unpublished Ph.D. thesis, Australian National University.

Molony, J.N. (1977) *The Emergence of Political Catholicism in Italy. Partito Popolare, 1919–1926*, London: Croom Helm.

Moody, J.N. (ed.) (1953a) *Church and Society. Catholic Social and Political Thought and Movements, 1789–1950*, New York: Arts.

—— (1953b) 'Introduction', in J.N. Moody (ed.) *Church and Society. Catholic Social and Political Thought and Movements, 1789–1950*, New York: Arts.

—— (1953c) 'The Church and the new forces in Western Europe and Italy', in J.N. Moody (ed.) *Church and Society. Catholic Social and Political Thought and Movements, 1789–1950*, New York: Arts.

—— (1953d) 'Catholicism and society in France. Catholic social and political movements, 1789–1950', in J.N. Moody (ed.) *Church and Society. Catholic Social and Political Thought and Movements, 1789–1950*, New York: Arts.

Müller, W. and Steiniger, B. (1994) 'Christian democracy in Austria: the Austrian People's Party', in D. Hanley (ed.) *Christian Democracy in Europe. A Comparative Perspective*, London and New York: Pinter.

Müller-Armack, A. (1989) 'The meaning of the social market economy', in A. Peacock and H. Willgerodt (eds) *Germany's Social Market Economy: Origins and Evolution*, London: Macmillan.

Muller, E.N. (1989) 'Distribution of income in advanced capitalist states: political parties, labour unions, and the international economy', *European Journal of Political Research* 17:367–400.

Murchland, B. (1982) *The Dream of Christian Socialism. An Essay on Its European Origins*, Washington and London: American Enterprise Institute for Public Policy Research.

Myles, J. (1989) *Old Age in the Welfare State: The Political Economy of Public Pensions*, Lawrence: University Press of Kansas (revised edition).

Neumann, S. (1973) *Die Parteien der Weimarer Republik*, Stuttgart: Kohlhammer.

Nitsch, T.O. (1986) 'Social Catholicism, Marxism and liberation theology: from antithesis to coexistence and synthesis', *International Journal of Social Economics* 13:52–74.

O'Brian, D.J. and Shannon, T.A. (eds) (1992) *Catholic Social Thought: The Documentary Heritage*, Maryknoll: Orbis.

O'Connor, J. (1973) *The Fiscal Crisis of the State*, New York: St. Martin's.

O'Connor, J.S. (1988) 'Convergence or divergence? Change in welfare effort in OECD countries, 1960–1980', *European Journal of Political Research* 16:277–99.

—— (1990) 'Definition and measurement of welfare effort and its correlates in cross-national analysis. A reply to Pampel and Stryker', *British Journal of Sociology* 41:25–8.

O'Connor, J. S. and Brym, R.J. (1988) 'Public welfare expenditure in OECD countries: towards a reconciliation of inconsistent findings', *British Journal of Sociology* 39:47–68.

OECD (1978) *The Tax/Benefit Positions of Selected Income Groups in OECD Member Countries, 1972–1976*, Paris: OECD.
—— (1980) *La Situation au regard de l'impôt et des transferts sociaux de certains groupes de revenue dans les pays membres de l'OCDE, 1974–1978*, Paris: OECD.
—— (1985) *Social Expenditure, 1960–1990. Problems of Growth and Control*, Paris: OECD.
—— (1986) *The Tax/Benefit Position of Production Workers, 1981–1985*, Paris: OECD.
—— (1988) *Reforming Public Pensions*, Paris: OECD.
—— (1992) *Economic Outlook, Historical Statistics 1960–1990*, Paris: OECD.
Olsson, S.E. (1987) 'Welfare state inc. The growth of a crisis industry', *Acta Sociologica* 30:371–8.
—— (1990) *Social Policy and Welfare State in Sweden*, Lund: Arkiv.
O'Neill, O. (1989) *Constructions of Reason. Explorations of Kant's Practical Philosophy*, Cambridge: Cambridge University Press.
Orfei, R. (1976) *L'Occupazione del Potere. I Democristiani '45–'75*, Milano: Longanesi.
Orloff, A.S. (1993) 'Gender and the social rights of citizenship: the comparative analysis of gender relations and welfare states', *American Sociological Review* 58:303–28.
O'Sullivan, N. (1993) 'Conservatism', in R. Eatwell and A. Wright (eds) *Contemporary Political Ideologies*, London: Pinter.
Paci, M. (1984) 'Il sistema di welfare Italiano tra tradizione clientelare e prospettive di riforma', in U. Ascoli (ed.) *Welfare State All'Italiana*, Bari: Laterza.
—— (1989a) *Pubblico e Privato nei Moderni Sistemi di Welfare*, Napoli: Liguori.
—— (1989b) 'Public and private in the Italian welfare system', in P. Lange and M. Regini (eds) *State, Market, and Social Regulation. New Perspectives on Italy*, Cambridge: Cambridge University Press.
Padgett, S. and Burkett, T. (1986) *Political Parties and Elections in West Germany. The Search for a New Stability*, London: Hurst.
Palme, J. (1990) *Pension Rights in Welfare Capitalism. The Development of Old-Age Pensions in 18 OECD Countries, 1930 to 1985*, Stockholm: Swedish Institute for Social Research.
Pampel, F.C. and Stryker, R. (1990) 'Age structure, the state, and social welfare spending: a reanalysis', *British Journal of Sociology* 41: 16–24.
Pampel, F. C. and Williamson, J.B. (1989) *Age, Class, Politics, and the Welfare State*, Cambridge: Cambridge University Press.
Pappi, F.U. (1984) 'The West German party system', *West European Politics* 7:7–27.
Pasquino, G. and McCarthy, P. (eds) (1993) *The End of Post-War Politics in Italy. The Landmark 1992 Elections*, Boulder: Westview.
Paterson, W.E. (1976) 'Social democracy: the West German example', in M. Kolinsky and W.E. Paterson (eds) *Social and Political Movements in Western Europe*, New York: St. Martin's.
Peacock, A. and Willgerodt, H. (eds) (1989) *Germany's Social Market Economy: Origins and Evolution*, London: Macmillan.
Pempel, T.J. (1990) 'Introduction. Uncommon democracies: the one-party dominant regimes', in T.J. Pempel (ed.) *Uncommon Democracies: The One-Party Dominant Regimes*, Ithaca and London: Cornell University Press.

Pennings, P. (1991) *Verzuiling en Ontzuiling: De Lokale Verschillen. Opbouw, Instandhouding en Neergang van Plaatselijke Zuilen in Verschillende Delen van Nederland na 1880*, Kampen: Kok.

Pierson, C. (1991) *Beyond the Welfare State? The New Political Economy of the Welfare State*, Cambridge: Polity.

Pijnenburg, B. (1993), 'De "C" van CDA: een analyse van het christen-democratisch electoraat', in K. van Kersbergen, P. Lucardie and H.-M. ten Napel (eds) *Geloven in Macht. De christen-democratie in Nederland*, Amsterdam: Het Spinhuis.

Piven, F.F. and Cloward, R.A. (1972) *Regulating the Poor. The Functions of Public Welfare*, London: Tavistock.

Platt, A.A. and Leonardi, R. (1979) 'The making of American foreign policy toward the Italian left in the postwar era', in D. Caraley and M. A. Epstein (eds) *The Making of American Foreign and Domestic Policy*, Farmingdale: Dabor.

Poggi, G. (1967) *Catholic Action in Italy: The Sociology of a Sponsored Organization*, Stanford: Stanford University Press.

—— (1972) 'The church in Italian politics, 1945–50', in S.J. Woolf (ed.) *The Rebirth of Italy, 1943–1950*, London: Longman.

Pontusson, J. (1988) *Swedish Social Democracy and British Labour: Essays on the Nature and Conditions of Social Democratic Hegemony*, Ithaca: Cornell University Press.

Prandi, C. (1983) *La Religione Popolare fra Potere e Tradizione*, Milano: Angeli.

Pridham, G. (1977) *Christian Democracy in Western Germany. The CDU/CSU in Government and Opposition*, London: Croom Helm.

Pryor, F.L. (1968), *Public Expenditure in Communist and Capitalist Countries*, London: Allen and Unwin.

Pütz, H. (1976) *Die CDU. Entwicklung, Aufbau und Politik der Christlich Demokratischen Union Deutschlands*, Düsseldorf: Droste.

Putnam, R.D. (with R. Leonardi and R.Y. Nanetti) (1993) *Making Democracy Work: Civic Traditions in Modern Italy*, Princeton: Princeton University Press.

Ragin, C.C. (1987) *The Comparative Method: Moving Beyond Qualitative and Quantitative Strategies*, Berkeley: University of California Press.

—— (ed.) (1991) *Issues and Alternatives in Comparative Social Research*, Leiden: Brill.

Rauch, R.W. (1972) *Politics and Belief in Contemporary France. Emmanuel Mounier and Christian Democracy, 1932–1950*, The Hague: Nijhoff.

Rein, M. (1985) 'Women in the social welfare labor market', *Discussion Papers 18, Labour Market Policy*, Berlin: Wissenschaftszentrum.

Righart, H. (1985) '"De ene ongedeelde KAB", vrome wens of werkelijkheid? Een historische schets van de Katholieke Arbeiders Beweging, 1945–1963', in J. Roes (ed.) *Katholieke Arbeidersbeweging. Studies over KAB en NKV in de Economische en Politieke Ontwikkeling van Nederland na 1945*, Baarn: Ambo.

—— (1986) *De Katholieke Zuil in Europa. Eem Vergelijkend Onderzoek naar het Ontstaan van Verzuiling onder Katholieken in Oostenrijk, Zwitserland, België en Nederland*, Meppel: Boom.

Rimlinger, G.V. (1971) *Welfare Policy and Industrialization in Europe, America and Russia*, New York: Wiley.

Ringen, S. (1987) *The Possibility of Politics. A Study in the Political Economy of the Welfare State*, Oxford: Clarendon.

Robertson, H.M. (1973) 'A criticism of Max Weber and his school', in R.W. Green (ed.) *Protestantism and Capitalism. The Weber Thesis and Its Critics*, Boston: Heath and Co.

Roebroek, J.M. (1993a) *The Imprisoned State. The Paradoxical Relationship Between State and Society*, Tilburg: Katholieke Universiteit Brabant.

—— (1993b) 'De confessionele verzorgingsstaat', in K. van Kersbergen, P. Lucardie and H.-M. ten Napel (eds) *Geloven in Macht. De Christen-Democratie in Nederland*, Amsterdam: Het Spinhuis.

Roebroek, J.M., Therborn, G. and Berben, T. (forthcoming) 'The Netherlands', in P. Flora (ed.) *Growth to Limits. The Western European Welfare States since World War II*, Berlin: de Gruyter.

Roes, J. (ed.) (1985) *Katholieke Arbeidersbeweging. Studies over KAB en NKV in de Economische en Politieke Ontwikkeling van Nederland na 1945*, Baarn: Ambo.

Rogier, J. (1980) *Een Zondagskind in de Politiek en Andere Christenen. Opstellen over Konfessionele Politiek in Nederland Van Colijn tot Cals*, Nijmegen: SUN.

Rosanvallon, P. (1981) *La Crise de l'État Providence*, Paris: Seuil.

Rueschemeyer, D., Stephens, E. Huber and Stephens, J.D. (1992) *Capitalist Development and Democracy*, Oxford: Polity.

Ruitenbeek, H.M. (1955) *Het Ontstaan van de Partij van de Arbeid*, Amsterdam: Arbeiderspers.

Ruppert, K. (1992) *Im Dienst am Staat von Weimar. Das Zentrum als Regierende Partei in der Weimarer Demokratie, 1923–1930*, Düsseldorf: Droste.

Sachße, C. (1992) 'Solidarität und Subsidiarität: Der deutsche Sozialkatholizismus in der Zeit des Kaiserreichs und der Weimarer Republik', unpublished manuscript, Gesamthochschule Kasselt.

Salvati, M. (1982) *Stato e Industria nella Ricostruzione. Alle Origini del Potere Democristiano, 1944–1949*, Milano: Feltrinelli.

Scharpf, F. (1984) 'Economic and institutional constraints of full employment strategies: Sweden, Austria and Germany, 1973–1982', in J.H. Goldthorpe (ed.) *Order and Conflict in Contemporary Capitalism*, Oxford: Clarendon.

—— (1987) *Sozialdemokratische Krisenpolitik in Europa*, Frankfurt: Campus.

Schmidt, M.G. (1980) *CDU und SPD an der Regierung. Ein Vergleich ihrer Politik in den Länder*, Frankfurt and New York: Campus.

—— (1982), *Wohlfahrtsstaatliche Politik unter bürgerlichen und sozialdemokratischen Regierungen*, Frankfurt and New York: Campus.

—— (1983) 'The welfare state and the economy in periods of economic crisis', *European Journal of Political Research* 11:1–26.

—— (1985) 'Allerweltsparteien in Westeuropa? Ein Beitrag zu Kirchheimers These vom Wandel des westeuropäischen Parteiensystems', *Leviathan* 3:376–98.

—— (1987) 'West Germany: the policy of the middle way', *Journal of Public Policy* 7:135–77.

—— (1988) *Sozialpolitik. Historische Entwicklung und internationaler Vergleich*, Opladen: Leske and Budrich.

—— (1989) 'Social policy in rich and poor countries: socio-economic trend and political-institutional determinants', *European Journal of Political Research* 17:641–59.

—— (1993) 'Gendered labour force participation', in F.G. Castles (ed.) *Families of Nations. Patterns of Public Policy in Western Democracies*, Aldershot: Dartmouth.

Schmidt, U. (1983) 'Die Christlich Demokratische Union Deutschlands', in R. Stöss (ed.) *Parteien-Handbuch. Die Parteien der Bundesrepublik Deutschland, 1945–1980*, Opladen: Westdeutscher Verlag.

—— (1987) *Zentrum oder CDU. Politischer Katholizismus zwischen Tradition und Anpassung*, Opladen: Westdeutscher Verlag.

Schmitt, C. (1986) *Political Romanticism*, Cambridge and London: MIT Press.

Schoenfeld, E. (1992) 'Militant and submissive religions: class, religion and ideology', *British Journal of Sociology* 43: 111–40.

Schwarz, H.P. (1986) *Adenauer: Der Aufstieg, 1876–1952*, Stuttgart: Deutsche Verlags-Anstalt.

Seifert, J. (1989) 'Die Verfassung', in W. Benz (ed.) *Die Geschichte der Bundesrepublik Deutschland, Band 1, Politik*, Frankfurt: Fischer.

Settembrini, D. (1977) *La Chiesa nella Politica Italiana (1944–1963). Alle Origini del Compromesso Storico*, Milano: Rizzoli.

Shalev, M. (1983) 'The social democratic model and beyond: two generations of comparative research on the welfare state', *Comparative Social Research* 6:315–51.

Shanahan, W.O. (1954) *German Protestants Face the Social Question, Vol. I, The Conservative Phase, 1815–1871*, Notre Dame: University of Notre Dame Press.

Sigmund, P.E. (1987) 'The Catholic tradition and modern democracy', *Review of Politics* 49:530–48.

Skocpol, T. (1992) *Protecting Mothers and Soldiers. The Political Origins of Social Policy in the United States*, Cambridge and London: Belknap Press of Harvard University Press.

Skocpol, T. and Amenta, E. (1986) 'States and social policies', *Annual Review of Sociology* 12:131–57.

Smeeding, T.M., O'Higgins, M. and Rainwater, L. (1990) *Poverty, Inequality and Income Distribution in Comparative Perspective. The Luxembourg Income Study (LIS)*, New York: Harvester and Wheatsheaf.

Soltau, R.H. (1965) *French Parties and Politics, 1871–1921, with a New Supplementary Chapter Dealing with 1922–1930*, New York: Russell and Russell.

Sombart, W. (1959) 'The role of religion in the formation of the capitalist spirit', in R.W. Green (ed.) *Protestantism and Capitalism. The Weber Thesis and Its Critics*, Boston: Heath and Co.

Spatano, G. (1969) *I Democratici Cristiani dalla Dittatura alla Repubblica*, Milano: Mondadori.

Spencer, P. (1973) *Politics of Belief in Nineteenth Century France. Lacordaire, Michon, Veuillot*, New York: Fertig.

Spotts, F. and Wieser, T. (1986) *Italy: A Difficult Democracy. A Survey of Italian Politics*, Cambridge: Cambridge University Press.

Spriano, P. (1978) *Storia del Partito Comunista Italiano, V, La Resistenza. Togliatti e il Partito Nuovo*, Torino: Einaudi.

SSIB: Data bank compiled in research project 'Svensk socialpolitik i internationell belysning', University of Stockholm: Swedish Institute for Social Research.

Steiner, J. (1986) *European Democracies*, New York and London: Longman.

Stegmann, F.J. (1969) 'Geschichte der sozialen Idee im deutschen Katholizismus', in W. Gottschalch, F. Kallenberg and F.J. Stegmann (eds) *Geschichte der sozialen Ideen in Deutschland*, München and Wien: Olzog.

Stephens, E. Huber and Stephens, J.D. (1982) 'The labor movement, political power and workers' participation in Western Europe', *Political Power and Social Theory* 3:215–50.

Stephens, J.D. (1979a) *The Transition from Capitalism to Socialism*, London: Macmillan.

—— (1979b) 'Religion and politics in three northwest European democracies', *Comparative Social Research* 2:129–57.

Stuurman, S. (1983) *Verzuiling, Kapitalisme en Patriarchaat. Aspecten van de Ontwikkeling van de Moderne Staat in Nederland*, Nijmegen: SUN.

Swank, D.H. and Hicks, A. (1984) 'On the political economy of welfare expansion: a comparative analysis of 18 advanced capitalist democracies, 1960–1971', *Comparative Political Studies* 17:81–119.

—— (1985) 'The determinants and redistributive impacts of state welfare spending in the advanced capitalist democracies, 1960–1980', in N.J. Vig and S.E. Schier (eds) *Political Economy in Western Democracies*, New York: Holmes and Meier.

Tamburrano, G. (1974) *L'Iceberg Democristiano*, Milano: Sugarco.

Tarrow, S. (1990) 'Maintaining hegemony in Italy: "the softer they rise, the slower they fall"', in T.J. Pempel (ed.) *Uncommon Democracies. The One-Party Dominant Regimes*, Ithaca and London: Cornell University Press.

Tawney, R.H. (1975) *Religion and the Rise of Capitalism. A Historical Study*, Harmondsworth: Penguin.

ter Heide, F.J. (1986) *Ordening en Verdeling. Besluitvorming over Sociaal-Economisch Beleid in Nederland, 1949–1958*, Kampen: Kok Agora.

Therborn, G. (1986a) *Why Some Peoples Are More Unemployed than Others. The Strange Paradox of Growth and Unemployment*, London: Verso.

—— (1986b) 'Karl Marx returning. The welfare state and neo-Marxist, corporatist and statist theories', *International Political Science Review* 7:131–64.

—— (1987) 'Welfare states and capitalist markets', *Acta Sociologica* 30:237–54.

—— (1989) '"Pillarization" and "popular movements". Two variants of welfare state capitalism: the Netherlands and Sweden', in F.G. Castles (ed.) *The Comparative History of Public Policy*, Cambridge: Polity.

—— (1994) 'Another way of taking religion seriously. Comment on Francis G. Castles', *European Journal of Political Research* 26:103–10.

Tilton, T. (1990) *The Political Theory of Swedish Social Democracy. Through the Welfare State to Socialism*, Oxford: Clarendon.

Titmuss, R.D. (1974) *Social Policy. An Introduction*, London: Allen and Unwin.

Troeltsch, E. (1931) *The Social Teaching of the Christian Churches*, London: Allen and Unwin.

Uertz, R. (1981) *Christentum und Sozialismus in der frühen CDU. Grundlagen und Wirkungen der christlich-sozialen Ideen in der Union, 1945–1949*, Stuttgart: Deutsche Verlags-Anstalt.

U.S. Department of Health and Human Services (various years) *Social Security Programmes throughout the World*, Washington: U.S. Government Printing Office.

Uusitalo, H. (1984) 'Comparative research on the determinants of the welfare state. The state of the art', *European Journal of Political Research* 12:403–22.

van Arnhem, J.C.M. and Schotsman, G.J. (1982) 'Do parties affect the distribution of income?', in F.G. Castles (ed.) *The Impact of Parties. Politics and Policies in Democratic Capitalist States*, London: Sage.

van den Tempel, J. (1946) *Nederland in Londen. Ervaringen en beschouwingen*, Haarlem: Tjeenk Willink.

van der Eijk, C. and van Praag, P. (1991) 'Partijen, kiezers en verkiezingen', in U. Becker (ed.) *Maatschappij, Macht, Nederlandse Politiek*, Amsterdam: Het Spinhuis (second edition).

van Doorn, J.A.A. (1989) 'Schets van de Nederlandse politieke traditie', in J.W. de Beus, J.A.A. van Doorn and P.B. Lehning (eds) *De Ideologische Driehoek. Neder- landse Politiek in Historisch Perspectief*, Meppel: Boom.

van Eijk, C.J. (1980) 'Counter-inflation policy in the Netherlands', in R.T. Griffiths (ed.) *The Economy and Politics of the Netherlands since 1945*, The Hague: Nijhoff.

van Kersbergen, K. (1991) 'De Nederlandse verzorgingsstaat in vergelijkend perspectief', in U. Becker (ed.) *Maatschappij, Macht, Nederlandse Politiek*, Amsterdam: Het Spinhuis (second edition).

—— (1994) 'The distinctiveness of Christian democracy', in D. Hanley (ed.) *Christian Democracy in Europe. A Comparative Perspective*, London and New York: Pinter.

van Kersbergen, K. and Becker, U. (1988) 'The Netherlands: a passive social democratic welfare state in a Christian democratic ruled society', *Journal of Social Policy* 17:477–99.

van Kersbergen, K. and Verbeek, B. (1994) 'The politics of subsidiarity in the European Union', *Journal of Common Market Studies* 32:215–36.

van Kersbergen, K., Lucardie, P. and ten Napel, H.-M. (eds) (1993) *Geloven in Macht. De Christen-Democratie in Nederland*, Amsterdam: Het Spinhuis.

van Lier, Th.J.H.M. (1981) 'Op weg naar de verzorgingsstaat (1950–1960)', in J. Bank and S. Temming (eds) *Van Brede Visie tot Smalle Marge*, Alphen a/d Rijn: Sijthoff.

van Putten, J. (1985) *Politieke Stromingen*, Utrecht and Antwerpen: Spectrum.

van Schendelen, M.P.C.M. (ed.) (1984) *Consociationalism, Pillarization and Conflict-Management in the Low Countries*, special issue of *Acta Politica* 19, 1.

van Wissen, G.J.M. (1982) *De Christen-Democratische Visie op de Rol van de Staat in het Sociaal-Economische Leven*, Amsterdam: Rodopi.

Veldkamp, G.J.M. (1978) *Inleiding tot de Sociale Zekerheid en de Toepassing ervan in Nederland en België, Deel 1, Karakter en Geschiedenis*, Deventer: Kluwer.

Vercellone, P. (1972) 'The Italian constitution of 1947–48', in S. J. Woolf (ed.) *The Rebirth of Italy, 1943–1950*, London: Longman.

Verwey-Jonker, H. (1961) 'De emanciepatiebewegingen', in A.N.J. den Hollander (ed.) *Drift en Koers. Een Halve Eeuw Sociale Verandering in Nederland*, Assen: van Gorcum.

Vis, J.J. (1973) *Kabinetsformatie 1973. De Slag om het Catshuis*, Utrecht and Antwerpen: Spectrum.

Visser, A. (1986) *Alleen bij Uiterste Noodzaak? De Rooms-Rode Samenwerking en het Einde van de Brede Basis, 1948–1958*, Amsterdam: Bert Bakker.

Visser, J. (1989) *European Trade Unions in Figures*, Deventer: Kluwer.

von Beyme, Klaus (1985) 'Policy-making in the Federal Republic of Germany: a systematic introduction', in M.G. Schmidt (ed.) *Policy and Politics in the Federal Republic of Germany*, New York: St. Martin's.

von der Dunk, H. (1982) 'Conservatism in the Netherlands', in Z. Layton-Henry (ed.) *Conservative Politics in Western Europe*, London and Basingstoke: Macmillan.

Walston, J. (1988) *The Mafia and Clientelism. Roads to Rome in Post-War Calabria*, London: Routledge.

Warner, G. (1972) 'Italy and the powers, 1943–49', in S.J. Woolf (ed.) *The Rebirth of Italy, 1943–1950*, London: Longman.

Waters, S. (1994) '"Tangentopoli" and the emergence of a new political order in Italy', *West European Politics* 17:169–82.

Weber, M. (1976) *The Protestant Ethic and the Spirit of Capitalism*, London: Allen and Unwin.

Weir, M., Orloff, A.S. and Skocpol, T. (1988) *The Politics of Social Policy in the United States*, Princeton: Princeton University Press.

Weiss, J. (1977) *Conservatism in Europe, 1770–1945. Traditionalism, Reaction and Counter-Revolution*, London: Thames and Hudson.

Welteke, M. (1976) *Theorie und Praxis der sozialen Marktwirtschaft. Einführung in die politische Ökonomie der BRD*, Frankfurt and New York: Campus.

Wertman, D.A. (1974) 'The electorate of religiously-based political parties: the case of the Italian Christian democratic party', unpublished Ph.D. thesis, Ohio State University.

—— (1981) 'The Christian democrats: masters of survival', in H.R. Penniman (ed.) *Italy at the Polls, 1979: A Study of the Parliamentary Elections*, Washington: The American Enterprise Institute for Public Policy Research.

Western, B. (1989) 'Decommodification and the transformation of capitalism: welfare state development in seventeen OECD countries', *Australian and New Zealand Journal of Sociology* 25:200–21.

Whyte, J.H. (1981) *Catholics in Western Democracies. A Study in Political Behaviour*, Dublin: Gill and Macmillan.

Widmaier, H.P. (1976) *Sozialpolitik im Wohlfahrtsstaat. Zum Theorie politischer Güter*, Reinbek bei Hamburg: Rowohlt.

Wilensky, H.L. (1975) *The Welfare State and Equality: Structural and Ideological Roots of Public Expenditures*, Berkeley: University of California Press.

—— (1981) 'Leftism, Catholicism, and democratic corporatism: the role of political parties in recent welfare state development', in P. Flora and A.J. Heidenheimer (eds) *The Development of Welfare States in Europe and America*, New Brunswick and London: Transaction.

Wilensky, H.L. and Lebeaux, C.N. (1965) *Industrial Society and Social Welfare. The Impact of Industrialization on the Supply and Organization of Social Welfare Services in the United States*, New York and London: Free Press and Macmillan.

Wilensky, H.L., Luebbert, G.M., Reed Hahn, S. and Jamieson, A.M. (1985) *Comparative Social Policy. Theories, Methods, Findings*, Berkeley: Institute for International Studies.

Williamson, P.J. (1985) *Varieties of Corporatism. A Conceptual Discussion*, Cambridge: Cambridge University Press.

Wilson, F.L. (1983) 'France', in V.E. MacHale and S.Skowronski (eds) *Political Parties of Europe*, Westport: Greenwood Press.

Windmuller, J. P. (1969) *Labor Relations in the Netherlands*, Ithaca: Cornell University Press.

Witte, E. and Craeybecks, J. (1987) *La belgique politique de 1830 à nos jours. Les tensions d'une démocratie bourgeoise*, Bruxelles: Editions Labor.

Woldendorp, J. (1993) 'Christen-democratie en neo-corporatisme in Nederland. Het CDA en het maatschappelijk middenveld', in K. van Kersbergen, P.

Lucardie and H.-M. ten Napel (eds) *Geloven in Macht. De Christen-Democratie in Nederland*, Amsterdam: Het Spinhuis.

Woldendorp, J., Keman, H. and Budge, I. (1993) *Political Data 1945–1990: Party Government in 20 Democracies*, Special Issue of *European Journal of Political Research* 24, Dordrecht: Kluwer.

Woldring, H.E.S. and Kuiper, D.Th. (1980) *Reformatorische Maatschappijkritiek. Ontwikkelingen op het Gebied van Sociale Filosofie en Sociologie in de Kring van het Nederlandse Protestantisme van de 19e Eeuw tot Heden*, Kampen: Kok.

Wolinetz, S.B. (1983) 'The Netherlands', in V.E. MacHale and S. Skowronski (eds) *Political Parties of Europe*, Westport: Greenwood Press.

—— (1989) 'Socio-economic bargaining in the Netherlands: redefining the post-war policy coalition', in H. Daalder and G.A. Irwin (eds) *Politics in the Netherlands. How Much Change?*, London: Frank Cass.

Woodward, E.L. (1963) *Three Studies in European Conservatism. Metternich, Guizot, the Catholic Church in the Nineteenth Century*, London: Frank Cass.

Zahn, E. (1989) *Regenten, Rebellen en Reformatoren. Een Visie op Nederland en de Nederlanders*, Amsterdam: Contact.

Zuckerman, A.S. (1979) *The Politics of Faction: Christian Democratic Rule in Italy*, New Haven: Yale University Press.

Zwart, R. (1993) 'Ideologie en macht. De christelijke partijen en de vorming van het CDA', in K. van Kersbergen, P. Lucardie and H.-M. ten Napel (eds) *Geloven in Macht. De Christen-Democratie in Nederland*, Amsterdam: Het Spinhuis.

Index

Numbers in **bold** represent main references. Numbers in *italics* represent pages with diagrams.

Hicks, A., and Misra, J. 20, 21, 22; and Swank, D.H. 17, 19, 21; Swank, D.H. and Ambuhl, M. 14, 17

Higgins, W. and Apple, N. 13

Hine, D. 59, 86, 165

Hitler, Adolf 40

Hockerts, H.G. 14, 111, 112–13, 115–16, 256

Hogan, W.E. 217, 218, 258

Huber, E. and Stephens, J.D. 21, 22, 24

Huber, E., Ragin, C. and Stephens, J.D. 20, 21, 22, 24; and Stephens, J.D. 107, 110, 140

Hulsman, T. 129

ideal-type 186–91

Immergut, E.M. 9

Immortali Dei (1885) 206

income 22; disposable 168–73, *169, 171*; distribution 17, 18–19, 21; policies 92

individuals 20

industrialism 10–11, 15; logic of 6

inequality 223–4

Inglehart, R. 240

institutionalism 7, 19

integration 182, 190

Interactive Simulation System (IAS) 255

interest group theories 7

International Christian Social Union 48

International Federation of Catholic Journalists 48

International Union of Social Studies 48

Irving, R.E.M. 34, 35, 36, 37, 40, 42, 44, 45, 59, 62, 65, 149, 183, 206

Irwin, G.A. 72

Istituto Nazionale della Previdenza Sociale (INPS) 155

Istituto Nazionale per l'Assicurazione contro le Malattie (INAM) 155

Istituto Nazionale per le Assicurazioni contro gli Infortuni sul Lavoro (INAIL) 155

Istituto per la Ricostruzione Industriale (IRL) 155

Italy, Catholicism in 40–3, 46;

Christian democracy in 57, 59, 61, 64–8, 233, 234; north–south divide 66; post-war political power 81–90; social policy in 153–67; welfare system in 176–7

Jackman, R.W. 10, 12

Janoski, T. 143; and Hicks, A.M. 20, 21

Janssen, G. and Berben, T. 128, 129

Jeune République 37

John XXIII, Pope 159

Johnson, E.A. 39

Jones, C. 199

Jones, H.M. 211

justice 224, 335

Kangas, O. 19, 255

Karvonen, L. 255

Katholieke Arbeidersbeweging 46

Katholieke Partij (KP) 35

Katholieke Vlaamsche Volkspartij 35

Katholieke Volkspartij (KVP) 54, 59, 70, 72, 73, 90, 91, 93–5, 131, 133, 134, 175

Katz, R.S. and Mair, P. 54

Katzenstein, P.J. 16

Kaufmann, F.-X. 39, 217, 255

Keman, H. 17, 19

Kenny, A. 199

Kerr, C. *et al.* 10

King, R. 83, 87

Klein, P.W. 60

Kogan, N. 67, 68, 85, 86, 89, 159–60, 161

Kohl, J. 10

Korpi, W. 13, 14, 19, 21, 99

Kossmann, E.H. 43, 255

Král, M.J.E. 34

Kuiper, D.Th. 134

Kulturkampf 38, 46, 214–15

Kuyper, A. 44

labour market 164, 183, 186, 187; cross-national comparisons 144–7; policy 132, 143–7

Lamennais, Félicité 209, 258

Lane, J.-E. and Ersson, S.O. 236; *et al.* 52